Economic Development of
Emerging East Asia

Economic Development of Emerging East Asia

Catching Up of Taiwan and South Korea

Frank S. T. Hsiao
and
Mei-Chu Wang Hsiao

ANTHEM PRESS

Anthem Press
An imprint of Wimbledon Publishing Company
www.anthempress.com

This edition first published in UK and USA 2017
by ANTHEM PRESS
75–76 Blackfriars Road, London SE1 8HA, UK
or PO Box 9779, London SW19 7ZG, UK
and
244 Madison Ave #116, New York, NY 10016, USA

British Library Cataloguing-in-Publication Data
A catalogue record for this book is available from the British Library.

Library of Congress Cataloging-in-Publication Data
A catalog record for this book has been requested.

ISBN-13: 978-1-78308-687-0 (Hbk)
ISBN-10: 1-78308-687-4 (Hbk)

This title is also available as an e-book.

In memory of
our parents

BRIEF CONTENTS

CONTENTS

LIST OF FIGURES

LIST OF TABLES

SOURCES OF THE CHAPTERS

Part I   Studies of Emerging East Asian Economies

1. "Some Development Indicators of Taiwan—A Comparative Study," *Journal of Economic Development*, 8(1), July 1983: 45–58. Copyright (1983) with permission from Professor Sung Y. Park, Editor, *Journal of Economic Development*.
2. "Capital Flows and Exchange Rates—Recent Korean and Taiwanese Experiences and Challenges," *The Journal of Asian Economics*, 12(3), Fall 2001: 353–81. Copyright (2001), with permission from Elsevier.
3. "Productivity Growth in Newly Developed Countries—The Case of Korea and Taiwan" (FSTH with Changsuh Park), *The Journal of the Korean Economy*, 3(2), Fall 2002: 189–230. (The lead article of the issue. The winner of the 2002 Best Paper Award with a cash prize from the editorial board of *The Journal of the Korean Economy*). Copyright (2002), with permission from Professor Sung Jin Kang, editor, *Korea and the World Economy* (formerly, *The Journal of the Korean Economy*).
4. "Korean and Taiwanese Productivity Performance—Comparisons at Matched Manufacturing Levels" (FSTH with Changsuh Park), *Journal of Productivity Analysis*, 23(1), January 2005: 85–107. Copyright (2005), with permission of Springer.

    Extended abstract published in Newsletter of North American Taiwanese Professors' Association, Winter 2002: 37–39. Extended abstract translated into Japanese by Kaoru Okayama, in *East Asia Prospective* (Higashi Azia e no Shiten), the International Centre for the Study of East Asian Development (ICSEAD), Kitakyushu, Japan. December 2002: 98–99.
5. "Colonialism, Learning and Convergence—A Comparison of India and Taiwan," *Journal of Asia Pacific Economy*, 10(2): 146–77. (The lead article of the issue). Reprinted by permission of the publisher (Taylor and Francis Ltd.). http://www.tandfonline.com.

Extended abstract translated into Japanese by Jun Sugawara, in *East Asia Prospective* (Higashi Azia e no Shiten), a publication of the *International Centre for the Study of East Asian Development* (ICSEAD), Kitakyushu, Japan. December 2002: 95–97.

Part II Catching Up and Convergence in East Asian Economic Growth

6. "Miracle or Myth of Asian NICs' Growth—The Irony of Numbers," in Richard W. Hooley and Zainal-Abidin Mahani, eds. *The New Industrial Revolution in Asian Economies, Research in Asian Economic Studies*, vol. 8. Greenwich, CT: JAI Press, 1998, 51–66. Copyright (1998) permission from the Emerald Group Publishing Limited.
7. "Miracle Growth in the Twentieth Century—International Comparisons of East Asian Development," *World Development*, 31(2), 2003: 227–57. (The lead article of the issue). Copyright (2003), with permission from Elsevier.
8. "Catching Up and Convergence: On the Long-Run Growth in East Asia," *Review of Development Economics*, 8(2), May 2004: 223–36. Copyright (2004) with permission from John Wiley and Sons.
9. Part of Chapter 9 was published as "How Bad is Taiwan's Economy? Compared to other economies around the world, Taiwan is doing just fine" in Features, Economy, East Asia, Taiwan. July 22. 2016. *The Diplomat*. Downloaded in July 2016 from the website of http://thediplomat.com/2016/07/how-bad-is-taiwans-economy/

ACKNOWLEDGMENTS

In preparing the chapters in this book, we are grateful to the original publishers of our papers, as listed in the Sources of Chapters section, for their quick response in granting permission to reprint the papers in this book. We also appreciate the comments and suggestions from three prepublication reviewers of this book.

We have a long list of economists and organizations to thank for helping us provide and collect data and references for our research. We are particularly grateful to the Council of Economic Planning and Development, Executive Yuan, Taiwan, for sending us *Taiwan Statistical Data Book* and monthly *Taiwan Economic Forum* (formerly, *Industry of Free China*) for many years, and to the Central Bank of China (Taiwan) for sending us many years of *Taiwan Economic and Financial Statistics Monthly*. These materials are particularly valuable since Taiwan's statistical data are not available from almost all international organizations. The comprehensive economic time-series dataset on East and Southeast Asian countries compiled by the *International Centre for the Study of East Asian Development* (ICSEAD), Kitakyushu, Japan, was also valuable for our work.

We are also very fortunate to be acquainted with many teachers, students and friends. At different stages of writing this book, we especially benefited from help from M. Jan Dutta, Toshiyuki Abe, Vei-Lin Chan, Song-Ken Hsu, Sheng-Cheng Hu, Cliff Huang, Hiroshi Ishida, William C. Kirby, Chi-Yuan Liang, Thomas Lindblad, Michael Luzius, Angus Maddison, Keith Maskus, Toshiyuki Mizoguchi, Naci Mocan, Robert McNown, Motoaki Moriya, Masao Oda, Osamu Takenaka, Changsuh Park, Eric D. Ramstetter, Hiroshi Setooka, Ron Smith, Henry Wan, Jr., Tsong-min Wu, Kenji Yamamoto and Tzong-shian Yu for discussions, exchange of publications and friendship.

The Dean's Office of the Leeds School of Business, University of Colorado Boulder, and Professor Kai R. Larsen, Ms. Brenda Engle, and many business faculty members provided us an excellent environment to work on this book. Dr. Salma Tariq Shukri and Mr. Richard Folsom helped read some chapters and gave many editorial comments and suggestions. Many current and previous staff members of the editorial office of Anthem Press, especially Ms. Kiran Bolla, the former acquisition editor, Mr. Vincent Devarajan, Ms. Abi Pandey and Leigh Westerfield spent a long time to see this book published. We are grateful for their patience and advice. Naturally, all errors of commission and omission are ours.

This is our second book on Asian economic development. As in the previous book, we wish to express our sincere and deep gratitude to our parents, who saw the importance of having us receive the best education we could. We also wish to express our profound appreciation to our teachers, in particular, Professors Ronald W. Jones, Lionel W. McKenzie, Richard N. Rosett, Hugh Rose, S. C. Tsiang and Shu-Ren Yang, who taught us rigorous economic analyses, and to our children, Edward and Victoria, for their patience and understanding throughout our research and teaching careers.

ABOUT THE AUTHORS

Frank S. T. Hsiao, professor emeritus of economics, Department of Economics, University of Colorado Boulder, United States, is an associate editor for the *Journal of Asian Economics*. He received his BA and MA in economics from National Taiwan University, Taipei, Taiwan, and MA and PhD (1967) in economics from the University of Rochester, Rochester, NY. From 1966 to 2007, he was a full-time professor in the Department of Economics, University of Colorado Boulder, United States. He has visited many East and Southeast Asian countries and authored and coauthored extensively articles in leading professional journals on growth models, production functions, Asian economic development and computer-assisted teaching, including a book on *Economic and Business Analysis: Quantitative Methods Using Spreadsheets* (2011).

Mei-Chu Wang Hsiao, professor emerita of economics, Department of Economics, University of Colorado Denver, United States, received her BA in accounting and banking from National Taiwan University, Taipei, Taiwan, and MA and PhD (1967) in economics from the University of Rochester, Rochester, NY. From 1981 to 2008, she was a full-time professor in the Department of Economics, University of Colorado Denver, United States. She has visited many East and Southeast Asian countries and has authored and coauthored many articles on econometric analysis of Asian economies, in addition to a recent book on *Economic Development of Taiwan: Early Experiences and the Pacific Trade Triangle*, with Frank Hsiao (2015).

INTRODUCTION

Asia is a vast, complex and diverse region. It has about one-third of the earth's land area and about one-half of the world's population. The world's major religions and cultures—Christianity, Islam, Hinduism, Confucianism/Daoism and Buddhism—originated in Asia. In addition, it has diverse climates, geology, races, cultures, country areas, population sizes and resources. According to Maddison (2006, Table B-18), India had the highest GDP from 0–1000 AD in the world, and China caught up with India after 1500 AD, which lasted until around 1820. China then fell behind the aggregate real GDP of 12 major European countries in 1870 and further fell behind that of the United Kingdom after 1913. The Industrial Revolution in the West during the nineteenth century did not spread to Asia, and Asia fell behind the West further during the era of Western colonialism. The economies of India, China and most of the Asian countries stagnated under colonialism and the imperialism of the European powers. Even two decades after World War II, "On the *per capita* basis the East [, *Southeast, and South*] Asian developing countries are in fact the world's poorest region" (Kirby 1967, 25; the brackets are the authors').

Japan was an exception in Asia. It was the only country in Asia to shed feudalism and start modernization in the late nineteenth century. Japan's policy of "Rich Country Strong Army" helped it rise up to annex Taiwan (1895) and Korea (1910), became a world power and eventually formed the "Greater East Asia Co-prosperity Sphere." While Japan tried to unite the East, Southeast and South Asians against European colonialism in the 1940s, it only proved to be another kind of Japan-centered imperialism and colonialism in Asia, and Japan was eventually defeated by the Allies in 1945.

Nevertheless, World War II brought a sea change in the world order. When the rest of Asia was still engaged in monocultural economic development and there was fighting among groups of nationalists, socialists, capitalists and communists, Japan recovered from the war damage quickly and, by benefiting from the Cold War and trading with the United States, achieved a high-growth "Japan Miracle" in the 1960s. Japanese foreign direct investment then moved to Taiwan and Korea in the 1970s.

In fact, the early 1970s was the threshold of a new world economy. It was the period of change from the era of resource-intensive heavy and chemical industries to energy saving as well as resource-saving high-tech industries, namely, the beginning of the era of electronics and computers. Japan was the first country to succeed in these industries. Its success set an example for the Taiwanese and Koreans, and it spilled over to Taiwan, Korea, Hong Kong and Singapore, the so-called Newly Industrializing Countries (NICs) or Asian Newly Industrializing Economies (NIEs) through learning by doing and a rapid increase in foreign trade and direct foreign investment from Japan and the United States. This set the stage for the East Asian Economic Miracle.

After the NIEs grew into advanced developing countries (ADC) in the 1980s and the 1990s, they found opportunities in nearby China. While the developed countries were experiencing lower one-digit GDP growth rates, these East Asian countries were experiencing close to two-digit growth rates. In the 1990s, the growth spread to the ASEAN countries, mainly Indonesia, Malaysia, Thailand and the Philippines, the second-generation NIEs. In the late 1990s, the growth also spread to Vietnam, Myanmar and India. This is in stark contrast to the slower growth of countries in Africa, Latin America and even Europe. Thus, the twenty-first century appears to be the century of the Asian Miracle.

In recent years, the fast-growing economies of the Asia-Pacific region have attracted the attention of economists, politicians, researchers and business communities. The economic dynamics of the ever-growing Asia-Pacific region necessitate that the United States adopt a "rebalancing strategy" toward Asia and propose the Trans-Pacific Partnership (TPP) and Free Trade Area of Asian-Pacific (FTAA). While the world is experiencing a recent slowdown and is facing uncertain circumstances in Brexit and the new Trump administration, it appears that "Asia-Pacific economies [...] remain the most dynamic region of the global economy" (IMF, 2016a), and "the near-term outlook for Asia remain[s] strong" in 2016 and 2017 (IMF, 2016b).

This book is a collection of our papers published mostly during the two decades at the turn of the century, the period economists generally consider the emergence of the Asia-Pacific century. The major players have been the NIEs: Taiwan, South Korea, Singapore and Hong Kong. But Singapore and Hong Kong are regarded as city-states, and thus, development economists usually see Taiwan and South Korea (hereafter Korea) as the countries that truly achieved a "miracle growth" during the postwar period.

Using quantitative and econometric analyses, this book studies the present and past economies of East Asia during the last century and provides future policy implications for economic development. This unique book provides comparative economic studies of Taiwan and Korea, and it compares them mostly with Japan and the United States. The book then finds that, in terms of the real GDP per capita in purchasing power parity (PPP), these emerging East Asian countries are still emerging in the world economy.

The topics of the chapters include development indicators, the effects of the 1997 Asian financial crisis, productivity growth, the catching up and convergence of long-run real GDP per capita growth, the time required for a country to catch up, and a special chapter on colonialism and economic development in Taiwan and India. Although written individually, all chapters, as explained further, relate to each other closely and cohesively. They are collected in one volume on similar themes to aid in the comprehensive understanding of emerging East Asian economies and are arranged systematically with the level of explanation proceeding from simple to more complex economic analyses.

Furthermore, the basic concepts of total factor productivity (TFP), Malmquist productivity index (MPI) and GDP in Purchasing Power Parity (PPP) are explained. Thus, the book, in addition to serving as references for regional economists and policy analysts, can also be used as a textbook on applications of these concepts in economics and business and for researchers at various stages.

In each chapter, as shown by the sections within the chapter, the first several sections explain the relevant economic conditions in detail, with an extensive literature review, to enable readers' understanding of the background of the countries and the objectives of the chapter. We then explain the need for the use of certain econometric models and the sources of data in detail.

Finally, the results of quantitative analysis are illustrated, acknowledging the limits of the model and analysis. The policy implications of the analysis are explored in the conclusion. While the quantitative analysis used in several chapters of this book requires a certain level of econometrics, readers may glance over the quantitative part and go directly to the concluding remarks on the policy implications of the chapter without much loss of understanding.

Overview of the Emerging East Asian Economies

It is well known that Korea and Taiwan are the two countries that had similar historical background before World War II (see Chapters 2 and 3). In 1979, both countries were designated in an OECD Report (1979) as two of the ten Newly Industrializing Countries (NICs), namely, Korea, Taiwan, Hong Kong and Singapore in Asia; Mexico and Brazil in South America; and Greece, Portugal and Spain, in addition to the former Yugoslavia, in Europe. However, by the end of the 1980s and into the 1990s, only the four Asian NICs remained as NICs.

In 1988, during the 14th G7 Summit in Toronto, Canada, Taiwan and Korea were viewed as the only two noncity-state countries of the Asian NIEs, along with Singapore and Hong Kong, to have achieved and maintained long-run rapid modern economic growth at a high employment level (Hirakawa and Park, 1994). By 1996, Korea was admitted to the prestigious OECD. Taiwan did not follow suit because of international political factors.

In the second half of the 1980s, while the Asian NIEs continued to grow, the ASEAN-4—namely Indonesia, Malaysia, Thailand and the Philippines, along with China—started rapid growth, and the growth fever spread to Vietnam and India in the new millennium. The rapid clustered sequential growth of Asia is unique in the history of economic development and is not shared by other regions or areas of the world (World Bank 1993; UNCTAD 1995). It is dubbed as the "flying-geese" model of development (Kojima, 2000).

This book studies the development of emerging East Asia, with an emphasis on Korea and Taiwan, comparing them with an early developed country, Japan, from a historical perspective, taking into account the interactions between these countries. We also compare Taiwan and India under colonialism. We hope that the East Asian economic experience and development can be valuable paradigms for emerging economies of African and Latin American countries in this age of globalization.

Overview of Chapters

Broadly speaking, the first half (Part 1) of this book compares the economic growth and development of Taiwan and Korea. The second half (Part 2) analyzes the catching up and the convergence of Korea and Taiwan on Japan, of Korea and Taiwan on the United States, and of Japan's catching up and convergence on the United States.

The first five chapters in Part 1 compare the economies of Taiwan and Korea, along with other countries. Chapter 1 compares the social indexes, political freedom, defense burden and development indicators of Taiwan with Korea and other Asian NIEs, along with Japan and China, during the 1970s at the time of their takeoff to fast economic growth. Although the book outlines the similarities between the two economies, after World War II, Taiwan's performance appears to have been better than that of Korea. Chapter 2 studies the effects of the 1998 Asian financial crisis on 22 macroeconomic fundamentals of the two countries. We found that they were basically similar. However, there were differences in nominal exchange rates and the ratios of the short-term external debt to international reserves. We then compare the causality of these two variables between Taiwan and Korea to show the cause and effect of the financial crisis.

Chapters 3 and 4 are more technical, using decomposition of the Malmquist Productivity Index to compare the productivity growth of Korea and Taiwan. We also identify and compare the leading industrial innovators of both countries. The last chapter of Part 1 is unique in the literature. It compares the colonial experiences of Taiwan under Japan and those of India under England, and then compares their effects on postwar economic development by estimating the learning coefficients of both countries. We then explain the consequences of the learning experience.

The three chapters in Part 2 compare the long-run growth of Taiwan, Korea and Japan. Chapter 6 discusses the number game on the measurement of total factor productivity. It centers upon the relationship between factor productivity and the real GDP growth rate. Specifically, it demonstrates that it is difficult to ascertain how low the percentage contribution of total factor productivity to real GDP growth rate should be in order to conclude that an economy is input-factor driven. Examination of several existing estimates could not give us a definite answer to conclude that the growth of Asian NICs is input-factor driven. Therefore, the argument that there may not be an Asian-centered world economy, as asserted by Krugman, may not be tenable.

Economically, the estimation of total factor productivity in Chapter 6 usually assumes that the production function has constant returns to scale, an assumption of long-run economic growth. Thus, in the next two chapters, we discuss the long-run growth trend of East Asian countries, Korea and Taiwan, and compare them with Japan. We then compare that of Japan with the United States.

Chapter 7 shows that, using Maddison's historical statistics (1901–92), Korea and Taiwan, along with Japan, grew very rapidly during the prewar period, and continued their rapid growth after the postwar periods, as compared with 53 other countries for which data are available. The chapter shows that the "East Asian miracle" started in the early years of the last century, only to be interrupted by World War II, and then continued after the mid-1970s, thus debunking the myth of no economic growth under colonialism.

However, despite the fast growth of Taiwan and Korea during the early postwar period, and even up to the 1990s, their real GDP per capita was still unable to surpass that of Japan in the 2010s, as shown in Chapter 7. Hence, a natural question is whether they are catching up with Japan and, if they are, when it will happen. In Chapter 8, we discuss the catching up and convergence of Taiwan and Korea with Japan, of Taiwan and Korea with the United States, and also of Japan with the United States. After estimating the convergence gap between the countries, we explore further by estimating the time required for convergence among these countries.

The above analysis is based on the data on the 1990s or the early 2000s. Thus, we may wonder what is the recent development of catching up and convergence in East Asia, whether the East Asian economies are still viable or whether they have dropped out of the scene like many other NICs several decades ago. In particular, we would like to know whether GDP per capita of Korea catches up with that of Taiwan, whether GDP per capita of Korea and Taiwan converges to Japan or to the United States, or more interestingly, their economic performance in comparison with some other OECD countries like the United Kingdom, Germany, France and the Netherlands.

Chapter 9 discusses these questions using recent international statistics published by International Monetary Fund, World Bank and the US CIA. Our study shows that the emerging East Asian countries are still emerging, and that despite the recent economic slowdown, the first- (the original Asian NIEs), the second- (the ASEAN-4) and the third- (China and India) generation NIEs are continuing to grow, probably toward an Asia-centered world economy.

Last, we are very fortunate to have three prepublication reviewers of this book give us valuable comments and suggestions on the book. To keep the consistency of the contents of the book, we added a separate section on questions and answers and two appendixes at the end of Chapter 9 to address their concerns. In particular, we took this opportunity to explain rather unknown facts about why Taiwan is acclaimed as the "Republic of Technology" and why Taiwan's catching up with some advanced European countries to become an advanced country is not a coincidence.

Since GDP per capita used in this book is mostly measured in the somewhat mysterious PPP, that is, the Geary-Khamis (or international) dollars, for the convenience of readers, and to gain some insight about the unfamiliar terminology, we have explained in detail the method of derivation and its interpretation in Appendixes 9A and 9B at the end of Chapter 9.

We have shown the sequence of our studies and the interrelation among the chapters in this Introduction. A more detailed abstract of the contents is given at the beginning of each chapter. For those who are interested in our econometric analysis, the detailed sources of data and extensive references are given in each chapter. All the tables and figures are generated using Microsoft Excel. We believe that the various statistical methods and arrangements of statistical data into tables and figures in this book are unique and innovative. The econometrics software program used in this book is the EViews software program (see www.EViews.com/home.html), as noted in each chapter.

For students and junior researchers, this book may serve as an example for writing research papers in regional development studies, as we have received many requests for information and questions about the papers collected in this volume. Some data sources may not be readily accessible or available. For simulation practice and practical purposes, data can be easily generated by using the Excel methods in Hsiao (2011, 182, 350, 494 and 526) applying the random number-generating function of Excel and by referring to the descriptive statistics given in the chapter.

This book is the second book in the sequel on our research on Asian economic development. We started from the study of *Economic Development of Taiwan—Early Experiences and the Pacific Trade Triangle* (Hsiao and Hsiao, 2015). This book then extends our studies on the economic development of Taiwan to that of East Asia, by comparing the economic development of Taiwan with Korea and Japan, and also with India and the United States. We plan to extend our inquiry to East and Southeast Asia in another project on *Trade, Investment, and Growth in East and Southeast Asia* (Hsiao and Hsiao, 2017).

References

Hirakawa, H., and I. Park (1994). *Asian NIEs—Korea, Taiwan, Hong Kong, and Singapore in Transition* (in Japanese). Kyoto: Sekai Shiso Sha.

Hsiao, Frank S. T. (2011). *Economic and Business Analysis-Quantitative Methods using Spreadsheets.* 700 pp. Singapore: World Scientific Publishing.

Hsiao, Frank S. T., and M. C. W. Hsiao (2015). *Economic Development of Taiwan-Early Experiences and the Pacific Trade Triangle.* 600 pp. Singapore: World Scientific Publishing.

——— (2018). *Trade, Investment, and Growth in East and Southeast Asia.* Forthcoming. London: Anthem Press.

IMF (2016a). *Regional Economic Outlook: Asia and Pacific. Building on Asia's Strengths during Turbulent Times.* April 16. Washington, DC: International Monetary Fund. Downloaded in November 2016 from https://www.imf.org/external/pubs/ft/reo/2016/apd/eng/pdf/areo0516.pdf

——— (2016b). *Regional Economic Outlook Update: Asia and Pacific Department.* Washington, DC: International Monetary Fund. October 6. Downloaded in November 2016 from http://www.imf.org/external/pubs/ft/reo/2014/apd/eng/areo0414.htm

Kirby, E. Stuart (1967). *Economic Development in East Asia.* New York: Frederick A. Praeger.

Kojima, K. (2000). "The Flying Geese Model of Asian Economic Development: Origin, Theoretical Extensions, and Regional Policy Implications," *Journal of Asian Economics* 11(4): 375–401.

Maddison, A. (1995). UNCTAD (United Nation Conference on Trade and Development) *World Investment Report,* New York and Geneva, Switzerland: United Nations.

——— (2006). *The World Economy,* in two vols. Development Centre Studies. Paris: OECD.

World Bank (1993). *The East Asian Miracle, Economic Growth and Public Policy.* World Bank Policy Research Report. Oxford: Oxford University Press.

Part I

STUDIES OF EMERGING EAST ASIAN ECONOMIES: TAIWAN AND KOREA

Chapter 1

SOME DEVELOPMENT INDICATORS OF TAIWAN: A COMPARATIVE STUDY OF EAST ASIA IN THE EARLY POSTWAR PERIOD

Abstract

This chapter presents the initial conditions of the pretakeoff period of Taiwan as compared with other comparable neighboring countries like South Korea, Japan and China. It presents the degree of "institutional readiness" of Taiwan, one of the newly industrializing economies (NIEs) in 1970s and 1980s, for takeoff to rapid economic development. We start from comparing the social indexes (including cultural, health and educational efforts), political freedom, defense burden and so forth. We then compare economic development ment indicators of Taiwan in the 1970s, the period in which Asia was just starting to emerge, with other Asian newly industrializing countries (NICs), namely, South Korea, Singapore and Hong Kong. In some comparisons, we also included Japan, China and the United States.

1.1 Introduction

Special interest in East Asia has been aroused again recently from Japan's emergence as a world industrial power (Patrick and Rosovsky 1976). After much acclaim of Japan as number one (Vogel 1979), people began realizing that not only Japan but also the smaller, newly industrializing countries (hereafter NICs) in Asia, such as Hong Kong, South Korea, Singapore and Taiwan, have followed closely and performed as well as Japan, although on a smaller scale (Little 1979). These five fast-growing countries, along with China and North Korea, are now viewed as a "challenge" and a "threat" to the United States and the Western world. They are known as the Eastasia Edge (Hofheinz and Calder 1982). With this perspective, this chapter examines some development ment indexes of Taiwan.

Taiwan's economic performance has been one of the best among the nations in the world after World War II. In fact, among 134 countries, for the period between 1950 and 1975, Taiwan's annual growth rate of per capita gross national product (GNP) in 1974 US dollars was 5.3%, ranking fifth, behind only Japan (7.6%), Swaziland (7.0%), Iraq (5.9%), and Greece (5.4%) (Morawetz, 1977, 77–80). In recent years the Taiwanese economy has been in the spotlight again as a new study has disclosed that Taiwan might be one of the few countries that has achieved this rapid growth with an equitable distribution of family income (Fei, Ranis and Kuo 1979). Since there currently exists extensive literature on the Taiwanese economy itself (e.g., Ho 1978; Galenson 1979), the purpose of this chapter is to compare some of its development indicators with those of selected countries.

1.2 Some Economic Indexes

It should be noted first that the term "development" has different meanings. Here we use it in a broad sense to include some economic, social and political aspects of Taiwanese society. Each of the indexes chosen is explained as it is introduced. Theoretically, an international comparison of these indexes may be made among all the countries in the world, as we have done previously (Hsiao and Hsiao 1981), or among countries in the same geographic area (WT 1980), or among those at similar levels of development (WDR 1980). Since most people like to compare themselves with a similar reference group, the emphasis of the comparisons in this chapter will be on the NICs, especially among the Asian NICs: Hong Kong, South Korea, Singapore and Taiwan. Whenever appropriate, we also compare the Taiwanese indexes with those of other countries not among the NICs.

With a population of 17 million in mid-1978, Taiwan is a large country, ranking 37th among 153 UN members,[1] and is comparable to the former East Germany, Sudan and Peru. Taiwan is rather small in terms of its area (36,000 km^2), ranking 116th among UN members. It is 70% larger than Belgium (21,000 km^2), but is slightly smaller than the Netherlands (41,000 km^2). The large population and small land area make Taiwan one of the most densely populated countries in the world. It has 472 persons per km^2, the sixth highest among UN members,[2] although it is only about one-eighth as dense as Singapore and Hong Kong. Apparently population density has little to do with the degree of development, as shown in Table 1.1.

---

1 For a detailed comparison with other countries in this paragraph, see Hsiao and Hsiao (1981, 7).
2 Exceeded only by Singapore (3,973), Malta (1,051), Barbados (590), Bangladesh (559), and Maldives (476). See WSB, 1979, as shown in Hsiao and Hsiao (1981, 7).

Table 1.1 Economic Development Indexes

	Twn	SKor	Sing	HK	Jpn	Chn	USA
1 Area (1,000 km2)	36 *	99 *	0.6	1 *	372	9,597	9,363
2 Population, in millions (Mid-1978)	17 *	37 *	2.3	4.6 *	115	952 *	218
3 Population Density (Mid-1977, persons/Km2)	472 *	376 *	3,973	4,408 *	307	90	23
4 GNP per capita, 1977 (Ranking in N=126)	1,179 *(51)*	977 *(56)*	2,820 *(30)*	2,622 *(33)*	6,511 *(18)*	230 * *(108)*	8,750 *(7)*
5 Energy consumption per capita 1978, in Kg. of coal equivalent	2,202	1,359	2,461	1,657	3,825	805	11,374
6 Average national savings rate in %,1972-7 (Ranking in N=126)	29.6 *(12)*	22.4 *(32)*	26.4 *(20)*	21.6 *(40)*	34.4 *(7)*	- -	18.2 *(56)*
7 % of urban population, 1980	77	55	100	90	78	25	73
8 % of labor force in agriculture (industry),1978	37 *(37)*	41 *(37)*	2 *(38)*	3 *(57)*	13 *(39)*	62 *(25)*	2 *(33)*
9 Current account balance before interest payment (US$ m), 1978	1,979	-455	-669	317 (1979)	17,528	na	-4,432
10 External public debt (US$ b, 1978)	2.9	12	1.1	0.2	0	na	0
11 External public debt as % of GNP, 1978	12.1	26.1	14.8	1.6	0	na	0
12 Public loans, net inflow (US$ m), 1978	227	2,777	40	38	0	na	0
13 Private Foreign investment (US$ m), 1978	110	61	422	-	-2,341	na	-10,404

Sources: Rows 1–3, WSB (1979); rows 4 and 6, WT (1980), tables 10–11. Other figures are based on WDR (1980). N = the total number of countries in the sample. b = billions, m = millions. *See WDR (1980).

The most important, although controversial, economic development index is per capita gross national product (GNP). GNP is a measure of the total gross domestic and foreign output claimed by the residents of a country. It is the sum of gross domestic product (GDP) and net factor income abroad (WT 1980, 6).[3] At current market prices, Taiwan's per capita GNP in 1977 was $1,179, ranking 51st among 126 countries according to the World Bank (WT 1980, 430). It is slightly higher than South Korea ($977) and

---

3 The source of data is quoted in initials, which are alphabetically ordered under the original title in the list of references. Thus WT = World Tables, WDR = World Development Report, etc.

Turkey ($1,110, not shown), and is almost the same as Mexico ($1,164, No. 52) and Panama ($1,195, No. 50).

Taiwan's per capita GNP in 1977 is also higher than all those of the Asian countries except Japan ($6,511), Singapore ($2,820), Hong Kong ($2,622) and Fiji ($1,326). An alternate index to per capita GNP is per capita energy consumption, which is measured in kilograms of coal equivalent to petroleum, natural gas, coal and lignite, hydroelectricity and nuclear power consumed, excluding traditional firewood. This is shown in row 5 of Table 1.1. Taiwan's figure is certainly high, indicating a vigorous industrial country. However, in contrast with GNP per capita, Taiwan's energy consumption seems too high, particularly when it is compared with Hong Kong and South Korea, which is probably an indication of a lack of effective energy conservation policies in the country.

Although per capita national income is rather low, Taiwan's average national savings rate is high. It is measured by the total gross national savings between 1972 and 1977 divided by the total GNP at current market prices for the same period. With average national saving ratio at 29.6%, Taiwan ranked 12th among 126 countries. Other countries with high average saving ratios are mostly oil-producing countries, except Japan, which had 34.4% and ranked seventh. High saving ratios result in high investment and consequently a high growth rate. Since Taiwan is a resource poor country, a high saving ratio depends only on the frugality of the Taiwanese people. This partly explains the rapid growth of the Taiwanese economy.

Industrialization requires some degree of urbanization. Urbanization is partially revealed in the size of the urban population and in the size of the industrial labor force vis-à-vis agricultural labor. These are shown in rows 7 and 8 of Table 1.1. About 77% of the Taiwanese population live in urban areas, almost the same as that of Japan and the United States. However, the percentage of the labor force in agriculture is still 37%, slightly lower than South Korea (41%), but much higher than that of Japan (13%) and the United States. (2%). The low percentages of agricultural labor in Singapore and Hong Kong are due to the city-state nature of these islands.

In addition to domestic saving, other sources of investment for development come from trade surplus, foreign loans and foreign investment. These are shown in rows 9 to 13. In 1978, the last year of the recovery from the first oil crisis of 1973–74 and just a year before the second oil crisis in 1979, the Taiwanese and Japanese economies had recovered from the initial crisis and experienced a large trade surplus, while South Korea, Singapore and the United States had trade deficits.

In terms of foreign loans that were disbursed by 1978, Taiwan's external public debt outstanding stood at US$ 2.9 billion, ranking 21st among 90 low-income and middle-income countries (WDR 1980, 138–39). Taiwan's external public debt is about one-fourth of Korea's debt, but it is well above those of Singapore and Hong Kong. Both Taiwan and Korea borrow heavily from outside to promote economic development.

Row 11, Table 1.1, shows the external public debt as a percentage of GNP. For Taiwan, the debt burden is 12.1%, ranking 64th among 90 low- and middle-income countries. Its debt burden in terms of GNP is not as heavy as most of the other developing nations. Rows 12 and 13 show the extent of the net inflow of public loans and private investment in 1978. Note the importance of public loans for Taiwan and South Korea. Japan and the United States had negative private investment, which shows the amount of foreign investment by firms of the developed countries.

1.3 Social Indexes

Social indexes include cultural, health and educational development (Harbison, Maruhnic and Resnick 1970, 15–17). Due to the availability of data, the following indexes are chosen for comparison.

Cultural Development Index (as a proxy for modernization):
1. Radio receivers per 1,000 population
2. Passenger cars and commercial vehicles per 1,000 population
3. Literacy rate of adult population over 15 years old

Health Index:
4. Population per physician
5. Population per hospital bed
6. Daily calorie supply per capita
7. Life expectancy at birth

Educational Effort Index:
8. Second-level enrollment
9. Third-level enrollment

Composite Index:
10. Physical quality of life index (PQLI)

These ten indexes are listed in Table 1.2. All data are based on the World Development Report (WDR, 1980), except rows 1, 2 and 5, which are taken from the most recent estimation (MRE) between 1974 and 1977 by the World Bank (WT 1980). The last index, the "physical quality of life index" (PQLI), was taken from Sewell (1980). The numbers with a plus sign are taken from

Table 1.2 Social Indexes

Country	Twn	SKor	Sing	HK	Jpn	Chn	USA
Cultural							
1 Radio/1,000 (MRE)	97	144	158	527	530	-	1,882
2 Cars/1,000 (MRE)	8	2.7	62.4	27	164		499
3 Percent of adult literacy (1975)	82 +	93	75 +	90	99	-	99 +
Health							
4 Population/physician (1977)	1,570 +	1,960	1,260	1,280	850		580
5 Population/hospital be (MRE)	450	1,430	280	240	100	-	150
6 Calorie/capita (1977)	120	119	134	126	126	105	135
7 Life expectancy (1978)	72	63	70	72	76	70	73
Educational Effort							
8 2nd level education in% (1977)	76 +	88 +	55	59	93	-	93 +
9 3rd level education in % (1976)	12 +	11 +	9 +	10 +	29	-	56 +
Composite Index							
10 PQLI (1980)	87	83	86	-	97	71	95

Sources: Data on MRE (Most recent estimates) are taken from WT (1980), on PQLI are based on Wright (1982) table; others are from WDR (1980). Note: + indicates the number taken from other years, see the text.

the data "for years other than, but generally not more than two years distant from, those specified" (WDR 1980, 158). Hence, most of the data are not strictly comparable. However, since social conditions change only gradually, the data provide some long-run trends of development and modernization.

In general, Taiwan's social indexes, like the economic indexes, are better than those of Korea but worse than those of Singapore and Hong Kong, as might be expected. However, the data reveal several surprises. Despite the fact that about 16% of Taiwan's exports consist of electric machinery and appliances, Taiwan's radio receivers per thousand population (97, row 1) is well below other countries. It seems that most of the electric and electronic equipment was produced in the Export Processing Zone and not directly accessible to the Taiwanese people themselves.

Another disappointment is the adult literacy rate (row 3), which is the percentage of adults aged 15 and over with the ability to both read and write. Despite well-touted achievements in the field of education, as much as 20% of the people in Taiwan were still illiterate, possibly well below all other countries in Table 1.2 except Singapore. The Taiwanese data are somewhat better in the number enrolled in the third (higher) level of education as a percentage of population aged 20–24 (row 9, Table 1.2). However, the differences among the four NICs are not significant and are still well below Japan and the United States.

Another interesting point is about the Taiwanese data on the population per physician and per hospital bed (rows 4 and 5), which are, respectively, "the total population divided by the number of practicing physicians qualified from medical school at a university level," and "by the number of hospital beds available in public and private hospitals and rehabilitation centers." Both numbers for Taiwan are high when compared with other countries except South Korea. The lack of physicians is not due to a lack of medical schools. It seems to reflect the brain drain. Many graduates of Taiwan's medical schools went abroad for "study," but as few as 4.4% came back to Taiwan from 1965 to 1980 (Hsiao and Kim 1982).

Taiwan's daily calorie supply per capita (row 6), which is the per capita calorie equivalent of food supplies as a percentage of requirement, is almost the same as Korea, but it is relatively low when compared with others. Nevertheless, life expectancy at birth (row 7), which indicates the number of years newborn children may expect to live, are more or less equivalent with other countries except Korea. Note that China's daily calorie equivalent per capita is estimated to be above the minimum daily requirement (105%), a feast for a country with a population close to one billion (India has only 91%, WDR (1980, Table 22). Similarly, China's life expectancy at birth is 70 years (WDR 1980, Table 1), which is comparable to most other countries except South Korea and Japan. This may reflect a good, if not better, medical care system in China (Hsiao and Hsiao 1981; Richman 1975, 353).

The last index is PQLI, which combines three indexes: literacy, life expectancy and infant mortality. The results are more or less expected from the above analysis. However, two things are worth noting. First, despite the difference in the economic and social indexes we have discussed above, the "physical quality of life" in Taiwan, South Korea and Singapore does not differ significantly. Second, the quality of Chinese life (71) is, although relatively low in the table, very respectable considering its population and the land area, especially when it is compared with the PQLI of India (43), Pakistan (38) and Indonesia (55) (Sewell 1980; Wright 1982, 16–17).

1.4 Political and Defense Development Indexes

Two of the most important aspects of the economic and social development indicators are the degree of political freedom and military defense. They are, however, often neglected in an international comparison since the concept of freedom is hard to measure and defense expenditures are always shrouded with much secrecy. We have tried to compare these two indexes based on the data published by Freedom House and the International Institute for Strategic Studies in London. These are shown in Tables 1.3 and 1.4.

Freedom House uses a seven-point scale for political and civil freedom, one corresponding to the most freedom and seven to the least. It then provides an overall judgment of each country as "free" (1 and 2), "partly free" (3 to 5), or "not free" (6 and 7) (Gastil, 1979, 15–24). Political rights rate electoral powers, existence of significant opposition parties, openness of voting procedures and the power of the elected representatives. The civil liberties are evaluated on the basis of independence of the news media, freedom of opinion, religion and movements, right to a fair trial and number of political prisoners. Economic freedom considers freedom to own property, of association, movement and information (Wright 1982, 15).

In Table 1.3, it can be seen that economic freedom is closely related to the status of freedom in each country. Except for Hong Kong, the political freedom of Taiwan, South Korea and Singapore are similar. The average rating between 1973 and 1982, however, shows Taiwan to be more restrictive in political rights (5.6, col. 2), with Korea being more restrictive in civil liberties (5.6, col. 4). In general, Taiwan's political freedom over the past ten years (col. 6) is rated more restrictive (4NF, 6PF) than any other except China (10NF). It may be interesting to know that the difference in the average rating of political rights between Taiwan and China is insignificant (5.6 for Taiwan and 6.5 for China, col. 2), although there is some difference in civil liberties (4.5 vis-à-vis 6.4). These ratings belie the "Free" China.

For many developed and developing countries, defense expenditures constitute the largest drain for social and economic development programs. This is certainly true for the countries in Table 1.4, except Hong Kong. Taiwan has to defend itself against China, as does South Korea against North Korea. Singapore has to protect its 55 islands and secure water supplies on the Malaysian mainland. Table 1.4 shows the defense expenditures and various burdens for 1975 and 1980 (in parentheses), respectively. However, the Taiwanese data are available only up to 1977, and the Chinese data are not available for 1975.

Military expenditures almost doubled between 1975 and 1980 (row 1), as did the per capita defense expenditure (row 2), and as a percentage of GNP

Table 1.3 Freedom Indexes

Year	Economic Freedom 1982 (1)	Political Rights 73-82 (2)	1982 (3)	Civil Liberties 73-82 (4)	1982 (5)	Status of Freedom 73-82 (6)	1982 (7)
Taiwan	Medium	5.6	5	4.5	5	NF4, PF6	PF
S. Korea	Medium	4.8	5	5.6	6	NF2, PF8	PF
Singapore	Medium	4.9	4	5.0	5	PF10	PF
HK	-	3.2*	4	2.0*	2	PF6, F3, NA1*	PF
Japan	High	1.8	1	1.0	1	F10	F
China	Low	6.5	6	6.4	6	NF10	NF
USA	High	1.0	1	1.0	1	F10	F

Notes: F = Freedom, PF = Partial Freedom, NF = No Freedom. *Average of 9 years, as Hong Kong's data for 1974 is not available.
Sources: For Economic Freedom, See Wright (1982), 16–17; other figures are based on the forthcoming edition of *Freedom in the World*, 1982, obtained through the courtesy of Ms. Lindsay M. Wright of Freedom House. Also see Gastil (1982).

Table 1.4 Defense Expenditures and Burden

Country Year	Taiwan 1975	*(1977)*	S. Korea 75	*(80)*	Singapore 75	*(80)*	Japan 75	*(80)*	China 75	*(80)*	USA 75	*(80)*
1 Defense Expenditures (Billions of US$)	1.0	*(1.7)*	0.9	*(3.5)*	0.3	*(0.5)*	4.6	*(9)*	-	*(57)*	89.0	*(143)*
2 per Capita (US$)	61	*(95*)*	28	*(91)*	152	*(239)*	42	*(75)*	-	*(56)*	417	*(644)*
3 % of Government spending	50	*(48.3*)*	29.2	*(30)*	18.1	*(16.5)*	6.6	*(4.7)*	-	*(0)*	23.8	*(23.3)*
4 % of GNP	6.9	*(8.3*)*	5.1	*(5.7)*	5.3	*(6.1)*	0.9	*(0.9)*	-	*(9.0*)*	5.9	*(5.5)*
5 Number in armed forces (millions)	0.5	*(0.4)*	0.6	*(0.6)*	0.03	*(0.04)*	0.2		-	*(4.5)*	2.1	*(2.1)*

*Based on IPA (1982). 403–4.
Sources: The Military Balance (198–82), 79, 112–13.

it increased slightly (row 4). Note that among the three countries, Singapore has the highest per capita expenditure, Taiwan has the highest ratio of defense expenditure to GNP,[4] while Korea maintains the largest armed forces.

---

4 Taiwan also has the highest percentage of defense expenditures in government spending (row 3, Table 1.4). Note that there are two budgets in Taiwan, "provincial" and "national." It is estimated that 50% of the "national" budget is for defense, which produced US$ 1 billion in defense expenditures in 1975. Sixty-five to seventy percent of defense equipment is locally manufactured. US military aid in 1974 was US $65 million (Keegan 1979, 696).

Although it is not clear at what point the ratio of defense expenditure to GNP becomes undesirably high, the military burden of the Taiwanese economy is certainly high as compared with other countries. It not only squeezes the developmental and social programs, but it also helps maintain the secretive authoritarian government in the name of anti-communism. Nobody will deny the importance of defense. The main problem is that, since the status of freedom is severely limited in Taiwan as well as many other developing countries, there is no discussion of, nor checks and balances, for military expenditures versus government expenditures for social and economic programs.

1.5 Concluding Remarks

In this chapter, we have shown that through the thrift and hard work of the Taiwanese, helped by foreign aid and investments, the Taiwanese economy has been one of the fastest growing economies in the world since World War II. Nevertheless, the general living standard, as shown by the social indexes, has been lagging behind and did not improve as much as we might have expected from rapid growth. From the data in the tables we have seen that Taiwan has a rather large population which has diluted the gain from economic progress. The data also suggest that the lack of political freedom may also keep the Taiwanese economy from achieving the delicate balance between military expenditures and other social programs. The sooner the people and the government of Taiwan identify these problems, the faster Taiwan will be able to join the ranks of developed countries.

Acknowledgments

The original version of this chapter was presented to the Annual Meeting of the Western Conference of the Association for Asian Studies held at Boulder, Colorado, September, 17–18, 1982. We are grateful to Charles Doering for editorial assistance.

References

Fei, John C. H., Gustav Ranis and Shirley W. R. Kuo (1979). *Growth with Equity: The Taiwan Case*. Oxford: Oxford University Press.

Galenson, Walter (1979). *Economic Growth and Structural Change in Taiwan*. Ithaca, NY: Cornell University Press.

Gastil, Raymond D. (1979). *Freedom in the World, Political Right and Civil Liberties*. Washington, DC: Freedom House.

———— (1982). "The Comparative Survey of Freedom," *Freedom at Issue* 64, January–February.

Harbison, F. H., J. Maruhnic and J. R. Resnick (1970). *Quantitative Analyses of Modernization and Development*. Princeton, NJ: Princeton University.

Ho, Samuel P. S. (1978). *Economic Development of Taiwan, 1960–1970*. New Haven, CT: Yale University Press.

Hofheinz, Roy Jr., and Kent E. Calder (1982). *The Eastasia Edge*. New York: Basic Books.

Hsiao, Frank S. T., and Inchul Kim (1982). "An Economic Model of the Brain Drain: Another View," Working Paper, University of Colorado.

Hsiao, Frank S. T., and Mei-chu Wang Hsiao (1981). "International Comparisons of the Taiwanese Economy," *Newsletter of the North America Taiwanese Professors Association* 1(2, 3): 5–9.

Information Please Almanac (IPA) (1982). 36th ed. New York: Simon and Schuster.

International Institute for Strategic Studies (1981). *The Military Balance 1981–82*. London: The International Institute for Strategic Studies.

Keegan, John (1979). *World Armies*. New York: Facts on File, Inc.

Little, Ian M. D. (1979). "An Economic Reconnaissance," chapter 7 of Galenson, 1979.

Morawetz, David (1977). *Twenty-Five Years of Economic Development, 1950 to 1975*. Baltimore: Johns Hopkins University Press.

Patrick, Huch, and Henry Rosovsky (1976). *Asia's New Giant, How the Japanese Economy Works*. Washington, DC: Brookings Institution.

Richman, Barry (1975). "Chinese and Indian Development: An Interdisciplinary Environmental Analysis," *The American Economic Review, Papers and Proceedings*, 345–55.

Sewell, John W. (1980). *The United States and World Development: Agenda 1980*. New York: Praeger Publications.

Vogel, Ezra F. (1979). *Japan as Number One: Lessons for America*. Cambridge, MA: Harvard University Press.

World Bank (1980). *World Development Report 1980* (WDR). New York: Oxford University Press.

———— (1980). *World Tables 1980*, 2nd ed. (WT). Baltimore: Johns Hopkins University Press.

World Statistics in Brief (WSB) (1979). *United Nations Statistical Pocketbook*. 4th ed. New York: United Nations.

Wright, Lindsay M. (1982). "A Survey of Economic Freedom," *Freedom at Issue* 64: 15–20.

Chapter 2

CAPITAL FLOWS AND EXCHANGE RATES DURING THE ASIAN FINANCIAL CRISIS: RECENT KOREAN AND TAIWANESE EXPERIENCES AND CHALLENGES

Abstract

In the face of the Asian financial crisis of 1997, the first part of this chapter carefully studies the characteristics of the financial crisis and its impacts on the Taiwanese and Korean economies. We examine 22 macroeconomic fundamentals, such as GDP, inflation rates, government budget, trade balance, external debt and so on, between Korea and Taiwan. We find that the macroeconomic fundamentals of both countries were basically the same, with the exception of the international finance sector. After defining the currency crisis and banking crisis, the causes of crises are identified as the nominal exchange rates and the short-term external debt to international reserves ratios. In view of this, in the second part of the chapter, we use cointegration and causality tests to examine the relationship between these two time series. We find a uni-directional causality from the short-term debt ratio to the exchange rate for Korea, but no causality is found between the two for Taiwan. The chapter ends with some discussion on the lessons and challenges from the experiences of these two countries.

2.1 Introduction

It is well known that Korea and Taiwan are the only two noncity-state countries, other than Japan, that have achieved and maintained rapid modern economic growth since the end of World War II. As such, most studies often lump them together as both countries achieved impressive growth through rapid industrialization and accelerated exports, like two wheels of a cart. Thus they are generally treated as twins, if not as identical, in world capitalistic development.

In recent years, however, their differences in the development process have also come to light. Taiwan relied more on domestic savings and direct foreign investment, along with emphasis on the contribution of small and medium-size enterprises. Korea depended on foreign borrowing, incurring large external debt, with a major role played by large conglomerates or chaebols in industrialization and trade. What are the impacts of the Asian financial crisis on these differences?

After the Asian financial crisis broke out in Thailand in mid-1997, it spread quickly to neighboring countries. The impact of the crisis and the response in these two countries are quite different. Taiwan seems to have fared much better than most of the neighboring countries, while Korea was severely affected. In 1998, the growth rate of current GDP in US dollars of Korea dipped to −32.6% (−8.5% in 1997), and that of Taiwan was −7.8% (4.0% in 1997), which is better than that of Japan, as Japan fell to −9.6% (−8.4% in 1997). This is shown by the columns in Figure 2.1 (the bars *[2]* using the secondary

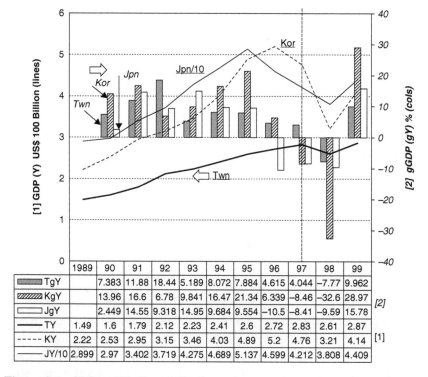

Figure 2.1 GDP and Its Growth Rate
US$ 100 Billion and Percent

vertical axis), indicating quite different responses of the twins.[1] However, the economy of these three countries recovered very quickly in the following year. In 1999, the above growth rate of Korea increased to a whopping 29%; that of Taiwan, to 10% and that of Japan, to 16%. It appears that both Taiwan and Korea, and for that matter, the Southeast Asian countries, are already on the way to full recovery, although some lingering problems still exist among them. What are the reasons for such large differences?

Due to the possible global contagion of the Asian financial crisis, an extensive literature already exists on it, including the crisis in Korea. However, few studies deal with Taiwan, as Taiwanese data are generally not available from international organizations, much less with comparisons of the different responses of Taiwan and Korea. The purpose of this chapter is to examine the economic characteristics and macroeconomic policy responses of the twins. We first discuss the causes and contagion of the recent financial crisis. We then study the characteristics of the crisis and the distinct impact on the Taiwanese and Korean economies. We submit that, since Korea was one of the four countries, along with Thailand, Indonesia and Malaysia, that were severely affected by the recent financial crisis, and Taiwan was only slightly affected, comparisons of the twins using time series analysis may contribute to an understanding of the cause and causality effects of the crisis.

Thus, after reviewing some explanations of the causes of the recent Asian financial crisis in Section 2.2, Section 2.3 examines 22 macroeconomic fundamentals of these two countries. In the real sector, we have examined current GDP and current GDP per capita, their percentage growth rates, inflation rate, the lending rates of banks, government budget, fiscal surplus-GDP ratios, unemployment rates and money supply (M2) to GDP ratios. In the external and financial sectors, we examine the balance of trade, the current account balance, international reserves, ratios of the average monthly imports to international reserves, ratios of cumulative inward portfolio investment to international reserves, the total external debt, ratios of total external debt to international reserves, short-term external debt, ratios of short-term external debt to international reserves, exchange rates and their percentage changes and, last, the year-end stock indexes and their percentage changes.

The sources and impact of the financial crisis in Korea and Taiwan are explained in Section 2.4. The financial crisis is considered as the interaction

---

1 The impact on the growth rates of real GDP in national currency were much less dramatic. For Korea, in terms of 1995 won, the percentage changes from 1997 to 1999 were 5.01%, −5.84% and 8.50%, respectively. For Taiwan, in terms of 1991 NT dollar, they were 6.77%, 4.65% and 5.50%, respectively. For Japan, in terms of 1990 yen, they were 1.59%, −2.50% and 1%, respectively (ICSEAD, 2000, 60).

between the currency crisis and the banking crisis. Section 2.5 examines the empirical findings of the linkage between the two crises, which are then reduced to the causality relation between the nominal exchange rate series and the ratios of short-term external debt to international reserves series.

Thus, in Sections 2.6 and 2.7, we examine first the stationarity of both time series data, and then their cointegration, and finally the causality relation by the error-correction model for Korea and the standard Granger causality test for Taiwan. Once again, we find the differences between Taiwan and Korea. Section 2.8 concludes by comparing the Korean case with that of Taiwan, and discusses the lessons and challenges from the experience of the two countries and prospects for the future.

2.2 Four Explanations of the Crisis

There are at least four explanations of the onset of Asian financial crisis:

(a) It is simply a phase of a growth cycle. There was an economic downturn during 1983–85, from which the region recovered, followed by over a decade of high growth. The pace of growth changed at the beginning of 1990, and a downturn was expected around 1994 (Ichimura et al., 1998, 1). Thus, the crisis in the mid-1997 was not unexpected.

(b) An oversupply of labor-intensive goods, such as footwear, textile products and electronic products, and the rise of China as a large exporter, has reduced export earnings of East and Southeast Asian countries (IMF, 1997; Park, 1996). China's 50% devaluation of the yuan in early 1994 accelerated the trend. The rise of Mexican exports and the enactment of the North American Free Trade Agreement (NAFTA) also intensified competition in East and Southeast Asia.

(c) There is a basic weakness in Asian financial management and capitalism. Financial liberalization in Asia began in the early 1990s. It was at best haphazard and incomplete. Increased banking activity, growth in short-term external debt and its exposure to the international capital market along with inadequate regulation and supervision, corruption and inefficiency led to an increase in real estate speculation and nonperforming loans (Krugman, 1998; Goldstein, 1998). The pegged exchange rates depleted the international reserves and aggravated the crisis.

(d) There is a self-fulfilling crisis and overreaction of the financial market. The macroeconomic fundamentals are, although not perfect, basically sound. However, once a liquidity crisis of a firm sets in, no creditor will make a loan if each creditor expects no other creditors will provide a new loan to repay the existing debt. Thus, when more and more foreign investors withdrew their loans, more and more domestic banks and firms were driven into illiquidity and eventual insolvency (Radelet and Sachs, 1998). The panic then spread to the whole country and was transmitted to other countries.

We submit that all four explanations reflect some aspects of the recent financial crisis and are consistent with our observations. Korea is one of the most affected countries in this financial crisis. What happened in Korea? We consider that the last two explanations seem more plausible.

2.3 Comparison of Taiwanese and Korean Economies in the 1990s

Several papers have discussed the macroeconomic background of the financial crisis (Kaminsky and Reinhart, 2000; Alba et al., 1999; Agenor, 2000). In this chapter, we select some macroeconomic fundamentals to show similarities and differences among the economies of Taiwan, Korea and Japan. For this purpose, instead of cluttering the chapter with numbers, we use charts to illustrate and dramatize the changes in some important macroeconomic variables over time from 1989 to 1999. To be consistent in the data collection, most of the annual data of 1989–99 in this section are taken from the latest issue of the International Centre for the Study of the East Asian Development (ICSEAD, 2000), except those few noted otherwise.

Figures 2.1 to 2.10 compare the economic conditions of Taiwan (in heavy solid lines or dark solid columns) and Korea (in heavy dotted lines or columns with an upward diagonal pattern fill), along with Japan (in solid lines or empty white columns), in 22 categories numbered in square brackets. Whenever possible, we have tried to compare the development patterns of these three countries, as they are closely related by international trade and historically had similar development patterns.[2]

Among the labels, J/10 in Figures 2.1, 2.2, 2.5, 2.6 and 2.8, or K/10 in Figure 2.9 suggest that the Japanese or Korean data were reduced to one-tenth of the original value to fit into the diagrams. Thus, if a curve has been so indicated, the curve itself may only be used to compare the differences in the shape or fluctuations. The reader should be aware that the actual curve is

---

2 Elsewhere we have shown that the real GDP per capita growth rates of these three countries in the postwar period (1951–92) were highest among the 56 countries listed in Maddison (1995, Appendix D): Taiwan, 6.03%, Korea, 5.90%; Japan, 5.57% (Hsiao and Hsiao, 2000b, Table 1).

ten times higher or larger than that plotted in the graph. To save space, we also created the secondary (right) Y-axis.

All the line charts use the left-hand side (LHS) primary Y-axis (also shown by the fat arrow). All column charts use the right-hand side (RHS) secondary Y-axis (shown by the fat arrow), the vertical axis titles and the axis labels that are set in italics. Each category of macroeconomic variables are numbered and enclosed in square brackets, set in italics for measuring from the RHS secondary axis and are underlined for measuring from the LHS primary axis. The legend and actual data for each figure are shown at the bottom of the figure. These 21 categories are explained briefly as follows.

2.3.1 The real sector

In Figures 2.1 and 2.2, the patterns of current GDP [1] and current GDP per capita (GDPpc) [3], all in US dollars and shown as the line graphs, for the three countries are very similar, all enjoying a robust economic growth until the peak year of both GDP and GDP per capita in 1995 for Japan, 1996 for

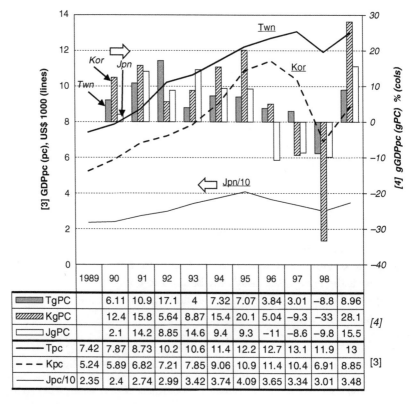

	1989	90	91	92	93	94	95	96	97	98		
TgPC		6.11	10.9	17.1	4	7.32	7.07	3.84	3.01	−8.8	8.96	
KgPC		12.4	15.8	5.64	8.87	15.4	20.1	5.04	−9.3	−33	28.1	[4]
JgPC		2.1	14.2	8.85	14.6	9.4	9.3	−11	−8.6	−9.8	15.5	
Tpc	7.42	7.87	8.73	10.2	10.6	11.4	12.2	12.7	13.1	11.9	13	
Kpc	5.24	5.89	6.82	7.21	7.85	9.06	10.9	11.4	10.4	6.91	8.85	[3]
Jpc/10	2.35	2.4	2.74	2.99	3.42	3.74	4.09	3.65	3.34	3.01	3.48	

Figure 2.2 GDP per Capita and Its Growth Rate
US$ and Percent

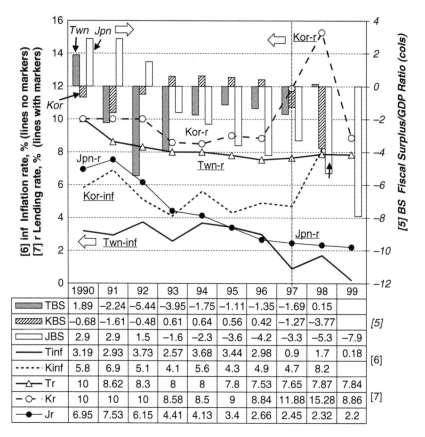

	1990	91	92	93	94	95	96	97	98	99	
TBS	1.89	-2.24	-5.44	-3.95	-1.75	-1.11	-1.35	-1.69	0.15		
KBS	-0.68	-1.61	-0.48	0.61	0.64	0.56	0.42	-1.27	-3.77		[5]
JBS	2.9	2.9	1.5	-1.6	-2.3	-3.6	-4.2	-3.3	-5.3	-7.9	
Tinf	3.19	2.93	3.73	2.57	3.68	3.44	2.98	0.9	1.7	0.18	[6]
Kinf	5.8	6.9	5.1	4.1	5.6	4.3	4.9	4.7	8.2		
Tr	10	8.62	8.3	8	8	7.8	7.53	7.65	7.87	7.84	
Kr	10	10	10	8.58	8.5	9	8.84	11.88	15.28	8.86	[7]
Jr	6.95	7.53	6.15	4.41	4.13	3.4	2.66	2.45	2.32	2.2	

Figure 2.3 Inflation Rates, Lending Rates and Overall Fiscal Surplus/GDP

Korea and 1997 for Taiwan. They then turned downward and reached a local minimum simultaneously in 1998.

In terms of the growth rates, *%gGDP [2]* in Figure 2.1 and *%gGDPpc [4]* in Figure 2.2 registered a negative value in 1998 for all three countries when the Thai baht plunged in mid-1997. Korea's growth rates were most severely affected and they decreased more than 30% in 1998, although Korea's GDP and GDP per capita growth rates were generally higher than those of Taiwan before 1995. It appears that Korea was catching up with Taiwan[3] in the 1990s.

---

3 In the prewar period (1911–40), Korea's real GDP per capita and its growth rate were consistently higher than those of Taiwan. Following the war (1951–92), they have been consistently lower. See Figure 2 and Table 1 in Hsiao and Hsiao (2000b) (ref. Chapter 6 of this book). The growth rate is calculated as a discrete percentage change between two consecutive years.

The inflation rates in terms of consumer prices,[4] [6] in Figure 2.3, of Taiwan and Korea (denoted as inf) also had a similar pattern. Both were decreasing up to 1997, but Korea's inflation rate almost doubled from 4.7% in 1997 to 8.2% in 1998, while that of Taiwan continued to decrease from 2.98% in 1996 to a mere 0.9% in 1997.

Their lending rates of banks,[5] denoted as r in [7], also tended to decrease until 1996. But Korea's lending rates increased from 8.84% in 1996 to 11.88% in 1997, and a whopping 15.28% in 1998, while those of Taiwan increased only slightly from 7.53% in 1996 to 7.65% in 1997 and 7.87% in 1998, the trend of which was similar to Japan.

Note that for both inflation rates and lending rates, Korea's rates are generally one to three percentage points higher than those of Taiwan, and that Taiwan's rates continue to decrease or maintain the same levels after the crisis. These probably indicate a better management of the Taiwanese monetary authority before and after the onset of the Asian financial crisis in mid-1997.

However, Figure 2.3 also shows that both Korea and Taiwan had fiscal budget deficits [5] (the columns measured from the right Y-axis with italic labels) in 1991 and 1992, but Korea's fiscal budgets turned positive after 1993, while those of Taiwan and Japan stayed negative. Korea had fiscal-surplus-to-GDP-ratios of about 0.4 to 0.6 during the four years just before the 1997 financial crisis, while Taiwan experienced 1.11 to 3.95 of deficit-to-GDP ratios and Japan, 1.6 to 4.2 deficit-to-GDP ratios. All three countries ran budget deficits in 1997.

Although we have not shown it in the figures here, we have confirmed that, in terms of percentage of GDP, all three countries also had similar patterns in private and government consumption and fixed investment, and that no drastic changes in these ratios before and after the 1997 crisis have been detected. The major difference is that Korea's fixed-investment-to-GDP ratios, which range from 35% to 38.8%, are much higher than those of Taiwan (20.7% to 23.7%), which probably explains Korea's higher GDP growth rates in the pre-crisis period of the early 1990s.

Figure 2.4 shows that, despite higher growth rates, the unemployment rates [9] (the columns measured from the right Y-axis in italic labels) of Korea are generally 0.5% to 1.0% higher than those of Taiwan before 1995. They are, however, very low as compared with those in the developed countries, except in 1998 and 1999, showing the dire effect of the impact of the financial crisis.

---

4   Taiwan's price changes are calculated from consumer price indices in TSDB (2000, 186). Korea's price changes are calculated from "all cities consumer price indexes," Bank of Korea (1999, 200).
5   Korea's lending rates are from IMF, 1999, and also ICSEAD, 2000. Taiwan's lending rates are secured loans bank interest rates from TSDB, 2000, 164. Also in ICSEAD, 2000.

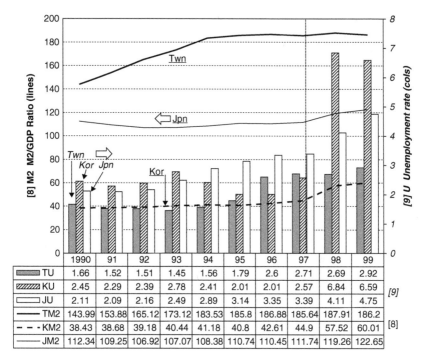

	1990	91	92	93	94	95	96	97	98	99
TU	1.66	1.52	1.51	1.45	1.56	1.79	2.6	2.71	2.69	2.92
KU	2.45	2.29	2.39	2.78	2.41	2.01	2.01	2.57	6.84	6.59
JU	2.11	2.09	2.16	2.49	2.89	3.14	3.35	3.39	4.11	4.75
TM2	143.99	153.88	165.12	173.12	183.53	185.8	186.88	185.64	187.91	186.2
KM2	38.43	38.68	39.18	40.44	41.18	40.8	42.61	44.9	57.52	60.01
JM2	112.34	109.25	106.92	107.07	108.38	110.74	110.45	111.74	119.26	122.65

Figure 2.4 Broad Money(M2)/GDP and Unemployment Rates

Throughout the 1990s, Korea's broad money-supply-(M2)-to-GDP ratios [8] (shown by the line graphs and measured from the left Y-axis with underlined labels) were much lower than those of Taiwan, and there were not many changes in the ratios for all three countries even after the 1997 crisis. Thus, in general, Korea's real sector macroeconomic foundation appeared to be as good as, or even better than, those of Taiwan before the crisis.

2.3.2 The external and financial sectors

The major differences between Korea and Taiwan appear in the external and financial sectors. While the data show that merchandise imports and exports increased steadily during the 1990s for all three countries, the balance of trade[6], *[11](TB)* in Figure 2.5 (the columns measured from the right Y-axis in Italic labels) and the current account balance, *[13]* CAB in Figure 2.6

---

6 Calculated as exports (#20) minus imports (#34) in Table 2 of each country in the ICSEAD (2000).

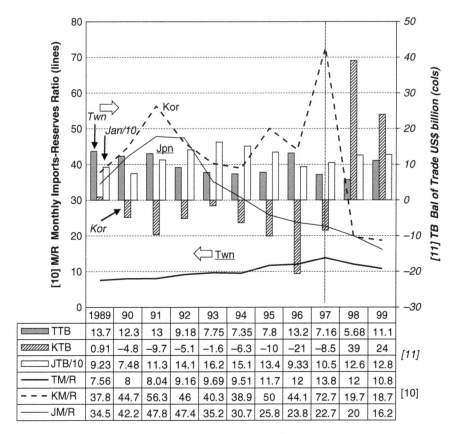

	1989	90	91	92	93	94	95	96	97	98	99
▬ TTB	13.7	12.3	13	9.18	7.75	7.35	7.8	13.2	7.16	5.68	11.1
▨ KTB	0.91	−4.8	−9.7	−5.1	−1.6	−6.3	−10	−21	−8.5	39	24
▭ JTB/10	9.23	7.48	11.3	14.1	16.2	15.1	13.4	9.33	10.5	12.6	12.8
— TM/R	7.56	8	8.04	9.16	9.69	9.51	11.7	12	13.8	12	10.8
- - - KM/R	37.8	44.7	56.3	46	40.3	38.9	50	44.1	72.7	19.7	18.7
— JM/R	34.5	42.2	47.8	47.4	35.2	30.7	25.8	23.8	22.7	20	16.2

[11]

[10]

Figure 2.5 BOT and Monthly Import-Reserves Ratios

(the columns measured from the right Y-axis in italic labels), of Taiwan and Japan have been consistently positive, while those of Korea have been almost always negative before 1997, except a mere US$ 1 billion current account surplus in 1993. Korea's current account balance even fell to US$ −23 billion in 1996 *[13]*.

Both balances of Korea increased quite dramatically from US$ −8 billion in 1997 to about US$ 40 billion in 1998, although both balances decreased to about US$ 24 billion in 1999. A reason given for the difference between Taiwan and Korea is the nature of outward foreign direct investment (OFDI). Taiwan's OFDI is export oriented, still using Taiwan's machinery and intermediate goods exported to the host countries, while that of Korea is local-market oriented, resulting in the misalignment of home and host countries' production structures (Chen and Ku, 2000, 142).

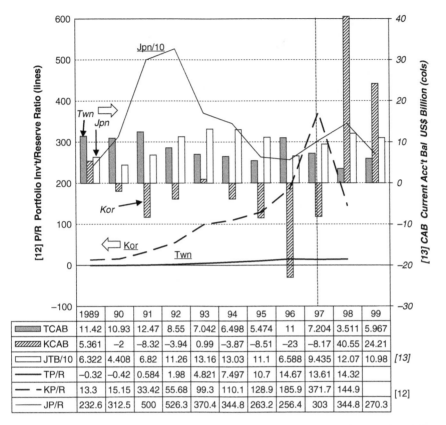

	1989	90	91	92	93	94	95	96	97	98	99	
TCAB	11.42	10.93	12.47	8.55	7.042	6.498	5.474	11	7.204	3.511	5.967	
KCAB	5.361	-2	-8.32	-3.94	0.99	-3.87	-8.51	-23	-8.17	40.55	24.21	
JTB/10	6.322	4.408	6.82	11.26	13.16	13.03	11.1	6.588	9.435	12.07	10.98	[13]
TP/R	-0.32	-0.42	0.584	1.98	4.821	7.497	10.7	14.67	13.61	14.32		
KP/R	13.3	15.15	33.42	55.68	99.3	110.1	128.9	185.9	371.7	144.9		[12]
JP/R	232.6	312.5	500	526.3	370.4	344.8	263.2	256.4	303	344.8	270.3	

Figure 2.6 Current Account Balance (CAB) and the Cumulative Inward Portfolio Investment/Reserves

The general trends in trade and the current account deficits of Korea and the surpluses of Taiwan and Japan are reflected in the much higher international reserves [16], R, in Figure 2.8 (the lines measured from the left Y-axis with underlined labels), of Taiwan (US\$ 73 billion to 90 billion, the heavy solid line) and Japan (US\$ 84 billion to 272 billion, the Jpn/10 line) than those of Korea (US\$ 14 billion to 52 billion, the dotted line) during the decade. Note that Korea's international reserves fell from US\$ 34 billion in 1996 to US\$ 20 billion in 1997, but increased to US\$ 52 billion in 1998.

The line charts of Figures 2.5 and 2.6 show the ratios of the average monthly imports to international reserves[7] [10] (M/R, the lines measured from the left

---

7   The original data were given as the ratio of international reserves to one-twelfth of the absolute value of the sum of the debits of goods, services, and income in balance

Y-axis) and the ratios of cumulative inward portfolio investment to international reserves[8] [12] (P/R, the lines measured from the left Y-axis), all of which are expressed as percentages. These are the indicators, along with the short-term external debt to international reserves ratios, *[17]* (SD/R, the columns measured from the right Y-axis with Italic labels) in Figure 2.8, that were closely related to the fluctuations in foreign exchange rates during the financial crisis.

Regarding the ratio of average monthly imports to international reserves [10] in Figure 2.5 (the lines measured from the left Y-axis with underlined labels), it is generally considered the lower, the better for an economy. Since its inverse, the ratio of international reserves to average monthly imports, indicates the ability of a country to pay for its imports in terms of months, it is generally considered that six months' worth of reserves is a minimum safety amount. Hence, if the monthly imports-to-international-reserves ratio is higher than 17% (1/6), that is, if the international reserves are not enough to pay for six months of imports, then the country is more vulnerable to financial crisis.

The line chart [10] in Figure 2.5 shows that Korea has the highest and most varied ratios among the three countries, ranging from 38% in 1989 to 73% in 1997. Japan's ratios are modest, ranging from 48% in 1991 and decreasing continuously to 16% in 1999, while those of Taiwan are the healthiest, ranging from mere 7.5% in 1989 to 14% in 1997.

Indicator [12] in Figure 2.6 (P/R) is the ratio of cumulative inward portfolio investment to international reserves.[9] This inward portfolio investment is highly speculative; it is the source of international hot money pursuing stock price changes. Here, the numerator is the cumulative sum of inward portfolio investment from 1980 and beyond. In fact, from 1991 to 1996, Korea's cumulative inward portfolio investment increased from US$ 2.3 billion to 21.2 billion, and that of Taiwan increased from US$ 0.8 billion to 3.2 billion. During this period, the inward cumulative portfolio investment is higher than foreign direct investment in Korea, with the former twice to 18 times higher than the latter, but in Taiwan, it ranged 0.6 to 2.6 times higher. This was another sources of vulnerability of the Korean economy.[10]

---

of payment. See the data sources and notes for each country in the ICSEAD, 2000, Tables 5.2, 6.2, #55. We take its inverse and then multiply by 100.

8 Calculated as the inverse of the ratio of international reserves to the cumulative sum of inward portfolio investment from 1980 forward. See the data sources and notes for each country in ICSEAD, 2000. The ratio is then multiplied by 100.

9 The original data were given as the ratio of international reserves to the cumulative inward portfolio investment, which is calculated as the cumulative sum of inward portfolio investment from 1981 forward (ICSEAD, Tables 5.2 and 6.2, #56 and footnote). We take its inverse and then multiply by 100.

10 It had been the general trend in East and Southeast Asia that during the early 1990s, capital flooded into the area and the share of foreign portfolio investment (FPI) was

Huge inward portfolio investment may not be a threat in the case of crisis if a country has enough international reserves. Thus, we have to look at the ratio [12] in Figure 2.6. It is generally considered that the lower the ratio, the better. Over the years, Korea has much higher ratios throughout the decade as compared with those of Taiwan. For Korea, it was only 13% in 1989, but increased rapidly and reached a whopping 372% in 1997, and then decreased to 145% in 1998. This can signal the danger of a currency crisis in won in case of a sudden flight of inward portfolio investment. For Taiwan, the ratios were maintained at a very low level. They were −0.32% in 1989, and increased slightly and steadily to mere 15% in 1996, well within the 100% threshold level.

Figures 2.7 and 2.8 show a similar discrepancy between Taiwan and Korea in the international finance sector. The total external debt [14a] (the lines measured from the left Y-axis without markers) for both Taiwan and Korea were increasing, very slowly for Taiwan, from US$ 17 billion in 1989 to only US$ 34 billion in 1997, an increase of 100%, but the increase was much more rapid for Korea, from US$ 42 billion in 1989 to US$ 143 billion in 1997, an increase of 240%. Apparently, Korea's high rate of GDP growth [1] (Figure 2.1) relied heavily on external debt. By doing so, however, Korea also greatly increased its financial vulnerability, as shown by the total external-debt-to-international-reserves ratios *[15]*.

Since Taiwanese international reserves [16] (lines in Figure 2.8 measured from the left Y-axis) are much higher than those of Korea, from *[15]* of Figure 2.7 (D/R, the columns measured from the right Y-axis in italic labels), Korea had much higher total debt-to-reserves ratios, 276% in 1989 to a huge 704% in 1997, as compared with Taiwan's ratios, which range from a mere 23% in 1989 to 40% in 1997. Note that Korea's short-term external debt [14b] (SD, the lines with markers measured from the left Y-axis) was more than doubled from US$ 28 billion in 1993 to US$ 66 billion in 1996, which consisted of about 50% of the total external debt for that year.

As we show below, since some economists regard short-term external debt as the culprit of the financial crisis, we also present the ratio of short-term external debt to international reserves *[17]* in Figure 2.8 (the columns measured from the right Y-axis with italic labels) for Taiwan and Korea. The contrast is staggering. Taiwan's ratios range from only 20% in 1989 to 27% in

---

higher than that of foreign diect investment, except in China, which did not deregulate foreign portfolio investment (EPA, 1998, 55). In comparing Korea and Taiwan, Chen and Ku (2000, 127) suggested that Korean chaebols crowded out FDI, and so foreign capital could only invest in security markets.

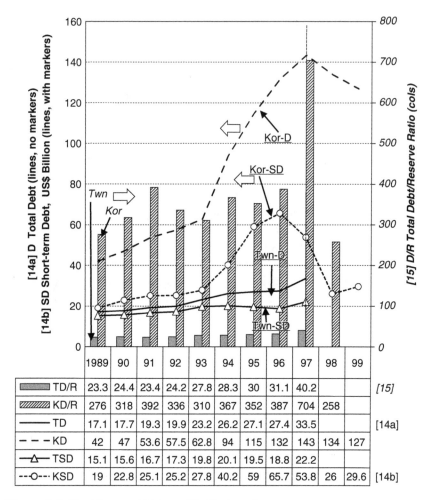

	1989	90	91	92	93	94	95	96	97	98	99	
TD/R	23.3	24.4	23.4	24.2	27.8	28.3	30	31.1	40.2			[15]
KD/R	276	318	392	336	310	367	352	387	704	258		
TD	17.1	17.7	19.3	19.9	23.2	26.2	27.1	27.4	33.5			[14a]
KD	42	47	53.6	57.5	62.8	94	115	132	143	134	127	
TSD	15.1	15.6	16.7	17.3	19.8	20.1	19.5	18.8	22.2			
KSD	19	22.8	25.1	25.2	27.8	40.2	59	65.7	53.8	26	29.6	[14b]

Figure 2.7 Total External Debt and Its Ratio to Reserves

1997, while those of Korea range from 125% in 1989 to 347% in 1997, about six to twelve times larger than those of Taiwan.

In general, the ratio of total external debt to international reserves *[15]* shown in Figure 2.7 indicates a country's solvency, and the ratio of short-term external debt to international reserves *[17]* shown in Figure 2.8 indicates the liquidity of the country at the time of the crisis. Both ratios for Korea are much higher than the critical point of 100%, at 390% and 160%, respectively, in 1996, and at 704% and 347%, respectively, in 1997, while those for Taiwan are much lower than the critical point of 100%. Herein lies the extreme vulnerability of the Korean economy to international capital market

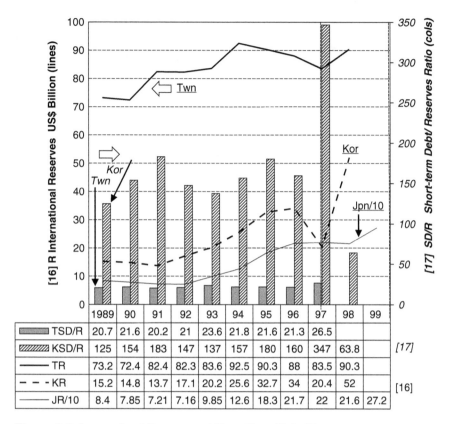

	1989	90	91	92	93	94	95	96	97	98	99
▨ TSD/R	20.7	21.6	20.2	21	23.6	21.8	21.6	21.3	26.5		
▨ KSD/R	125	154	183	147	137	157	180	160	347	63.8	
—— TR	73.2	72.4	82.4	82.3	83.6	92.5	90.3	88	83.5	90.3	
- - - KR	15.2	14.8	13.7	17.1	20.2	25.6	32.7	34	20.4	52	
—— JR/10	8.4	7.85	7.21	7.16	9.85	12.6	18.3	21.7	22	21.6	27.2

Figure 2.8 International Reserves and Short-Term Debt/Reserves

fluctuations. Both column graphs of Figure 2.7 and Figure 2.8 show the differences dramatically.

The last two figures show the exchange rates and stock market indexes. Figure 2.9 shows the average exchange rate, with US dollars, of the Korean won, the New Taiwan dollar, and the Japanese yen (per US dollar exchange rates) [18] and their percentage changes [19]. Figure 2.10 shows the levels and percentage changes of the year-end stock indexes[11] [20] [21]. Unlike Japan, whose yen continued to appreciate until 1995, Taiwan and Korea maintained more or less at constant levels and small percentage changes in exchange rates until 1996, moving somewhat around NT$ 26.5 per US dollar for Taiwan and about 760 won per US dollar for Korea [18]. All three currencies started

---

11 The indexes are taken as follows: for Taiwan, 1991 = 1; for Korea, 1995 = 1; and for Japan, 1990 = 1 (ICSEAD, 2000, no. 43 of Table 1 of each country)

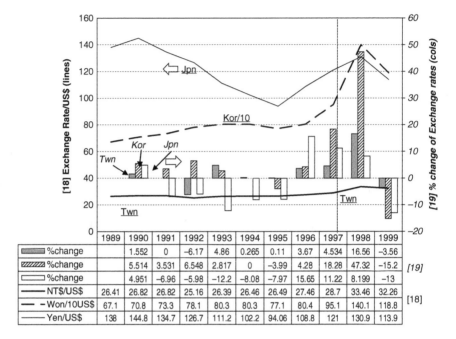

	1989	1990	1991	1992	1993	1994	1995	1996	1997	1998	1999	
%change		1.552	0	-6.17	4.86	0.265	0.11	3.67	4.534	16.56	-3.56	
%change		5.514	3.531	6.548	2.817	0	-3.99	4.28	18.28	47.32	-15.2	[19]
%change		4.951	-6.96	-5.98	-12.2	-8.08	-7.97	15.65	11.22	8.199	-13	
NT$/US$	26.41	26.82	26.82	25.16	26.39	26.46	26.49	27.46	28.7	33.46	32.26	
Won/10US$	67.1	70.8	73.3	78.1	80.3	80.3	77.1	80.4	95.1	140.1	118.8	[18]
Yen/US$	138	144.8	134.7	126.7	111.2	102.2	94.06	108.8	121	130.9	113.9	

Figure 2.9 Average Exchange Rates per US Dollar and Percentage Changes

depreciating in 1996 (see the columns in Figure 2.9), and the depreciation of New Taiwan dollar and Korean won reached their peak in 1998, at NT$33.5 per US dollar and 1,400 won per US dollar, although both fell back slightly in 1999 [18]. Along with other indicators mentioned above, there were signs of a quick recovery from the financial crisis in 1999.

Figure 2.10 shows that the year-end stock price indexes, however, were rather erratic during the whole period. The indexes of Taiwan and Korea moved together before 1995 and deviated in opposite directions to each other [20] (the lines measured from the left Y-axis with underlined labels), indicating quite different impacts of the financial crisis on the two countries. The Taiwan index reached its high of 1.8 in 1997 and fell to 1.4 in 1998 [20]. The Korea index reached its low of 0.4 in 1997 and recovered slightly to 0.6 in the following year [20]. Both indexes reached a ten-year high of 1.8 and 1.2, respectively, in 1999.

2.4 Short-term Debt, Exchange Rates and Crisis in Korea

We have seen that the real sectors of the macroeconomic fundamentals of Korea and Taiwan basically have had similar performance during the last decade. The major differences between these two countries lie in the external

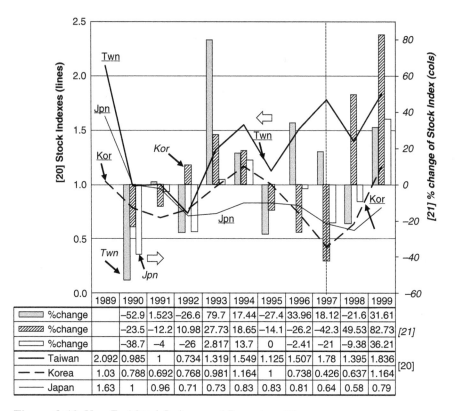

	1989	1990	1991	1992	1993	1994	1995	1996	1997	1998	1999	
%change		−52.9	1.523	−26.6	79.7	17.44	−27.4	33.96	18.12	−21.6	31.61	
%change		−23.5	−12.2	10.98	27.73	18.65	−14.1	−26.2	−42.3	49.53	82.73	[21]
%change		−38.7	−4	−26	2.817	13.7	0	−2.41	−21	−9.38	36.21	
Taiwan	2.092	0.985	1	0.734	1.319	1.549	1.125	1.507	1.78	1.395	1.836	[20]
Korea	1.03	0.788	0.692	0.768	0.981	1.164	1	0.738	0.426	0.637	1.164	
Japan	1.63	1	0.96	0.71	0.73	0.83	0.83	0.81	0.64	0.58	0.79	

Figure 2.10 Year-End Stock Indexes and Percentage Changes

and financial sectors. Among the variables, we find that the greatest discrepancy is shown by the ratios of total external debt to international reserves, that is, series [15] D/R in Figure 2.7. Since total external debt also includes long-term external debt, which is bound by long-term contracts, the immediate cause of the financial crisis may be attributable to short-term external debt (Radelet and Sachs, 1998; Rodrik and Velasco, 1999).

In fact, series *[17]* SD/R, in Figure 2.8, of the ratios of short-term external debt to international reserves also yields a similar discrepancy as series [15] between the two countries. Since Taiwan barely faced the recent Asian financial crisis as compared with Korea, our finding points to short-term external debt as the cause of the 1997 financial crisis in Korea, and possibly other Southeast Asian countries. This is consistent with the observation presented in Rodrik and Velasco (1999).

As Korea sought to join the Organization for Economic Cooperation and Development (OECD) in the early 1990s, it started financial reform in

earnest.[12] The prospects for prosperity that would come along with deregula-
tion, reform and openness attracted foreign capital to Korea in droves.[13] This
is reflected in the sweeping increase of total external debt [14a], Figure 2.7,
especially short-term external debt [14b], Figure 2.7. The waves of optimism
and the government policy of controlling commercial banks to support the
government's economic development plans fostered moral hazard of excessive
lending and borrowing in the expectation that the central bank, the government, or an international organization would bail out the banks or firms out
when things went wrong.[14]

Ironically, it has been often pointed out that this crony relation between the
government and business was one of the factors in Korea's rapid growth.[15]
Under these circumstances, "the Korean banks kept lending to chaebols
which the government preferred [...] Korean banks [...] developed few skills
in credit analysis or risk management [...] Reflecting the history of directed
lending, banks generally did not insist on, or receive, full financial information from chaebols" (Shim, 2000, 154). However, with easy money, Korean
firms expanded. "The debt-to-equity ratio of Korean cooperates was approximately 450% by the end of 1996, three times the comparable US ratio, and
more than five times the comparable Taiwanese ratio."[16]

This is not the case with Taiwan. While the Taiwanese government also
encouraged domestic savings and allocated capital to selected industrial sectors, capital was invested in large public enterprises and a few large private
firms. Private small and medium-size enterprises seldom received funds from
the government or banks except export financing. This resulted in low debt-
to-equity ratios of the Taiwanese firms. Furthermore, the government did not
adopt the policy of investment risk sharing with private enterprises, and thus,
the Taiwanese economy remained centered around small and medium-size

---

12 Korea joined the prestigious OECD in 1996.
13 Herd behavior is not the monopoly of a financial crisis. For an overview of the pull and
    push of capital flow and exchange rates, see Glick, ed. (1998). Kaminsky and Reinhart
    (2000, 480) find that "in the 1980s and 1990s most liberalization episodes have been
    associated with financial crises of varying severity. [...] the twin crises may have com-
    mon origins in the deregulation of the financial system."
14 The problem of moral hazard was prevalent in East Asian countries before the 1997
    crisis, and it was one of the reasons that attracted massive foreign capital to the area
    during the 1990s. Other reasons are the deregulation of capital inflows, relatively high
    rates of interest, and so on (EPA, 1998, 83).
15 EPA, 1998, 145. More generally, a long-term view is that "the system that produced
    the Asian crisis of 1997–98 also produced the impressive economic performance of the
    previous two decades" (Crockett, 2000).
16 Shim (2000, 146) quoted from another source.However, according to EPA (1998, 82),
    the external capital ratios (external capital/(internal and external capital)) of Korea in
    1995–96 were 74%–76%, for Taiwan were about 55% and for Japan and the United
    States were 61%–66%, for Malaysia and Indonesia were 44%–58%. While Korea's
    ratio was high, it did not seem particularly alarming.

enterprises,[17] thus avoiding the problem of moral hazard that occurred in other East Asian countries.

In the case of Korea, the foreign banks (Japanese, European or US) borrowed yen or dollars at low interest rates and re-lent the money at higher rates for short periods to Korean banks, which in turn re-lent the money to local firms for longer periods with higher interest rates (Uchitelle, 1998; Shim, 2000, 156). Before June 1997, Korean commercial banks were not required to maintain adequate liquidity ratios on foreign currency assets. About 20% of local foreign borrowings were also invested in foreign securities in Thailand, Indonesia, Russia and Latin America (Shim, 2000, 156). The mismatched foreign currency dominated borrowings, and speculative investment in foreign countries added to the vulnerability of the banking system and possible contagion effects when a financial crisis occurred. Using a simple two-period model, Rodrik and Velasco (1999) have concluded that the banking crisis (bank run) "can only occur when investors take on sufficiently large amounts of short-term debt." They point out that the larger the stock of such debt, the larger the size of a crisis, and the larger the consequences in terms of liquidation and reduced output and consumption.

However, a currency crisis occurs when the monetary authority tries to maintain fixed (or fixed within a band) foreign exchange rates (Fukushima and Takii, 1998, 11). Most developing countries peg their exchange rates to one currency (US dollar or French franc) or a few currencies so as to reduce the currency risk, to attract inward foreign direct investment from developed countries. Korea was no exception. Since March 1990, Korea had adopted the market average exchange rate system,[18] but loosely pegged to the US dollar. It was abandoned only when Korea moved to a complete floating system in November 1997 in the midst of the financial crisis (EPA, 1998, 270).

In 1996, Korean exports declined and the trade deficit (series [11] TB, Figure 2.5) increased due to the decrease in demand for semiconductors and the appreciation of the won against the yen, which was induced by the appreciation of the US dollar against the yen (ibid., 119; Fukushima and Takii, 1998, 146). The decrease in demand for steel in China and the increasing competition in Asian markets forced Hanbo Steel, the flagship of the fourteenth-largest chaebol in terms of total assets in 1996, with US$ 6 billion in debt, declared bankruptcy in January 1997 (Fukushima and Takii, 1998, 142).

---

17 EPA, 1998, 85–86. This may be seen from the fact that the ruling government has been an émigré regime (Gold, 1986), which has no roots in local business. On Taiwan's small and medium-size enterprises, see Hsiao and Hsiao, 1996, 1999.

18 In this system, the won-per-US-dollar rate was "allowed to float in the interbank market within a daily range around the weighted average of the previous day's interbank rates for spot transactions" (Shim, 2000, 146). The allowed range of variation was ±1.5% up to December 1995, and expanded to ±10% in November 1997.

The bankruptcy of Sammi Steel (Sammi Chaebol, ranked twenty-sixth) followed in March. Then Kia Motors (Kia Chaebol, ranked seventh), the third-largest Korean automaker, with US$ 10.6 billion in debt, followed on July 15 (ibid., 143). The government reacted by letting some chaebols go under, but defended the won at the end of 1997 (Radelet and Sachs, 1998, 1999). This action resulted in the sharp depletion of international reserves, and a marked increase in the ratio of short-term external debt to international reserves in 1997.[19] This then triggered a chain reaction.

Foreign creditors, who were already alarmed at Thailand's financial crisis in July 1997, refused to roll over the short-term debt. They started pulling capital from Korea, and as borrowers could not pay back lenders fast enough, the won devaluated further. On July 5, 1997, the won plummeted to 905.60 per US dollar, the lowest in a decade (Fukushima and Takii, 1998, 148). The news of the depletion of international reserves sent the won further down to 2,000 won per US dollar by the end of 1997 (EPA, 1998, 119). The turmoil in the exchange rate market continued well into 1998. The average annual exchange rate shot up almost 50%, from 951 won in 1997 to 1,400 won per US dollar in 1998, as shown in series [18] and [19], Figure 2.9. At the same time, the assets value plummeted. The year-end stock price index decreased 26% in 1996 and 42% in 1997, as shown by series [20] and [21], Figure 2.10. The government's defense of the won was ineffective. The pegged exchange rate system gave way to the complete floating system on December 16, 1997, and the Korean won continued to depreciate.

2.5 On the Currency and Banking Crises

We have seen from the analysis in Section 2.3 that the differences in macroeconomic performance between Korea and Taiwan can be found in the external and financial sectors. The fluctuations of Korean exchange rates (won/US$, [18], Figure 2.9) and the short-term external-debt-to-international-reserves ratios (hereafter, short-term debt ratios, [17], Figure 2.8) seem to be closely related. Section 2.4 explains the process of their interaction. We have also shown that, while the financial crisis in Korea and the Southeast Asian countries appears to have been triggered suddenly by the financial crisis in Thailand in July 1997, the signs of the crisis were already revealed in 1996,

---

19 The year 1997 was also the year of the presidential election in Korea. Uncertainty about the election outcome reduced the propensity to invest (EPA, 2000, 146), which, coupled with the decrease in exports, turned the 1997 GDP growth rate to a near negative 10% (see [2] in Figure 2.1). Thus, the effect of the Asian financial crisis was manifested only in 1998, during which the nominal GDP growth rate decreased more than 30%.

and the roots of the Korean crisis may be traced back to the early 1990s when the government started preparing to join the OECD. We may say that a long-run undercurrent of crisis had been snowballing for a long time,[20] and it erupted as a financial crisis only in July 1997. This may also be the case in Thailand and other Southeast Asian countries.[21]

In the literature, banking crises are difficult to identify empirically. They are "a combination of events, such as forced closure, merger, or government takeover of financial institutions, run of banks [...] failure to roll over interbank deposits [...] the share of nonperforming loans in banks' portfolios, large fluctuations in real estate and stock prices" and so forth (IMF, 1998, 76). In this chapter, we follow Radelet and Sachs (1998) and Rodrik and Velasco (1999) to consider short-term debt ratios as the major source of the financial crisis. However, in the literature, a currency crisis is either "identified simply as a substantial nominal currency devaluation" or by an index of foreign exchange market pressure (IMF, 1998, 76). In this chapter, we consider nominal currency devaluation as the source of the financial crisis.

Based on various definitions, the IMF (1998, 77) has identified, between 1975 and 1997, 158 episodes of currency crisis and 54 banking crisis. "For emerging market countries, the frequency of currency crises shows no marked trend, while banking crises are clustered in the early 1980s and the 1990s" (ibid., 77–78). This is "possibly related to the financial sector liberalization" during this period (ibid., 77). As the IMF (and some other scholars) has observed,

Given that the two types of crises may have common origins, or that one type of crisis may induce the other, it is not surprising that countries appear to have banking and currency crises at around the same time. In these instances, banking crises preceded currency crises more often than the other way round. [...] banking crises led currency crises by one year on 13 occasions, and by two years on 10 other occasions. The crises were contemporaneous in 12 instances. Currency crises preceded banking crises by one year only seven times and by two years another four times.

---

20 In addition to the London-based *Economist*, as early as in the beginning of 1996, the IMF and the Institute of Developing Economies in Tokyo, had warned of the vulnerability of the Thai economy (Abe, 1998, 3).

21 Abe (1998) conducted fieldwork in Thailand in September 1997 and pointed out that the change from a fixed exchange rate system to a managed floating exchange rate system, in July 2, 1997, signaled the change from export-led growth to a bad-loans-ridden economy, and triggered the Thai financial crisis. He delineates Thailand's ten underlying problems, which "are rather inherent, structural and long-term" (ibid. 5, 41). See also Appendix: Thailand, A stylized chronology in Corbett and Vines (1999).

This evidence, while suggestive, should be interpreted with caution in view of the difficulties in dating the beginning of banking crisis. (ibid., 78)

In view of our interest in the linkage between the currency crisis and the banking crisis, we would like to go a step further and examine econometrically the causality between the two crises. This way, we may also avoid the ambiguity problem in dating, namely, timing the beginning and the ending of the crises (Park, 2000). So far as we are aware, a time series analysis of the causality between the two crises has not been done in the literature, as most of the analyses have been based on cross-section data.

2.6 The Causality Test—The Case of Korea

We now would like to use recently developed econometric techniques to examine the relationship and the causality between the nominal exchange rates and the short-term debt ratios using annual data from 1979 to 1998 given in the ICSEAD (1999, 2000).

2.6.1 The unit root test

It is well known that many macroeconomic time series are nonstationary. Therefore, before examining the cointegration and the causality between the variables, we employ the augmented Dickey-Fuller (ADF) unit root test (Dickey and Fuller, 1979, 1981) to examine the stationarity of Korea's nominal exchange rate[22] (hereafter, exchange rate) and the short-term debt ratio. The general equation for the ADF test is,

$$\Delta x_t = a_0 + a_2 t + a_1 x_{t-1} + \sum_{i=1}^{k} \beta_i \Delta x_{t-i} + \epsilon_t, \qquad (2.1)$$

where x_t (level series) is the natural logarithm of Korea's exchange rate series (or, x_t may also be the short-term debt ratio series), and Δx_t is the first-difference series of x_t. The variable t is the time trend. The variable x_{t-1} is the one-period lag of xt for the unit root test, and Δx_{t-i} is the ith lag of the dependent variable. The optimal lag length k is chosen by minimum Akaike information criterion (AIC) (Enders, 1995; Maddala and Kim, 1998).

---

22 Since foreign lenders' and speculators' behavior is generally based on anticipation of daily changes in the nominal exchange rate, we adopted this as our variable. Real exchange rates are useful in explaining changes in trade performance and current account balance over the years.

Table 2.1 ADF Unit Root Test
Korean Exchange Rate and the Short-Term Debt Ratio

Part 1: Level Series			MacKinnon
Variable	k	Test-statistic	critical values
			10%
Exchange rate (c, t)	1	-0.140	-3.286
Short-term debt ratio (c, t)	2	-2.743	-3.296

Part 2: First-difference Series			MacKinnon	
Variable	k	Test statistic	critical values	
			1%	10%
Exchange rate (c, t)	7	-8.077 ***	-5.115	
Short-term debt ratio (c)	5	-2.805 *		-2.704

Notes: (1) The optimal lag length k is chosen at the minimum AIC from lag = 1 to lags = 7.
(2) (c, t) denotes that the testing equation has included constant term (c), and significant time trend (t). (3) *** (*) denotes significant at the 1% (10%) level.

Part 1 of Table 2.1 presents the ADF unit root test results on the level series. For a unit root test, the null hypothesis is H_0: $a_1 = 0$ (unit root), against the alternative hypothesis H_1: $a_1 < 0$. For Korea's exchange rate series and the short-term debt ratio series, the test equation (2.1) includes a constant and a statistically significant trend. Both calculated test statistics are greater than their critical values at the 10% significance level. Therefore, we cannot reject H_0. Since both level series are not stationary, we proceed to test their first-difference series. The test results are presented in Part 2 of Table 2.1. In both cases, the calculated test statistics are less than their critical values at 1% significance level, so we can reject H_0. Hence, both of the first-difference series of Korea's exchange rate and the short-term debt ratio are I(0), and their level series are I(1).

2.6.2 *The cointegration test*

Although Korea's exchange rate and short-term debt ratio are both I(1) series, it is quite possible that they can be cointegrated, and there exists a long-run equilibrium relationship between the two series. There are several testing procedures available for a cointegration test, and each method has its own merits and weaknesses (Enders, 1995). Since we have a bivariate case and our sample has only 20 observations, it is appropriate to use Engle and Granger's two-step cointegration test to estimate the cointegrating equations from both directions and then test the stationarity of both residual series (Engle and Granger, 1987, 1991; Enders, 1995; Maddala and Kim, 1998).

For this purpose, we generate the residual series from the estimated cointe-grating equation (step 1) and then use the ADF unit root test to examine the stationarity of the residual series (step 2). The ADF test equation for a unit root in the residual series is

$$\Delta e_t = \alpha e_{t-1} + \sum_{i=1}^{k} \beta_i \Delta e_{t-i} + v_t, \tag{2.2}$$

where Δe_t is the first-difference series of residuals e_t, and Δe_{t-i} is the ith lag of Δe_t. The value of optimal lag length k is selected by the minimum AIC method. v_t is the random error term. Since the residual series is calculated from a cointegrating equation, we do not need to include an intercept or time trend in Equation (2.2).

Table 2.2 presents the results of the two-step cointegration test for Korea. On the one hand, when we use the exchange rate as the dependent variable in cointegrating regression, the estimated cointegrating equation is

$$x_t = 6.119 + 0.035t + 0.071y_t, \tag{2.3}$$

where x_t is the logarithmic series of exchange rate, y_t is the short-term debt ratio and variable t is the time trend. From Equation (2.3), we generate the residual series e_t, and then apply the ADF unit root test on e_t series using the test equation (2.2).

On the other hand, when we use the short-term debt ratio as the dependent variable, the estimated cointegrating equation is

$$y_t = -27.445 - 0.290t + 4.970x_t. \tag{2.4}$$

We then generate the residual series u_t from Equation (2.4) and perform the ADF unit root test using Equation (2.2), where e_t is replaced by the u_t series. In both cases, the test statistics are less than the critical values at the 10% significance level.[23] Hence, we can reject H_0: $\alpha = 0$ in both cases, and e_t and u_t series are stationary. This implies that Korea's exchange rate series and the short-term debt ratio series are cointegrated and that there exists a long-run equilibrium relationship between these two series.

2.6.3 The ECM causality test

We have shown above that Korea's exchange rate and the short-term debt ratio are individually I(1) series and that they are cointegrated with order one.

---

23 See Engle and Yoo (1987), Table 3. We use the available critical value for sample size = 50.

Table 2.2 The Engle-Granger Cointegration Test
Korean Exchange Rate and Short-Term Debt Ratio

Step 1: Cointegrating regression					Step 2: ADF test of residual		Engle-Yoo critical values
Cointegrating	const.	t	Indep. vari.	adj			test
equation	a_0	a_1	a_2	R^2	k	statistic	10%
x = f(c, t, y)	6.119	0.035	0.071	0.578	e 2	-3.031 *	-2.90
equ. (2.3)	(0)a	(0)a	(0.01)a				
y = f(c, t, x)	-27.445	-0.290	4.970	0.574	u 2	-3.168 *	-2.90
equ. (2.4)	(0.02)b	(0)a	(0.01)a				

Notes: (1) The p-values are in parentheses. (2) For step 1: H0 is that the coefficient equals zero in the standard t-test. a and b denote that the test is significant at the 1% and 5% levels, respectively. (3) For step 2: * denotes rejection of H0: a unit root (no cointegration) at the 10% significance level.

Hence, the error-correction model (ECM) is appropriate to use in testing their causality relationship (Engle and Granger, 1987). The test involves the estimation of the following two equations:

$$\Delta x_t = \alpha + \sum_{i=1}^{m} \beta_i \Delta x_{t-i} + \sum_{j=1}^{n} \gamma_j \Delta y_{t-j} + \eta e_{t-1} + \mu_t, \qquad (2.5)$$

$$\Delta y_t = \delta + \sum_{i=1}^{p} \lambda_i \Delta x_{t-i} + \sum_{j=1}^{q} \theta_j \Delta y_{t-j} + \phi u_{t-1} + v_t, \qquad (2.6)$$

where Δx_t and Δy_t are the first-difference series of Korea's exchange rate and the short-term debt ratio. They are individually I(0) stationary series. The optimal lag lengths for m, n, p and q of the lagged variables Δx_{t-i} and Δy_{t-j} are selected by the minimum AIC method. The e_{t-1} is the lagged residual series from the cointegrating Equation (2.3), and u_{t-1} is the lagged residual series from the cointegrating Equation (2.4). μ_t and v_t are the random error terms in the ECM. The causal relationship in Equation (2.5) is seen from the joint significance of the coefficients γ_j's of Δy_{t-j}'s. The causal relationship in Equation (2.6) is seen from the joint significance of the coefficients λ_j's of Δx_{t-i}'s (Granger, 1969; Hsiao, 1987). The significance of the negative coefficients η and ϕ represents the long-run adjustment process and the convergence of the two series.

The left-hand side of Table 2.3 presents the ECM regression results (note that the variable resid(-1) is e_{t-1} in Equation (2.5) and resid(-1) is u_{t-1} in Equation

Table 2.3 The ECM Causality Test
Korean Exchange Rate and the Short-Term Debt Ratio

ECM Regression							Wald's coeff test		
Dep var.	Const	$\Delta x(-1)$	$\Delta x(-2)$	$\Delta y(-1)$	resid(-1)	adj R^2	Ho	F-stat	Causality
Δx equ.(2.5)	0.000 *(0.99)*	1.679 *(0)a*	-0.442 *(0.20)e*	-0.032 *(0.20)e*	-0.527 *(0.13)d*	0.599	$\gamma_1=0$	1.844 *(0.19)e*	D.R.→ Ex.R.(e) / D.R.→ Ex.R.(d)
Δy equ. (2.6)	-0.053 *(0.87)*	0.993 *(0.82)*	---	0.125 *(0.74)*	-0.836 *(0.04)b*	0.162	$\lambda_1=0$	0.055 *(0.82)*	Ex.R -\-> D.R. / Ex.R.→ D.R.(b)

Notes: (1) The p-values are in parentheses. (2) The a, b, c, d and e denote that the test is significant at the 1%, 5%, 10%, 15% and 20% level, respectively. (3) Ex.R. = Exchange Rate; D.R. = Short-term Debt Ratio.

(2.6)). The right-hand side of the table presents Wald's coefficient test, the results of causality direction and the long-run adjustment process of the series. For Equation (2.5), the optimal lag lengths are m = 2 and n = 1. The Wald's test for H_0: γ_1 = 0 shows that the F-statistic is 1.844, which has p-value = 0.19. This means that the test is significant at the 20% level. Although this significance level is slightly higher than the usual practice of the 10% or 15% level, nevertheless, it did imply that there is a causality relationship running from Korea's short-term debt ratio to the exchange rate. In addition, the coefficient η is −0.527, which is significant at the 15% level. This implies that there exists a significant long-run adjustment process between the two variables.

However, for Equation (2.6), the optimal lag lengths are p = 1 and q = 1. The Wald's test for H_0: λ_1 = 0 shows that the F-statistic is 0.055, which is very small and has a large p-value at 0.82. This means that the test is not significant even at the 20% level. This implies that there is no feedback causality from Korea's exchange rate to its short-term debt ratio. In addition, the coefficient φ is −0.836, which is significant at the 5% level. This means that there exists a significant long-run adjustment process between the two variables, which is consistent with the results from Equation (2.5).

In sum, at the 20% significance level (a rather weak case), our results from the ECM causality test indicate a unidirectional causality from Korea's short-term debt ratio to the exchange rate. Furthermore, the test results also show that there exists a long-run adjustment process between the two variables.

2.7 The Causality Test—The Case of Taiwan

For comparisons, we would like to use the same econometric techniques in the case of Korea above to examine the causality relation between Taiwan's nominal exchange rate (NT$/US$) and the short-term debt ratio using the

Table 2.4 The ADF Unit Root Test
Taiwan's Exchange Rate and the Short-Term Debt Ratio

Part 1: Level Series			MacKinnon
Variable	k	Test-stat	critical values, 10%
Exchange rate (c)	1	-2.027	-2.693
Short-term debt ratio (c, t)	5	-3.168	-3.446
Part 2: First-difference Series			MacKinnon
Variable	k	Test-statistic	critical values, 1%
Exchange rate (c, t)	3	-5.382 ***	-5.115
Short-term debt ratio (c)	2	-4.298 ***	-4.137

Notes: Same as notes (1), (2) and (3) in Table 2.1.

annual data from 1979 to 1998. The data are taken from the same sources in the ICSEAD (1999, 2000).

2.7.1 The unit root test

In the case of Taiwan, for the ADF unit root test equation (2.1), the variable x_t (level series) is the natural logarithm of Taiwan's exchange rate series (or, x_t may also be the short-term debt ratio series), and the other variables have the same definition. Part 1 of Table 2.4 presents the test results of the level series. Since both test statistics are greater than their critical values at the 10% significance level, Taiwan's exchange rate series and the short-term debt ratio series are not stationary.

Part 2 of Table 2.4 shows the test results of the first-difference series. Since both calculated test statistics are less than their critical values at the 1% significance level, the first-difference series of Taiwan's exchange rate and the short-term debt ratio are stationary, I(0), and their level series are I(1).

2.7.2 The cointegration test

Table 2.5 presents the Engle-Granger cointegration test results. When we use Taiwan's exchange rate (x_t) as the dependent variable, the estimated cointegrating equation is

$$x_t = 3.619 - 0.032t + 0.180y_t, \qquad (2.7)$$

Table 2.5 The Engle-Granger Cointegration Test
Taiwan's Exchange Rate and the Short-Term Debt Ratio

Step 1: Cointegrating regression					Step 2: ADF unit root test on residual series			Engle-Yoo critical values
Cointegrating equation	const. a_0	t a_1	Indep. vari. a_2	adj. R^2	Series	k	Test-statistic	10%
x = f(c, t, y) equ. (2.7)	3.619 (0)a	-0.032 (0)a	0.180 (0.83)	0.643	e	1	-1.817	-2.90
y = f(c, x)n equ. (2.8)	0.194 (0.27)	---	0.008 (0.88)	0.002	u	3	-1.149	-2.90

Notes: (1) Same as note 1 in Table 2.2. (2) Same as note 2 in Table 2.2, and n denotes that the equation has no significant time trend. (3) For step 2: H0 is that the residual series has a unit root.

where y_t is the level series of Taiwan's short-term debt ratio. When we use Taiwan's short-term debt ratio as the dependent variable, the estimated cointegrating equation is

$$y_t = 0.194 + 0.008x_t. \tag{2.8}$$

The ADF unit root tests on the residual series e_t from Equation (2.7) and u_t from Equation (2.8) above yield test statistics that are greater than their critical values at the 10% significance level. Hence, e_t and u_t series are not stationary. Therefore, Taiwan's exchange rate series and the short-term debt ratio series are not cointegrated. This finding is different from the case of Korea.

2.7.3 The standard Granger causality test

Although the level series of Taiwan's exchange rate and the short-term debt ratio are not stationary and not cointegrated, their first-difference series are stationary. We can use them in the short-run dynamic model of the standard Granger causality test (SGCT) to examine their causality relationship. The SGCT model involves the estimation of the following two equations (without resid(-1)):

$$\Delta x_t = \alpha + \sum_{i=1}^{m} \beta_i \Delta x_{t-i} + \sum_{j=1}^{n} \gamma_j \Delta y_{t-j} + \mu_t, \tag{2.9}$$

$$\Delta y_t = \delta + \sum_{i=1}^{p} \lambda_i \Delta x_{t-i} + \sum_{j=1}^{q} \theta_j \Delta y_{t-j} + v_t, \tag{2.10}$$

Table 2.6 The Granger Causality Test
Taiwan's Exchange Rate and the Short-Term Debt Ratio

Regression	constant	$\Delta x(-1)$	$\Delta y(-1)$	$\Delta y(-2)$	$\Delta y(-3)$	adj R^2	Ho	F-stat	Causality
Dep. var.									
Δx	-0.015	0.427	-0.294			0.093	$\gamma_1=0$	0.234	D.R. does not
equ.(2.9)	*(0.45)*	*(0.17)e*	*(0.64)*					*(0.64)*	cause Ex.R.
Δy	0.006	-0.028	-0.248	-0.356	-0.166	0.095	$\lambda_1=0$	0.067	Ex.R. does not
equ.(2.10)	*(0.41)*	*(0.80)*	*(0.45)*	*(0.18)e*	*(0.53)*			*(0.80)*	cause D.R.

Notes: Same as notes (1), (2) and (3) in Table 2.3.

where Δx_t and Δy_t are the first-difference series of Taiwan's exchange rate and the short-term debt ratio, respectively, and the other variables have the same definition as in Equations (2.5) and (2.6).

Table 2.6 presents the causality test results for Taiwan. For Equation (2.9), the optimal lag lengths are m = 1 and n = 1. The Wald's test for H_0: $\gamma_1 = 0$ shows that the F-statistic is small at 0.234, which has large p-value at 0.64. Therefore, we cannot reject the null hypothesis even at the 20% significance level. This implies that Taiwan's short-term debt ratio does not cause the exchange rate. However, for Equation (2.10), the optimal lag lengths are p = 1 and q = 3. The Wald's test for H_0: $\lambda_1 = 0$ shows that the F-statistic is very small at 0.067, which has a large p-value at 0.80. Hence, like in Equation (2.9), we cannot reject the null hypothesis even at the 20% significance level. This implies that Taiwan's exchange rate does not cause the short-term debt ratio.

In sum, the test results from the SGCT indicate that there is no causality relationship between Taiwan's nominal exchange rate and the short-term debt ratio. This finding is different from the case of Korea. Again, our study has demonstrated that the short-term-external-debt-to-the-international-reserves ratio has a very different impact on Korea's and Taiwan's exchange rates.

2.8 Conclusion: Lessons and Challenges

We have shown that macroeconomic fundamentals of the Korean economy were at least as good as those of Taiwan before the onset of the Asian financial crisis. Yet Taiwan has fared better than most of the Asian countries, while Korea was severely affected. Our figures show that the major difference between the two countries appears to be the external and financial sectors. Korea has an extremely high ratio of total external debt, in particular, the ratio of short-term external debt to international reserves, along with a high ratio of cumulative inward portfolio investment to international reserves. It is conceivable that a nation that has too much indebtedness heightens vulnerability to the speculative attack of foreign capital. When this occurs, all four factors that cause the crisis, as we have explained in Section 2.2, will be set in motion, resulting in currency and banking crises.

The wave of the financial crisis reached Taiwan by the end of July 1997, resulting in currency devaluation and stock price decline until the end of the year. However, Taiwan consistently had large trade and current account surpluses (see series [11] and [13] in Figures 2.5 and 2.6), abundant international reserves (see series [16] in Figure 2.8) and, above all, very low short-term external debt (see series [14b] in Figure 2.7). In contrast, unlike Korea, as early as 1989, Taiwan had already moved from the market average exchange rate system to a completely flexible exchange rate regime (EPA, 1998, 270), thus avoiding extreme vulnerability to both the banking and the currency crisis.

Furthermore, amply available internal capital funds, the large current account surpluses, the large share of government-held banks (55% by the end of 1996), the fear of capital flows from China and so forth did not motivate the Taiwanese to seek external borrowing actively. The slower pace of Taiwan's financial liberalization and internationalization[24] also did not attract massive international indirect foreign investment inflows either[25] (Fukushima and Takii, 1998, 138; EPA, 1999, 177–80). Ironically, while its slower pace of financial liberalization saved Taiwan, the planned acceleration of liberalization in the postcrisis era may pose a great challenge and renew instability in the future.[26]

---

24 However, Chen and Ku (2000, 127) suggest "the timing and sequencing of capital account liberalization in Taiwan was quite similar to that in Korea." According to a short chronology of financial liberalization in EPA (1998, 57), Korea seems to have run faster. It is also not clear when local banks were allowed to borrow money from foreign financial institutions. Indonesia did so in March 1989.

25 Fukushima and Takii, 1998, 138; EPA, 1999, 177–80. For a discussion of economic and political liberalization from a historical perspective, see Hsiao and Hsiao (2000a). For Taiwan's globalization process, see Hsiao and Hsiao (2001). Incidentally, China did not deregulate its capital market and strongly favored FDI. This is the major reason that China also weathered the financial crisis relatively well (EPA, 1998, 57).

26 Recently, *The Economist* (November 11, 2000) and *Business Week* predicted debt problems in Taiwan in early next year. Standard & Poor's recently downgraded Taiwan's economic rating from "stable" to "negative," *Taipei Journal*, December 22, 2000, 3. To our knowledge, none of the studies from Taiwan has concerned about possible instability due to accelerated financial reform. Unlike foreign reports, Taiwanese scholars

Our causality test results show that the ratio of short-term external debt to international reserves and the nominal exchange rate have a quite different causality relationship between Taiwan and Korea. The two series for Taiwan are not cointegrated, and there is no causality relation between the two series. However, the two series for Korea are cointegrated, showing the existence of a long-run equilibrium relationship between the two series. Furthermore, the causality test results for Korea shows that the ratio of short-term external debt to international reserves causes unidirectional exchange rate fluctuations but not vice versa. Considering the different impacts of the financial crisis on Taiwan and Korea, these findings are consistent with our expectation.

They are consistent with the fact that national currency depreciation and stock market fluctuations are the results of the self-fulfilling herd behavior of highly speculative international short-term debt. The unidirectional causality result is also consistent with a recent cross-sectional study by Kaminsky and Reinhart (2000, 478) in which they state that "a banking crisis increases the probability of that a country will fall prey to a currency crisis." The unidirectional causality may also rise from the fact that a banking crisis due to sudden reversal of capital flow has more severe and protracted effects on an economy than a currency crisis (Calvo and Reinhart, 1999). A prolonged attempt by the government to defend the national currency and to bail out failed firms might aggravate the crisis (Radelet and Sachs, 1998). The Taiwanese government intervened in the foreign exchange market heavily only for a very short period from July to October 1997, preserving precious international reserves[27] and keeping the already low short-term-debt-to-reserves ratio reasonably low.

In Korea, after considerable debate, the government finally, in December 3, 1997, accepted the rescue aid of US$ 57 billion from international organizations, including the IMF, World Bank and so on, under stringent conditions of economic reform (Fukushima and Takii, 1998, 141–42; Shim, 2000, 159–60). These conditions, which were challenges to the Korean government, included orderly reductions of the current account deficit ; buildup international reserves and containment of inflationary pressures; improvement in financial sector transparency, market-oriented practice and supervision; risk management; reduction of reliance on short-term debt; the allowing of foreign investment in Korean financial institutions; and the establishment of foreign financial subsidies to promote competition (Shim, ibid., 159–60).

---

generally consider that Taiwan got around the recent Asian financial crisis through "sound" monetary and fiscal policies. See conference papers in Policy Studies (1999).

27 Hu et al., 1998; Yang, 1998. Regarding the surprisingly few other studies that deal with the financial crisis in Taiwan, see Chen and Ku (2000) and Wang (2000).

As the financial reform and restructuring programs of chaebols proceeded rapidly and smoothly under the newly elected government, the economy started recovering during the first quarter of 1999. Reduction in domestic demand and imports (EPA, 1999, 158) prompted unprecedented surpluses in the trade balance and the current account balance in 1998 (Figures 2.5 and 2.6), and spurred GDP growth in 1999 (Figures 2.1 and 2.2). The economy has continued recovering and the recovery seems real and lasting (EPA, 2000, 151–61).

What is the economic future of these two countries? The recent prediction by the Asian Development Bank (2000, 242–43) is that the growth rate of real GDP (and real GDP per capita) for Korea is 7.5% and 6.0% (6.4% and 5.0%) in 2000 and 2001, respectively. For Taiwan they predict 6.3% and 6.2% (5.1% and 5.4%) in 2000 and 2001, respectively. The estimated figures are higher than for most of the Asian countries, including China. The continuous growth of the Korean and Taiwanese economies in the near future may be expected.

It is likely that the 1997 financial crisis will induce a vigorous restructuring of the Korean financial system and rationalization of its economy, and Korea and other Asian countries will come out as stronger competitors of Taiwan. While Taiwan has fared better in the recent crisis, the need for the restructuring and rationalization of its economy has also been revealed in this crisis, as its economy has also slowed down in recent years. If Taiwan does not complete its own economic reform resolutely, its future exports competitiveness may suffer irrevocably. The final impact of the Asian financial crisis is yet to be seen. A great challenge to these two countries, as well as other Asian countries, is to complete the restructuring of the financial and corporate sectors (Kawai, 2000), to improve regional integration and to cooperate in taking lessons from the eurozone (Letiche, 2000). These are basic steps to make the economic recovery last and to revive the "East Asian economic miracle" in the new millennium and the new international economic order (Dutta, 2000).

Sources of Data

The datasets in this chapter are taken from the IMF (1988; 1999) and the ICSEAD (1999; 2000), as noted in the text. All the tables in this chapter are the authors' own calculations.

Acknowledgments

This chapter was presented at the AEA/ACAES Session at the 2001 ASSA Annual Meeting in New Orleans, LA. We are grateful to Professors Richard Hooley, Hugh Patrick and Stephen Reynolds for helpful comments and suggestions. We are also indebted to Professors Steven R. Beckman, Charles Engel, Ronald W. Jones, Henryk Kierzkowski, Robert McNown, Ron P. Smith and Myles Wallace for helpful comments, and to Professors Peter C. Y. Chow, Jin-Lung Henry Lin, Keith Maskus, Eric D. Ramstetter, Don Roper, Hiroshi Setooka, Dr. Tatsufumi Yamagata and Messrs. Pao-Jui Chen, Jirawat Panpiemras and Changsuh Park for help in data collection. All errors of omission and commission are ours.

References

Abe, Kiyoshi (1998). "Thai Economic Disease: Ten Problems of the Footless Economy," *Economic Journal of Chiba University* (Keizai Kenkyu) 13 (June).

Agenor, Pierre-Richard (2000). *The Economics of Adjustment and Growth*. San Diego: Academic Press.

Agenor, Pierre-Richard, Marcus Miller, David Vines and Axel Weber, eds. (1999). *The Asian Financial Crisis: Causes, Contagion and Consequences*. Cambridge: Cambridge University Press.

Alba, Pedro, Amar Bhattacharya, Stijn Claessens, Swati Ghosh and Leonardo Henandez (1999). "The Role of Macroeconomic and Financial Sector Linkages in East Asia's Financial Crisis." In Agenor et al., 1999, chapter 1.

Asian Development Bank (ADB) (2000). *Asian Development Outlook 2000*. Oxford: Oxford University Press.

Bank of Korea. (1999). *Economic Statistics Yearbook*. Seoul: Bank of Korea.

Calvo, Guillermo A., and Carmen M. Reinhart (1999). "Capital Flow Reversals, the Exchange Rate Debate, and Dollarization," *Finance and Development*, September, 13–15.

Chen, Tain-Ji, and Ying-Hua Ku. (2000). "Differing Approaches, Differing Outcomes: Industrial Priorities, Financial Markets, and the Crisis in Korea and Taiwan." In Peter C. Y. Chow and Bates Gill, eds. *Weathering the Storm: Taiwan, Its Neighbors, and the Asian Financial Crisis*. Washington, DC: Brookings Institution Press, chapter 5.

Chow, Peter C. Y., and Bates Gill, eds. (2000). *Weathering the Storm: Taiwan, Its Neighbors, and the Asian Financial Crisis*. Washington, DC: Brookings Institution Press.

Corbett, Jenny, and David Vines (1999). "The Asian Crisis: Lessons from the Collapse of Financial Systems, Exchange Rates and Macroeconomic Policy." In Agenor et al., 1999, chapter 2.

Crockett, Andrew (2000). "Lessons from the Asian Crisis." In Joseph R. Bisignano, William C. Hunter and George G. Kaufman, eds., *Global Financial Crisis: Lessons from Recent Events*. New York: Kluwer Academic Publishers, Chapter 2.

Dickey, D. A., and W. A. Fuller (1979). "Distribution of the Estimators for Autoregressive Time Series with a Unit Root," *Journal of the American Statistical Association* 74(366): 427–31.

——— (1981). "Likelihood Ratio Statistics for Autoregressive Time Series with a Unit Root," *Econometrica* 49(4): 1057–1072.

Dutta, M. (2000). "The Euro Revolution and European Union: Monetary and Economic Cooperation in the Asia-Pacific." Working Paper, Department of Economics, Rutgers University.

Economic Planning Agency (EPA) (1998, 1999, 2000). Asian Economy 1998, Asian Economy 1999, *Asian Economy 2000* [in Japanese]. Tokyo: EPA.

Enders, Walter (1995). *Applied Econometric Time Series*. New York: John Wiley & Sons.

Engle, R. F., and B. S. Yoo (1987). "Forecasting and Testing in Co-integrated Systems," *Journal of Econometrics* 35: 143–59.

Engle, Robert F., and Clive W. J. Granger (1987). "Co-integration and Error-correction: Representation, Estimation, and Testing," *Econometrica* 55(2): 251–76.

——— (1991). *Long-run Economic Relationships-Readings in Cointegration*. Oxford: Oxford University Press.

Fukushima, Mitsuo, and Mitsuo Takii, eds. (1998). *The 1997 Asian Currency Crisis: An Analysis of Its Background and Impact on 9 East Asian Countries and Regions [in Japanese]*. Ajiken Topic Report, January. Tokyo: Institute of Developing Economies (Ajia Keizai Kenkyujo).

Glick, Reuven, ed. (1998). *Managing Capital Flows and Exchange Rates: Perspective from the Pacific Basin*. Cambridge: Cambridge University Press.

Gold, Thomas B. (1986). *State and Society in the Taiwan Miracle*. New York: M. E. Sharp.

Goldstein, Morris (1998). *The Asian Financial Crises: Causes, Cures, and Systemic Implications*, June. Policy Analyses in International Economics, 55. Washington, DC: Institute for International Economics.

Granger, Clive W. J. (1969). "Investigating Causal Relations by Econometric Models and Cross-Spectral Methods," *Econometrica* 37 (3): 424–38.

Hsiao, Frank S. T., and Mei-Chu W. Hsiao (2015). *Economic Development of Taiwan: Early Experiences and the Pacific Trade Triangle*. Singapore: World Scientific Publishing.

——— (2001). "Taiwan in the Global Economy: Past, Present, and Future." In Peter Chow, ed. *Taiwan's Modernization in Global Perspective*. Westport, CT: Praeger, 2002, 161–221. (Reprinted in Chapter 2 of Hsiao and Hsiao, 2015, 171–235).

——— (2000a). "Economic Liberalization and Development: The Case of Lifting Martial Law in Taiwan." In Taiwan Study Promotion Committee, ed. *The Transformation of an Authoritarian Regime: Taiwan in the Post-Martial Law Era*. Institute of Taiwanese History Preparatory Office. Taipei: Academia Sinica. 353–79. (Reprinted in chapter 12 of Hsiao and Hsiao, 2015, 505–31.).

——— (2000b). "International Comparisons of Taiwanese Economic Growth: A Long-run Perspective," 45 pp. Working Paper, Department of Economics, University of Colorado.

——— (1999). "The Historical Traditions of Taiwanese Small-and-Medium Enterprises." In Fu-San Huang and Ka-im Ang, eds. *Taiwan's Commercial Traditions: Collected Papers*. Taipei: Academia Sinica, 465–524. (Reprinted in Chapter 6 of Hsiao and Hsiao, 2015).

——— (1996). "Taiwanese Economic Development and Foreign Trade." In John Y. T. Kuark, ed. Comparative Asian Economies, in *Contemporary Studies in Economic and Financial Analysis* (vol. 77, part B). Greenwich, CT: JAI Press, 211–302. Originally published in Fairbank Center Discussion Paper No. 9, 1994, Harvard University, and also in William Kirby and Megan Greene, eds. (1995). *Harvard Studies on Taiwan: Papers of the Taiwan Studies Workshop, volume 1*. The John King Fairbank Center for East Asian Research, Harvard University, 1995. (Reprinted in Chapter 1 of Hsiao and Hsiao, 2015).

Hsiao, Mei-Chu W. (1987). "Tests of Causality and Exogeneity between Exports and Economic Growth: The Case of Asian NICs," *Journal of Economic Development* 12(2): 143–59.

Hu, Sheng-Cheng, Jin-Lung Lin, Jia-Dong Shea and Chung-Shu Wu (1998). "The Asian Financial Crisis: A Comparative Analysis of Taiwan Experience." Working paper, Institute of Economics, Academia Sinica, Taipei.

Ichimura, Shinichi, William James and Eric D. Ramstetter (1998). "On the Financial Crisis in East Asian Economies," International Center for the Study of East Asian Development (ICSEAD), Kitakyushu, Japan, Working Paper Series, vol. 98-14, June.

International Centre for the Study of the East Asian Development (ICSEAD) (1999). Recent Trends and Prospects for Major Asian Economies, *East Asian Economic Perspectives* (EAEP). 10, Special Issue. February.

——— (2000). Recent Trends and Prospects for Major Asian Economies, *East Asian Economic Perspectives* (EAEP). 11, Special Issue. February.

International Monetary Fund (IMF) (1997). "Philippines: Recent Economic Development," IMF Staff Country Report, No. 97/28. April.

——— (1998). *World Economic Outlook: A Survey by the Staff of the International Monetary Fund.* May. Washington, DC: International Monetary Fund.

——— (1999). *International Financial Statistics.* Washington, DC: International Monetary Fund.

Kaminsky, Graciela L., and Carmen M. Reinhart (1999). "The Twin Crises: The Causes of Banking and Balance-of-Payments Problems," *American Economic Review* 89(3): 473–500.

Kawai, Masahiro (2000). "The Resolution of the East Asian Crisis: Financial and Corporate Sector Restructuring," *Journal of Asian Economics* 11(2): 133–68.

Krugman, Paul (1998). "What Happened to Asia?" Manuscript, January.

Letiche, John M. (2000). "Lessons from the Euro Zone for the East Asian Economies," *Journal of Asian Economics* 11(3): 275–300.

Maddala, G. S., and In-Moo Kim (1998). *Unit Roots, Cointegration, and Structural Change.* Cambridge: Cambridge University Press.

Maddison, Angus (1995). *Monitoring the World Economy, 1820–1992.* Paris: Development Centre, OECD.

Park, Won-Am (2000). "Was Korea's Financial Crisis Self-fulfilling?" *Journal of the Korean Economy* 1(2): 301–23.

Park, Yung Chul (1996). "East Asian Liberalization, Bubbles, and Challenges from China," *Brookings Papers on Economic Activity*, 2.

Policy Studies (1999). "Conference Papers on Taiwan Economic Policy in Post-Asian Financial Crisis" [in Chinese], *Taiwan Economic Forecasting and Policy* 30(1). Taipei: Academia Sinica.

Radelet, Steven, and Jeffrey Sachs (1999). "What Have We Learned, So Far, from the Asian Financial Crisis?" Working Paper, Harvard Institute for International Development.

——— (1998). "The East Asian Financial Crisis: Diagnosis, Remedies, Prospects," Working Paper, Harvard Institute for International Development.

Rodrik, Dani, and Andres Velasco (1999). "Short-term Capital Flow," NBER, Working Paper no. 7364, September.

Shim, Young (2000). *Korean Bank Regulation and Supervision: Crisis and Reform,* London: Kluwer Law International.

Taiwan Statistical Data Book (TSDB) (2000). Taipei: Council for Economic Planning and Development.

Uchitelle, Louis (1998). "Economists Blame Short-Term Loans for Asian Crisis," *New York Times*, Business section, January 8.

Wang, Jiann-chyuan. (2000). "Taiwan and the Asian Financial Crisis: Impact and Response." In Chow and Gill, 2000, chapter 6.

Yang, Ya-Hwei (1998). "Coping with the Asian Financial Crisis: The Taiwan Experience," *Seoul Journal of Economics* 11(4): 423–45.

Chapter 3

PRODUCTIVITY GROWTH IN NEWLY DEVELOPED COUNTRIES: THE CASE OF KOREA AND TAIWAN

Abstract

Using the weighted Malmquist productivity index, the efficiency index and the technical index, this chapter compares the productivity growth of 15 matched manufacturing sectors of Korea and Taiwan. The distance functions are derived by using industry-wide production frontiers from 1979 to 1996. We find that the efficiency growth rates for both countries are high and are the predominant component of productivity. We also find that technology and productivity growth rates are much higher in Taiwan than in Korea. At a disaggregated level, there is more similarity in technology growth, but less or no similarity in efficiency growth. In both countries, productivity growth is similar, but traditional industries rely more on efficiency, basic industries on technology and high-tech industries on both. Lastly, in the innovator analysis, we found that the petroleum and coal products sector was consistently the major innovator of the manufacturing industry in both countries, but the minor innovators differed.

3.1 Introduction

Since the Asian financial crisis of 1997, it has become clear that the "East Asian Economic Miracle" has its limits. The Asian NIEs and the Association of Southeast Asian Nations (ASEAN) countries have fallen into recession and face the prospect of a productivity slowdown.[1] Taiwan and South Korea (hereafter Korea), the most prominent "twins" among the impressive Asian

---

1 Recovery is on the way in 2002, although "growth in the region will continue to be uneven. And there's plenty that can go wrong" *(Business Week, 2002)*. Note that we are examining the economy from the real side and that the crisis is on the financial side of the economy. Hsiao and Hsiao (2001a) have shown that the macroeconomic fundamentals of the two countries were basically sound before 1997 and that the disturbance occurred in the international finance sector. Thus, it appears that the estimated trend of

performers, are no exception. This chapter compares productivity growth and its two components, technical progress and efficiency change, at the matched manufacturing levels of the two countries during 18 years (1979–96) before the financial crisis set in.

The importance of productivity growth in the study of the economic development of nations cannot be overemphasized. Productivity growth is "the single most important indicator of any nation's economic performance in the long run" (Lester, 1998), and "for real economic miracles you have to look to productivity growth [...] In terms of human welfare, there is nothing that matters as much in the long run" (Baumol et al., 1989). Indeed, Korea and Taiwan can claim long-run "miracle growth" in the twentieth century. From 1911 to 1992, the average annual growth rate of real GDP per capita of Taiwan was 3.04%, and of Korea, 2.98%. The two ranked second and third in long-run world development, surpassed only by Japan, which had 3.34%.

If we restrict our calculation to the postwar period from 1951 to 1992, then Taiwan's real GDP per capita average annual growth rate was a whopping 6.03%, which was ranked number one in the world, followed by Korea's, at 5.98%, which was even higher than that of third-ranked Japan (5.57%) (Hsiao and Hsiao, 2003a). For almost a century, the real GDP per capita of Korea and of Taiwan, measured either by levels or by growth rates, grew like twins. By 1996, Korea was admitted to the OECD. Taiwan should have followed suit, but was prevented from doing so by international politics. Thus, one would expect a similar pattern of productivity growth in these two newly developed countries.

Productivity may be partial, either labor or capital productivity, or total (multifactor). Partial productivity is the value of output produced per unit of labor or capital, and total productivity measures the value of output when both factors are used. In this chapter we discuss both partial and total productivities in the manufacturing industry. Both Taiwan and Korea are manufacturing-oriented countries with a high share of manufacturing goods exports to total exports (Syrquin and Chenery, 1989). The manufacturing industry played a crucial role in the rapid growth of both countries in the postwar period (Timmer, 2000).

The traditional method of productivity analysis is to calculate productivity growth based on production or cost functions with some restrictive neoclassical assumptions.[2] Despite much discussion in the literature, there is no consensus about the size of total factor productivity growth rates (Hsiao and Hsiao,

---

productivity growth in this chapter, unless the crisis is due to overproduction, may not foretell the impending financial crisis like that in 1997.

2 See Stiroh (2001) for exposition on the restriction and a survey that is not inclusive and comprehensive of total factor productivity (TFP) studies. For survey articles, see

1998). This chapter, instead, proposes to employ the recently developed method of the Malmquist productivity index and its composition using non-parametric data envelopment analysis (DEA). There are a few papers that use the Malmquist index methodology to study productivity growth in Korea and Taiwan separately by decomposing the index into two components: technological change and efficiency change. These include Lee, Kim and Heo (1998) and Kim and Park (2002) for Korea, and Färe, Grosskopf and Lee (1995) and Lee (1997) for Taiwan. However, as far as we are aware of, no one has used this index to make direct comparisons of productivity growth between these two newly developed countries, even though they are so similar in history and stage of economic development.

One of the problems with comparisons of productivity among countries is that we may compare the productivity of economies at different stages of economic and social development. This happens in cross-section analyses when many countries are involved. Fortunately, this is not the case with Korea and Taiwan. Figure 3.1 presents a long-run historical view of both countries. It shows the ten-year moving average of real GDP per capita in 1990 Geary–Khamis dollars for Taiwan, South Korea and some OECD countries in the logarithmic scale since the colonial period (Hsiao and Hsiao, 2001a; Maddison, 1995). It visualizes and confirms the distinctively twinlike relation between the two countries. In the prewar period, both economies grew rapidly and attained the highest real GDP per capita just before World War II, and both then plunged to a level that was even lower than the level of the early 1910s.

The diagram shows that the "miracle" of economic growth in both countries started as early as the 1910s and was disrupted by World War II and the chaos of the early postwar period for almost 20 years. The economies recovered to their prewar peak during the late 1950s and the mid-1960s, and then continued to show rapid economic growth[3] thereafter. Their real GDP per capita is even expected to converge with that of Japan and the United States (Hsiao and Hsiao, 2003b). As economic growth is determined by productivity, we may expect that the pattern of productivity growth of these two countries would be similar. This is one of the points we would like to explore in this chapter.

Hsiao and Hsiao (1998) and Dowling and Summers (1998). A recent study of TFP growth in Korea is provided in Kwack (2000). There are several papers that compare directly the TFP of Korea and Taiwan, including Oshima (1987), Kawai (1994), Okuda (1997) and Timmer (2000). None, however, use the decomposition of the Malmquist productivity index.

3 Using the Perron's test of time-series analysis, Hsiao and Hsiao (2003a) have shown that the plunge in GDP per capita in 1944 was indeed very significant in both countries.

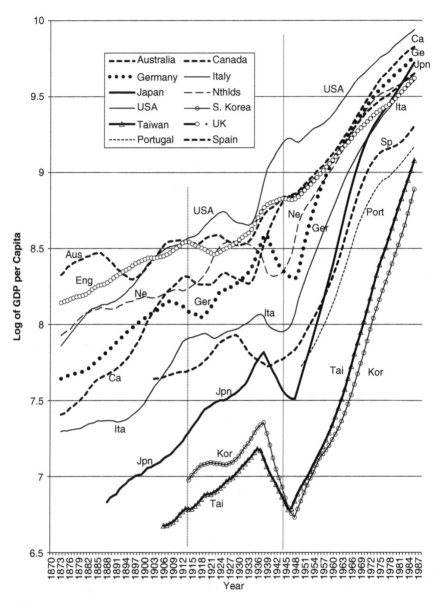

Figure 3.1 Real GDP per Capita of Taiwan, Korea and Some OECD Countries
The Ten-Year Moving Average

Figure 3.1 also shows that the real GDP per capita of Korea was consistently higher than that of Taiwan in the prewar period and that it became consistently lower than that of Taiwan in the postwar period. We would like to shed some light on this question from the vantage point of productivity growth of the matched manufacturing levels of both countries.

The major technical contribution of this chapter is to use the Malmquist output index and its composition, efficiency and technological changes in comparing the matched manufacturing sectors of Korea and Taiwan. We derive the composition in a very simple way in Section 3.2, followed by an explanation of the sources of data in Section 3.3. We use the three-digit matched industry levels of 15 manufacturing industries so that the differences in productivity are not due to the product composition of each industry. Torii and Caves (1992) also use the matched manufacturing sectors. However, they appear to be more concerned with the different estimation methods of frontier functions and with the determinants of the productivity of Japan and the United States.

Section 3.4 examines the overall industrial structure of Korea and Taiwan by comparing real output, real capital, the number of workers and partial productivity of labor and capital between Korea and Taiwan. This is the conventional analysis of productivity in the literature, as may be seen in various papers collected in Wagner and van Ark (1996).

In Section 3.5, we go beyond traditional analysis and studies and compare efficiency, technology and productivity of the cross-section of 15 manufacturing sectors, which are grouped into three categories: traditional, basic and high-tech industries as well as the time series of these indexes. We believe our method of presentation and analysis of international comparisons of productivity growth is innovative and unique in the literature. In Section 3.6, the time-series data are divided into period A, 1979–86, and period B, 1987–96. We then compare efficiency, technology and productivity of the three industrial categories in each subperiod. Section 3.7 asks an important question: which sectors are the real movers of the manufacturing industry in these newly developed countries each year, the sectors that help form the social metaproductivity frontier that serves to measure the efficiency and technology of other industries. We also discuss briefly the effects of industrial policy in both countries. Section 3.8 presents some conclusions.

3.2 The Malmquist Productivity Index

Unlike the neoclassical model of productivity analysis, the Malmquist productivity index method allows inefficiency in production and can be decomposed into efficiency change (catching up) and technical change (innovation). Let the pair of observed input vector x^t at time t and the corresponding observed output vector y^t at time t be denoted as $a^t = (x^t, y^t)$. Then the output distance function at *time* t is defined as

$$D^t\left(a^t\right) = \inf\{\delta \mid y^t / \delta \text{ is in } P^t(x^t)\}$$
$$= [\sup\{\delta \mid \delta y^t \text{ is in } P^t\left(x^t\right)\}]^{-1} , \qquad (3.1)$$

where $P^t(x^t) = \{y^t \mid x^t \text{ can produce } y^t\}$ is the production set at time t, which is convex, closed, bounded and satisfies the strong disposability of x^t and y^t (Coelli, 1996, 62). The scalar δ is a fraction, $0 < \delta \leq 1$ for all $y \geq 0$, and $\delta = 1$ if y^t is in the production set. Then, the Malmquist productivity index (MPI) at time t when the production set (technology) is $P^t(x^t)$ is defined as $M^t = D^t(a^{t+1})/D^t(a^t)$, which is the ratio of the maximum proportional changes in the observed outputs required to make each of the observed outputs efficient in relation to the technology at t.

Similarly, the MPI at time t +1 when the production set is $p^{t+1}(x)$ is $M^{t+1} == D^{t+1}(a^{t+1})/D^{t+1}(a^t)$, which refers to the technology at t +1. To avoid ambiguity in choosing the indexes, the output-oriented MPI is then defined as the geometric mean of the MPI in two consecutive periods (Coelli et al., 1998, 128; Färe et al., 1994):

$$\text{MPI}^t = (M^t M^{t+1})^{1/2} = \left[\left(\frac{D^t\left(a^{t+1}\right)}{D^t\left(a^t\right)}\right)\left(\frac{D^{t+1}(a^{t+1})}{D^{t+1}(a^t)}\right)\right]^{1/2} , \qquad (3.2)$$

where $\text{MPI}^t > = < 1$ implies productivity change is positive, zero or negative from period t to period t +1. In this chapter, we refer to the MPI simply as the productivity index. We estimate the four distance functions in Equation (3.2) by nonparametric linear programs. The objective is to construct an annual cross-industry best-practice meta production frontier from the sample, and then compare the observed annual output of each industry with this cross-industry frontier.

Following Färe et al. (1994, 1995) and Lee et al. (1998), we use a cross-industry frontier for the whole manufacturing industry, instead of category-specific frontiers,[4] since, in this chapter, we are interested in the relative performance among all the sectors of the manufacturing industry as a whole, reflecting

---

4 Elsewhere we have constructed the category-specific frontiers with further decomposition of the efficiency index into the pure efficiency change and the scale efficiency change, based on the variable-returns-to-scale technology (Hsiao and Park, 2002). For the definition of category in this chapter, see Section 3.3 below.

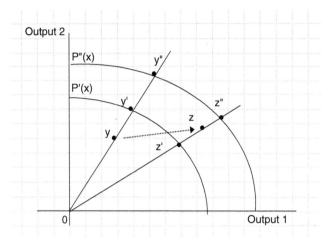

Figure 3.2 The Production Possibility Curves (PPC) and the Malmquist Productivity Index (MPI)

the social capacity of the economy-wide production system (Nishimizu and Hulten, 1978).

The MPI in (3.2) is the standard definition. It is enigmatic and not intuitively clear. In the literature, the diagram with one-input one-output of Färe et al. (1994) is often reproduced to illustrate the concept. Instead, we present it and show its decomposition using the familiar diagram of a production possibility curve[5] (PPC) (see Figure 3.2).

To avoid the cluttering of superscript in Figure 3.2, we denote the observed outputs for periods t and t +1 as y and z, respectively, and the corresponding efficient outputs at time t as y' and z' along the PPC P'(x), and those at time t +1 as y" and z" along the PPC P"(x), respectively. Then, in Figure 3.2, for two inputs case, definition (3.1) means that $D^t(a^t) = y/y'$, which is the ratio of actual output y at t to the corresponding output y' on the best-practice production frontier at time t, and $D^t(a^{t+1}) = z/z'$ is the ratio of the actual output z at time t +1 to the corresponding output z' on the best-practice production frontier at time t. These two distance functions show the degree of deficiency of the observed outputs (y, z) from the production frontier or technology (y^t, z^t) at time t. The ratio of these two distance functions then measures the change in the relative efficiency of the observed output at time t.

Similarly,

$$D^{t+1}(a^t) = y/y'' \text{ and } D^{t+1}(a^{t+1}) = z/z''$$

5 We submit that our method of illustration is unique in the productivity literature.

measure the degree of deficiency of observed outputs (y, z) from the best technology production (y", z") at t +1. Substituting them into the definition of the
MPI above and simplifying, we have

$$MPI = \left(\frac{z}{y}\right)\left[\left(\frac{y'}{z'}\right)\left(\frac{y''}{z''}\right)\right]^{1/2}.$$

(3.3)

Multiplying (y'/z")(z"/y') to the right side,

$$MPI = \left(\frac{z/z''}{y/y'}\right)\left[\left(\frac{y''}{y'}\right)\left(\frac{z''}{z'}\right)\right]^{1/2} = EI * TI.$$

(3.4)

Writing y"/y' as (y/y')/(y/y"), and z"/z' as (z/z')/(z/z") in the square brackets, then, in terms of the original distance function (3.2), (3.4) is equivalent to

$$MPI\left(a^{t+1}, a^{t}\right) = \underbrace{\frac{D^{t+1}\left(a^{t+1}\right)}{D^{t}\left(a^{t}\right)}}_{EI}\left[\underbrace{\left(\frac{D^{t}\left(a^{t+1}\right)}{D^{t+1}\left(a^{t+1}\right)}\right)\left(\frac{D^{t}\left(a^{t}\right)}{D^{t+1}\left(a^{t}\right)}\right)}_{TI}\right]^{\frac{1}{2}} = EI * TI. \quad (3.5)$$

Thus, the MPI is decomposed into a product of two terms. Each term in
the square root in (3.5) measures the ratio of the outputs on the PPC at time
t and t +1. The geometric average of the ratios is used as an index of the "technological change" over the two periods, and is denoted in this chapter[6] as TI
(the technology index). It shows the degree of expansion (or contraction) of
PPC due to new product and process innovation, new management system or
external shock.

The first term in (3.5) shows the ratio of the degree of deficiency of the
observed y and z relative to the corresponding output along the PPC at each
period. This term is an index of the relative "efficiency change" by comparing
the actual output with possible output the technology allows at each period,
and is denoted in this chapter as EI (the efficiency index). It reflects the results
of technology learning, knowledge diffusion and spillover across the industrial
sectors, improvement in market competitiveness, cost structure, capacity uti-
lization and so on.

---

6 We prefer to use the words "technical index" (TI), like price index, instead of the conventional name "technical change" to avoid confusion between the ratio y''/y' and the
percentage change $(y'' - y') * 100 / y'$.

When the observed outputs are on the PPC curve at each period, that is, y = y' and z = z", then EI = 1. In this case, if the technological progress is Hicks neutral, the PPC moves proportionately outward along the ray from the origin, and then, as shown in Fare et al., we have y"/y' = z"/z' = z/y. Hence, TI = z/y, where y is on P'(x) and z on P"(x). z/y is the same as the conventional definition (using the growth accounting method) of the total factor productivity (TFP) ratio between two periods. Hence, the TFP ratio is a special case[7] of the MPI when EI = 1.

When 1 is deducted from this ratio, TFPG ≡ (z/y −1) x 100 is the discrete growth rate[8] (or percentage change) of TFP (Färe et al., 1994) between the two consecutive periods. Similarly, MPG ≡ (MPI − 1) x 100 is the growth rate of productivity, EG ≡ (EI − 1) x 100 is the growth rate of efficiency, and TG = (TI −1) x 100 is the growth rate of technology. These three indicators will be used in this chapter to compare the industrial structures of Korea and Taiwan.

The output-oriented Malmquist productivity index (MPI), efficiency index (EI), and technology index (TI) are calculated using the method of nonparametric data envelopment analysis used in Färe et al. (1994) and programmed in Coelli (1996). The growth rates of the productivity (MPG), efficiency (EG) and technology (TG) are then obtained by subtracting one from the indexes and multiplying by 100. Comparisons of productivity are performed using indexes as well as growth rates, both of which are pure numbers, independent of the units of measurement used in each county.

Differentiating the MPI in (3.5) logarithmically, we have the unique relationship

$$\widehat{MPI} = \widehat{EI} + \widehat{TI} ,$$

where X with hat $\hat{X}$ denotes the growth rate $\hat{X} \equiv \Delta X/X$. It shows that the continuous growth rate of the MPI is the sum of the growth rate of the efficiency index (EI) and the growth rate of the technology index (TI). Since we use discrete growth rates, the relation between MPG, EG and TG is only approximate, that is,

$$MPG \approx EG + TG,$$

which may deviate considerably in some empirical studies.

---

7 Thus, it is confusing, if not in error, to refer to the MPI as the TFP or the TFP ratio.

8 However, if we define TFPG = ln z- ln y, then it is a continuous growth rate, which is compounded instantaneously. In the continuous case, the sum from period 0 to period 17 will cancel out the middle terms and the average growth rate is (ln y^{17} − ln y^0) /17. Since some growth rates are negative, we use the discrete growth rates.

3.3 Sources of Data

For Korea, the real value added and the number of workers by industry are taken from OECD (2000), STAN Database for Industrial Analysis 1970–1997. For the physical capital stock, see Pyo (1998). GDP by industry is taken from the Korea National Statistics Office (2002) home page: http://www.nso.go.kr.

For Taiwan, the data were made available to the authors courtesy of Drs. Sheng-cheng Hu and Vei-lin Chan. Real GDP (calculated by dividing the GDP deflator for each industry) is from *Taiwan Area National Income*, which has data on 22 manufacturing sectors. Due to the lack of consistency among the data, Hu and Chan (1999) selected 15 industries, which are used in this chapter. Real capital (at the 1991 constant price) is adopted from the table on Series of Real Net Fixed Capital Stock (excluding land) of Industrial and Service Sectors in *The Trends and Multifactor Productivity, Taiwan Area*, published every four years by the Directorate-General of Budget, Accounting and Statistics, Executive Yuan, Taiwan. The number of workers is taken from *Monthly Statistics of Manpower Allocation, Taiwan Area*, published by the Ministry of Economic Affairs (Hu and Chan, 1999).

Since Taiwan's dataset consists of 15 sectors, as shown on the left-hand side of Table 3.1, and ranges[9] from 1978 to 1996, the Korean data are rearranged and matched with the Taiwanese data and are reduced to 15 sectors, as noted in the last column of Table 3.1.

To calculate the Malmquist productivity index of (3.2), we need four distance functions for the initial two periods for each sector. Each additional period requires three more distance functions (Coelli, 1996). Thus, for 18 years, each sector requires 52 (= 3 x 18 −2) distance functions.

For 15 sectors and 18 years, we have found 780 linear program solutions of distance functions to construct the time series of the productivity index. The productivity index of each sector in each year is decomposed into indexes of efficiency and technology. At the end, we have generated a sample of 810 (= 3 x 15 x 18) panel data of the three indexes.

In addition to the evidence of a break in the data in the mid-1980s, especially for Taiwan, as presented in Section 3.4 below, since the years in the mid-1980s are considered as a time of transition from traditional industrialization to the high-tech and service-oriented industrialization for both countries, the time-series data have been divided into two subperiods: Period A covers 1979 to 1986 and Period B, 1987 to 1996. Taiwan lifted its 37-year-long martial law in 1987 and entered a new era of political freedom and economic liberalization and reform (Hsiao and Hsiao, 2001b).

---

9 The data range from 1978 to 1996. We lost one year in calculating the indexes and the growth rates.

Table 3.1 Classification of 15 Manufacturing Industries

Category			STAN Industry Category for Korea
A. No.		Taiwan's 15 Sectors	Combination of Korean Mfg Sectors
T	01	1 Food, Berages & Tabacco	311, 312, 313, 314
T	02	2 Textiles	321
T		3 Apparel and Ornaments (a)	322
T		4 Leather, Fur, and Products	323
T	03	5 Wood Products & Non-metalic Furniture	331, 332
T	04	6 Paper, Paper Products & Printing	341, 342
B	05	7 Chemical Products, Rubber, and Plastics	351, 352, 355, 356
B	B.	8 Petroleum, Coal, and Products	353, 354
B	06	9 Non-Metallic Mineral Products	361, 362, 369
B	07	10 Basic Metal Industries	371, 372
B	08	11 Fabricated Metal Products	381
H		12 Machinery Products and Repairs	382
H		13 Electric, Electronic Machinery Products and Repairs	383
H		14 Transportation Products and Repairs	384
H	09	15 Precision Instruments and Other Manufacturing (b)	385, 390

Notes: (a) The Korean list includes "#324 Footwear," which may be "wearing apparel" or "leather products." Since we do not have detailed information, we divide the number in 324 in two: one half in Apparel (322), and the other half in Leather and Products (323). (b) The title of 385 in the Korean list is "Professional Goods."

Similarly, Korea passed the 6.29 Declaration on Democratization to change the presidential election method from indirect to direct election by the people and promulgated seven other laws to democratize the society. One of the consequences of this, as in Taiwan, has been the gain in power of labor unions (Lee et al., 2001).

Following Hu and Chan (1999), the 15 sectors in the cross-section dataset are further grouped into three categories: the traditional industry category (T, Sectors 1 to 6), the basic industry category (B, Sectors 7 to 11) and the high-tech industry category (H, Sectors 12 to 15), as shown in the "Category" column in Table 3.1.

3.4 Labor and Capital Productivities

The conventional method of comparing the productivity of manufacturing sectors within and between countries is to examine average labor productivity and average capital productivity of the manufacturing industry (Wagner and van Ark, 1996).

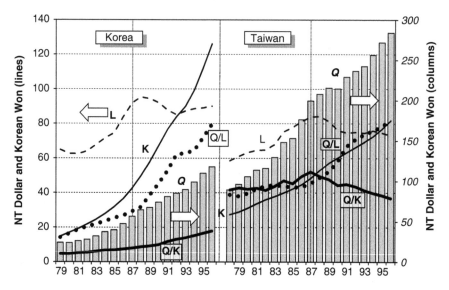

Figure 3.3 Real Output, Labor and Capital Productivities
Korea and Taiwan

Figure 3.3 draws the time series of real output (Q) and real capital (K), and
the number of workers (L), labor productivity (Q/L) and capital productivity (Q/K), measured in New Taiwan dollars for Taiwan and won for Korea,
except that labor is given by the number of workers. The units of the data
are adjusted to fit the time series in one diagram. They are drawn to show
merely the trend and shape of the lines within the country and between the
countries over the years, but the height of the lines and columns between the
two countries are not comparable, as the lines and columns are measured in
each country's national currency in different units (to show in one chart). With
the exception of real output, which is drawn in columns, measured from the
right-hand side secondary Y-axis, and labeled in italic, all lines are measured
from the left-hand side primary Y-axis.

    In both countries, there is a steady increase in real output (Q, the col-
umns), real capital stock (K, the light solid line), labor (L, the light dashed line)
and labor productivity (Q/L, the heavy dotted line) during the longer period.
However, in both countries, there is a surge in the number of workers in the
first half of the 1980s, when then tapers off and decreases afterward. The
difference between the two countries is apparent in capital productivity (Q/
K, the heavy solid line), which increases steadily in Korea during 1979–96,
but which in Taiwan increases up to 1987 and then decreases after 1988, corresponding to the decrease in the output share of the manufacturing sector
in GDP, as Taiwan enters a service-oriented stage of development after the

mid-1980s (Hsiao and Hsiao, 2001b). Since the manufacturing sector is generally more capital intensive, it is not clear that the decrease in the share of the manufacturing industry in the industrial output is due to the decrease in capital productivity. To determine whether that is the case, we need to look into the experience of other advanced countries.

3.5 Total Productivity Growth 1979–96

Having calculated efficiency, technology and productivity growth rates for Korea and Taiwan covering the cross-section of 15 manufacturing sectors, each of which has a time-series of the three growth rates from 1979 to 1996, we now discuss their properties separately.

3.5.1 Analysis of the cross-section data

Figure 3.4 shows the three indexes[10] of each manufacturing sector for the period from 1979 to 1996. EG is shown by an empty column on the left, TG by a filled dark column on the right and MPG by a marked line with circles. The number next to the circle mark is the value of MPG. We also calculated the weighted grand average[11] growth rates, EG, TG and MPG, for the whole manufacturing industry. We weighted the average by value-added output shares for an obvious reason, that is, to take into account the importance (or size) of a sector in the industry. In Figure 3.4, the weighted grand average (Grd Avg) and its values are shown in large circles. The lower section of the chart also indicates whether a sector is in the traditional (T), basic (B) or high-tech (H) category.

Comparisons at the aggregate level

At an aggregate level of weighted grand average growth rates of the manufacturing industry as a whole, both countries have almost the same

---

10 Figure 3.4 is constructed as follows. We first take the geometric mean of EI (and also TI and MPI) of each manufacturing sector for the period from 1979 to 1996; thus, we have 15 means of EIs, one each for 15 sectors. We do the same for TI and MPI. We then subtract one from each mean and multiply it by 100 to obtain EG, TG and MPG.

11 To derive the weighted grand average, we first weight the index EI (and similarly TI and MPI) using the value-added output share of each sector for each year as weight, and then sum the weighted index for each year over the 15 sectors. This will aggregate the EI for 15 sectors. We do the same for TI and MPI. After taking the geometric mean of EI, TI and MPI for 18 years, respectively, and subtracting one from the index and multiplying by 100, we have the weighted grand average growth rates of the manufacturing industry for the three indexes.

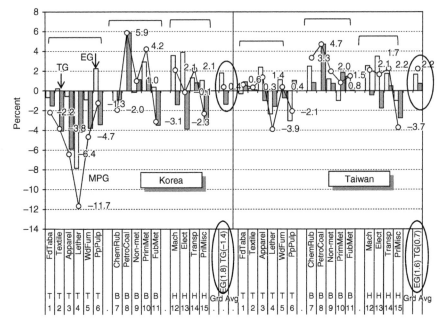

Figure 3.4 Efficiency, Technology and MPI Growth Rates
Korea and Taiwan. 15 Manufacturing Sectors, 1979–96
Arranged by Table 3.1

positive efficiency growth (see the circled numbers in the X-axis labels), 1.80% for Korea and 1.65% for Taiwan. However, the similarity ends here. The overall weighted technology growth rates (TG) are quite different, −1.38% for Korea and 0.72% for Taiwan, resulting in a low-weighted MPG for Korea (0.38%) and a much higher weighted MPG for Taiwan (2.23%) (See the circle marker of "Grd Avg" (Grand Average) column in Korea and Taiwan sections). Thus, efficiency growth is the dominant factor in productivity growth in both countries, and they are almost the same.

However, considering that the manufacturing industry plays a prominent and leading role in a country's industrialization, negative technology growth and the resulting low productivity growth in Korea may, at least partially, explain[12] why GDP per capita of Korea falls behind that of Taiwan in Figure 3.1. It is rather surprising that technology growth rates, and therefore

---

12 Other explanations are that there may be systematic errors in the data; the aftermath of the evils of colonialism may have been worse in Korea than in Taiwan; it may also be due to different government policies or to different patterns of development and industrial structure (Hsiao and Hsiao, 2003a).

productivity growth rates, can be so different between these two newly developed countries.

While a detailed analysis is beyond the scope of this chapter, we may venture an explanation as follows. Korean industries are generally dominated by large chaebols (Hattori, 1997), the main concern of which is efficiency and cutting cost to remain competitive (Schive, 1990, 282), while the Taiwanese industries consist of small and medium-sized enterprises (Numazaki, 1997), their success depends on a quick response to demand changes, and hence, new technology and new design play an important role for their survival.

A very clear similarity can be found in the high-tech industry category (H). Except for the efficiency growth rate of the "Precision Instruments and Others Manufacturing" sector (15), the sign pattern of the growth rates of efficiency, technology and productivity and the order of the productivity growth rates among the sectors are all remarkably the same between the two countries, and the size difference is also small, showing a similar industrial structure in the hightech category in both countries.

As we elaborate below, this is due to the fact that both countries have enforced the development of the electric and electronic sector, machinery and so forth, and the high-tech industries are more exposed to the same international market and multinational investment in both countries. In contrast, the traditional category is more local in character and differs considerably between the two newly developed countries.

The similarities and differences among the three categories are clearer if the three indexes are arranged in descending order of productivity growth rates (MPG). This is shown in Figure 3.5. In all categories, Korea has much larger and more negative growth rates than Taiwan, especially in technology growth. Note the similarity of the shape and location of the columns and lines in all categories, especially the same ranking of sectors in the High-tech category. They are indeed visually similar.

Similarity in the high-tech industries, especially in the electronics industry is due to technology transfer through TNC (transnational corporation) investment, joint ventures, foreign buyers, foreign licensing and capital goods imports from foreign countries, especially from Japan and the United States (Hobday, 1995). This is a large and complex issue that should be a topic of another discussion. We may point out briefly a few observations as follows. In Korea, from 1982 to 1986, 50% and 33% of the value of FDI came from Japan and the United States, respectively (Kim, 1999, 195). During the same period, Japan and the United States provided 27% and 51% of the total value of technical licensing, 27% and 48% of the total value of technical

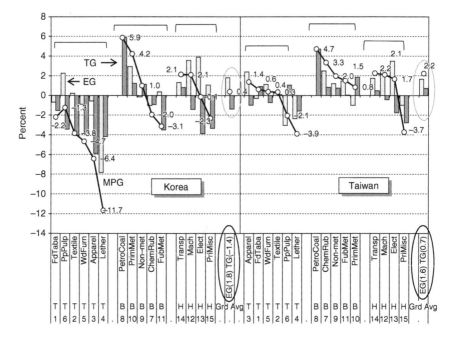

Figure 3.5 Efficiency, Technology and MPI Growth Rates
Korea and Taiwan, 15 Manufacturing Sectors, 1979–96
Sorted by MPG in Each Category

consultancy and 25% and 14% of capital goods imports, respectively (ibid.), mostly in the field of high-tech industries[13] (Hobday, 1995).

In Taiwan, from 1982 to 1986, an equal amount of 33% of the value of FDI came from Japan and the United States (TSDB, 2002, 268). About one-quarter of Japanese investment and one-half of American investment (all in value terms) were in electronic and electric appliances.[14] From 1989 to 1995, Japan and the United States provided 37% and 33% of the value of technical

---

13 Urata (1996, 152) shows that from 1986 to 1993, the value of Japanese investment in Korea was 27% in electric machinery, 20% in transportation equipment and 10% in general machinery, for a total of 57% in high-tech industries, while those in Taiwan were 27%, 10% and 9%, respectively, for a total of 46%.
14 This is estimated from the cumulative data from 1952 to 1995, see IC (1995, 40–43). During 1952–95, the Japanese and US investments in Taiwan's high-tech industries (general machinery, electronic and electric appliances, transportation equipment, and precision instruments) were 41% and 53% of their total investment (ibid.).

transfer, respectively.[15] Similar to Korea, these were mostly in the field of high-tech industries (Hobday, 1995). Since Japan and the United States have been prominent providers of investment and technology in the high-tech industries, and much less, or none, in the traditional industries, in Korea and Taiwan, similarity in efficiency and technology in the high-tech industries in the two countries can be expected.

Correlation coefficients

To find the degree of relationship among the sectors between Korea and Taiwan, we have calculated Pearson correlation coefficients[16] among EG, TG and MPG between Korea and Taiwan, shown in Table 3.2. This table shows the correlation coefficients of weighted indexes[17] for the 15 manufacturing sectors in the two countries, using the data in Figure 3.4. Table 3.2A indicates the coefficients of the manufacturing industry as a whole, and Tables 3.2B to 3.2D indicate the coefficients for the three categories. In each subtable (B, C, D), the upper left block (along columns 1 and 2) shows the correlations among the pairs from EGk, TGk and MPGk for Korea alone, and the lower right block (along columns 4 and 5) shows the correlations among the pairs from EGt, TGt and MPGt for Taiwan alone. The coefficients along the diagonal line in the enclosed range with bold-faced numbers are the direct comparisons of EG, TG and MPG between Korea and Taiwan, and the off-diagonal numbers are cross-comparisons of growth rates between the two countries.

---

15 NSC (1998, 86–87). Earlier data (M. Hsiao, 1992, 158) show that the value of technical transfer from Japan and the United States to Korea (1962–85) was 55% and 23%, respectively, and to Taiwan (1952–83) was 66% and 21%, respectively.

16 Correlation analysis is often used in intercountry comparisons, as seen in O'Mahony and Wagner (1996). For the use of the t distribution in productivity analysis, see Torii and Caves (1992). Note that t(0.01, 16) = 2.921, t(0.05, 16) = 2.120, t(0.10, 16) = 1.746, etc. When p = 0 is rejected at a level of significance, then the industry in the two countries correlates at that level of significance.

17 The correlation coefficient r's of the weighted indexes are taken as follows. For Table 3.2B to 3.2D in each country, we weigh each of the three indexes EI, TI and MPI in each category by the corresponding value-added output shares within that category for each year. Squaring the weighted index in each category, we have the average weighted index for each category, with each index containing 18 time-series observations. The correlation coefficients are taken among the six weighted indexes, EIk, EIt, within a category, the degree of freedom being 16. For Table 3.2A, the r's are calculated by summing a weighted index of the 15 manufacturing sectors, the weights being the value-added output shares of the 15 manufacturing sectors of that country each year. Thus, each of the six indexes contains 18 time-series observations. Note that the calculations of the r's among the indexes (EIk, EIt, ...) and of the r's among the growth rates (EGk, EGt, ...) are the same.

Table 3.2 Pearson Correlation Coefficients of Manufacturing Industry Korea and Taiwan, 1979–96

A. Mfg Industry n = 15

	Mfg	EGk	TGk	MPGk	EGt	TGt
1	TGk	0.045				
2	MPGk	0.808 a	0.625 a			
3	EGt	**-0.11**	0.165	0.022		
4	TGt	0.514 b	**0.01**	0.408 c	-0.727 a	
5	MPGt	0.622 a	0.206	**0.62** a	0.133	0.580 b

B. Traditional Category n = 6

		EGk	TGk	MPGk	EGt	TGt
6	TGk	-0.444 c				
7	MPGk	0.671 a	0.365 d			
8	EGt	**0.061**	0.097	0.158		
9	TGt	-0.073	**0.15**	0.049	-0.606 a	
10	MPGt	-0.012	0.266	**0.22**	0.482 b	0.402 c

C. Bsic Category n = 5

		EGk	TGk	MPGk	EGt	TGt
11	TGk	-0.121				
12	MPGk	0.628 a	0.695 a			
13	EGt	**-0.15**	0.245	0.093		
14	TGt	0.238	**-0.16**	0.042	-0.885 a	
15	MPGt	0.292	0.056	**0.26**	-0.297	0.701 a

D. High-tech Category n = 4

		EGk	TGk	MPGk	EGt	TGt
16	TGk	0.422 c				
17	MPGk	0.966 a	0.640 a			
18	EGt	**0.193**	-0.141	0.128		
19	TGt	0.488 b	**0.45** c	0.542 b	-0.143	
20	MPGt	0.572 b	0.348 d	**0.59** b	0.458 c	0.813 a

Notes: a, b, c and d = significant at 1%, 5 %, 10 % and 15%, respectively, of the t distribution for the null hypothesis, H_0: $\rho = 0$.

We submit that if the Korean and Taiwanese economies are at the same stage and the structures of production are similar, then the growth rates of efficiency, technology and productivity will be more or less similar and of the same magnitude and trend, as the sample may be regarded as drawn from the same population. This implies that the Pearson and rank correlation coefficients between the variables and countries should be high. With this understanding, we may observe several interesting patterns in Table 3.2.

Intercountry coefficients

For the manufacturing industry as a whole (Table 3.2A), along the bold-faced diagonal elements in the small box, the correlation coefficient is high and very significant for productivity growth (MPGt, MPGk), but that of technology growth (TGt, TGk) is almost zero and not significant, and that of efficiency growth (EGt, TGk) is negative and not significant. The two newly developed countries are very similar in the pattern of productivity growth, and yet have quite different, or even opposite patterns of efficiency and technology growth at the aggregate level of the manufacturing industry.

Along the diagonal of other subtables (Tables 3.2B, 3.2C, 3.2D), correlation coefficients in the traditional sector are positive but not significant, and in the basic sectors, they tend to be negative but not significant. Only technology growth and productivity growth in the high-tech category are significant at the significant levels of 5, 10 or 15%. This reinforces our observation above that new technology comes from the same international market, which both Korea and Taiwan face, resulting in high correlation coefficients. In contrast, efficiency improvement, similar to the traditional industries, is more country specific and is local in character, independent of international influence. This seems to be the case in general for all the boxes in the subtables. In the traditional and basic categories the correlation coefficients are not significant or even negative. That is, these sectors in the two countries are generally not correlated, in other words, not similar.

Intracountry coefficients

The triangle matrices in the upper left corner along columns 1 and 2 and the lower right corner along columns 4 and 5 show the relation of the three growth rates within each country. The withincountry comparisons also reveal several interesting similarities between the two countries.

For the manufacturing industry as a whole (Table 3.2A), in both countries, there is a very high correlation between MPG and EG or TG, especially in Korea, but low or negative and significant correlation between EG and TG. Thus, even though EG and TG are the components of MPG, they are generally independent of each other inside each country.

This relation, however, differs with the industry category. In the traditional sector (Table 3.2B), EG and TG in both countries, and especially EG, have high and significant correlations with MPG. Thus, for both countries, the main source of productivity growth in the traditional category comes from improvement in efficiency rather than in technology.

In contrast, in the basic category (Table 3.2B), TG in both countries has a very high and significance correlation (1%) with MPG, but EG has a different relation in the two countries. EG is highly correlated with MPG in Korea, but negatively and insignificantly correlated with MPG in Taiwan. Thus, we may consider that the main source of productivity improvement in the basic category comes mostly from technology growth rather than from efficiency growth, as the effects of EG on MPG in these newly developed countries differ.

In the high-tech industry category (Table 3.2D), we notice that, unlike the other two categories, both EG and TG have a very high correlation with MPG at the 1% significance level, although the correlation coefficient between EG and MPG in Taiwan is rather low at the level of significance of 10%. Thus, in both countries, the source of growth of productivity in the high-tech industry category comes from both efficiency improvement and technology growth, greatly increasing the output growth of the high-tech industries in both countries.

The overall effect of the three categories on the manufacturing industry, as shown in Table 3.2A, is that in Korea both efficiency and technology improvements contribute to productivity growth (at 1% level of significance), but in Taiwan, efficiency growth does not contribute to productivity growth, and only technology growth does so in all categories.

Aside from the bold-faced diagonal coefficients, the off-diagonal coefficients relate one index of one country to another index in the other country. The coefficients may be small or negative and generally not significant, as expected. However, a strange finding is that in the high-tech category, Korea's technology growth and efficiency growth are significantly correlated with Taiwan's productivity growth, and so is Taiwan's technology growth with Korea's productivity growth. The explanation is not clear.[18] Both growth indexes may be influenced by a third factor, such as the international technology market or the pattern of technology transfer in the high-tech industries, or perhaps there is a learning process between the countries. In any case, this interpretation is consistent with our other observations.

Figure 3.5 above shows, when each category is arranged in decreasing order of productivity growth rates (MPG), the shape, trend and position of the three indexes are visibly very similar between the two countries. Thus, we have also calculated the cross-country rank correlation coefficients of the ranking

---

18 There are a few studies comparing the industrialization of Korea and Taiwan separately, but none have examined the relationship between these two countries. See Okuda (1997) and other articles in the same issue. Also see Wade (1990) and Schive (1990). Schive (ibid.,278) stated that a Taiwanese firm (Mosel) sold its 64K CMOS SRAM to Hyundai of Korea.

of the sectors in each category between the indexes (not shown here). It turns out that the correlation coefficients of the rankings in each category are very similar to Table 3.2. For the manufacturing industry as a whole, the rank correlation for the technology index is large (0.7) and that of the efficiency index is very small (0.2). The rank correlation coefficients of EG in traditional and basic categories are negative and small and insignificant, while the coefficient in the high-tech category is 1.0. Thus, the efficiency growth in both countries is not only country specific, but the ranking of the sectors is also country specific. In contrast, technology growth in both countries is not only highly significantly correlated, but the ranking of the sectors is also exactly the same. This again seems to reflect the international character of technological growth.

Correlation at the sectoral levels

Instead of comparing the weighted indexes in each category, we may go one step further and find the correlation coefficients of unweighted indexes EG, TG and MPG between the two countries sector by sector.[19] This is presented in Figure 3.6, diagrammatically. The left-hand side of Figure 3.6 shows the direct correlation coefficients of each manufacturing sector between Korea and Taiwan. Clearly, the coefficients for EG (the empty bars, EGkt) are generally lower than those for TG (the filled bars, TGkt). Thus, technology growth shows more similarity between the two countries than does efficiency growth. There are more positive and high correlation coefficients in TG, more negative correlations in EG and MPG in the traditional category and more negative correlations in TG and positive correlations in MPG in the basic category. Thus, more diverse trends are shown in the traditional and basic categories between the two countries.

In particular, in traditional industries, the "Food, Beverage, and Tobacco" (#5), "Apparel" (#2) and "Leather, Fur, and Products" (#4) sectors have a negative correlation coefficient in productivity (the solid line with circle markers, MPGkt), but the "Food, Beverage, and Tobacco" (#5), "Wood Products" (#3) and "Leather" (#4) sectors have very high correlation coefficients in TG and low or negative coefficients in EG.

In the traditional and basic industry categories, the correlation coefficient of TG and EG tend to be opposite: if one is positive, the other tends to be negative. This is not the case in the high-tech category, in which TG and EG

---

19 The correlation coefficient *r* of each sector between the two countries is found by correlating the time series data of EI (or TI or MPI) of a sector in Taiwan with the time series data of EI of the same sector in Korea. The same for TI and MPI. In this exercise, the indexes are not weighted.

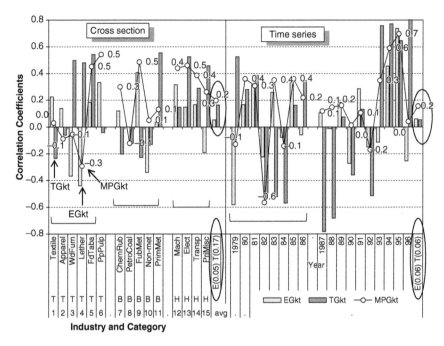

Figure 3.6 Correlation Coefficients of Growth Rates
Korea and Taiwan, Each Industry and Period, 1979–96

often have relatively strong and positive correlation coefficients, except EG in the "Precision Instruments and Other Manufacturing" (#15) sector.

Our diagram confirms our observation in Table 3.2 that there is more similarity among the indexes in the high-tech categories than the other categories. Thus, whether from the weighted indexes in Table 3.2 or the unweighted indexes in Figure 3.6, we have the same observations and conclusion.

We have also calculated the (arithmetic) average of the correlation coefficients of the 15 sectors. The average EG of the whole manufacturing industry is close to zero (0.05), while the average TG is 0.17, and the average MPG is 0.2. These numbers are indeed small, mainly due to the cancellation effect of the positive and negative correlation coefficients. It also suggests that analyses based on aggregated numbers alone may be misleading.

3.5.2 Analysis of time-series data

The right-hand side of Figure 3.6 presents correlation coefficients of unweighted indexes for the 15 manufacturing sectors for each year between

Korea and Taiwan[20] separating period A and period B. The correlation coefficients fluctuate considerably over the years: more fluctuating and more negative in the early 1980s, and mostly negative in the late 1980s, which shows the trend of deviation between the two countries. The correlation coefficients in the 1980s are either small but positive or large but negative. The technology growth rates (TG), in particular, have a large but negative correlation (above 0.5). However, in the first half of the 1990s, the industrial structure of both countries seems to converge in all three indexes, as both governments emphasize high-tech industries during this period.

3.6 Productivity Growth of Three Categories in Subperiods

We have examined the productivity performance of the manufacturing industry of Korea and Taiwan in the 1979–96 period in the previous section. In this section, we would like to examine sector by sector[21] the performance of three categories, traditional, basic and high-tech industries, in each subperiod, called period A (1979–86) and period B (1987–96). A much clearer similarity between the two countries in the industrial structure of the manufacturing industry emerges in the subperiods.

Figures 3.7 and 3.8 show the three categories of the manufacturing industry for period A and period B for Korea and Taiwan, respectively: the sectors are arranged in the original order for easy comparison sector by sector. When the sectors in each category are rearranged in accordance with a decreasing order of productivity growth rates (MPG), the similarity is much more striking (not shown) than that in Figure 3.5 above. Note the great similarity in terms of the shape, size and position between the two countries in each period, especially those of the productivity index in period B.

In period A, Korea has a mixture of signs of the efficiency growth rates (EG), the technology growth rates (TG) and productivity growth rates (MPG), while Taiwan has mostly positive growth rates for almost all sectors and

---

20 The correlation coefficient r of each year between the two countries is found by correlating the cross-section data of EI (or TI or MPI) of a year in Taiwan with the corresponding cross-section data of EI of the same year in Korea. The same holds for TI and MPI. In this exercise, the indexes are not weighted.

21 Since we do not aggregate the data, the indexes are not weighted by the value-added output shares. Notice that, in both countries, the time trend of the manufacturing sector in period B, 1987–96, appears to be different, and thus we take 1987 as the year of demarcation. See Appendix 3A and Figure 3A.1

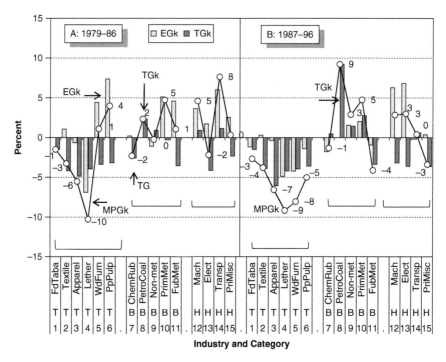

Figure 3.7 Efficiency, Technology and MPI Growth Rates
Korea, 15 Manufacturing Sectors, 1979–86 and 1987–96

categories, showing the vitality of the Taiwanese manufacturing industry over
Korean industry in period A. Referring to Figure 3.8, we see that the gain
in productivity growth of Taiwanese traditional industries is mostly due to
efficiency growth, with very little due to technology growth, except probably
in the Food and Tobacco sector (#1). The Taiwanese basic industry shows
strong technical growth, especially in the Petroleum, Coal and Products sector
(#8) and the Basic Metal (#10) sector. Both countries show positive efficiency
growth and negative technology growth in Fabricated Metal Products (#11).
In the high-tech category, both countries have positive efficiency growth in all
sectors, especially in the Transportation sector (#14), and negative technology
growth in the Electric, Electronic Machinery (#13) and Precision Instruments
and Other Manufacturing (#15) sectors. The similarity is almost complete in
this high-tech category.

In period B, the similarity of the two countries is even greater. The advantages of the traditional industry category in EG, TG and MPG have mostly
disappeared, and negative growth rates are registered for almost every sector in
both countries. In this category, Korea continues to show negative technology

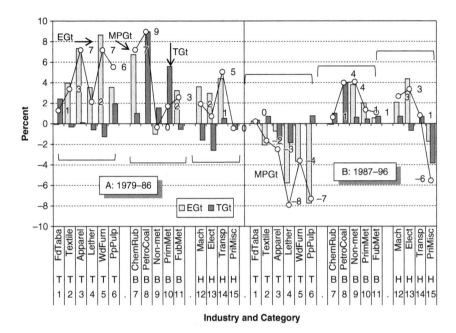

Figure 3.8 Efficiency, Technology and MPI Growth Rates
Taiwan, 15 Manufacturing Sectors, 1979–86 and 1987–96

growth, while Taiwan shows negative efficiency growth. Indeed, the change is striking and dramatic in both sets of the figures. In the basic industry category, Korea's Petroleum and Coal and Products (#8) sector grows almost five times, while the growth of the same sector in Taiwan decreases by half. However, Taiwan continues to show positive growth in efficiency and technology in this category, and Korea also shows improvement in technology in other sectors, except the Fabricated Metal Products (#11) sector. In the high-tech industry category, both countries have the same pattern of EG, TG and MPG in every sector, and there is an increase in EG in the Electric, Electronic Machinery Products and Repair (#13) sector in both countries, reflecting the results of the economic policy of both countries.

3.7 The Innovators of the Manufacturing Industry

In the process of deriving the distance functions in Equation (3.1), we have compared the actual output of each sector each year with the corresponding maximum output on the manufacturing-wise best-practiced beta frontier of that year (see Figure 3.2). The two components of the Malmquist productivity index (MPI), namely, the efficiency index (EI) and the technical index (TI), are interpreted as catch-up and shift of production frontier, respectively. Therefore, it is important to identify which industries, called the innovators by Färe et al. (1994), shift the production possibility curve of the manufacturing industry each year. If we can find the same innovators, that would be additional evidence for the same pattern of manufacturing structure in these two countries.

Färe et al. (1994) define an innovator as

$$\{TI_i > 1, D_i^t\left(a^{t+1}\right) > 1, \quad D_i^{t+1}\left(a^{t+1}\right) = 1\}, \quad (3.6)$$

where TI_i is the technology index of manufacturing sector i, and $D_i^t(a^{t+1})$ and $D_i^{t+1}(a^{t+1})$ are the estimated values of distance functions of industry i. An innovator is the industry i that has technical progress at time t, whose output is located beyond the previous production frontier but on the current frontier based on the constant-returns-to-scale technology.

Table 3.3 shows the innovators of the manufacturing industry in both countries. We find both similarity and dissimilarity in the innovators of the overall manufacturing industry. First, the petroleum sector (Pe) (#8) is the main innovator of the manufacturing industry in both countries. The petroleum sector in Korea is an innovator over almost the whole period, except for the five years before 1990, and in the case of Taiwan, it is an innovator in the early 1980s and the 1990s. This can also be seen in Figure 3.4. On average, from 1979 to 1996, the technology and productivity indexes of the Petroleum sector are consistently higher than those of any other sectors in Korea and Taiwan. We may also see this clearly in periods A and B in both countries in Figures 3.7 and 3.8.

Another common innovator between Korea and Taiwan is the Precision Instrument sector in period A. Because the economies are growing rapidly, this sector in both countries probably includes all other innovative products that cannot be classified into the conventional definitions of the existing sectors, yet these products play a leading role in technical progress in the manufacturing industry. Other minor innovators are different in each country. Korea has the Food (Fd) and the Apparel (Ap) sectors as occasional innovators, and Taiwan has a larger variety, including the Leather (Le), the Electric and Electronic Machinery (El) and Transportation (Tp) sectors as occasional innovators. No innovator is listed in 1985, in which no technical progress occurred in the manufacturing industry in either country. It is not clear whether this is a coincidence or due to some third factor in the international economy.

Table 3.3 Innovators in the Manufacturing Industry
By Category Each Year

Year	Korea Tradition		Basic	High-tech	Taiwan Tradition	Basic	High-tech
1979	Fd		Pe			Pe	
80						Pe	
81		Ap	Pe			Pe	
82	Fd				Le		Pr
83			Pe	Pr			Pr
84	Fd		Pe			Pe	Pr
85							
86			Pe	Pr			Pr
Count	3	1	5	2	1	4	4
1987				Pr		Pe	Pr
88			Pe				Pr
89							Tp
90	Fd		Pe			Pe	
91			Pe				Tp
92	Fd	Ap	Pe				Tp
93			Pe				
94			Pe			Pe	
95			Pe			Pe	El
96			Pe			Pe	
Count	2	1	8	1		5	1 2
Total	5	2	13	3	1	9	1 3 6

Note: Fd = 1Food, beverage & tobacco, Ap = 3Apparel and Ornaments, Pe = 8Petroleum, coal, and products, Le = 4Leather, fur, and products, El = 13Electric, electronic machinery products and repairs, Tr = 14Transportation products and repairs, Pr = Precision instruments and other manufacturing.

In terms of the category of the Korean manufacturing industry, the dominant innovators are in the traditional industries (Fd and Ap) and basic industries (Pe). High-tech industries play weak roles as innovators. In Taiwan, the basic and high-tech industries are the major innovators, and the traditional industries have not been in the position of innovators.

In general, both countries have the same two major innovators and different minor innovators. Both countries embarked on heavy and chemical projects in the mid-1970s: Taiwan in 1974 as part of the "Ten Major Construction Projects" (Hsiao and Hsiao, 1996, 251–52), and Korea also in 1974 by establishing the National Investment Fund (Bae, 2001). So far as the Petrochemical and Coal sector is concerned, Table 3.3 shows that both countries have apparently succeeded in their industrial policy of promoting this sector, although other projects have been lackluster or have failed.

In the 1980s, however, both governments started promoting capital and skill/high-tech industries, which included, in addition to chemicals and their products, electronics, basic metal, machinery, transport equipment and precision instruments (Hsiao and Hsiao, 1996, 254; Okuda, 1997). In view of this, it is rather surprising that the Electric and Electronic Machinery Products sector has not played any innovator role in Korea and has played only a very minor role in Taiwan in the overall manufacturing industry. A further study of the role of innovators and the effectiveness of the government industrial policy is called for.

3.8 Some Concluding Remarks

The "East Asian Miracle" has generated an extensive and varied literature. However, there is still little consensus on productivity growth (Hsiao and Hsiao, 1998), and no study has even considered productivity growth at matched manufacturing levels of Taiwan and Korea, the two most outstanding economies among the developing countries since the end of World War II. This chapter attempts to fill this gap and to stimulate research in this area.

From an economic point of view, there is much similarity in industrial structure between Korea and Taiwan. At the aggregate level, the similarity of the growth patterns and the trends in labor, capital and output are obvious, except that the capital productivity of Korea continued to grow, while that of Taiwan began to decrease in 1987, coinciding with a decrease in the share of the manufacturing industry in GDP.

Against this general background, we have examined the productivity performance of Korea and Taiwan from 1979 to 1996, using the efficiency, technology and productivity indexes of the matched manufacturing sectors. For the overall cross-section data, both countries have similarly positive and high weighted efficiency growth (1.8% for Korea and 1.6% for Taiwan). However, the weighted technology growth rate of Korea in this period is negative (−1.4%), while that of Taiwan is positive (0.7%), resulting in a much smaller but positive weighted productivity growth for Korea (0.4%) and a large and positive weighted productivity growth for Taiwan (2.2%). The weighted growth rates of efficiency, technology and productivity in Korea fluctuate more than those of Taiwan, indicating a rather uneven industrialization process in Korea.

The negative technical index for Korea in this chapter is consistent with three previous papers on international cross-section analysis (Kim and Park, 2001), but is different from a country analysis of Korea. Using the data of 28 manufacturing sectors from 1970 to 1996, Kim and Park (2002) found EG, TG and MPG for Korea as 1.18, 0.76 and 1.87, respectively. Lee et al. (1998), using Korean data of 36 manufacturing sectors from 1967 to 1993, found EG, TG and MPG for Korea as −0.86, 1.14 and 0.29, respectively. A similar discrepancy for Taiwan is found in Färe et al. (1995). Using four aggregated manufacturing sectors from 1978 to 1989, they found EG, TG and MPG for Taiwan as −0.22, 3.84 and 3.59. The results are different from the 1.47, 0.09 and 1.56 in Lee (1997), who calculated the indexes only for the six "essential goods industries" (Sectors 1, 2, 3, 5, 9 and 15 in Table 3.1) from 1978 to 1994. Unlike ours, all these indexes are not weighted, and the methods of computation are not indicated. Apparently, more studies on this field need to be done to find some consensus.

In both countries, productivity improvement in traditional industry comes from efficiency growth, that in basic industries from technology growth, and that in high-tech industries from both efficiency and technology growth. However, correlation analysis reveals that the processes of efficiency improvement and technology change are different in the two countries. The high-tech industry is an exception, since both efficiency improvement and technology growth are positively and highly correlated between the two countries, showing that both countries have the common factor that they are exposed to the international market and influenced by multinational investment.

The analysis from the time-series data leads to the same conclusion as the analysis from the cross-section data. However, the time-series data do not reveal much about the common trend of the three indexes between the two countries. The correlation analysis shows that the similarity between the manufacturing sectors in period B, 1987–96, has increased, indicating that due to government policies of emphasizing high-tech industries, there is a sign of convergence in this industry between the two countries. However, the innovator analysis reveals that only the Petrochemical sector dominated the production frontier in countries, and that the Electric and Electronic Machinery Products sector played no role or a very minimal one as an innovator. While the future is hard to predict, the policy implication of our analysis is that each country shows similarity in recent years at the aggregate level and that the two countries can learn from each other: Korea from Taiwan on technology adoption, and Taiwan from Korea on efficiency improvement.

Appendix 3A Overall Industrial Structure of Korea and Taiwan

Figure 3A.1 shows the overall industrial structures of Korea and Taiwan as the composition of GDP by industries: the primary, secondary and tertiary

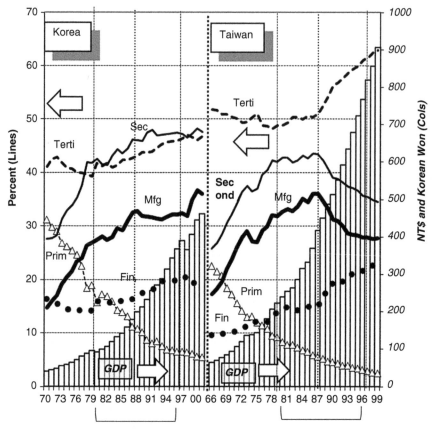

Figure 3A.1 Composition of GDP by Industry
South Korea and Taiwan

industries from 1970 to 1999. We also present the trends of the manufacturing and financial sectors, as the manufacturing industry is the prominent factor in a country's industrialization and modernization, and the financial industry[22] is a fast-growing sector in both countries in the 1980s and 1990s. The extended time period is to put the industrial structures from 1978 to 1996, the range of which our matched data are available, in time perspective.

For both countries, we see almost the same steady growth of real GDP (shown as columns that are drawn from the right-hand-side secondary Y axis labeled in italic). Note that the GDP levels are measured in Korean won for Korea and New Taiwan dollars for Taiwan; thus, the sizes of the columns are

---

22 The percentage of the manufacturing sector and the financial sector is calculated as a percentage of the whole industry, not as a percentage of the secondary or the tertiary industry.

not directly comparable except for the trends and growth rates between the two countries. The lines are percentage distribution of each industry in real GDP in each year, and they are comparable between the two countries.

Korea has a higher percentage of the secondary industry (Sec) and a lower percentage of the tertiary industry (Terti). Its manufacturing industry increased from 15% of total output in 1970 to 33% in 1988, and flattened out at about 32% between 1989 and 1997, then started increasing again to 35% in 1999. Taiwan's manufacturing industry was at a higher rate of 24% in 1970 and increased to 36% in 1987, and started decreasing after 1988 to 28% in 1999. There seems a clear change in the time-series trend after 1987 or 1988 in both countries. This justifies the division of the whole matched industry period at 1987. It appears that Taiwan has experienced deindustrialization (and the rise of the tertiary industry) after the lifting of martial law in 1987. Although Auty (1997) pointed out that Korea outpaced Taiwan in macroeconomic performance, Taiwan's trend of deindustrialization is similar to more advanced countries and may be taken as the advancement to an industrial society in Taiwan as compared with that in Korea. Except for the secondary industry, especially the manufacturing industry, after the mid-1980s, the trend of each pair of the corresponding curves in both countries looks very similar.

Acknowledgments

We are indebted to Professors Vei-lin Chan, Song-ken Hsu, Sheng-cheng Hu and Ms. Li-Min Weng for making the data on Taiwan and Korea available to the authors. Without their help, this chapter could not have been written. This chapter was presented at the Conference on Korea and the World Economy, Seoul, Korea, 2002. We are indebted to Dr. Chang Soo Lee for helpful discussions. Comments and suggestions from the audience and from Professors Martin Boileau, Mei-chu W. Hsiao, Cliff Huang, Murat F. Iyigun, John Y. T. Kuark, Robert F. McNown, Keith E. Maskus and two anonymous referees were most helpful. Most of the figures and tables have been redrawn using the new version of the Microsoft Excel program. All errors of omission and commission are ours.

References

Auty, R. M. (1997). "Competitive Industrial Policy and Macro Performance: Has South Korea Outperformed Taiwan?" *Journal of Development Studies* 33(4): 445–63.
Bae, Jin-Young (2001). "Incentive Structure and Its Changes in the Korean Industrial Policy Regimes from 1962–1997," *The Journal of the Korean Economy* 2(2): 297–331.

Baumol, William S., Batey Blackman and E. N. Wolff (1989). *Productivity and American Leadership: The Long View*. Cambridge, MA: MIT Press.

Business Week (2002). "Asia: Is This the Rebound?", Business Week online, March 25.

Coelli, Tim (1996). "A Guide to DEAP Version 2.1: A Data Envelopment Analysis (Computer) Program," CEPA Working Paper 96/08, University of New England.

Coelli, Tim, D. S. P. Rao and George E. Battese (1998). *An Introduction to Efficiency and Productivity Analysis*. Boston: Kluwer Academic Publishers.

Dowling, Malcolm, and Peter M. Summers (1998). "Survey Article-Total Factor Productivity and Economic Growth-Issues for Asia," *The Economic Record* 74(225): 170–86.

Färe Rolf, Shawa Grosskopf, Marry Norris and Wen-Fu Lee (1995). "Productivity in Taiwanese Manufacturing Industries," *Applied Economics* 27: 259–65.

Färe Rolf, Shawa Grosskopf, Marry Norris and Zhongyang Zang (1994). "Productivity Growth, Technical Progress, and Efficiency Change in Industrialized Countries," *American Economic Review* 84: 66–83.

Hattori, Tamio (1997). "Chaebol-Style Enterprise Development in Korea," *The Developing Economies* 25(4): 458–77.

Hobday, Michael (1995). *Innovation in East Asia: The Challenge to Japan*, Brookfield, VT: Edward Elgar.

Hsiao, Frank S. T., and Mei-Chu W. Hsiao (2003a). "'Miracle Growth' in the Twentieth Century–Comparisons of East Asian Development," *World Development* 31(2): 227–57.

——— (2003b). "Catching Up and Convergence: Long-run Growth in East Asia," *Review of Development Economics* 8(2): 223–36.

——— (2002). "Taiwan in the Global Economy—Past, Present, and Future." In Peter C. Y. Chow, ed. *Taiwan in Global Economy: From an Agrarian Economy to an Exporter of High-Tech Products*. Westport, CT: Greenwood Press, 161–222.

——— (2001a). "Capital Flows and Exchange Rates: Recent Korean and Taiwanese Experience and Challenges," *Journal of Asian Economics* 12: 353–81.

——— (2001b). "Economic Liberalization and Development: The Case of Lifting Martial Law in Taiwan." In Academia Sinica, ed. *Change of an Authoritarian Regime: Taiwan in the Post-Martial Law Era*, Taiwan Studies Promotion Committee, Taipei: Preparatory Office of Institute of Taiwan History, Academia Sinica, 353–79.

——— (1998). "Miracle or Myth of Asian NICs' Growth—The Irony of Numbers." In M. Jan Dutta and Richard W. Hooley, eds. *The New Industrial Revolution in Asian Economies*. Greenwich, CT: JAI Press, 51–68.

——— (1995). "Taiwanese Economic Development and Foreign Trade." In John Y. T. Kuark, ed. *Comparative Asian Economies*. Greenwich, CT: JAI Press, 1996, 211–302. Originally published in William C. Kirby and J. Megan Greene, eds. *Harvard Studies on Taiwan: Papers of the Taiwan Study Workshop*, 1, The Fairbank Center for East Asian Research, Harvard University, 199–270.

Hsiao, Frank S. T., and Changsuh Park (2002). "Korean and Taiwanese Productivity Performance-Comparisons at Matched Manufacturing Levels," Discussion Papers in Economics, University of Colorado 02-12. Published in (2005). *Journal of Productivity Analysis* 23(1): 85–107.

Hsiao, Mei-Chu W. (1992). "Direct Foreign Investment, Technology Transfer, and Industrial Development—The Case of Electronic Industry in Taiwan." In M. Dutta, ed. *Research in Asian Economic Studies*, vol. 4, pt. A: *Asian Economic Regime: An Adaptive Innovation Paradigm*. Greenwich, CT: JAI Press, 145–64.

Hu, Sheng-Cheng, and Vei-Lin Chan (1999). "The Determinants of Taiwan's Total Factor Productivity" [in Chinese], *Industry of Free China*, September, 1–50.

Investment Commission (IC) (1995). *Statistics on Overseas Chinese and Foreign Investment, Technical Cooperation, Outward Investment, Outward Technical Cooperation, Indirect Mainland Investment*. Taipei: Ministry of Economic Affairs.

Kawai, Hiroki (1994). "International Comparative Analysis of Economic Growth: Trade Liberalization and Productivity," *The Developing Economies* 32(4): 373–97.

Kim, Linsu (1999). *Learning and Innovation in Economic Development*. Northampton, MA: Edward Elgar.

Kim, Taegi, and Changsuh Park (2001). "*Productivity Growth in Korea: Efficiency Improvement or Technical Progress?*" Working Paper, University of Colorado Boulder.

Kwack, Sung Yeung (2000). "Total Factor Productivity Growth and the Source of Growth in Korean Manufacturing Industries, 1971–1993," *Journal of the Korean Economy* 1(2): 229–65. Also in Inchul Kim, Sung Yeung Kwack and Se-Il Park, eds. *Growth, Productivity and Vision for the Korean Economy*. Seoul: Pakyoungsa, 308–53.

Lee, Jeong-Dong, Tai-Yoo Kim and Eunnyeong Heo (1998). "Technological Progress versus Efficiency Gain in Manufacturing Sectors," *Review of Development Economics* 2(3): 268–81.

Lee, Ju-Ho, Young-Kyu Moh and Dae-Il Kim. (2001). "Do Unions Inhibit Labor Flexibility? Lessons from Korea," KDI School of Public Policy and Management, Korea Working Paper, WO1-05.

Lee, Wen-Fu (1997). "Productivity, Efficiency and Technical Change: The Case of Taiwan's Essential Goods Industries." Paper presented at the Taipei International Conference on Efficiency and Productivity Growth, The Institute of Economics, Academia Sinica, 1997, Taipei.

Lester, Richard K., ed. (1998). *The Productivity Edge: A New Strategy for Economic Growth*. New York: W. W. Norton.

Maddison, Angus (1995). *Monitoring the World Economy, 1820–1992*. Development Center. Paris: OECD.

National Science Council (NSC) (1998). *Indicators of Science and Technology, Republic of China*. Taipei: Executive Yuan.

Nishimizu, Mieko, and Charles R. Hulten (1978). "The Sources of Japanese Economic Growth: 1955–1971," *Review of Economics and Statistics* 60: 351–61.

Numazaki, Ichiro (1997). "The *Laoban*-Led Development of Business Enterprises in Taiwan: An Analysis of the Chinese Entrepreneurship," *The Developing Economies* 25(4): 440–57

OECD (2000). *STAN Database for Industrial Analysis*, 1970–1977. Paris: OECD.

Okuda, Satoru (1997). "Industrialization Policies of Korea and Taiwan, and Their Effects on Manufacturing Productivity," *The Developing Economies* 25(4): 358–81.

O'Mahony, Mary, and Karin Wagner (1996). "Anglo-German Productivity Performance since 1973." In David G. Mayes, ed. *Sources of Productivity Growth*. Cambridge: Cambridge University Press.

Oshima, Harry T. (1987). *Economic Growth in Monsoon Asia: A Comparative Survey*. Tokyo: University of Tokyo Press.

Pyo, Hak Kil (1998). "Estimation of Korean Physical Capital Stock by Industry and Type of Asset" [in Korean]. Working Paper. Seoul: Korea Institute of Public Finance.

Schive, Chi (1990). "The Next Stage of Industrialization in Taiwan and South Korea." In Gary Gereffi and Donald L. Wyman, eds. *Manufacturing Miracles: Paths of Industrialization in Latin American and East Asia*. Princeton, NJ: Princeton University Press. 267–91.

Stiroh, Kevin J. (2001). "What Drives Productivity Growth?" *FRBNY Economic Policy Review*, Federal Reserve Bank of New York, March, 37–59.

Syrquin, Moshe, and Hollis B. Chenery (1989). "Three Decades of Industrialization," *World Bank Economic Review* 3(2): 145–81.

Taiwan Statistical Data Book (TSDB) (2002). Taipei: Council for Economic Planning and Development.

Timmer, Marcel (2000). *The Dynamics of Asian Manufacturing, A Comparative Perspective in the Late Twentieth Century*. Northampton, MA: Edward Elgar.

Torii, Akio, and Richard E. Caves (1992). "Technical Efficiency in Japanese and U.S. Manufacturing Industries." In Richard E. Caves, ed. *Industrial Efficiency in Six Nations*. Cambridge, MA: MIT Press, 425–57.

Urata, Shujiro (1996). "Production of Electronic Products in East Asia and New Mode of Foreign Trade: The Role of Foreign Direct Investment" [in Japanese]. In Ryutaro Komiya and Yutaka Yamada, eds. *Economic Development of East Asia: How Long Will Growth Last?* [in Japanese]. Tokyo: Toyo Keizai Shimposha, 145–65.

Wade, Robert (1990). "Industrial Policy in East Asia: Does It Lead or Follow the Market?". In Gary Gereffi and Donald L. Wyman, eds. *Manufacturing Miracles: Paths of Industrialization in Latin American and East Asia*. Princeton, NJ: Princeton University Press, 231–65.

Wagner, K., and R. van Ark, eds. (1996). *International Productivity Differences, Measurement and Explanations*. Contributions to Economic Analysis. North Holland: Elsevier.

Chapter 4

KOREAN AND TAIWANESE PRODUCTIVITY PERFORMANCE: COMPARISONS AT MATCHED MANUFACTURING LEVELS

Abstract

In growth theory, industrial productivity is the major factor driving economic growth. Instead of using conventional measures of total factor productivity, we use the weighted Malmquist productivity index, which was developed only recently, and its components, the efficiency index and the technology index.

Following the previous chapter, this chapter also compares the productivity performances of 15 matched manufacturing sectors in Korea and Taiwan. Using Maddison's data, we first ascertain that Taiwan and Korea are at the same development stage. The distance functions are derived by using the Malmquist productivity indexes, based on category-wise metafrontiers, 1978–96. Comparisons at the sector levels are made using sequential multiplicative products of the indexes.

We find that during this period, the overall productivity and technology growth rates of Taiwan were higher than those of Korea. This is also shown at disaggregated levels. While there are many similarities between the two countries, the productivity and technology growth rates of the high-tech industries in Korea are much larger than those of Taiwan, and more high-tech sectors in Korea are leading innovators compared to Taiwan. In contrast, Taiwan's high overall growth rate rested mainly on its traditional and basic industries. The differences are chronic rather than transient.

Our results indicate that there are several signs that Korea is catching up with Taiwan in productivity at long last. Their performance in the next decade will be of interest to watch.

4.1 Introduction

The rapid postwar growth of Taiwan and of the Republic of Korea (hereafter Korea) has been a focus of studies among scholars of development economics. The development of these two countries began in the early years of the twentieth century (Hsiao and Hsiao, 2003a), and accelerated after World War II (Hsiao and Hsiao, 2002, 2003a; Page, 1994). Beginning in the late 1960s, they entered the world production process, achieving impressive growth through rapid industrialization and accelerated exporting in the 1970s and the 1980s, with double dependence on Japanese imports (capital equipment and intermediate goods) and US markets (Hattori and Sato, 1997; Hsiao and Hsiao, 1996; Okuda, 1997).

Figure 4.1 compares the long-run GDP per capita levels of four Asian countries.[1] The two newly developed countries, Korea and Taiwan, and two more recently fast-growing developing countries, China and Thailand.

The long-run growth of the real GDP per capita of Taiwan (the heavy solid line) and Korea (the light solid line) has been extraordinary among developing countries, especially during the postwar period (Hsiao and Hsiao, 2003a). These two economies have grown almost like twins, showing fairly rapid prewar growth, and then presenting very high export-GDP ratios and import-GDP ratios and equally rapid growth in manufacturing, in the postwar period (Hattori and Sato, 1997; Timmer, 2000). As Figure 4.1 shows, the real GDP per capita growth of both countries accelerated markedly during the 1970s and 1980s, and is expected to converge with that of Japan and the United States (Hsiao and Hsiao, 2004).

However, Figure 4.1 also shows that in the postwar period, in contrast to the prewar period, the real GDP per capita level and the growth rate of Korea were consistently lower than those of Taiwan. This difference was not due to historical background or to the two countries being at different stages of development. In fact, the situation was reversed before the war, as Figure 4.1 shows. After the war, despite the destruction of the Taiwanese economy by Allied air raids (1944–45) and the war in Korea (1950–53), Korean real GDP per capita was almost the same as that of Taiwan from 1953 to 1955 (Hsiao and Hsiao, 2003a). Korea and Taiwan were at the same developmental stage by the mid-1950s, and continued to be so until recently.[2]

---

1 The diagram is taken from Figure 1 of Hsiao and Hsiao (2003a). This article also showed that, according to Maddison's data (1995), the real per capita GDP growth rates of Korea and Taiwan from 1951 to 1992 were the highest in the world: Korea 5.8%, Taiwan 6.03%, per annum, exceeding third-ranking Japan, 5.57% (ibid. Table 1).

2 Note that we use the analysis of growth rates in explaining differences in levels of real GDP per capita. As we mentioned above, during the early postwar period, Korean real GDP per capita was almost the same as that of Taiwan, but since then the real GDP per capita level of Korea has been consistently lower than that of Taiwan. As shown in this

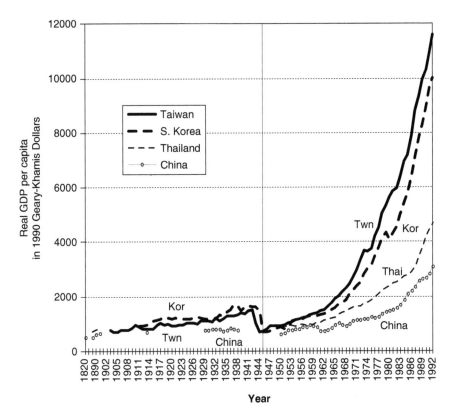

Figure 4.1 Levels of GDP per Capita—Four Asian Countries 1820–1992

One of the reasons for the different growth rates may be difference in the performance of productivity growth between these two countries. A study of the productivity growth of their manufacturing sectors thus may yield useful information about differences in the development pattern of the two economies. It may also throw light on a second question: whether Korea can catch up with Taiwan in the future, or whether Taiwan is likely to maintain its superiority. We propose to explore these questions here.

The remainder of this chapter is organized as follows. Section 4.2 briefly explains the Malmquist productivity index and its components, which are used in this chapter. In Section 4.3, we explain the data of 15 matched manufacturing industries and the derivation of the productivity indexes for these two countries. Section 4.4 compares the structure of the manufacturing industry

---

chapter, one of the reasons is the different performance of productivity growth between these two countries.

by industrial categories: traditional, basic and high-tech. We then compare the aggregate productivity performances of the whole manufacturing industry in Section 4.5. Section 4.6 compares the trend of each of five indexes among the three categories, and Section 4.7 compares the trend of five indexes in each category. Section 4.8 finds the innovators that push the category-wise meta-production frontier outward each year. Section 4.9 concludes.

4.2 The Malmquist Productivity Index

There are several methods of computing productivity growth, either at the aggregate level or at industrial levels. Before the mid-1990s, most studies estimated the total factor productivity (TFP) growth rate, using Solow's residual method or the growth accounting method. There are several papers that directly compare the TFP of Korea and Taiwan, including Oshima (1987), Kawai (1994), Okuda (1997), and Timmer (2000). Despite the considerable amount of literature (Hsiao and Hsiao, 1998), there is no consensus about adequate rates of TFP growth in the process of economic growth, as they fluctuate greatly among countries and over periods (ibid.). The residual method is often considered to be rather misleading and to provide little insight into the determination of productivity growth (Nelson, 1973; Nelson and Pack, 1999).

In this chapter, we instead adopt the Malmquist productivity index (MPI), which has become popular since the mid-1990s. While the data envelopment analysis (DEA) was originally meant for firm- or industry-level analysis (Forsund and Sarafoglow, 2002), it has been applied to the comparison of productivity among industrialized countries by Färe et al. (1994), to Taiwanese manufacturing industries by Färe and Lee (1995) and to Korean manufacturing sectors by Lee et al. (1998).

Let the pair of observed input vector x^t at time t and the corresponding observed output vector y^t at time t be denoted as $a^t = (x^t, y^t)$. Then the output distance function at time t is defined as

$$D^t\left(a^t\right) = \inf\left\{\delta \mid \frac{y^t}{\delta} \text{ is in } P^t\left(x^t\right)\right\}, \tag{4.1}$$

where $P^t(x^t) = \{y^t \mid x^t \text{ can produce } y^t\}$ is the production set at time t, which is convex, closed, bounded and which satisfies the strong disposability of x^t and y^t (Coelli, 1996, 62). The scalar δ is a fraction, $0 < \delta \leq 1$ for all $y^t \geq 0$, and $\delta = 1$ if yt is in the production set. The output-oriented MPI is then defined as the geometric mean of the MPI in two consecutive periods (Coelli et al., 1998, 128; Färe et al., 1994):

$$MPI^t = (M^t M^{t+1})^{1/2} = \left[\left(\frac{D^t \left(a^{t+1} \right)}{D^t \left(a^t \right)} \right) \left(\frac{D^{t+1}(a^{t+1})}{D^{t+1}(a^t)} \right) \right]^{1/2}, \quad (4.2)$$

where MPI $>$ $=$ $<$ 1 implies productivity growth (or change) is positive, zero or negative[3] from period t to period t + 1. Definition (4.2) may be decomposed into two parts, the efficient index EI and the technology index TI (Färe et al., 1994),

$$MPI^t = \underbrace{\frac{D^{t+1}(a^{t+1})}{D^t(a^t)}}_{EI} \left[\underbrace{\left(\frac{D^t \left(a^{t+1} \right)}{D^{t+1}(a^{t+1})} \right) \left(\frac{D^t \left(a^t \right)}{D^{t+1}(a^t)} \right)}_{TI} \right]^{1/2}, \quad (4.3)$$

and EI in turns decomposes into PI and SI in the presence of variable returns to scale (VRS)[4] (Färe et al., 1997) as shown in Equation (4.4) below.

The first term in (4.3) is called the efficiency change index (or simply efficiency index, EI hereafter), and the second term is the technology change index (or simply technology index, TI hereafter). The term in the square root measures the relative movement of the productivity curves, based on the constant-returns-to-scale benchmark between two periods, and is the technology index TI. It represents new product and process innovation, new management systems or external shock shifting the productivity curves.

If the concept of the distance function is applied to a variable-returns-to-scale (VRS) benchmark rather than a constant-returns-to-scale (CRS) benchmark, EI in Equation (4.3) may be decomposed into two terms, and MPI in (4.3) becomes

---

3 The statement here is true only under constant-returns-to-scale technology. According to Grifell-Tatje and Lovell (1995, 174), (4.2) will "understate the magnitude of productivity growth when input growth occurs in the presence of increasing returns-to-scale," and overstate it under decreasing returns-to-scale. The biases are reversed when input contraction occurs. Thus, we could assume constant-returns-to-scale technology like neoclassical theory and ignore PI and SI in Equation (4.4) below; or assume that Taiwan and Korea have the same kind and degree of returns-to-scale technology, making the indexes still comparable between the two countries. In view of the very long-run contemporaneous development process of the two countries, the latter assumption may not be as strong as it appears.

4 Ray and Desli (1997) emphasize the importance of VRS in using a reference technology. However, the method of VRS in some cases has an infeasible solution (see Ray and Desli, 1997, 1037). One of the comments of Färe et al. (1997) in response to Ray and Desli (1997) is that the CRS captures the long run, and the VRS is appropriate for the short run. Since our study analyzes the long-run productivity trend, we use the method of Färe et al. (1997).

$$\text{MPI}^t = \underbrace{\frac{V^{t+1}\left(a^{t+1}\right)}{V^t\left(a^t\right)}}_{\text{PI}} \underbrace{\left[\frac{\left(\dfrac{V^t\left(a^t\right)}{D^t\left(a^t\right)}\right)}{\left(\dfrac{V^{t+1}\left(a^{t+1}\right)}{D^{t+1}\left(a^{t+1}\right)}\right)}\right]}_{\text{SI}} \cdot \underbrace{\left[\left(\frac{D^t\left(a^{t+1}\right)}{D^{t+1}\left(a^{t+1}\right)}\right)\left(\frac{D^t\left(a^t\right)}{D^{t+1}\left(a^t\right)}\right)\right]^{\frac{1}{2}}}_{\text{TI}}, \quad (4.4)$$

where $V^t(a^t)$ is the output distance function (4.1) based on the VRS benchmark. The ratio $V^{t+1}(a^{t+1})/V^t(a^t)$ is the pure efficiency change index (or simply pure efficiency index, PI, hereafter) from time t to t + 1, based on the VRS technology. The ratio $V^t(a^t)/D^t(a^t)$ is the scale efficiency index at time t, which measures the output difference between the VRS technology and the CRS technology at time t. The ratio of this difference at t and t + 1 is the scale efficiency change index from time t to t + 1, and is called the scale efficiency change index (or simply scale index, SI hereafter). It indicates the change in efficiency due to the scale of production between the two periods.

In this chapter, we refer to the output-oriented MPI simply as the productivity index. When the observed outputs are on the productivity curve at each period, then EI = 1, and as shown in Färe et al. (1994), MPI is the same as the conventional definition of the TFP ratio between two periods. In this case, when 1 is subtracted from this ratio, we have the discrete growth rate[5] (that is, the percentage change) of TFP. Hence, the TFP growth rate is a special case[6] of the MPI growth rate when EI = 1. Similarly, we define MPG ≡ (MPI − 1) × 100 as the growth rate of productivity, EG ≡ (EI − 1) × 100 as the growth rate of efficiency, and TG ≡ (TI − 1) × 100 as the growth rate of technology. SG ≡ (SI − 1) × 100 and PG ≡ (PI − 1) × 100 are growth rate (or percentage change) of scale efficiency and pure efficiency, respectively. Comparisons of productivity performance of Taiwan and Korea are carried out using indexes as well as growth rates, both of which are pure numbers, independent of the units of measurement used in each country.

---

5 Using the conventional notation in Färe et al. (1994), for a production function y(t) = A(t)F(L(t), K(t)), TFPG = (A(t + 1)/A(t)) − 1 is a discrete growth rate, which is compounded once at the end of the year. However, if we define TFPG = ln A(t + 1) − ln A(t), then it is a continuous growth rate, which is compounded instantaneously during the year. In the continuous case, the sum from period 0 to period 17 will cancel out the middle terms, and the average continuous growth rate is (ln A(17) − ln A(0))/17. Since some growth rates are negative, we use the discrete growth rate.

6 Thus, it is confusing, if not in error, to call MPI defined above simply as TFP or the TFP ratio.

4.3 The Data and Estimation of Productivity Growth Rates

The dataset for 15 manufacturing sectors for Korea and Taiwan consists of one output, the real value-added output of each sector, net of intermediate goods,[7] two inputs, the number of workers and the real capital stock from 1978 to 1996. The dataset consists of 15 sectors, as shown on the left-hand side of Table 4.1, and has a range of 19 years. The 15 sectors in the cross-section dataset are further grouped into three categories:[8] the traditional industry category (T, Sectors 1–6), the basic industry category (B, Sectors 7–11), and the high-tech industry category (H, Sectors 12–15), as shown in the first "Category (Ca)" column in Table 4.1.

We estimate the distance functions (4.4) by nonparametric one-output two-input linear programs following Coelli (1996) for each category.[9] Our derivation of the category-wise cross-industry metafrontier is different from the current practice of finding the distance functions for all manufacturing sectors by constructing the manufacturing industry-wide frontier. Our method takes into account that the meta production frontiers for the three categories in each year are different. For example, the technology used in traditional industries is quite different from that used in high-tech industries. Thus, we submit that technology used in an individual manufacturing sector in an industrial category should be compared with the production frontier of that category, not with the manufacturing industry as a whole.[10]

---

7 The Taiwanese data are available only in value-added output and inputs; thus, we also use the same data for Korea. This implies that we made a strong assumption that the sectoral production function is additively separable between factor inputs and intermediate inputs, and the value-added productivity measure may fail to capture the full impact on productivity (Sudit and Finger, 1981). Unless welfare implications of productivity are to be analyzed, this may pose a problem, as pointed out by a referee of this chapter, due to increasing intermediate materials inputs such as capital imports, outsourcing, quality and so on in Korea and Taiwan. For a theoretical discussion of substitutability between material and value-added inputs, see Buccola (2000).

8 We follow the classification made by Hu and Chan (1999) for the manufacturing industry in Taiwan.

9 The category-wise cross-industry best-practice meta production frontier is estimated each year by linear constraints $\{-y_j^t + Y^t w \geq 0, -x_j^t + X^t w \geq 0, w \geq 0\}$, where for our problem, Y^t is $1 \times N$ output vector, X^t is $2 \times N$ input matrix, w is $N \times 2$, $j = 1, 2, ..., N$, and N is the number of manufacturing sectors in each category in Table 4.1. We then compare the actual output of each manufacturing sector in the category with the corresponding maximum outputs on the category-wise frontier and construct the distance functions $D^t(a^t)$ and so on for consecutive years by maximizing the inverse of the distance δ subject to the frontier technology. For each category, we calculated $N \times (4 \times 18 - 2)$ distance functions using linear programs, where $N = 6$ for the traditional category, 5 for the basic category and 4 for the high-tech category, a total of 1,050 distance functions.

10 We owe this point to Professor Tim Coelli. However, the current literature uses the industry-wide production frontier rather than the category-specific frontier. See Färe et al. (1994, 1995), Lee et al. (1998) and Nishimizu and Hulten (1978). Elsewhere we

Table 4.1 Classification of 15 Manufacturing Industries
Taiwan and Korea

Ca	ISIC	No.	Taiwan's 15 Sectors	STAN Industry Category for Korea Combination of Korean Mfg Sectors
T	01	1	Food, Beverage & Tobacco	311, 312, 313, 314
T	02	2	Textiles	321
T		3	Apparel and Ornaments (a)	322
T		4	Leather, Fur, and Products	323
T	03	5	Wood Products & Non-metalic Furniture	331, 332
T	04	6	Paper, Paper Products & Printing	341, 342
B	05	7	Chemical Products, Rubber, and Plastics	351, 352, 355, 356
B		8	Petroleum, Coal, and Products	353, 354
B	06	9	Non-Metallic Mineral Products	361, 362, 369
B	07	10	Basic Metal Industries	371, 372
B	08	11	Fabricated Metal Products	381
H		12	Machinery Products and Repairs	382
H		13	Electric, Electronic Machinery Products & Repairs	383
H		14	Transportation Products and Repairs	384
H	09	15	Precision Instruments and Other Manufacturing (b)	385, 390

Notes: (a) The Korean list includes "#324 Footwear," which may be "wearing apparel" or "leather products." Since we do not have detailed information, we divide the numbers in 324 in two: one half in Apparel (322), and another half in Leather and Products (323). (b) The title of 385 in the Korean list is "Professional Goods."

For each category we have constructed five indexes, TI, EI, PI, SI and MPI, for each sector in each category for 18 years.[11] Since the importance of each sector is different in terms of the value-added share in each category,[12] each index in each year in each category is weighted by the share of the corresponding value-added output in that year and in that category.[13] The sums

---

have also experimented with the industry-wide cross-section frontier method with constant returns to scale technology (Hsiao and Park, 2002). The results are different (see Footnote 16).

11 We lose one year since the indexes start from the second year of the sample. We have a total of $1,350 (= 5 \times 15 \times 18)$ indexes.

12 See Figure 4.2. For example, in Figure 4.2b, the value-added output in the "1Food" (food, beverage and alcohol) sector for Korea consistently maintained 41%–50% of the total value-added output in the traditional category between 1979 and 1997, while that of "4Lethr" (leather fur, and products) sector ranged only between 0.4% and 1%. Clearly, it is inappropriate to give the same weight to the indexes of these two sectors.

13 For example, for the six MPIs in the traditional category in 1979, we calculated the weighted MPI, say, by $w_i MPI_i$, where $w_i = q_i / \sum q_i$, $i = 1, 2, ..., 6$, and q_i is the value-added output of the ith sector in 1979 in the traditional category. The sum $\sum^6 w_i MPI_i$ multiplied

of the weighted indexes within each category in selected years are presented in Table 4.2. The column of manufacturing (Mfg) each year is the geometric mean of the indexes of three categories of the same year. The rows of "geomean" are the geometric mean of the indexes of 18 years in each category.[14] Note that the multiplicative decomposition of the MPI indexes (4.3) and (4.4) still holds approximately even though the original indexes are weighted by value-added outputs in each category.

4.4 The Structure of the Manufacturing Industry

Since the value-added output shares weight the indexes, we first examine the differences and similarities between the structures of the manufacturing industries in terms of the value-added output shares of Korea and Taiwan. This is shown in Figure 4.2. The number in parentheses after each sector label, like 1Food (94a), shows the sector's correlation coefficient (94% in this case) between Korea and Taiwan, and the letter after the number shows the level of significance of the student t distribution under the null hypothesis that the population correlation coefficient is zero for a two-sided test: a means that the level of significance of the sample correlation coefficient is a, 1%; similarly, b, 5%; c, 10%; and d, 20%.

The upper three curves in Figure 4.2a show the output shares of the three categories in the whole manufacturing industries (the lower three curves will be explained shortly). All three show quite similar trends between the two countries over time. Their correlation coefficients are all positive and high and significant at the 1% level, showing that there were very strong common features in the aggregate structures of their manufacturing industries. In both countries, the importance of the traditional industries was replaced by high-tech industries, especially in Taiwan after 1987, and both countries were apparently climbing the technology ladder for rapid growth, as evidenced by constantly increasing shares of high-tech and basic categories, especially after 1987. This is a source of the parallel growth of Taiwan and Korea shown in Figure 4.1.

At a disaggregate level, as might be expected, there were differences in importance among the manufacturing sectors in each category. Figure 4.2b shows that in the traditional category the food industry was the most important

---

by 100 is given as 0.972 in the "79 row" under the "Trad" column in Table 4.2. Note that a weighted growth rate is the same as its weighted index minus one: $\sum w_i MPG_i = \sum w_i(MPI_i - 1) = \sum w_i MPI_i - 1$, since $\sum w_i = 1$. This relates Figure 4.3 to Table 4.2.

14 It can be shown easily that the geometric mean of the "Mfg" column is also the geometric mean of the three geometric means of the categories.

Table 4.2 Weighted Malmquist Indexes, within Each Category

Year	Korea				Taiwan			
	Mfg	Trad	Basic	Hi-tech	Mfg	Trad	Basic	Hi-tech
Productivity Index (MPI)								
79	0.970	0.972	0.961	0.979	1.020	1.035	1.099	0.931
80	0.896	0.958	0.894	0.838	1.035	1.055	1.060	0.992
81	1.060	1.004	0.978	1.215	1.068	1.092	1.130	0.988
82	0.993	0.979	0.977	1.023	0.986	1.002	0.952	1.005
83	1.073	0.996	1.101	1.125	1.070	1.041	1.071	1.099
84	1.078	1.020	1.050	1.171	1.070	1.057	1.083	1.070
85	0.960	0.969	0.968	0.943	0.981	0.993	1.003	0.950
86	1.073	1.022	1.012	1.197	1.104	1.101	1.065	1.148
87	1.062	1.021	1.021	1.148	1.066	1.039	1.038	1.124
88	1.017	1.028	0.978	1.047	0.983	0.926	0.983	1.045
89	0.957	0.977	0.973	0.921	0.993	0.987	0.956	1.037
90	1.015	1.005	0.945	1.100	0.967	0.967	0.953	0.982
91	1.020	0.943	1.078	1.043	1.037	1.025	1.037	1.050
92	0.994	0.965	0.954	1.066	0.993	0.990	0.992	0.998
93	0.997	0.978	1.077	0.942	0.987	0.960	1.002	1.001
94	1.023	0.969	1.038	1.064	1.010	0.980	1.047	1.004
95	1.004	0.936	0.978	1.105	1.007	0.969	1.015	1.038
96	0.976	0.922	0.974	1.035	0.994	0.995	1.016	0.972
geomean	1.008	0.981	0.996	1.049	1.020	1.011	1.027	1.023
Efficiency Index (EI)								
79	1.000	0.996	1.040	0.966	0.961	1.000	0.867	1.024
86	0.999	1.030	0.933	1.036	1.118	1.070	1.260	1.036
87	1.069	1.028	1.054	1.129	0.946	0.977	0.877	0.989
96	0.969	0.983	0.931	0.994	0.960	0.979	0.898	1.007
geomean	1.006	1.007	0.994	1.018	1.006	0.997	0.997	1.023
Technology Index (TI)								
79	0.970	0.976	0.923	1.014	1.061	1.036	1.269	0.909
86	1.075	0.992	1.082	1.157	0.988	1.030	0.845	1.108
87	0.994	0.994	0.971	1.017	1.126	1.063	1.182	1.136
96	1.007	0.937	1.045	1.042	1.035	1.016	1.131	0.965
geomean	1.002	0.974	1.003	1.031	1.014	1.014	1.029	0.999
Pure Efficiency Index (PI)								
79	0.991	0.983	0.994	0.995	0.993	1.023	0.959	0.998
86	1.034	1.017	1.018	1.069	1.041	1.065	1.059	1.000
87	1.023	1.012	0.988	1.071	0.968	0.983	0.923	1.000
96	0.986	0.983	0.985	0.990	0.989	0.980	0.975	1.011
geomean	1.001	0.997	0.999	1.006	0.997	0.993	1.000	0.998
Scale Index (SI)								
79	1.010	1.014	1.045	0.971	0.969	0.979	0.907	1.025
86	0.967	1.013	0.918	0.974	1.076	1.004	1.199	1.036
87	1.046	1.016	1.068	1.056	0.987	0.994	0.978	0.989
96	0.983	1.001	0.946	1.004	0.972	0.999	0.922	0.996
geomean	1.007	1.011	0.994	1.015	1.011	1.005	1.003	1.027

Notes: All geomeans are taken for 18 years from 1979 to 1996. In the table, except the productivity indexes, all other indexes show only the values of 1979 and 1996.

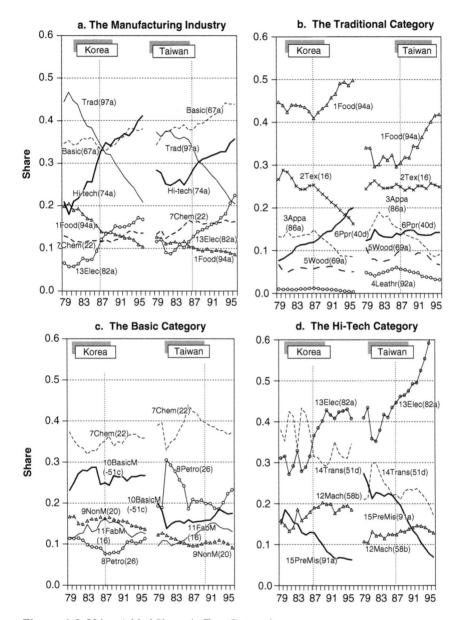

Figure 4.2 Value-Added Shares in Four Categories
Korea and Taiwan

sector in both countries, with a very high correlation coefficient (0.94) and significant at 1% level (a), followed by 2textiles, 6paper, 3apparel, 5wood and 4leather. Interestingly, the ranking was almost the same between Korea and Taiwan in the mid-1990s, and their patterns were also very similar, except for the 2textile and 6paper sectors, whose correlation coefficients were only 0.16 and 0.40, respectively. The two sectors showed opposite trends in the two countries. The 2textiles sector of Korea was declining, while that of Taiwan was staying flat, and the share of the 6paper industry sector was increasing in Korea, while in Taiwan it was also staying flat.

The value-added output shares of the five sectors in the basic category, as shown in Figure 4.2c, were quite different. The correlation coefficients were generally low and not significant, and the 10basic metal sector had a negative and low (10%) level of significance between the two countries. In contrast, the ordering of the importance of the high-tech industries, shown in Figure 4.2d, was the same in both countries in the mid-1990s, and was also highly correlated and significant, except for the 14transportation sector, which had a low 20% level (d) of significance.

Note that the importance of the industries in each category is examined by comparing the industries in that category. In both countries, the most important industry in each category was the same, that is, 1food sector in the traditional category, 7chemicals in the basic category and 13electronics in the high-tech category.

We have plotted these three sectors at the bottom of Figure 4.2a, in which comparisons are made for all 15 manufacturing sectors. It turns out that these three sectors were the largest sectors among the 15 sectors in both countries (not shown in Figure 4.2), and they were highly correlated with a high significance level between Korea and Taiwan except for the chemical sector. In both countries, the importance of the value-added output of the 1food sector in the whole manufacturing industry continued to slide after 1987, to about 10% of the whole manufacturing industry. But in the traditional category, it increased to 50% for Korea and 40% for Taiwan (Figure 4.2b). The trend was similar in both countries.[15] Apparently the 1food sector was squeezed out by the high-tech industries, especially by the 13electric and electronic sector.

In general, so far as the structure of manufacturing industry is concerned, Korea and Taiwan were similar, except for the basic industry sectors. Thus, the next question is whether this means that their productivity growth rates were also similar.

---

15 It turns out that the 2textile and 6paper sectors are the only two sectors that have clearly different trends in the whole manufacturing industry of each country, as compared with their trends in the category.

4.5 Aggregate Productivity Performances

Figure 4.3 shows the growth rates of the five indexes in overall manufacturing industries (the line with circle markers) and three manufacturing categories (the traditional in solid darker columns, the basic in slanted line columns and the high-tech in dot-filled columns) for the period from 1979 to 1996. All growth rates are derived by subtracting 1 from the rows of geometric means in Table 4.2 multiplied by 100.

It appears that the overall variation of performance indexes for Korea was much larger than that for Taiwan, and the performance among the sectors was also quite different. The overall productivity growth rate (MPG) in Korea (0.8%, the last row of the table below the chart) was only 40% of that of Taiwan (2.0%). Similarly, the technology growth rate (TG) and the scale efficiency growth rate (SG) in Korea were only 20 and 60%, respectively, of those of Taiwan, and only the efficiency growth rate (EG) was the same as

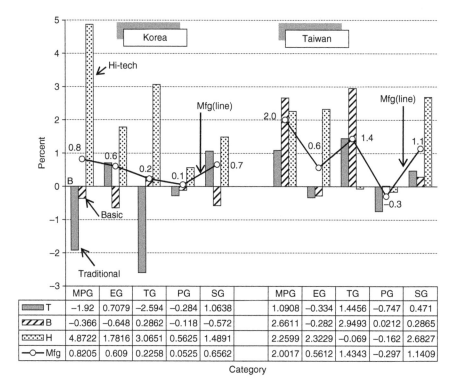

	MPG	EG	TG	PG	SG		MPG	EG	TG	PG	SG
T	−1.92	0.7079	−2.594	−0.284	1.0638		1.0908	−0.334	1.4456	−0.747	0.471
B	−0.366	−0.648	0.2862	−0.118	−0.572		2.6611	−0.282	2.9493	0.0212	0.2865
H	4.8722	1.7816	3.0651	0.5625	1.4891		2.2599	2.3229	−0.069	−0.162	2.6827
Mfg	0.8205	0.609	0.2258	0.0525	0.6562		2.0017	0.5612	1.4343	−0.297	1.1409

Category

Figure 4.3 Growth Rates of the Composition of Output Indexes
Manufacturing Overall and Three Categories, 1979–96

that of Taiwan (0.6%). According to Kaldor's first law, the growth of GDP is positively related to the growth of manufacturing output, and his second law states that the growth of manufacturing output is positively related to the growth of manufacturing productivity (Thirlwall, 2002). Thus, our finding of slower MPI growth (namely, low MPG) may explain why the per capita GDP growth rate of Korea consistently fell behind that of Taiwan.[16]

Note that the pure efficiency index growth rate (PG) was low for both countries but that Taiwan registered a negative growth rate (−0.3%), due mostly to the large negative growth rate (−0.7%) in the traditional category. The Korea PG had a growth rate of 0.1%, mainly due to a high pure efficiency growth rate (0.6%) in the high-tech category. On the other hand, the overall SG of Korea (0.7%) was lower than that of Taiwan (1.1%).

While Taiwan's average productivity growth rate (MPG, 2.0%) from 1979 to 1996 was more than twice as large as that of Korea (0.8%), a closer look at the structure of the productivity indexes may reveal different prospects for the future economic growth of the two countries. Among individual categories, the most conspicuous feature is that Korea's technology growth rate (TG) in the traditional category was on average −2.6%, the largest negative growth rate among all the categories in the two countries. Thus, we see from Table 4.2 that this resulted in a large negative productivity growth (−1.9%) in that sector, and also in a very low technology growth rate (0.2%) in the manufacturing industry as a whole. This appears to be an important reason for the low productivity growth rate in the overall manufacturing industry (MPG, 0.8%) in Korea. Other contributing factors were much lower technical and efficiency growth rates in Korea's basic category. However, Korea had much higher technology (TG) and pure efficiency index growth (PG) (3.1% and 0.6%, respectively) in the high-tech category, as compared with those of Taiwan (in negative values).

Taiwan's higher productivity growth rate was derived mainly from technology growth rate (TG) in the basic and traditional categories. Its average technology growth rate (TG) in the high-tech industry was only −0.1%, much lower than that of Korea (3.1%), although its average efficiency growth rate (EG, 2.3%) was slightly higher. Thus, Korea's low productivity growth was mainly caused by low technology growth (TG) in the traditional and basic categories, while Taiwan's high productivity growth rate reflected a high growth rate in these same two categories. As the governments in this region place top priority on promoting the information and computer technology

---

16 When the indexes are estimated using the industry-wide best-practice frontier, the industry-wide weighted MPG, EG and TG for the manufacturing industry are 0.4, 1.8 and −1.4% for Korea, and 2.2, 1.6 and 0.7% for Taiwan, respectively (Hsiao and Park, 2002). Korean MPG and TG are still much lower than those of Taiwan, and we have the same interpretation.

(ICT) revolution (Hsiao and Hsiao, 2003b), and the future of their economies depends very much on the development of high-tech industries, it seems problematic whether Taiwan can maintain its superiority in real per capita GDP level as well as its growth rate in the future.

4.6 The Trend of Each Index among the Three Categories

Figures 4.4 and 4.5 are a disaggregated version of the table[17] in Figure 4.3, and show the time series profile of sequential multiplicative products of the indexes[18] for the whole manufacturing industry as well as for each category from 1979 to 1996. They are normalized cumulative indexes (not growth rates). Figure 4.4 is drawn from the cumulative indexes of the columns in Table 4.2 grouped by categories for each index. Figure 4.4a is the cumulative productivity index (MPI). Its time trend shows the growth pattern of the index. The manufacturing sequential multiplicative index ranges from 87% to 120% in the case of Korea, and from 102% to 143% in the case of Taiwan (the heavy solid line). When the levels of the productivity index in both countries were normalized to 100, Korea's cumulative index increased very slowly, while Taiwan's index accelerated until around[19] 1987 and leveled out afterward, but still remained about 20% higher than that of Korea after 1987.

The performances of the categories over the years were quite different, however. As can be seen in Figure 4.4a, the productivity of Korea's high-tech category accelerated tremendously but unevenly throughout the whole period, while that of Taiwan accelerated at the beginning but then decelerated slightly after 1987. (The arrows in Figure 4.4a and also Figure 4.5d show that the cumulative productivity index of Korea in 1995 and 1996 exceeded

---

17 We have also used correlation analysis to examine the differences and similarities among the five indexes in the overall manufacturing industries as well as in each of the three industrial categories of the two countries. However, for simplicity, the results are not reported here.

18 See Färe et al. (1994). Our series are constructed as follows. Let m_i be one of the Malmquist indexes, MPI, TI, etc. Then, the multiplicative series at time t is defined as $s_t = 100 \times \Pi_{i=1}^{t} m_i$, where $s_0 \equiv 100$, with time 0 taking at 1978, and m_i is the index at t, t = 1979, 1980, ..., 1996. This is applied to all the 40 time series in Table 4.2. Note that, s_t is a "normalized" cumulative index, and the original index can be derived from $s_t/s_{t-1} = m_t$. The discrete growth rate of s_t is $100 \times ((s_t - s_{t-1})/s_{t-1}) = (m_t - 1) \times 100$, the growth rate of index m_t at t, which we have denoted as MPG, TG, etc. Thus, in Figures 4.5 and 4.6, the sign of the vertical difference $s_t - s_{t-1}$ shows whether the growth rate is positive, zero or negative, and also indicate approximately the magnitude of change.

19 In the previous version of this chapter, we showed that 1987 was a turning point for productivity growth in both countries, and compared the differences in productivity performance between 1979–86 and 1987–96.

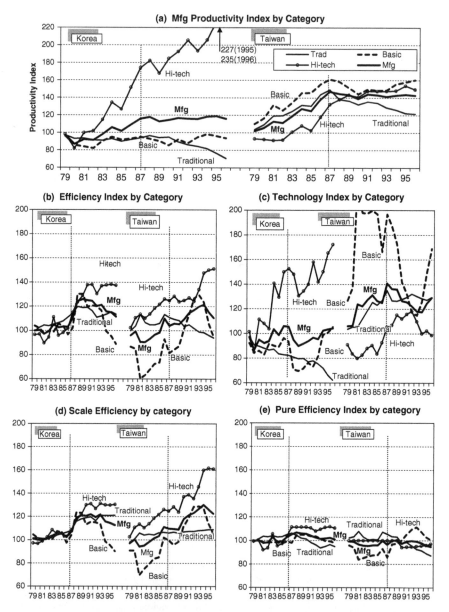

Figure 4.4 Trends of Five Indexes (MPI, EI, TI, SI and PI) by Category

the range of the Y-axis.) Taiwan's indexes in the basic category also tended to decelerate after 1987, but still remained about 60 points higher than those of Korea. In Korea, productivity of the traditional category grew horizontally, and after 1987 started to decrease considerably. By 1996, Korea's cumulative

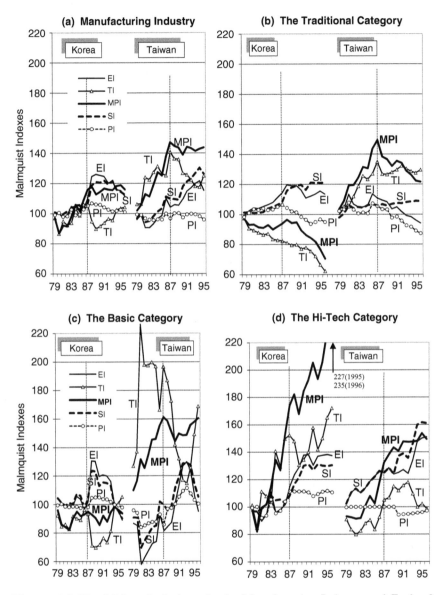

Figure 4.5 Five Malmquist Indexes in the Manufacturing Industry and Each of Three Categories

index in the traditional category had fallen from a high of 97% to 71%. But in Taiwan, it accelerated until 1987, and then fell from a high of 147% to 122%, still maintaining a much higher position than that of Korea. In general, throughout the period, productivity in Korea's basic and traditional categories was consistently much lower than that of Taiwan. It has been a long-range phenomenon.

We have seen the time trend difference in productivity performance in two countries, and also the source of the strength of the Taiwanese manufacturing sector during the years under study here. It appears that as far as the three industrial categories are concerned, Korea pursued a big-push unbalanced industrialization, encouraging the productivity growth of high-tech industries at the expense of basic and traditional industries. In comparison, Taiwan more or less pursued a balanced-productivity growth industrialization, with productivity of all three categories expanding at a similar pace. Our analysis throws further light on the different development patterns to achieve rapid economic growth discussed by Hattori and Sato (1997): the Korean economy has been characterized by government-led development, in which the government pushed the high-tech industries to their limits, while the Taiwanese economy has been characterized by market-led development of small and medium-size enterprises (no major players like Samsung or Hyundai), leading to more or less balanced development of manufacturing productivity. These differences are clearly shown in our productivity analysis.

In terms of the components of the productivity index, the differences are also significant. Korea and Taiwan showed more or less the same level of overall efficiency over the years (Figure 4.4b). However, Taiwan's efficiency in the high-tech category grew slightly faster than that of Korea, while its efficiency in the traditional category declined faster, and its efficiency in the basic category fluctuated much more widely than that of Korea. However, Figure 4.4c shows that the main reason for Korea's overall low productivity in the manufacturing industry was due to consistently very low technical progress in the traditional and basic sectors: it had a much lower rate of overall technical change in these two categories than Taiwan throughout the whole period.

Figure 4.4c also shows that technical change in the high-tech category in Korea was uneven but accelerated, while that of Taiwan stayed low and even decelerated in the early 1990s. In fact, Taiwan's cumulative technology index in the high-tech category was the lowest among the three categories, although the index in the resource-intensive basic sector fluctuated greatly at exceptionally high levels. Here again, considering the lack of natural resources in Taiwan, and in view of the accelerated technology growth (as shown by the steeper slope) of Korea in high-tech industries, it is not clear how far Taiwan can maintain its productivity superiority over Korea in the near future.

Compared with other indexes, the changes in the cumulative scale and pure efficiency indexes are very much subdued for most of the categories. We only note that Taiwan's overall cumulative scale index (Figure 4.4d) was slightly higher than that of Korea in the early 1990s, and that of the high-tech category accelerated after 1987, as compared with Korea, which leveled out. This may reflect the trend in the size of the enterprises in two countries: enterprise size in Korea was decreasing and that of Taiwan increasing (Abe and Kawakami, 1997). The overall cumulative pure efficiency index in Korea was slightly higher than that of Taiwan (Figure 4.4e), and the cumulative pure efficiency index in Taiwan's basic category fluctuated much more than that of Korea.

4.7 The Trend of Five Indexes in Each Category

Figures 4.5a to 4.5d provide category-by-category time series performances of the five indexes as derived in Equations (4.3) and (4.4): MPI (the heavy solid line) is the product of EI (the light solid line) and TI (the light solid line with triangle markers), and EI is the product of PI (the dotted line with circle markers) and SI (the dashed line). As with Figures 4.4a–4.4e, these were cumulative indexes of columns in Table 4.2, grouped by indexes for each category. Note first that the traditional category consists mostly of labor-intensive industries, while the basic category, resource-intensive industries and the high-tech category consist mostly of technology-intensive industries. Most of the indexes in each category show a clear turning point at 1987.

Figure 4.5a reveals the history of the five cumulative indexes in the manufacturing industry as a whole. The indexes are normalized to 100 in 1978. The figure then shows that, after 1979, the overall cumulative productivity index (MPI) of Korea stumbled, but that of Taiwan grew rapidly and leveled out only after 1987. It is a similar case for the cumulative technology index (TI), except that Taiwan's TI fell precipitously after 1987, but still maintained a much higher position than Korea's. Figure 4.5a reveals that, throughout the period, Taiwan's higher cumulative productivity index was driven by its higher overall cumulative technology index as compared with that of Korea.

In the labor-intensive traditional category (Figure 4.5b), all indexes, except the scale index, decreased after 1987. However, Taiwan's cumulative productivity and technology indexes were still constantly much higher than those of Korea, while Korea's cumulative efficiency and scale efficiency indexes exceeded those of Taiwan in the early 1990s. In the resource-intensive basic category (Figure 4.5c), the cumulative productivity index of Taiwan was consistently much higher than that of Korea, which stagnated during the whole period of study. Note the extremely volatile cumulative technology index (TI) in Taiwan's basic category (Figure 4.5(c)): it rapidly increased before 1987 and rapidly fell afterward. Other indexes in both countries were also volatile, especially those for Taiwan, which may reflect scarcity of natural resources in both countries.

The high-tech industries in both countries (Figure 4.5d) have been export-oriented internationally competitive sectors, but, surprisingly, Taiwan's cumulative productivity index, and for that matter, the cumulative technology index, have been persistently very low compared with those of Korea. Korea's cumulative productivity index in the high-tech industries has shown a superior performance over those of Taiwan throughout the period, helped greatly by the equally impressive growth of technology (TI) and efficiency (EI). Here is another warning sign for the future of Taiwanese export competitiveness vis-à-vis Korea in the high-tech category.

4.8 The Innovators

Lastly, we ask which manufacturing sector in each category made the category-wise best-practice production frontier shift in each year. We follow Färe et al. (1994) in identifying the "innovators," which exhibit the following properties:[20]

$$\left\{ TI > 1, \ D^t\left(a^{t+1}\right) > 1, \ D^{t+1}\left(a^{t+1}\right) = 1 \right\} \tag{4.5}$$

That is, an innovator is a manufacturing sector that has technology growth at time t, located beyond the previous technology set but on the current technology set, based on the constant-returns-to-scale technology. We find again that, at first glance, Korea and Taiwan have the same general pattern, as shown in Table 4.3. The leading innovator in each category in both countries was the same: the food sector (1Fd) in the traditional category, the petroleum sector (8Pe) in the basic category and the transportation sector (14Tr) in the high-tech category. Furthermore, these innovators kept their leading positions throughout most of the period, except that, in the mid-1990s, the food sector lost its innovator position in Korea as did the transportation sector in Taiwan.

There were also differences between the countries. In the traditional category, the apparel sector (3Ap) was an innovator, but twice as often in Taiwan as in Korea, while the leather sector (4Le) played a role as an innovator in Taiwan but not in Korea. Considering relatively high technology growth and low efficiency growth in Taiwan (Figure 4.3), it appears that in general Taiwan's metafrontiers shifted more often than Korea's, confirming more innovation activities in Taiwan's traditional industries.

---

20 See Färe et al. (1994), 79, for more detail.

Table 4.3 Innovators by Category, Each Year

	Korea			Taiwan		
Yr	Tradition	Basic	High-tech	Tradition	Basic	Hig-tech
79	1Fd	8Pe	14Tp	4Le	8Pe	
80				1Fd	8Pe	
81	1Fd 3Ap	8Pe 11Fm	14Tp 15Pr	3Ap	8Pe	14Tp
82	1Fd			1Fd 3Ap 4Le		14Tp 15Pr
83		8Pe 11Fm	15Pr	1Fd		14Tp 15Pr
84	1Fd	8Pe	14Tp	1Fd 3Ap 4Le	8Pe	14Tp 15Pr
85				1Fd		
86	1Fd	8Pe 11Fm	14Tp 15Pr	1Fd 3Ap 4Le		14Tp 15Pr
87	3Ap	11Fm	15Pr	1Fd 3Ap	8Pe	14Tp 15Pr
88	1Fd 3Ap	8Pe	14Tp			14Tp 15Pr
89	1Fd	11Fm		3Ap		14Tp
90	1Fd	8Pe 11Fm 12Ma	14Tp	1Fd		14Tp
91	1Fd	8Pe	13El 14Tp	1Fd 3Ap	8Pe	14Tp
92	1Fd 3Ap	8Pe	14Tp	1Fd		14Tp
93	1Fd	8Pe	15Pr	1Fd		
94		8Pe	13El 15Pr	1Fd	8Pe	
95		8Pe	13El 14Tp 15Pr	1Fd	8Pe 13El 14Tp	
96		8Pe	14Tp	1Fd 3Ap	8Pe	
No.	11 4	13 6	1 3 10 7	14 8 4	9 1	12 6

Note: See Table 4.1. 1Fd = Food, etc., 3Ap = Apparel, 8Pe = Petroleum, Coal, etc., 11Fm = Fabricated Metal, 12Ma = Machinery, 13El = Electric, Electronic Machinery, etc. 14Tp = Transportation, 15Pr = Precision Instruments and Other Manufacturing Goods.

In the basic category, the fabricated metal (11Fm) sector was an innovator in Korea but never in Taiwan. The petroleum and coal sector (8Pe) was an innovator for many years in both countries, especially in Korea after 1990. For the high-tech category, all four high-tech sectors played a role as innovators at one time or another in Korea, indicating vigorous innovative activities in this sector in Korea and confirming again the results in Figures 4.3 and 4.5d. Also in Korea, the machinery sector (12Ma) was an innovator only once (in 1990), while the electric and electronic sector (13El) was an innovator in the early 1990s.

In Taiwan, the precision instrument and other manufacturing goods sector (15Pr) was a prominent innovator only in the early years before 1988, but it was an innovator for Korea even after 1993. However, unlike in Korea, the machinery sector (12Ma) has never been an innovator, and curiously, the electric and electronic sector (13El) has been an innovator only once (1995), while Korea scored three times (1991, 1994 and 1995). Here again, in terms of innovators, Taiwan appeared to be more innovative in the 1980s and fell behind Korea in the 1990s.

The fact that the precision instruments and other manufacturing goods sector could have been an innovator in both countries indicates that, as rapidly developing countries, both constantly produced new products and adopted new technology, which did not fall easily into the conventional classification of the manufacturing sectors.

In general, the innovators in each category in both countries were basically similar,[21] showing the same economic vitality. Note that an innovator may not be the largest manufacturing sector in a category or in the whole manufacturing industry (see Figure 4.2). As an example, in both countries, the 3Apparel sector was an innovator for several years, but the value-added output of this sector never exceeded 20% of that of the traditional category, indicating that small sectors may be the leading sectors of the manufacturing industry. Another interesting finding is that, curiously, the electric and electronic sector (13El), which both governments tried so hard to protect and promote in the late 1980s to early 1990s, was neither an important nor a consistent innovator throughout the period.[22] Considering the recent advancement and importance of information and computer technologies in both countries and the developed world[23] (Hsiao and Hsiao, 2003b), we expect this sector to become a leading innovator in the near future.

---

21 For the manufacturing industry-wide best-practice production frontiers, the leading innovators were also the same in both countries: the 1food, 8petroleum and 15precision and other manufacturing sectors (Hsiao and Park, 2002).

22 It is not clear whether this is due to a "productivity paradox" of information technology or a mismeasurement of productivity (Lester, 1998, 228). However, we do not find the "paradox" in Figures 4.4 and 4.5.

23 Korea and Taiwan for the most part adopted their technology from the best-practice frontiers in the world, and the speed with which a frontier in the two countries could be pushed outward seems to have been heavily dependent upon how fast innovation occurred in the world. However, since the indexes in this chapter are derived within each country relative to its own best-practice frontier, the patterns and the differences in productivity performances between Korea and Taiwan might not be expected to change even if the world frontiers were taken into account.

4.9 Conclusions

In this chapter, we have examined the productivity performances of the world's two most rapidly growing countries, using the Malmquist output index and its components for the panel data of 15 matched manufacturing sectors, over the period of 1978–96.

We found that there is a clear similarity between Taiwan and Korea in the structure of value-added output shares in the traditional and high-tech categories, but quite large differences in the resource-intensive basic category. In both countries, the importance of the food sector in the overall manufacturing industry has been declining rapidly, and, in contrast, that of the electric and electronic sector has been increasing quite fast since 1987.

However, when we examine the productivity performance indexes, a difference appears. Korea's average growth rates of overall productivity, technology and scale efficiency have been well below those of Taiwan, and the average efficiency growth rate has just equaled that of Taiwan. This may explain why the per capita GDP growth rate of Korea has consistently fallen behind that of Taiwan in the postwar period. However, a closer look at the composition of the productivity index reveals that the low overall average productivity growth of Korea has been caused by low overall average technology growth in the traditional and basic categories, while its average technology growth in the high-tech category has been twice as high as that of Taiwan.

When the five cumulative indexes are grouped by categories for each index, we find that the productivity and technology indexes of Korea's basic and traditional sectors have been consistently lower than those of Taiwan for the whole period, indicating consistent bias against these two categories, which has resulted in a low average productivity growth rate for Korea. Thus, the Korean problem is chronic rather than transient. It also shows an extraordinary growth of productivity in the high-tech category at the expense of basic and traditional categories in Korea, while the productivity growth of the three categories in Taiwan has expanded at about the same pace. Thus, we have identified different development patterns in the two newly developed countries: Korea has pursued a government-led unbalanced growth strategy, while Taiwan pursued a market-led balanced growth strategy. It will be interesting to see which policy contributes more to sustainable economic growth.

When the cumulative indexes are grouped by indexes for each category, it is clear that, although Taiwan's average productivity performance and the technology index in the traditional and basic categories have been generally superior to those of Korea over the whole period, they have been much inferior in the internationally competitive high-tech industries, especially in recent years. Furthermore, we have found that, while the food, petroleum and transportation sectors have been the common leading innovators in the three categories, respectively, in both countries, Taiwan has had many more frontier sectors (26) in the traditional category and Korea has had more frontier sectors (21) in the high-tech category, especially in the electronics sector (3), showing again the consistent productivity superiority of Korea's high-tech industries. Thus, our results indicate that there are several signs that Korea is catching up with Taiwan in productivity. Their performance in the next decade will be interesting to watch.

Appendix 4A: Sources of Data

For Korea, the real value-added output (at the 1995 constant price) and the number of workers by industry are taken from OECD (2000), STAN Database for Industrial Analysis 1970–1997. Korea has 28 three-digit manufacturing sectors, based on the ISIC Rev. 2, in the period from 1970 to 1996. The Korean data are rearranged and matched with the Taiwanese data and are reduced to 15 sectors as shown in Table 4.1. Some problems in comparability of the data are noted in the footnote to Table 4.1. We do not use the "Report on Mining and Manufacturing Survey" since its industry classification has been changed several times over the years, and it is difficult to find the matched classification. For the physical capital stock, see Pyo (1998). For GDP by industry, see the Korea National Statistic Office (2002) home page: http://www.nso.go.kr.

The data on Taiwan were made available to the authors by courtesy of Drs. Sheng-cheng Hu and Vei-lin Chan, who used the data to find the total factor productivity at the industrial level in Hu and Chan (1999), applying the growth accounting method. Real GDP (calculated by dividing GDP deflator for each industry) is from *Taiwan Area National Income*, which has data on 22 manufacturing sectors. Due to the lack of consistency among the data, Hu and Chan (1999) selected 15 industries, which are used in this chapter. Real capital (at 1991 constant price) is adopted from the table on Series of Real Net Fixed Capital Stock (excluding land) of Industrial and Service Sectors in *The Trends and Multifactor Productivity, Taiwan Area*, published every four years by the Directorate-General of Budget, Accounting and Statistics, Executive Yuan, Taiwan. The number of workers is taken from *Monthly Statistics of Manpower Allocation, Taiwan Area*, published by the Ministry of Economic Affairs, Taiwan.

Acknowledgments

We are indebted to Professors Vei-lin Chan, Song-ken Hsu, Sheng-cheng Hu, Keith E. Maskus and Ms. Li-Min Weng for making the data on Taiwan and Korea available to the authors. Without their help, this chapter could not have been written. Comments and suggestions from Professors Been-Lon Chen, Tim Coelli, Mei-Chu W. Hsiao, two anonymous referees, the conference participants at the Asia Conference on Efficiency and Productivity Growth, Academia Sinica, Taipei, Taiwan, July 2002, and seminar participants at the University of Colorado Boulder were most helpful. All errors of omission and commissions are ours.

References

Abe, M., and M. Kawakami (1997). "A Distributive Comparison of Enterprise Size in Korea and Taiwan," *Developing Economies* 35(4): 382–400.

Buccola, S. T. (2000). "Material and Value-Adding Inputs in Manufacturing Enterprises," *Journal of Productivity Analysis* 13: 231–47.

Coelli, T. (1996). "A Guide to DEAP Version 2.1: A Data Envelopment Analysis (Computer) Program." *CEPA* Working Paper No. 96/08, University of New England.

Coelli, T., D. S. P. Rao and G. E. Battese (1998). *An Introduction to Efficiency and Productivity Analysis*. Boston: Kluwer Academic Publishers.

Färe, R., S. Grosskopf and M. Norris (1997). "Productivity Growth, Technical Progress, and Efficiency Change in Industrialized Countries: Reply," *American Economic Review* 87(5): 1040–43.

Färe, R., S. Grosskopf and W. F. Lee (1995). "Productivity in Taiwanese Manufacturing Industries," *Applied Economics* 27: 259–65.

Färe, R., S. Grosskopf, M. Norris and Z. Zang (1994). "Productivity Growth, Technical Progress, and Efficiency Change in Industrialized Countries," *American Economic Review* 84: 66–83.

Forsund, F. R., and N. Sarafoglow (2002). "On the Origins of Data Envelopment Analysis," *Journal of Productivity Analysis* 17: 23–40.

Grifell-Tatje, E., and C. A. K. Lovell (1995). "A Note on the Malmquist Productivity Index," *Economics Letters* 47(2): 169–79.

Hattori, T., and Y. Sato (1997). "A Comparative Study of Development Mechanisms in Korea and Taiwan: Introductory Analysis," *Developing Economies* 35(4): 341–57.

Hsiao, F. S. T., and C. Park (2002). "Productivity Growth in Newly Developed Countries—The Case of Korea and Taiwan." *Journal of the Korean Economy* 3(2), 189–230.

Hsiao, F. S. T., and M. C. W. Hsiao (1996). "Taiwanese Economic Development and Foreign Trade." In J. Y. T. Kuark, ed. *Comparative Asian Economies*. Greenwich, CT: JAI Press, 211–302. Originally published in W. C. Kirby and J. M. Greene, eds. *Harvard Studies on Taiwan: Papers of the Taiwan Study Workshop* I. The Fairbank Center for East Asian Research, Cambridge, MA: Harvard University, 1995, 199–270. (Also Chapter 1 in Hsiao and Hsiao [2015].)

——— (1998). "Miracle or Myth of Asian NICs' Growth—The Irony of Numbers." In M. J. Dutta and R. W. Hooley, eds. *The New Industrial Revolution in Asian Economies*. Greenwich, CT: JAI Press, 51–68.

——— (2002). Taiwan in the Global Economy—Past, Present, and Future. In P. C. Y. Chow, ed. *Taiwan in Global Economy—From an Agrarian Economy to an Exporter of High-Tech Products*, Westport, CT: Greenwood Press, 161–222. (Also Chapter 2 in Hsiao and Hsiao, 2015.)

———— (2003a). "'Miracle Growth' in the Twentieth Century—Comparisons of East Asian Development." *World Development* 31(2): 227–57. (Also in Chapter 6 of the present volume.)

———— (2003b). "The Impact of the US Economy on the Asian-Pacific Region: Does It Matter?", *Journal of Asian Economics* 14(2): 219–41.

———— (2004). "Catching Up and Convergence: Long-run Growth in East Asia," *Review of Development Economics* 8(2): 223–36. (Also in Chapter 7 of the present volume.)

———— (2015). *Economic Development of Taiwan—Early Experiences and the Pacific Trade Triangle.* Singapore: World Scientific Publishing.

Hu, S. C., and V. L. Chan (1999). "The Determinants of Taiwan's Total Factor Productivity" [in Chinese]. *Industry of Free China (Taiwan).* September, 1–50.

Kawai, H. (1994). "International Comparative Analysis of Economic Growth: Trade Liberalization and Productivity," *Developing Economies* 32(4): 373–97.

Lee, J. D., T. Y. Kim and E. Heo (1998). "Technological Progress versus Efficiency Gain in Manufacturing Sectors," *Review of Development Economics* 2(3): 268–81.

Lester, R. K. (1998). *The Productivity Edge, A New Strategy for Economic Growth.* New York: W. W. Norton.

Maddison, A. (1995). *Monitoring the Word Economy, 1820–1992.* Development Center. Paris: OECD.

Nelson, R. R. (1973). "Recent Exercises in Growth Accounting: New Understanding or Dead End?", *American Economic Review* 63: 462–68.

Nelson, R. R., and H. Pack (1999). "The Asian Miracle and Modern Growth Theory," *Economic Journal* 109: 416–36.

Nishimizu, M., and C. R. Hulten (1978). "The Sources of Japanese Economic Growth: 1955–1971," *Review of Economics and Statistics* 60: 351–61.

OECD (2000). *STAN Database for Industrial Analysis,* 1970–1997. Paris: OECD.

Okuda, S. (1997). "Industrialization Policies of Korea and Taiwan and Their Effects on Manufacturing Productivity," *Developing Economies* 25(4): 358–81.

Oshima, H. T. (1987). *Economic Growth in Monsoon Asia: A Comparative Survey.* Tokyo: University of Tokyo Press.

Page, J. (1994). "The East Asian Miracle: Four Lessons for Development Policy." In S. Fisher and J. J. Rotemberg, eds. *NBER Macroeconomics, Annual 1994.* Cambridge, MA: MIT Press.

Pyo, H. K. (1998). "Estimation of Korean Physical Capital Stock by Industry and Type of Asset" [in Korean]. Working paper, 1998. Seoul: Korea Institute of Public Finance.

Ray, S., and E. Desli (1997). "Productivity Growth, Technical Progress, and Efficiency Change in Industrialized Countries: Comment," *American Economic Review* 87(5): 1033–39.

Sudit, E. F., and N. Finger (1981). "Methodological Issues in Aggregate Productivity Analysis." In A. Dogramaci and N. R. Adam, eds. *Aggregate and Industry-Level Productivity Analyses.* Boston: Martinus Nijhoff Publishing.

Thirlwall, A. P. (2002). *The Nature of Economic Growth: An Alternative Framework for Understanding the Performance of Nations.* Northampton, MA: Edward Elgar.

Timmer, M. (2000). *The Dynamics of Asian Manufacturing: A Comparative Perspective in the Late Twentieth Century.* Northampton, MA: Edward Elgar.

Chapter 5

COLONIALISM, LEARNING AND CONVERGENCE: A COMPARISON OF INDIA AND TAIWAN

Abstract

Before World War II, Taiwan was a colony of Japan, and India was a colony of the United Kingdom. This chapter is unique and different from other chapters in that we compares the colonial experiences of Taiwan and India before World War II and their effects on the economic development of the postwar period. The chapter combines the traditional learning model with recent theory of economic growth using Maddison's long-run real GDP per capita data.

We first discuss the performance of India and Taiwan in the world economy. While economic theory suggests that, due to its large area and population, India could have grown faster than Taiwan, this was not the case after World War II. We identify differences in terms of learning in the development experience of the two countries under colonial rule. The colonial distortion in industrial and agricultural development appeared to be more important in India than in Taiwan. It appears that the most important factors, however, were health and education.

We then derive learning coefficients of India with the United Kingdom, Taiwan with Japan, and Japan with the United States through the prewar and postwar periods. Long-run coefficients of learning are estimated. Using the conventional unit root–based test of convergence, we show that the model of learning leads to a logistic model of economic growth. We then confirm that real GDP per capita of Taiwan was converging to that of Japan, whereas that of India showed only slight convergence to the United Kingdom or Taiwan. Our results underscore the importance of studying colonial experiences of the two countries, and for that matter, of any country in order to understand its postwar economic development.

5.1 Introduction

The study of the economic convergence of developing to developed countries as well as the convergence of some developed countries to dominant developed countries, such as the United States, is one of the most intriguing and difficult matters in the recent literature on economic growth and development. Few works, however, have focused on whether former colonies could catch up with the colonizer country once the colony achieved independence and cast off colonial institutions deemed inimical to economic development. This may be so since most former colonies in Africa and Asia, which gained independence after World War II, are still struggling and remain low-income countries. Here, an income convergence appears out of the question. The few exceptions of noncity-states are Taiwan and South Korea (hereafter Korea). They were colonies of Japan from 1895 to 1945 and from 1911 to 1945, respectively. Elsewhere, we have studied and confirmed the convergence of GDP per capita of Taiwan and Korea to that of Japan and the United States (Hsiao and Hsiao, 2004). We also pointed out that the foundation of human capital and social and economic infrastructure in Taiwan began during the Japanese period (Hsiao and Hsiao, 2002, 2003) and continued after the war (Hsiao and Hsiao, 1998, 2003), eventually catapulting Taiwan into rapid growth (Hsiao and Hsiao, 1996, 2003).

A stark contrast to Taiwan is India, which was under full-fledged British colonial rule for almost one century (1858–1947). Under the British regime, India already possessed modern textile and steel industries, transcontinental railways, a banking system and a capital market. It was arguably the most industrialized colony in the world. And yet, the general impression is that India remained "poor and stagnant" for several decades after World War II (Higgins, 1968; Dreze and Sen, 1995, Chapter 1).

India gained independence in 1947 and Taiwan in 1949, and the current constitution was laid down in both countries in 1950. What then explains the difference in economic development between India and Taiwan? Was there a difference in colonial policies as pursued by the United Kingdom and Japan? What is the colonial linkage in determining the postwar development of the two countries? Does GDP per capita converge to that of their former colonial masters? These questions are addressed in this chapter.

In a highly competitive world, no nation can afford to stand still. Contrary to Krugman's predictions of an essentially factor-driven growth (1994), Taiwan and Korea, along with Hong Kong and Singapore, the so-called newly industrializing economies (NIEs), climbed the technology ladder during the final three decades of the twentieth century (Hsiao and Hsiao, 2001b). They learned and advanced their technological abilities through education, foreign trade and inward and outward foreign direct investment, in order to stay competitive and sustain rapid growth. Why was this not the case in India during the postwar decades, or at any rate up to the onset of the Asian financial crisis in 1997?

In the next section, we compare India and Taiwan in the world economy by comparing absolute and relative "size" in terms of geographical area, population and economic activity. In the section following, colonial heritages are compared. We point out that institutional reform and agricultural self-sufficiency were achieved already during the colonial period in Taiwan but not in India. The different learning experiences are quantified in the fourth section in order to corroborate our qualitative observations.

The fifth section uses a conventional unit root–based test of convergence to study convergence between, respectively, India and the United Kingdom, Taiwan and Japan, and Japan and the United States. We also examine the convergence between India and Taiwan, between Taiwan and the United Kingdom and between Taiwan and the United States. The sixth section derives a logistic model and sets up a nonlinear regression model for the convergence of India and Taiwan to Japan and the United Kingdom as well as between Japan and the United States. Concluding remarks are given in the final section.

5.2 India and Taiwan in the World Economy

It might appear a bit unusual, if not strange, to compare India and Taiwan, as India is considered a "large" country while Taiwan is "small." However, the qualifications "large" and "small" above all depend on the eye of the examiner (Perkins and Syrquin, 1989). India is indeed a large country. It is 91 times of Taiwan in geographical area and 44 times of Taiwan in terms of population. In 1995, India ranked seventh in area and second in population in the world, whereas Taiwan ranked respectively 113th and 39th (World Bank, 1997). Nevertheless, India and Taiwan are at similar levels of population density and aggregate GDP, which may be more important in economic analysis (Perkins and Syrquin, 1989). India's population density is only 48% that of Taiwan and its aggregate GDP exceeds Taiwan's GDP by only 25%. The ranks of India and Taiwan in the world are, respectively, 11th and 4th as to population density and 15th and 19th by aggregate GDP. However, Taiwan obviously exceeds India by far in terms of GDP per capita. In 1995, GDP per capita in Taiwan was 36 times higher than that of India, with Taiwan ranking 25th and India ranking 108th in the world.

It has been stated that "large countries do appear to grow faster than small ones," and that "size" matters for both structure and performance. "Large countries have less choice in determining development strategy than small ones, but having a wider range of options is not necessarily an advantage in efforts to achieve modern economic growth" (Perkins and Syrquin, 1989, 1747).

Elsewhere we have drawn attention to Taiwan's extraordinary performance in electronics production (Hsiao and Hsiao, 2002). In 1995, Taiwan produced more than 10% of the world's personal computers. Its production of keyboards and motherboards ranked number one in the world (*Nikkei Sangyo Shinbun*, February 11, 1996). In 1998, Taiwan's share in production volume was as follows: scanners (85%), cases (75%), motherboards (66%), SPS (66%), keyboards (65%), mouse (60%), monitors (58%), sound cards (49%), video cards (40%), notebooks (39%) and graphics cards (31%), all ranking first in the world. In 1998, Taiwan therefore was "the number three producer of information technology worldwide, only behind the United States and Japan" (Underwood, 1999, 22).[1]

Indeed, Taiwan is certainly a very large country in the world by almost any measure except land area. In recent studies of endogenous theories of economic growth, "size" also matters. A larger labor stock, more consumers and a greater land area all lead to higher growth rates through economies of scale and a variety of intermediate inputs and opportunities to reduce fixed costs (Feenstra, 2004). Thus, although no definite conclusions may be drawn about the impact of land area and economic performance, the theory does suggest that in many respects India has a better chance to grow faster than Taiwan, as indeed happened before World War II. We are interested in explaining why this did not happen during the postwar period, at least until the early 1990s.

If we ignore differences in the size of the area and population as a determinant factor behind economic performance, we can ask what past performances of the two countries look like. Figure 5.1 shows real GDP per capita levels in ten Asian countries, using the right-hand side of the Y-axis for both the pre-war and the postwar period. The data are based on internationally comparable real GDP per capita figures for 56 countries during the years 1820–1992 (Maddison, 1995, Appendix D), based on 1990 Geary–Khamis dollars compiled from international purchasing power parities.[2] From Maddison's data,

---

1 The original source is the Market Intelligence Center of the Institute for Information Industries in Taiwan. According to this institution, "Taiwan IT companies produced more than $19 billion in hard-ware products in 1998. Adding offshore production, the total reached $32 billion, an increase of 8.4% over 1997" (Underwood, 1999, 22).
2 For a discussion of the Geary–Khamis method and references, see Kravis et al. (1982, 89–93). Also see Appendix 9A of this book.During the 2003 conference at Groningen, the Netherlands, Angus Maddison pointed out that updated data series are available up to 2002. However, in order to avoid possible distortions due to the Asian financial crisis and since this chapter is concerned with long-run convergence, we kept the original series running from 1911 to 1992 or 1994.

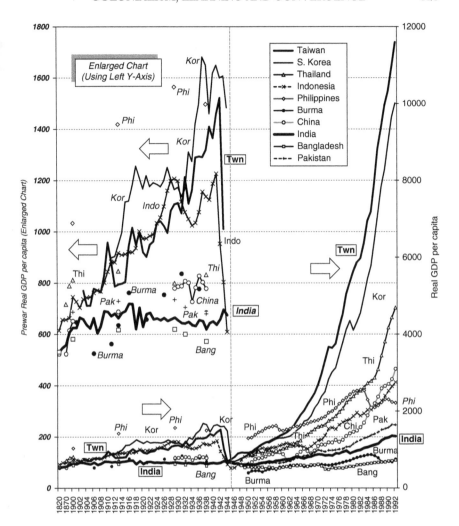

Figure 5.1. Levels of Real GDP per Capita in 10 Asian Countries
In 1990 Geary–Khamis Dollars, 1820–1992

we see clearly that the ranking of countries can hardly stay constant over time. The upper part of the left-hand side of Figure 5.1 shows the enlarged pre-war performance using the left-hand side of the Y-axis (in italics). GDP per capita in India reached its prewar peak in 1916 at $719 and stayed almost constant, around $650 until 1947. After independence, in 1947, real GDP per capita increased, gradually doubling from $641 in 1947 to $1,360 in 1991. Throughout the prewar and postwar periods, its GDP per capita level was almost the lowest among the ten Asian countries shown.

By contrast, in 1904, real GDP per capita in Taiwan was $712, as compared with India's $636 in that year. The difference is $76, the smallest difference between the two countries in the last century. However, Taiwan's real GDP per capita doubled to $1,522, the prewar peak, in 1942, as compared to India's $658. In the postwar period, after Taiwan recovered slowly until reaching the prewar peak by 1962, it has increased more than seven times, reaching $11,590 in 1992, as compared with India's $1,348. Why are there such differences in real GDP per capita between these two countries?

5.3 The Colonial Heritage

In the introduction, we pointed out that India was probably one of the most industrialized colonies in the world during the prewar period. The British invested heavily in India during the 1930s. India was one of the eight industrial powers of the world and was the world's sixth-largest trader, surpassed only by the United States, Great Britain, Germany, France and Canada. "Compared with her huge population and with her resources, however, the degree of industrialization was quite meager and insufficient" (Wallbank, 1958, 18).

India's growth rate of manufacturing value added, measured at constant prices, averaged 10.36% during the period 1868–1900 but fell to 6% during the years 1900–13 and further, to 4.8% in the 1919–39 period (Lal, 1999, 19). However, in another study, it is shown that during the interwar period, manufacturing output in India increased at a rate well above the world average for 28 countries, surpassed only by the Soviet Union, Japan, Finland and South Africa. The rate of growth was higher than in the United Kingdom, the United States and Germany (Morris, 1983, 609). Between 1922 and 1939, the production of several manufacturing goods increased markedly, especially cotton textiles (2.5 times), steel (6 times), paper (2.5 times) and sugar (1.2 times) but also including machinery, matches, glass and soap. The number of factories increased four times, and employment rose by 40% (Ito, 1973, 192; based on Chakravarti et al., 1965).

By contrast, in the second half of the nineteenth century, Taiwan was "economically backward" (Ho, 1978, 24). The first short 107 km railway was built only in 1893, half a century later than the first railway in India in 1853 (Ito, 1978, 23; Rothermund, 1993, 28). Nothing in Taiwan before the Japanese occupation appeared to be comparable to India. During the years 1912–40, that is, under Japanese occupation, Taiwan's real annual rate of growth in manufacturing industry was 5.3%–5.9%, depending on the estimate, that is, at best slightly higher than that in India (Mizoguchi and Umemura, 1988, 47; Shinohara, 1971, Table 16). Throughout the prewar period, Taiwan's manufacturing industry consisted mainly of food processing. Its share in total manufacturing output amounted to 78% in 1930 and 65% in 1940, with sugar alone accounting for, respectively, 63% and 39% (Mizoguchi and Umemura, 1988, 48).

However, as the Taiwanese economy entered the war stage after the Second Sino–Japanese War in the mid-1930s, the emphasis in manufacturing shifted toward metal processing and oil refining, the production of machinery and the chemical, petrochemical and pharmaceutical industries. Light industry of daily consumer goods was developed to attain full self-sufficiency in wartime (Hsiao and Hsiao, 2002; Kusui, 1944, 69–74; Chang, 1980). By 1939, the value of industrial output for the first time exceeded that of agricultural output (Hsiao and Hsiao, 2002). Although Taiwan's prewar industrialization began too late and amounted to too little, it did include all basic light and heavy industries for postwar development. By contrast, Indian scholars tend to emphasize the distorted and unbalanced colonial development of Indian industry, which catered only to the needs of the British empire (Joshi, 1985).

In the 1920s and 1930s, the Japanese authorities were inclined to make full use of the comparative advantage of Taiwanese agriculture. Through intensive research and development, extensive rural reorganization and institutional reform, the Japanese authorities introduced new plants and crops, improved methods of cultivation and erected extensive flood control and modern irrigation systems (Hsiao, 1997; Hsiao and Hsiao, 2002; Ho, 1978, 36–37, 57–65). The rate of growth in Taiwan's agriculture averaged 3.1% over the years 1911–39 and climbed to 8% in 1945–60 due to massive aid from the United States (Lee, 1975, 1406).[3] Annual population growth was 3.8% during 1951–55 and 3% in 1966–70, one of the highest rates in the world. Yet, the agricultural output growth rate, 4.8% over the years 1953–63, was higher still, supporting the influx of Chinese refugees and rapid natural population growth in Taiwan with additional resources for industrialization (Lee and Liang, 1974; Hsiao and Hsiao, 1996, 227–28, 240–41).

By the end of the 1930s, Taiwan's production of bananas and canned pineapple ranked third in the world, whereas sugar and sweet potatoes ranked fourth, tea sixth, rice and peanuts tenth and salt thirteenth. Most of the products were exported, especially to Japan. Few countries were indeed endowed with so many kinds of products in such large quantities. India, by contrast, achieved self-sufficiency in agriculture only after 1970 (Kojima, 1993).

---

3 Lee was a consultant of the Sino-American Joint Commission on Rural Reconstruction. The scholar-cum-politician became the President of Taiwan in 1988 and was reelected for another four years in 1990.

In stark contrast to the positive appraisal of the Japanese contribution to agricultural development in Taiwan and its large impact on postwar economic growth, Indian scholars tend to condemn the "neglect of agriculture" and "agricultural stagnation" under British colonial rule as well as "the connection between the parasitical role of the landlords and absence of entrepreneurial initiative from the peasants with the structural constraints of the colonial economy and the political necessities of imperial rule," which all "resulted in the tragic poverty of the Indian people" (Joshi, 1985, 26–28). Thus, in the postindependence period, the "agricultural sector recorded a growth of 2.7% during 1950/51 to 1983/84 compared with a meager rate of less than 1% during 1904/05 to 1944/45" (Joshi, 1985, 39).

Perhaps for this reason, India's advanced industrial development before World War II was not reflected in the growth of its GDP per capita. India's real GDP per capita remained low during and after the wartime years. Real GDP per capita growth rates in India averaged −11% during the prewar period (1911–40) and 1.94% during the immediate postwar period (1952–92), whereas, in Taiwan, average growth rates were 1.18% and 6.03%, respectively, during the same periods (Hsiao and Hsiao, 2003, Table 5.1).

A possible and favorite argument is that while Indian's real GDP did increase, its increase was offset by the increase in population, resulting in a low GDP per capita (Lal, 1999). Therefore, we compare, in Figure 5.2 for India and in Figure 5.3 for Taiwan, the level of real GDP (GDP, heavy line) and its growth rate (gGDP, generally in longer empty columns, using the right-hand side Y-axis) as well as the level of population (POP, dotted line) and its growth rates[4] (gPOP, generally in shorter dark columns, using the right-hand side Y-axis). In both figures, real GDP is measured in million 1990 Geary–Khamis dollars, whereas population is given on the left-hand side Y-axis in thousands of persons. The lower part of Figure 5.2 shows that levels of both real GDP and population in India were rather stagnant before the war but increased considerably after the war.

Figure 5.3 shows that levels of real GDP and population in Taiwan were also stagnant before the war (same as other countries, see Figure 5.1). However, if we enlarge the prewar real GDP levels for both countries, 5 times for India and 50 times for Taiwan, it is clear that, as in the case of real GDP per capita in Figure 5.1, Indian real GDP level (the line marked with circles on the upper left part of Figure 5.2) increased almost linearly before 1945, while that of Taiwan (the line marked with triangles on the upper left part of Figure 5.3)

---

4 The growth rate here is defined as the rate compounded at the end of each year, $g = (X_t - X_{t-1})/X_{t-1}$.

Table 5.1 Social and Economic Conditions of India and Taiwan
Late 1950s

COUNTRY	Indi	%tl		Twn	%tl	Diff
	(1)	(2)		(3)	(4)	(5)
Per Capita GNP in 1961 (in US$)	80	24	(56th)	145	43	(42nd)
Factor score	-0.28	43	(42nd)	1.05	84	(12th)
F1. Sociocultural Indicators						(2)-(4)
1 6 Extent of Social Mobility	C	5		A	78	-73
2 9 Degree of Cultural and Ethnic Homogeneity	D+	15		A	68	-53
3 8 Extent of Mass Communication	C-	26		B	66	-41
4 3 Extent of Urbanization	C	45		B+	77	-32
5 7 Extent of Literacy	C-	34		B	65	-31
6 2 Extent of Dualism	B	54		A	85	-31
7 5 Importance of the Indigenous Middle Class	B	57		A	84	-27
8 11 Crude Fertility Rate	C+	16		B	32	-16
9 4 Character of Basic Social Organization	B	47		B	47	0
10 12 Degree of Modernization of Outlook	A	76		A	76	0
11 1 Size of the Traditional Agricultural Sector	C+	41		C	19	22
12 10 Degree of Social Tension	B+	65		B-	26	39
F2. Political System						
13 13 Degree of National Integration and Sense of National Unity	D+	19		A	85	-66
14 14 Extent of Centralization of Political Power	C	14		A	74	-61
15 17 Degree of Competitiveness of Political Parties	B-	36		B-	36	
16 18 Predominant Basis of the Political Party System	A	81		B	57	24
17 16 Degree of Freedom of Political Opposition and Press	A	70		C	14	57
18 19 Strength of the Labor Movement	B+	80		D	4	76
19 15 Strength of Democratic Institutions	A	88		D	8	80
F3. Sociopolitical Characteristics						
20 24 Extent of Political Stability	D	3		A	68	-65
21 21 Political Strength of the Military	C	0		B	51	-51
22 20 Political Strength of the Traditional Elite	C	11		C-	0	11
23 22 Degree of Administrative Efficiency	A	86		A-	70	16
24 23 Extent of Leadership Commitment to Economic Development	A	88		B	55	32
F4. Economic Indicators						
25 32 Level of Modernization of Techniques in Agriculture	C	31		A	96	-65
26 31 Character of Agricultural Organization	C	27		A-	84	-57
27 34 Level of Adequacy of Physical Overhead Capital	C	26		A	82	-57
28 28 Gross Investment Rate	D	39		B	85	-46
29 30 Change in Degree of Industrialization since 1950	B	38		A	73	-35
30 29 Level of Modernization of Industry	C+	54		A	88	-34
31 33 Degree of Improvement in Agricultural Productivity since 1950	B	58		A	89	-31
32 26 Rate of Growth of Real Per Capita GNP: 1950/51 - 1963/64	C+	57		A	86	-30
33 39 Degree of Improvement in Financial Institutions since 1950	A-	68		A+	97	-30
34 36 Level of Effectiveness of the Tax System	C+	50		B+	70	-20
35 40 Rate of Improvement in Human Resources	B+	73		A	81	-8
36 41 Structure of Foreign Trade	A	89		A+	95	-5
37 35 Degree of Improvement in Physical Overhead Capital since 195	A-	72		A-	72	0
38 38 Level of Effectiveness of Financial Institutions	B+	73		B+	73	0
39 37 Degree of Improvement in the Tax System since 1950	A-	86		B+	73	14
40 27 Abundance of Natural Resources	C	16		D	0	16

Source: Adelman and Morris 1967. Also see Appendix.

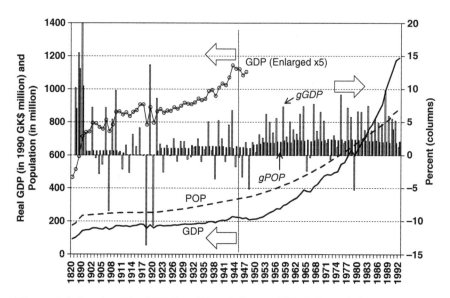

Figure 5.2 Levels of Real GDP and Population, and Their Growth Rates
India

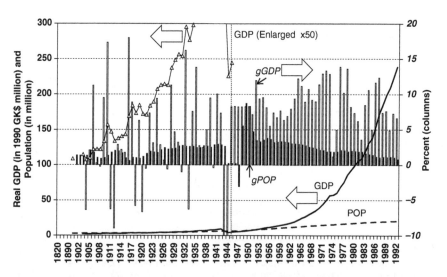

Figure 5.3 Levels of Real GDP and Population, and Their Growth Rates
Taiwan

increased exponentially before 1945. Thus, the difference emerged in the colonial period.

Moreover, in terms of growth rates of real GDP and population, we also see quite a different picture. The columns showing percentage growth rates of real GDP and population are measured from the right-hand Y-axis, which has the same scales for both charts. That is, the column heights in Figures 5.2 and 5.3 are fully comparable. Between 1900 and 1992, Taiwan's population growth rates were almost consistently higher than those of India. Taiwan overcame the population growth by increasing GDP growth rates to well above population growth rates during the prewar and postwar periods, even if GDP growth rates were rather erratic during the prewar period. The argument that India's population increase reduced the fruits from industrialization appears untenable.

Many reasons have been given for the stagnant performance of the Indian economy before and after World War II. It is understandable that many Indian scholars blame it on the exploitation and evils of British colonialism and its sequel after independence. They argue that "British imperialism has discouraged industries, prevented the creation of necessary tariffs to encourage Indian industry, established a parasite landlord—zamindar—class, taxed the Indian masses too much, and neglected social services, such as education" (Wallbank, 1958, 32). Other scholars, however, found the causes of Indian poverty in socioreligious traditions and customs in Indian culture.

However, if we consider the prewar economic performance of Taiwan and Korea as well as their success after the war, we find that the crucial problem here seems to be how much the colonial government should interfere with local custom and culture to prepare for the basic institutional reform necessary for postwar economic development, in addition to developing local industry. Different from the Japanese colonial regime, the British government in India upheld liberal principles and shunned interventionist measures (Rothermund, 1993, 119). The "serious weakness of the post-Mutiny British bureaucracy" was "the impersonal nature of the official machine and its lack of contact with the people it ruled. Day-to-day efficiency rather than the preparation of the people of India for some objective, such as self-rule, was the hallmark of the Indian civil service" (Wallbank, 1958, 81).

When Japan invaded Taiwan in 1895, the island was found to be uninhabitable and facing high mortality rates due to infectious diseases such as malaria and cholera. The Japanese authorities did not convert Taiwan into an "extractive state" as did some European powers pursuing a colonization strategy influenced by the feasibility of settlements (the disease environment), which in turn influenced the postwar development of the one-time colony

(Acemoglu et al., 2001). Apparently, the Japanese had no choice but to stay in Taiwan, despite epidemic diseases.

The first thing the Japanese did was to enforce private and public hygiene, including "ventilation and lighting of a house, building of a lavatory inside the house, the habit of bathing, washing hands after relieving, spittoons and garbage cans in public places" (Wu, 1999; Tsurumi, 1977, 154–55). Other micromanagement included using waste baskets, making waste disposal arrangements and setting dates for household cleaning, in addition to implementing a ban on binding women's feet and on the pigtail hairstyle for men. By the end of the 1930s, all the common infectious diseases had been eradicated. This was in great contrast to India (and, for that matter, China). Even in the 1950s, the thatched huts in Indian villages had no chimneys or windows, "filth and smells were everywhere. Sewage ran along the narrow alleyways" (Wallbank, 1958, 19). In the 1940s, malaria infected 100 million people every year, and tuberculosis, hookworm, cholera, smallpox and typhoid took a heavy toll (Wallbank, 1958, 23).

The next focus of attention of the Japanese colonial government was education. In a loosely defined caste system of Confucianism, inherited from China, status descends from scholars to peasants, craftsmen and merchants in that order. The Japanese tried to change this. In the 1910s, the Japanese government wrote that "the [upper class] Taiwanese despised manual labor and had nothing but contempt for honest and useful occupations which required physical skill or exertion." Teachers' responsibility was to "make the next generation of native leaders less prejudiced against agriculture, commercial, and manual occupations" (Tsurumi, 1977, 50–51).

We submit that the nurturing of a positive attitude toward manual labor and work ethics has contributed tremendously to Taiwanese industrialization, especially the growth of small and medium-size enterprises in the rural and urban areas before and after the war (Hsiao and Hsiao, 1999).

By contrast, the British did little to change social custom in India. "The Indian ryot was bound down by custom, caged within the confine of his caste, he tended to be satisfied with a bare minimum of substance, and [...] showing little interest in improving his lot. [...] they would be the most difficult to arouse to the necessity of basic reforms" (Wallbank, 1958, 33).

By 1944, 81% of the boys and 61% of the girls (71% on average) among Taiwanese school-aged children were enrolled in elementary schools (Hsiao and Hsiao, 1996, 220). A Chinese general coming to Taiwan after the war even likened the elementary school buildings to university buildings in China. Again, this is in contrast to India, where a 77% primary school enrolment ratio was achieved only in 1997 (World Bank, 1999, Table 10).

The Japanese colonial government promoted the national language vigorously in Taiwan. They established continuing education classes in Japanese in every village and enforced the Japanization movement (Kominka Undo) among the Taiwanese, including the spread and daily use of Japanese (Wu, 1992, 357–60). In 1930, about one million Taiwanese or 23% of the population, knew Japanese, and by 1942, numbers of Japanese-speaking Taiwanese had increased to 3.3 million, or 58% of the total population.

We do not have comparable figures for Indian school enrollments. However, "in 1941 only 12.5 percent of the population of British India were literate in their own language; only 2 percent were literate in English; and for all of India, only 14 percent were estimated to be literate. Most serious was the lack of schooling for girls. [...] In 1941 barely 5 percent of all women were literate" (Wallbank, 1958, 24). The difference between Taiwan and India was large. The ability to understand Japanese and English was important since these are the languages that opened the eyes of the colonial people to the Western world of modern arts and sciences.

According to the educational development indicators used by UNESCO, the earliest data available are from 1950, five years after a period of war and chaos and preparation for postcolonial transformation (UNESCO, 1963). Postwar Taiwanese economic performance has been a continuation of the prewar growth pattern, and standards of living did not recover to the prewar peak until the mid-1960s (Hsiao and Hsiao, 1998, 2002, 2003). A takeoff only occurred in the late 1960s. Similarly, India's GDP per capita did not recover to the 1940 peak level at $696 until 1958 (Maddison, 1995). The period between 1950 and the early 1960s may therefore be considered a time of recovery during which the influence of the colonial heritage was still very strong.

In 1950–51, Taiwan's literacy rate was 50% as compared to 20% in India.[5] The adjusted school enrollment ratio, adjusted for duration-of-schooling, for the age group 5–19 years was 47% as compared to India's 21% (UNESCO, 1963). This shows that India lagged considerably behind Taiwan in educational development.

Comparing India with Taiwan in 1950 with regard to ratios of teaching staff and pupils in total population, India scored much worse than Taiwan in first-level education (staff: 0.15 % versus 0.27%, enrollment: 5% versus 12%) and second-level vocational education (staff: 0.002% versus 0.03%, enrollment: 0.03% versus 0.45%). India exceeded Taiwan only slightly in general

5 Compared with Korea and Japan, this illiteracy rate (the other 50%) in Taiwan in the early 1950s was unusually much higher. It is not clear whether this is due to the fact that the new Chinese émigré regime after the war considered those Taiwanese who could speak only Japanese but not Chinese as illiterate. More study is called for.

second-level education (staff: 0.06% versus 0.05%, enrollment: 1.37% versus 1.05%) and general third-level education (staff: 0.01% versus 0.01%, enrollment: 0.11% versus. 0.09%) (UNESCO, 1963, 137–38, 163–64, 184–85, 216–17).[6] The far higher proportions of enrollment in first-level and vocational second-level schooling in Taiwan were the results of Japanese colonial policy (Hsiao and Hsiao, 1999; Tsurumi, 1977).

Table 5.1 compares the social, cultural, political and economic conditions of India and Taiwan in the late 1950s. The data are based on Adelman and Morris (1967), who studied 41 variables of "salient sociopolitical and economic features" for 74 developing countries. Columns 1 and 3 show the original ratings by Adelman and Morris. In columns 2 and 4, ratings are converted into percentiles. The method of conversion is described in Appendix 5A.

Column 5 shows the differences in ranking between India and Taiwan: a negative sign indicates that India was relatively worse off than Taiwan, while a positive sign means the reverse. It should be noted that the difference in GNP per capita was very small in the early stage of postwar development. In 1961, Taiwan's GDP per capita was only 1.8 times that of India. However, India's factor score was negative, whereas that of Taiwan was positive and large, with the 84th percentile corresponding to the twelfth rank among the 74 developing countries covered by the survey. Taiwan's lead superiority is also reflected in the last column. The percentiles of Taiwan were higher than those of India in almost every category except Political System (F2) (see Figure 5B.1 in Appendix 5B).

In Taiwan, the Japanese left behind an extensive irrigation system, effective farm organizations, a pervasive educational system, massive facilities for the generation of electricity and elaborate transportation and communication networks (Hsiao and Hsiao, 1996, 219–21). In addition, customs and habits conducive to a modern industrial society were introduced, such as an appreciation of manual labor, the propensity to innovate, habits of keeping time and being on time, concepts of law and order, respect for rule by law and formal instructions.[7] In other words, the social, cultural and psychological

---

6 Ratios calculated by dividing the original data by the midyear population of 1950 (UNESO, 1963, 33).
7 In 1959/60 the former President of Taiwan, T. H. Lee, then a member of the Joint Committee of Rural Reconstruction (JCRR), a US aid organization, remarked to a group of graduate students at the National Taiwan University (including the first author of this chapter) that Taiwanese farmers read Japanese magazines even before the JCRR experts, learning how to diversify and improve their methods of farming (Hsiao and Hsiao, 1996, 240n32; on the use of the Japanese language in rural Taiwan, see Tsurumi, 1977, 154).This is in contrast to reports that the Japanese used the police force to compel Taiwanese farmers to shift to new rice seeds (Ponlai rice) during the initial stage of

preconditions for an economic takeoff were already in place in the 1930s and early 1940s, although some of them originated from coercion by the colonial government for the sake of the mother country and military purposes. In modern terminology, Taiwan's "institutional reform" was completed long before the end of World War II. The reform facilitated the prewar rapid development of agriculture and industry. Although often not acknowledged in the literature, it was essential for the rapid economic growth after the war. This was clearly not the case in India.

There were some similarities between Taiwan and India in the control of dominant public enterprises in the early postwar period. After World War II, the Chinese émigré regime of the Nationalist (Kuomintang, KMT) government confiscated Japanese-owned firms and banks, amalgamating them into about 50 public enterprises. Non-Taiwanese-speaking Chinese bureaucrats and managers replaced non-Taiwanese-speaking Japanese capitalists. The KMT perpetuated the Japanese-controlled wartime economy and industries on a large scale due to massive American aid supporting the influx of Chinese refugees and 600,000 Chinese soldiers (Hsiao and Hsiao, 1996, 2000, 2003; Twu, 1975, 499).

Until the end of the 1970s, banks and financial institutions, insurance companies, the stock exchange, education, transportation, communication, utilities and public media were all under government control with operations highly regulated. Nowhere could Taiwanese small and medium-sized enterprises enter, not even in local transport, newspapers, shipping, aviation or gas and electricity facilities. By contrast, private electricity companies and plants had thrived under the Japanese occupation (Hsiao and Hsiao, 2002, section V).

Taiwan's postwar economic development may be divided into six stages, that is, chaos (August 1945–49); transition (1950–53); recovery and import substitution (1953–63); takeoff and export promotion (1964–73); the second import substitution (1974–80); and accelerated growth and high-tech industrialization (since 1980) (Hsiao and Hsiao, 1996). By contrast, India's postwar development may be divided into the following three stages: initial growth (1947–65), stagnant industrialization (1965–80) and growth recovery (since

---

the Green Revolution in the 1920s. This policy at any rate did alter attitudes among Taiwanese farmers. In India, however, "the village was the great fortress of conservatism. Without benefit of education, suspicious of new methods of agriculture, the Indian ryot, or peasant, dimly appreciated the fact that his standard of living was tragically low, but at the same time he was often the despair of those who tried to improve his lot" (Wallbank, 1958).Around 1969, the following remark was made by a Chinese mainland resident of Taiwan in his 50s: "Those stupid Taiwanese. All they learned under the Japanese was to line up in queues" (Tsurumi, 1977, 156).

1980) (Kojima, 1993). Compared with Taiwan, India missed the takeoff and export promotion stages as well as the second import substitution stage.

Nevertheless, numerous Taiwanese private small- and medium-sized firms survived from the Japanese period and continued to grow, thanks to Japanese foreign direct investment in Taiwan and US support of free markets and free trade as well as US influence on KMT policies through US aid (Hsiao and Hsiao, 1999). Between 1929 and 1936, the number of firms employing fewer than 30 workers and using motors rose from 5,546 to 7,503, an average rate of increase of 4.7% per year (Hsiao and Hsiao, 1999, Table 1a, 495.) The further increase was to an estimated 13,655 firms by 1954, corresponding to an annual average rate of growth of 3.3%. It needs to be noted that in 1954, there were still 27,618 firms not using power. Comparable data for the prewar period are not available (ibid. Table 1b. 503.).

Elsewhere we have pointed out that, "unlike large-scale [capital-intensive] American multinationals, by the end of 1975, 58.6% of Japanese multinationals in Taiwan were themselves SMEs [small and medium-size enterprises] in Japan [...] [They] preferred joint ventures and accepted minority ownership [...] by seeking out their Taiwanese counterparts. Thus, Taiwanese SMEs were able to maximize the benefits of imitation and learning [...] the Japanese multinational probably contributed more to the vitality of the Taiwanese SMEs" (Hsiao and Hsiao, 1996, 285).

Geographical proximity, cultural similarities and historical links with Japan undoubtedly helped the Taiwanese private enterprises prosper. American markets were opened up through Japanese Sogo Shosha (trading companies), which by the mid-1970s had become more influential than the public enterprises (Hsiao and Hsiao, 1996). Throughout the prewar and postwar periods, the Taiwanese were able to learn from the Japanese. This was very different from the Indian experience. While India, like Taiwan, maintained predominantly public enterprises, its socialist ideology, strong anticapitalism and anti–United States stances kept the country from developing viable small and medium-size enterprises to compete with public enterprises and monopolies.

5.4 A Simple Model of Learning

With respect to the rapid economic growth in Taiwan before and after World War II, we have elsewhere shown that real income per capita of Taiwan is indeed catching up with that of its one-time colonial mother country Japan and also with the United States (Hsiao and Hsiao, 2004). It is of interest to find out whether the real income per capita of India has been catching up with that of the United Kingdom in the long run. Catchup by learning can be achieved mainly through technology transfers and spillovers between two trading partners. In this section, we formulate a simple model of learning between developing and developed countries. It is "simple" since data other than real GDP per capita, for instance, capital and labor, are not available for the prewar period.

The basic assumption here is that the wider the gap of real GDP per capita between two trading partners, the faster the learning process and the stronger the effect of learning. Let y and y* be real GDP per capita of developing and developed countries, respectively. Then

$$\ln\left(\frac{y*}{y}\right) = \ln y* - \ln y \qquad (5.1)$$

is taken as an indicator of the "advantages of backwardness" (Gerschenkron, 1962), that is, a technological gap that can be exploited by developing countries such as Taiwan and Korea.

Following Nelson and Phelps (1966), and more recently Verspagen (1994), the growth rate of real GDP per capita of a developing country, denoted as $d(\ln y)/dt$, is proportional to the discrepancy between developed and developing countries' real GDP per capita (in logarithms):

$$\frac{d(\ln y)}{dt} = r(\ln y* - \ln y), \qquad (5.2)$$

or in discrete form,

$$\ln y_t - \ln y_{t-1} = r(\ln y_{t-1}^* - \ln y_{t-1}), \qquad (5.3)$$

where r is a constant nonnegative fraction measuring the degree of learning through technological transfer or imitation of industries in the developing country.[8] It ranges from zero to one, and may be called more explicitly the coefficient of learning or catching up.[9]

---

8 Technology may also be transferred through foreign direct investment and cost-free diffusion (Gomulka, 1990, 161). Our analysis here is consistent with the emphasis on the role of technological progress and human capital development in achieving productivity growth and a process of catch up as emphasized by Abramowitz in an interview (1999).

9 In this interpretation, the constancy of r is unrealistic as it implies that the least developed country is the most innovative (Gomulka, 1990, 160). However, Hsiao and Hsiao (2001b) show that Taiwan and Korea surpassed the threshold of development already during the colonial period, both possessing the ability to absorb foreign technology during the early stage of postwar development.

When r = 0, there is no learning and so no growth takes place, and when r = 1, the growth rate equals to the income discrepancy (in logarithms).

We use Maddison's data (1995) from the early 1900s to 1992 for India, Taiwan, Japan, the United Kingdom and the United States. Figure 5.4 shows values of r for the learning process of each pair of countries, Taiwan with Japan (T with J, light solid line), India with the United Kingdom (I with UK, heavy solid line), and Japan with the United States (J with US, dotted line).

In general, the coefficients fluctuate more during the transition period (1945–50) in the cases of Taiwan with Japan, and Japan with the United States, but not for India and the United Kingdom. This suggests a smooth postwar transition in the latter two countries.

In all cases, the coefficients fluctuate far more in the prewar period than after World War II. The coefficients for Taiwan with Japan in particular fluctuate more in the prewar period than afterward, which indicates a rather erratic transfer of technology from Japan to Taiwan during the colonial period. This is contrary to intuition considering that Taiwan was a colony of Japan and that the same Japanese were the prime movers of the colonial economy. Ignoring the transition before the war, Taiwan and Japan experienced the largest fluctuations in coefficients, followed by Japan and the United States, and then India and the United Kingdom.

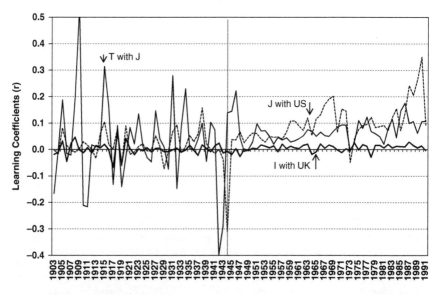

Figure 5.4 Learning Coefficients
India with the United Kingdom, Taiwan with Japan, and Japan with the United States

During the prewar period, positive learning coefficients seem to be cancelled out by negative ones, although net results appear positive (Figure 5.4). This explains the slow growth in the prewar period in Taiwan, India and Japan.

Postwar coefficients behaved quite differently. Annual coefficients are mostly positive, but here there is a clear difference among the three pairs of countries. Japan's learning coefficients with the United States are consistently the highest for the entire period as well as for the postwar period alone, especially in the late 1960s and late 1980s. Taiwan's learning coefficients with Japan are consistently higher than those of India with the United Kingdom for both the entire period and the postwar years.

Apparently, the difference in learning ability of India, Taiwan and Japan explains, at least in part, the difference in growth rates of the three countries during the whole period and the postwar period.

Using Maddison data (1995), Hsiao and Hsiao (2003) show that during the postwar period from 1951 to 1992, the average annual growth rate of real GDP per capita in Taiwan, measured in Geary–Khamis dollars, was 6.03%, higher than anywhere elsewhere among the 57 countries for which long-run data are available. Taiwan's growth rate was above that of Korea, which ranked second at 5.8%, whereas Japan ranked third at 5.57% and Thailand, fourth at 4.07%.

We estimated long-run coefficients of learning between any two countries by using a polynomial distributed lag (or Almon lag) model (Greene, 2003). When we assume that the growth rate of real GDP per capita, $\ln y_t - \ln y_{t-1}$, is a distributed lag function of the indicator of the advantages of backwardness, $\ln y^*_{t-1} - \ln y_{t-1}$, the long-run learning relationship between two countries can be written as the finite distributed lag model:

$$\left(\ln y_t - \ln y_{t-1}\right) = c + \sum_{j=0}^{k} \beta_j \left(\ln y^*_{t-1-j} - \ln y_{t-1-j}\right) + e_t, \qquad (5.4)$$

where k is the lag length, β_j's are the distributed lag weights and e_t is the error term.

We apply the technique of the polynomial distributed lag to estimate the coefficient's β_j in the model, that is,

$$\beta_j = \sum_{i=0}^{p} \gamma_i j^i, \qquad (5.5)$$

where p is the degree of polynomial and γ_i are polynomial coefficients. The sum of the β_j's in Equation (5.4) is the long-run coefficient of learning, which

Table 5.2 The Long-Run Coefficients of Learning
India with the United Kingdom, Taiwan with Japan, and Japan with the United States

	Total period			Prewar period			Postwar period		
Relation	1911-1992 Long-run			1911-1940	Long-run		1951-1992 Long-run		
	k	p	Coeff	k	p	Coeff	k	p	Coeff
India with UK	7	1	0.040	1	1	0.030	5	1	0.090
			(2.05) **			(0.33)			(1.27)
Twn with Jpn	4	1	0.101	7	1	0.176	5	1	0.046
			(2.45) **			(0.40)			(2.04) **
Jpn with USA	5	2	0.012	3	2	-0.054	7	2	0.026
			(0.51)			(-0.59)			(2.41) **

Notes: (1) The optimal lag length k is chosen at the minimum AIC from lag 1 to 8. (2) p = degree of polynomial distributed lags. (3) The t-values are in the parentheses. (4)** denotes significant at the 5% level.

represents the long-run effect of the discrepancies in the real GDP per capita between an advanced country and a less advanced country on the growth rate of real GDP per capita of the less advanced country.

Table 5.2 presents estimates of long-run coefficients of learning for the different pair of countries in three time periods: the entire period, 1911–92, the prewar period, 1911–40 and the postwar period, 1951–92 (the same periods as in Hsiao and Hsiao, 2003). The total period includes the transitional years between 1941 and 1950.[10]

The most interesting and striking results refer to Taiwan and Japan. For the entire period, the long-run coefficient of learning is 0.101, which is positive and significant at the 5% level. Historically, this means that Taiwan's GDP per capita growth has benefited from the learning with Japan. Taiwan's prewar learning coefficient is high at 0.176, but it is not significant. However, in the postwar period, the long-run learning coefficient is 0.046, which is also positive and significant at the 5% level. This implies that, on the whole, Taiwan learned considerably and continuously from Japan, especially in the postwar period. This is consistent with our observations in previous articles (Hsiao and Hsiao, 1989, 1996, 2003; Hsiao, 2001).

Since we specify measurement of Taiwan's learning from Japan, we have no information about its learning from other OECD countries. However,

---

10 In the estimation process, we apply the parsimony principle by first assuming that β_j is a decreasing linear function (p = 1) to estimate the model. If this assumption does not hold, then we re-estimate the model by assuming that β_j is a concave quadratic function (p = 2). We have estimated the model from a lag length (k) varying from 1 to 8, with the optimal lag length chosen by the minimum Akaike information criterion (AIC).

since Taiwan's foreign trade and inward foreign direct investment rely heavily on Japan and the United States, ranging from 34% to 89% over the period 1952–98, and since most Taiwanese businessmen in the early postwar period understand Japanese, it is safe to argue that Taiwan's learning from other OECD countries was marginal (Hsiao and Hsiao, 1996, 2002). In this context, we note that Japan supplied almost 66% and the United States another 21% of the 1871 cases of technology transfer registered with the Taiwanese authorities over the period 1952–83 (Hsiao and Hsiao, 1996, 274).

The results also show that, for the entire period, India learned little from the United Kingdom (a small positive coefficient, 0.04, yet significant at the 5% level). However, the coefficients are small and statistically insignificant for the prewar and postwar periods separately.

Our results also reveal that, for the entire period, the long-run learning coefficient of Japan with the United States is 0.012, but it is not significant. The prewar coefficient has the wrong sign and is insignificant, but the postwar coefficient is 0.026 and is significant at the 5% level. This reflects Japanese learning from, and catching up with, the United States after World War II, which in turn may be ascribed to the fact that GDP per capita differences between Japan and the United States are small and Japan was capable of absorbing lessons from the United States in that period.

5.5 Unit Root-Based Tests of Convergence

Bernard and Durlauf state that "countries i and j converge if the long-term forecasts of (log) per capita output for both countries are equal at a fixed time t" (1996, 165, definition 2). More specifically, "if $y_{i,t} - y_{j,t}$ contains either a nonzero mean or a unit root, then definition 2 of convergence is violated" (Bernard and Durlauf, 1996, 170, proposition 5). Using this definition, the convergence hypothesis has been tested in time series among the Nordic countries (Oxley and Greasley, 1999), between Australia, the United Kingdom and the United States (Oxley and Greasley, 1995) and also between OECD countries at large (Bernard and Durlauf, 1995).

Here, we use Maddison's data from 1950 to 1992 (without discontinuities) and the Augmented Dickey–Fuller (ADF) unit root test (Dickey and Fuller, 1979, 1981) in order to test for convergence between Taiwan, India, the United Kingdom, Japan and the United States. The general equation for the ADF test is,

$$\Delta x_t = a_0 + a_1 x_{t-1} + a_2 t + \sum_{i=1}^{k} \beta_i \Delta x_{t-i} + \varepsilon_t, \tag{5.6}$$

where x_t (level series) is $(y_{i,t} - y_{j,t})$, the annual difference of natural logarithms of real GDP per capita between the developed country and the developing country. Δx_t is the first-difference series of x_t. The variable x_{t-1} is the one-period lag of xt for the unit root test, t is the time trend and Δx_{t-i} is the ith lag of the dependent variable.

The optimal lag length k is chosen by minimum Akaike information criterion (AIC) from k = 0 to k = 6 (Enders, 1995; Maddala and Kim, 1998; Hsiao and Hsiao, 2001a). For a unit root test, the null hypothesis is H_0: $a_1 = 0$ (contains unit root), against the alternative hypothesis H_1: $a_1 < 0$ (does not contain unit root).

Table 5.3 presents the ADF unit root test results for six pairs of countries. For India with the United Kingdom, test results show that the difference series of real GDP per capita contains a unit root and that it is not a stationary series, that is, India is not converging with the United Kingdom. Although there is a small positive time trend, it is not significant at the 10% level so there is no convergence on this account either. For India and Taiwan, there is no convergence, but there is a positive and significant (at the 10% level) time trend, which implies that India's real GDP per capita has a weak tendency of divergence from that of Taiwan.

Table 5.3 ADF Unit Root Tests
Differences of (log) GDP per Capita, 1950–92

Countries	k	Test statistic	MacKinnon critical value at 10%	Convergence as equality	Coefficient of time trend (p-value)	Narrowing gap?
1 India-UK	0	-1.551	-3.190	No	0.0002 (0.778)	No(diverg)
2 Twn-Jpn	1	-0.992	-3.191	No	-0.0015 (0.015)**	Yes
3 Jpn-USA	1	-2.937**	-2.934(a)	Yes	---	
4 India-Twn	0	-1.949	-3.190	No	0.0069 (0.052)*	No(diverg)
5 Twn-UK	2	-2.639	-3.193	No	-0.0068 (0.006)***	Yes
6 Twn-USA	4	-2.449	-3.197	No	-0.0082 (0.011)**	Yes

Notes: (1) *** (**) (*) denotes significance at the 1% (5%) (10%) level. (2) The optimal lag length k is chosen by the minimum AIC from k = 0 to k = 6. (3) (a) denotes MacKinnon critical value at the 5% level. (4) – denotes that the time trend is not significant. It is excluded in the test equation.

For Taiwan with Japan, although it is not converged yet, there is a negative and significant (at the 5% level) time trend, which implies that real GDP per capita differences between Taiwan and Japan are narrowing over time, that is, Taiwan is catching up with Japan. We obtained the same results for Taiwan with the United Kingdom as well as for Taiwan with the United States. These findings demonstrate that rapid economic growth in Taiwan during the past four or five decades has made Taiwan's real GDP per capita catch up, although not yet converge, with Japan, the United Kingdom and the United States.

For Japan with the United States, test results show a rejection of H0 at the 5% level of significance, that is, the difference series of real GDP per capita does not contain a unit root and it is a stationary series. This implies that Japan's real GDP per capita has converged to that of the United States, the world leader in productivity development from the mid-nineteenth century until now. However, "the technological potential already explored in the United States that faces us in the first twenty-five years of the new century is such that some country, perhaps this country, will again have advantages over other countries in exploiting the new technology. Or it might be a united Europe. For a while, many thought it might be Japan" (Abramovitz, 1999). Our unit root test shows that Japan has indeed caught up with the United States.

5.6 A Logistic Model of Convergence

Instead of using a time-series analysis with unit root tests, we suggest a more direct approach to the problem of convergence. There is an abundant literature on convergence using cross-section data. However, we are interested in comparing two countries, a former colony and its former colonist. The most appropriate method of studying convergence in such a situation is to make use of a logistic model (Hsiao and Hsiao, 2004).

Given growth rates of real GDP per capita and coefficients of learning in the past, we look toward the future asking whether real GDP per capita of India and Taiwan could catch up with that of the United Kingdom and Japan, respectively. Many studies have been done using cross-country data involving several countries and applying linear regression analysis after linearizing the growth equation under the assumption of a Cobb-Douglas production function. Instead, we use time-series analysis for two countries only.

To compare growth paths in two countries, we only need to modify Equation (5.2) slightly, thus preserving the basic form of conventional growth analysis. We replace real GDP per capita (y) on the left-hand side of Equation (5.2) by the ratio p of real GDP per capita of developing and developed countries, $p = y/y^*$, where, empirically, $0 < p < 1$.

The right-hand side of Equation (5.2) can be written as ln (y*/y) = ln (1/p) = − ln p. In addition, we write p ≡ 1 − g, where g is a small positive fraction. Then, by Taylor's approximation, ln p = ln (1 − g) ≈ − g = p − 1, or ln (y*/y) = 1 − p. Substituting into Equation (5.2) and noting that d(ln p)/dt = d(ln y)/dt − d(ln y*)/dt reduces to the left-hand side of Equation (5.2) if y* is constant, we get, for nonconstant y*,

$$\frac{d(\ln p)}{dt} = r(1 - p).$$

(5.7)

This is a simple S-shaped logistic model with the solution

$$\ln\left[\frac{p}{(1-p)}\right] = a + bt,$$

(5.8)

where we write b for r in accordance with econometric convention (see Equation (5.10) below). Equation (5.8) may be solved for p as

$$p = \frac{1}{[1 + A exp(-bt)]},$$

(5.9)

where A = exp(−a), and a is a constant of integration. From Equation (5.8), the slope of the ratio ln[p/(1 − p)] depends on the sign of b, and the point of inflection exists at t = −a/b (Johnston, 1984).

Since the logistic curves ln[p/(1 − p)] for the five pairs of the countries show that the time-series are nonlinear, we modified Equation (5.8) into a cubic function of time as follows:

$$\ln\left[\frac{p}{(1-p)}\right] = a + bt + ct^2 + dt^3.$$

(5.10)

Solving for p, we get,

$$p = \frac{1}{[1 + A exp(-bt - ct^2 - dt^3)]}.$$

(5.11)

In (5.10), t^3 is the dominant term; hence, the convergence of p = y/y* in (5.11) depends ultimately on the sign of coefficient d regardless of the signs of coefficients b and c. If d is positive, p converges to 1 as t goes to infinity, and y converges to y* as t increases. If d is negative, p tends to zero as t goes beyond any limit, and y diverges from y*. If d = 0, Equation (5.10) becomes quadratic, and the convergence of p depends on the sign of c, regardless of the sign of b.

Before estimating the logistic model in Equation (5.10), we first employ the ADF unit root test described above to examine the stationarity of ln[p/(1 − p)] series. Since India became independent in 1947, we use sample data from 1947 to 1992 in pairs 1, 2 and 4, as shown in Table 5.4.

For pair 3, Japan with the United States, we use a slightly larger sample covering the period 1945–94. Part 1 of Table 5.4 presents test results on the level series. For India with the United Kingdom, and Japan with the United States, ln[p/(1 − p)] series have no unit root, so they are stationary series and can be used in the estimation of logistic model.

But for Taiwan with Japan and India with Taiwan, the ln[p/(1 − p)] series contains a unit root. Hence, they are not stationary. Therefore, we proceed to apply the ADF test on the first-difference series of ln[p/(1 − p)]. Results are presented in Part 2 of Table 5.4. In both cases, the first-difference series are stationary and can be used in the estimation of the logistic model.

Part 1 of Table 5.5 presents estimated logistic curves for India with the United Kingdom, and Japan with the United States using the level series of ln [p/(1 − p)]. First, we use the ordinary least squares (OLS) method to estimate Equation (5.10), but the Durbin–Watson d-test shows the existence of serial autocorrelation at the 5% level of significance. We then re-estimate Equation (5.10) by the first-order autocorrelation model (AR(1)). In the case of India with the United Kingdom, the coefficient d is very small (1.99×10^{-5}), although

Table 5.4. ADF Unit Root Test
ln [p/(1−p)]

Countries	k		Test-statistic	MacKinnon critical value
Part 1: Level Series				
1 India-UK (1947-1992)	0		-3.083 **	-2.927 b
2 Taiwan-Japan (1947-1992)	1	(t)	-1.301	-3.187 c
3 Japan-USA (1945-1994)	1	(t)	-3.253 *	-3.182 c
4 India-Taiwan (1947-1992)	1		-0.533	-2.602 c
Part 2: First-difference Series				
2 Taiwan-Japan (1947-1992)	0	(t)	-5.049 ***	-4.178 a
4 India-Taiwan (1947-1992)	0		-7.491 ***	-3.585 a

Notes: (1) The optimal lag length k is chosen at the minimum AIC from k =0 to k = 6. (t) denotes that the testing equation has significant time trend. (2) *** (** or *) denotes significant at the 1% (5% or 10%) level. (3) a (b or c) denotes critical value at the 1% (5% or 10%) level.

Table 5.5 Estimation of Logistic Model and Convergence

Part 1: Use Level Series: ln[p/(1-p)]

Countries	Sample period		const a	t b	t^2 c	t^3 d	adj R^2	DW-d
1 India-UK	1947-92	AR(1)	-2.379 *** (0)	0.013 (0.101)	-0.001 *** (0.002)	1.99E-05 *** (0)	0.829	1.906
3 Jpn-USA	1945-94	AR(1)	-1.656 *** (0)	0.074 *** (0)			0.991	1.087

Part 2: Use First-difference Series of ln[p/(1-p)]

Countries	Sample period		const α	t β	t^2 γ	Implication	adj R^2	DW-d
2 Twn-Jpn	1947-92	AR(1)	-0.090 *** (0.001)	0.004 *** (0)		c > 0 and significant	0.525	1.923
4 India-Twn	1947-92	OLS	-0.084 *** (0)	0.0008 (0.308)		c > 0, but not significant	0.024	1.914

Notes: (1) AR(1) denotes that the regression is estimated by the first-order autocorrelation method. (2) p-values are in the parentheses. (3) *** (** or *) denotes significant at the 1% (5% or 10%) level.

positive and significant. This implies that there is very slight tendency (or it will take a long time) for India to converge to the United Kingdom.

For Japan with the United States, the coefficient d is insignificant (at the 10% level) in the cubic logistic model, and the coefficient c is also insignificant in the quadratic logistic model. Therefore, a linear logistic model is estimated in this case. The coefficient b is 0.074, which is positive and significant at the 1% level. This implies that Japan's real GDP per capita converges, at a fast speed, with that of the United States.

Part 2 of Table 5.5 presents the estimated logistic curves for Taiwan with Japan, and India with Taiwan using first-difference series of ln [p/(1 − p)]. The logistic model of Equation (5.10) in the first-difference series can be written as,

$$\Delta \ln\left[\frac{p}{(1-p)}\right] = \alpha + \beta t + \gamma t^2. \tag{5.12}$$

Taking the difference and using algebra, we can prove that coefficient d in Equation (5.10) and the coefficient γ in Equation (5.12) should have the same sign, and the coefficient c in Equation (5.10) and the coefficient β in Equation (5.12) should also have the same sign. In both cases, Taiwan with Japan, and India with Taiwan, the estimated coefficients of γ are insignificant. Therefore, a linear logistic model in Equation (5.12) is estimated in both of these cases.

For Taiwan with Japan, the coefficient β is positive and significant at the 1% level. This indicates that the coefficient c is also positive, which implies that Taiwan's real GDP per capita is catching up with that of Japan. For India with Taiwan, the coefficient β is a small and positive but insignificant at the 10% level, which indicates that India's real GDP per capita is not catching up with that of Taiwan.

In general, for each pair of countries, observations from the estimation of the logistic model concur with the results of the unit root–based test of convergence.

5.7 Concluding Remarks

While there are many reasons for the different development paths taken by India and Taiwan, we can now point out some major differences. With specific reference to Taiwan's path of development, we downplayed the government's industrial policy and asserted in previous papers that Taiwan's sustained economic growth up to the early 1990s was largely due to the outward-looking attitude of the Taiwanese people and the Chinese bureaucrats in Taiwan in combination with the Taiwan–Japan–United States Pacific triangle relationship spurred by the depreciation of the US dollar (Hsiao & Hsiao, 1996, 268–69; 2000, 190–92). It is not clear whether a similar constellation of factors can also be applied to India.

Despite the fact that India's manufacturing industry developed early and continued to grow before World War II, its development appears to have been lopsided, as it was primarily serving British interests. At the same time, the British colonial government neglected agricultural development, depriving India of a postwar agricultural growth that could support population growth and further industrialization after independence.

This was in stark contrast to Taiwan where the motto of industrialization in the early postwar period was "Using agriculture to nurture industry" and where the surplus in agriculture was appropriated by the government through taxation and a barter system in order to maintain low wage rates in industry (Hsiao and Hsiao, 1996, 241–42). We also found the common assertion attributing India's slow GDP per capita growth to rapid population growth untenable.

During the early years of Japanese occupation, the emphasis in Taiwan was on rice and sugar production to satisfy demand in Japan. The manufacturing industry was almost confined to food processing. However, after the 1930s, light and heavy industries started to emerge for purposes of wartime self-sufficiency. Thus, by the end of World War II, agriculture in Taiwan had a very strong foundation. Industrial and agricultural developments were more or less balanced, at least as compared to India. The value of output in industry exceeded that of agriculture for the first time in Taiwan in 1939 and in India only in 1990. In 1990, agriculture accounted for 31% and industry for 29% of India's GDP (World Bank, 1992, 222).

The unbalanced growth between agriculture and industry, and also across branches of industry, is clearly important in explaining the postwar development of India, as indeed is done by many Indian scholars. However, by comparing colonial developments and using recent growth theory, we find more compelling reasons why India fell behind Taiwan in the postwar period. The most conspicuous differences were in health and education, that is, what we generally call human capital accumulation or institutional reform. This was neglected by the British colonial government in India but not by the Japanese authorities in Taiwan. These differences are also implied in the social, cultural and political conditions in the late 1950s to an extent reflecting the long-run effects of colonialism in the two countries.

In the second part of the chapter, we argued that major differences in the development process in Taiwan and India are due, at least in part, to differences in learning capability, which in turn reflects educational and institutional reform during the colonial period. Thus, we first set up a model of learning in accordance with the idea of "advantages of backwardness" in terms of technology, which is interpreted as a function of the difference of real GDP per capita between developing and developed countries.

Learning coefficients of India with the United Kingdom, Taiwan with Japan and, for comparison, Japan with the United States are estimated. The coefficients are high for both India and Taiwan for the entire period under study, but not so for Japan, which suggests that the colonial heritage did exert influence over a long period of time. The coefficients are also significant in the postwar period for Taiwan and Japan, indicating that Taiwan had a closer relationship with Japan, and Japan with the United States, during the postwar years.

Given past growth rates and coefficients of learning, we examined whether real GDP per capita of India could catch up with that of the United Kingdom, Taiwan with Japan, and Japan with the United States, in the future. For this purpose, we adopted two methods: conventional time-series analysis and a new logistic model. Our new logistic model of convergence is an extension of the learning model and belongs to the same family of the dynamic equation used in the current literature, adapted to the case of time-series data.

The advantage of our logistic model is that the convergence process is formulated explicitly between the per capita incomes of any pair of two countries, not as a convergence of per capita incomes to the steady-state growth path of developing countries. It does not depend on the initial condition of the country's per capita income but, more realistically, depends on the learning coefficient or similar coefficients (the coefficients of time trend).

In general, we were able to show that real GDP per capita of Taiwan converges to that of Japan, although the speed of convergence is rather slow, as Japan and the United States are also growing rapidly over time. Thus, while diminishing returns will eventually set in and the economic growth rate of the NIEs may be tapering off (cp. Krugman, 1994), the convergence of the Taiwanese economy to advanced countries like Japan and the United States may ultimately be realized. However, in the case of India, our results show that there is no sign of convergence with the United Kingdom, or it will take very long time to converge (see Chapter 9).

In this chapter, we have examined the different colonial experience of India and Taiwan and its impact on postwar economic development. There may be many explanations about the differences. However, by using long-run data, this chapter emphasizes that differences in growth performance already started during the colonial period. We suggest that more attention should be given to development policies during the colonial period and the way in which such policies are linked to the postcolonial period.

Another implication is that, through the comparison with India, it is apparent that Taiwan's oft-touted "Economic Miracle" is indeed not a miracle. It all started from the social and economic reforms during the colonial period.[11] It took almost a century of economic development for Taiwan to become the advanced country it is today (Hsiao and Hsiao, 2002, 2003).

Finally, comparison between India and Taiwan also brought out again the importance of "institutional reform" in the process of economic development. While India was one of the industrialized and export-oriented countries in the early twentieth century, especially compared with Taiwan, the lack of institutional reform during the prewar period under colonialism played a key role in India's slow economic performance after independence, at any rate until the mid-1990s.

Appendix 5A: Explanations of Table 5.1

The percentiles are based on the 74 countries studied by Adelman and Morris (1967). They include Afghanistan, Algeria, Argentina, Bolivia, Brazil, Burma,

---

11 During the Groningen conference in 2003, Thomas Lindblad questioned whether the relationship between Japan and Taiwan was similar to that between the United Kingdom and Singapore or Hong Kong). Offhand, we think that Singapore and Hong Kong are city-states with much smaller economies than Taiwan and are probably closer to the United Kingdom/India than to Japan/Taiwan in terms of human capital development. More research is called for in this area.

Cambodia, Cameroon, Ceylon, Chad, Chile, Colombia, Costa Rica, Cyprus, Dahomey, Dominican Republic, Ecuador, El Salvador, Ethiopia, Gabon, Ghana, Greece, Guatemala, Guinea, Honduras, India, Indonesia, Iran, Iraq, Israel, Ivory Coast, Jordan, Kenya, Korea (South), Laos, Lebanon, Liberia, Libya, Malagasy Republic, Malawi, Mexico, Morocco, Nepal, Rhodesia, Senegal, Sierra Leone, Somali Republic, South Africa, Syrian Arab Republic, Taiwan, Tanganyika, Thailand, Trinidad, Tunisia, Turkey, Uganda, United Arab Republic, Uruguay, Venezuela, Vietnam (South), Yemen, Zambia.

The percentiles in Table 5.1 are calculated as follows:

(1) The letter score of A+, A, A−, etc. for each country for each variable is from Adelman and Morris (1967).

(2) We assigned a numerical score linearly, for example, A+ for 1, A for 2, A− for 3, B+ for 4, …, E for 14, E− for 15.

(3) For each variable, the countries are sorted in ascending order of numerical scores. For the second key of sorting, we used "factor scores" (from Adelman and Morris, 1967, 170). Each country is then allotted a natural number, called rank, which indicates its position in the ascending sequence of the scores.

(4) The ranks of Taiwan and India are found. If several countries have the same score, say 3, 3, 3, with Taiwan, then the rank corresponding to the last repeated score, say, 22, is recorded as Taiwan's rank.

(5) Taiwan's rank is subtracted from 74, and divided by 74, multiplied by 100, to obtain the "percentile" for Taiwan, i.e., $(74 − 22) \times 100/74 = 70.27$. This means that 70% of developing countries are ranked below Taiwan's rank (22). In statistical theory, the term "percentile" is often taken to mean the percentage of countries equal to or below the current ranking number in question. The method of calculation applied here appears more logical.

Appendix 5B: Illustration of Table 5.1

Figure 5B.1 illustrates columns 2, 4 and 5 of Table 5.1. It is intended to give a bird's eye view of the general trend of the difference between India and Taiwan, without pay much attention to the title of each item, as the titles are barely visible.

The percentiles of India (column 2, the light solid line), those of Taiwan (column 4, the dotted line) and the difference in percentiles between India and Taiwan (column 5, the heavy solid line) are drawn in the chart. Note that from the difference curve, India excelled Taiwan (the heavy solid line is above the

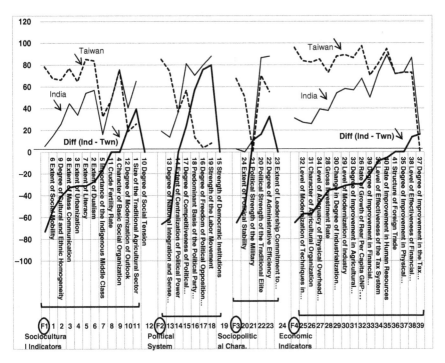

Figure 5B.1 Social and Economic Conditions of India and Taiwan
Late 1950s

zero line) in most of the political system (F2) and sociopolitical characteristics (F3), but Taiwan excelled India (the heavy solid line is below the zero line) in most of the sociocultural indicators (F1) and economic indicators (F4).

Acknowledgments

This chapter was presented at the conference on "Catch-up Growth and Technology Transfer in Asia and Western Europe" at the Groningen Growth and Development Centre, University of Groningen, The Netherlands, in October 2003. We are grateful to Professor Thomas Lindblad of the University of Linden, Professor Angus Maddison of OECD, and other participants at the Groningen conference for comments and suggestions. Earlier versions of this chapter were presented at a joint session of the 2002 Annual Convention of the Allied Social Science Associations (ASSA)/Association of Indian Economic Studies (AIES) in Atlanta, Georgia, and also at Kansai University in Osaka, the International Centre for the Study of East Asian Development (ICSEAD) in Kitakyushu, Japan. We are indebted to participants in these seminars and also to Professors Ann Carlos, Shinichi Ichimura, Teng-hui Lee, Hiro Lee, Robert McNown, Naci Mocan, Motoaki Moria, Masao Oda, Eric Ramstetter and Ron Smith for help in reference search, discussions and suggestions. As usual, all errors of omission and commission are ours.

References

Abramovitz, M. (1999). "What Economists Don't Know about Growth: Interview with Moses Abramovitz," *Challenge* 42(1): 81–101.

Acemoglu, D., S. Johnson and J. A. Robinson (2001). "The Colonial Origins of Comparative Development: An Empirical Investigation," *American Economic Review* 91(5): 1369–1401.

Adelman, I., and C. T. Morris (1967) *Society, Politics, and Economic Development: A Quantitative Approach*. Baltimore: Johns Hopkins University Press.

Bernard, A. B. and S. N. Durlauf (1995). "Convergence in International Output," *Journal of Applied Econometrics* 10: 97–108.

——— (1996). "Interpreting Tests of the Convergence Hypothesis," *Journal of Econometrics* 71: 161–73.

Chakravarti, S. C., K. B. Kundu and M. M. Pattra (1965). *Economic Development of India*. Calcutta: Nababharat.

Chang, Z. H. (1980). *Industrialization of Prewar Taiwan* [in Chinese]. Taipei: Lian-jin Publishing.

Dickey, D. A., and W. A. Fuller (1979). "Distribution of the Estimators for Autoregressive Time Series with a Unit Root," *Journal of the American Statistical Association* 74(366): 427–31.

——— (1981). "Likelihood Ratio Statistics for Autoregressive Time Series with a Unit Root," *Econometrica* 49(4): 1057–72.

Dreze, J., and A. Sen, (1995). *India: Economic Development and Social Opportunity*. Delhi: Oxford University Press.

Enders, W. (1995). *Applied Econometric Time Series*. New York: Wiley.

Feenstra, R. C. (2004). *Advanced International Trade: Theory and Evidence*. Princeton, NJ: Princeton University Press.

Gerschenkron, A. (1962). *Economic Backwardness in Historical Perspective*. Cambridge, MA: Harvard University Press.

Greene, W. H. (2003). *Econometric Analysis*. Upper Saddle River, NJ: Prentice-Hall.

Gomulka, S. (1990). *The Theory of Technical Change and Economic Growth*. London: Routledge.

Higgins, B. (1968). *Economic Development, Principle, Problems, and Policies*, rev. ed. New York: Norton.

Ho, S. P. S. (1978). *Economic Development of Taiwan, 1960–1970*. New Haven, CT: Yale University Press.

Hsiao, F. S. T. (1997). "Colonialism or Comparative Advantage? On Agricultural Development in Colonial Taiwan," Proceedings of the National Science Council, Part C: Humanities and Social Sciences (Taiwan) 7(4): 497–513.

Hsiao, F. S. T., and M. C. W. Hsiao (1989). "Japanese Experience of Industrialization and Economic Performance of Korea and Taiwan: Tests of Similarity." In Sheng-Cheng

Hu and C. F. Lee, eds. *Advances in Financial Planning and Forecasting, Supplement 1: Taiwan's Foreign Investment, Exports, and Financial Analysis*, 157–90. Greenwich, CT: JAI Press.

—— (1996). "Taiwanese Economic Development and Foreign Trade." In W. C. Kirby and J. M. Greene, eds. *Harvard Studies on Taiwan: Papers of the Taiwan Studies Workshop*, vol. 1, 199–270. Cambridge, MA: John King Fairbank Center for East Asian Research, Harvard University. Also in John Y. T. Kuark, ed., *Comparative Asian Economies: Contemporary Studies in Economic and Financial Analysis*, 211–302. Greenwich, CT: JAI Press.

—— (1998). "Colonial Linkages in Early Postwar Taiwanese Economic Development." Vol. 1, in W. C. Kirby and M. S. Weiss, eds. *Harvard Studies on Taiwan: Papers of the Taiwan Studies Workshop*, vol. 2, 91–117. Cambridge, MA: John King Fairbank Center for East Asian Research, Harvard University.

—— (1999). "The Historical Traditions of Taiwanese Small- and Medium-Size Enterprises." In F. S. Huang and K. I. Ang, eds. *Taiwan's Commercial Traditions: Collected Papers*. Taipei: Academia Sinica, 464–524.

—— (2000). "Economic Liberalization and Development: The Case of Lifting Martial Law in Taiwan." In Fu-san Huang and Ka-im Ang, eds. *The Transformation of an Authoritarian Regime: Taiwan in the Post-Martial Law Era*. Taipei: Academia Sinica, 353–79. Also in University of Colorado Boulder, Department of Economics, Discussion Paper 99-29.

—— (2001a). "Capital Flows and Exchange Rates: Recent Korean and Taiwanese Experiences and Challenges," *Journal of Asian Economics* 12(3): 353–81.

—— (2001b). "Diminishing Returns and Asian NIEs: How They Overcome The Iron Law." In Sheng-Cheng Hu, ed. *Conference Proceedings on Economic Development in Memory of Professor Mo-huang Hsing*, 239–86. Taipei: Institute of Economics, Academia Sinica.

—— (2002). "Taiwan in the Global Economy: Past, Present, and Future." In P. C. Y. Chow, ed. *Taiwan in the Global Economy: From an Agrarian Economy to an Exporter of High-Tech Products*. Westport, CT: Praeger, 161–221.

—— (2003). "'Miracle Growth' in the Twentieth Century: International Comparisons of East Asian Development," *World Development* 31(2): 227–57.

—— (2004). "Catching Up and Convergence: Long-Run Growth in East Asia," *Review of Development Economics* 8(2): 223–36.

Hsiao, M. C. W. (2001). "Pacific Trade Triangle and the Growth of Korea and Taiwan: Cointegration and Causality Analysis," Working Paper, University of Colorado Denver.

Ito, M. (1973). "On India's Industrialization during the 1930s." In H. Yamada, ed. *Some Problems on Colonial Economic History* [in Japanese]. Tokyo: Institute of Asian Economies.

Johnston, J. (1984). *Econometric Methods*, 3rd ed. New York: McGraw-Hill.

Joshi, P. C. (1985). "Agriculture." In J. N. Mongia, ed. *India's Economic Development Strategies, 1951–2000 A.D.* Dordrecht: D. Reidel, chapter 2.

Kojima, M. (1993). *An Analysis of the Modern Indian Economy: The Trace and Problems of Large Country Economic Development* [in Japanese]. Tokyo: Keiso Shobo.

Kravis, I. B., A. Heston and R. Summers (1982). *World Product and Income: International Comparisons of Real Gross Product*. Baltimore: Johns Hopkins University Press.

Krugman, P. (1994). "The Myth of Asia's Miracle," *Foreign Affairs* 73(6): 62–78.

Kusui, R. (1944). *A Study of the Wartime Taiwanese Economy* [in Japanese]. Taihoku, Taiwan: Nampo Jimbun Kenkyu Sho.

Lal, D. (1999). *Unfinished Business: India in the World Economy.* New Delhi: Oxford University Press.

Lee, T. H. (1975) "Growth Rate of Taiwan Agriculture 1911 - 1992." In T. H. Lee (1983). *Agriculture and Economic Development in Taiwan*, vol. 2. 1364–1445. Taichung, Taiwan: Ta-Kung Printing Co.

Lee, T. H., and K. S. Liang (1974). "Process and Pattern of Economic Development in Taiwan." In S. Ichimura, ed. *Economic Development of East and Southeast Asia.* (Honolulu: University Press of Hawaii). Also in T. H. Lee (1983). *Agriculture and Economic Development in Taiwan*, vol. 2, 1–67. Taichung, Taiwan: Ta-Kung Printing.

Maddala, G. S., and I. M. Kim (1998). *Unit Roots, Cointegration, and Structural Change.* Cambridge: Cambridge University Press.

Maddison, A. (1995). *Monitoring the World Economy, 1820–1992.* Paris: OECD.

Mizoguchi, T., and M. Umemura, eds. (1988). *Economic Statistics of Prewar Japanese Colonies: Estimation and Analysis* [in Japanese]. Tokyo: Toyo Keizai Shimpo Sha.

Morris, M. D. (1983). "The Growth of Large Scale Industry to 1947." In D. Kumar, ed. *The Cambridge Economic History of India*, vol. 2: c. 1757–c. 1970. London: Cambridge University Press, chapter 7.

Nelson, R. R., and E. S. Phelps (1966). "Investment in Humans, Technological Diffusion and Economic Growth," *American Economic Review* 56(1/2): 66–75.

Oxley, L., and D. Greasley (1995). "A Time-Series Perspective on Convergence: Australia, UK and USA since 1870," *Economic Record* 71(214): 259–70.

——— (1999). "A Nordic Convergence Club?" *Applied Economics Letters* 6: 157–60.

Perkins, D. H., and M. Syrquin (1989). "Large Countries: The Influence of Size." In H. Chenery and T. N. Srinivasan, eds. *Handbook of Development Economics*, vol. 2, 1691–1753. Amsterdam: North-Holland.

Rothermund, D. (1993). *An Economic History of India from Precolonial Times to 1991*, 2nd ed. London: Routledge.

Shinohara, M. (1971). "Industrialization and Trade." In M. Shinohara and S. Ishikawa, eds. *Economic Growth of Taiwan: Quantitative Studies on its Economy* [in Japanese]. Tokyo, Japan: Institute of Asian Economies, chapter 2.

Tsurumi, P. E. (1977). *Japanese Colonial Education in Taiwan, 1895–1945.* Cambridge, MA: Harvard University Press.

Twu, J. Y. (1975). *Taiwan under Japanese Imperialism* [in Japanese]. Tokyo: Tokyo University Press.

Underwood, L. (1999). "The Park That Chips Built," *TOPICS, The Magazine of International Business in Taiwan* (published by the American Chamber of Commerce in Taipei) 29(3): 17–30.

UNESCO (1963). *Statistical Yearbook 1963.* Paris: UNESCO.

Verspagen, B. (1994). "Technology and Growth: The Complex Dynamics of Convergence and Divergence." In G. Silverberg and L. Soete, eds. *The Economics of Growth and Technical Change: Technologies, Nations, Agents.* Brookfield, VT: Elgar, 154–84.

Wallbank, T. W. (1958). *A Short History of India and Pakistan, from Ancient Times to the Present.* New York: New American Library.

World Bank (1992, 1997). *World Development Report.* New York: Oxford University Press.

——— (1999). *Human Development Report.* New York: Oxford University Press.

Wu, W. S. (1992). *A Study of Leadership Class of Taiwanese Society during the Japanese Occupation Period*. Taipei: Cheng Chung Book Co.

——— (1999). "Transformation of Taiwanese society under Japanese Colonialism and Its Historical Implications" [in Chinese]. In *Proceedings of the Fourth Conference of East Asian History Education*. Tokyo: Society for the Comparative Study of History and History Education, chapter 8.

Part II

CATCHING UP AND CONVERGENCE IN EAST ASIAN ECONOMIC GROWTH

Chapter 6

MIRACLE OR MYTH OF ASIAN NICS' GROWTH: THE IRONY OF NUMBERS

Abstract

Krugman (1994) has argued that the East Asian NICs' economic growth has been input-driven, that is, not attributable to technical progress or "efficient growth"; therefore, their growth presents no economic miracle. His argument is based on total factor productivity (TFP) studies of other economists. This chapter carefully compares their results with other similar calculations of TFP growth rates. Section 6.2 recaptures the essence of the so-called Asian miracle in terms of real GDP growth rates. Section 6.3 explains TFP. We then compare TFP growth rates and TFP contributions of Asian NICs and some OECD countries in Section 6.4. Comparisons with similar estimates of other developing countries are given in Section 6.5. Section 6.6 presents some concluding remarks. We find that under the current state of the art, it is not convincing to make any prediction on the future of Asian NICs and Asian development based on a few statistical results.

6.1 Introduction

In 1979, an OECD report (1979) defined ten newly industrializing countries (NICs). In addition to the four "Asian NICs," namely, South Korea, Taiwan, Hong Kong and Singapore, the group also included Mexico, Brazil, Greece, Portugal, Spain and the former Yugoslavia. The NICs "are characterized by a fast growth of the level and share of industrial employment, and enlargement of export market shares in manufactures." In addition, a rapid growth of real per capita GDP since the 1960s has also been pointed out (6 and 19). By the end of the 1980s, it turns out that only the four Asian NICs remained as NICs. The rapid growth rates of other NICs were not sustained (WDR, 1989). Thus, economic growth of the Asian NICs has been regarded as an economic "miracle." Furthermore, in the place of other non–East Asian newly industrializing countries, the four ASEAN countries (referred here as ASEAN-4), Malaysia, Thailand, Indonesia and the Philippines, started growing so rapidly after the 1970s that they are now considered as quasi-NICs. The performance of China after the 1978 reform, especially since the mid-1980s, along with Vietnam and India in recent years, has also been very respectable. Thus, it is said that the Pacific Century has already begun, led by Japan and the United States in the region (Kim and Young, 1987; Park and Park, 1989).

In recent years, however, Krugman (1994) has presented a contrarian view. His argument may be summarized syllogistically: One, the East Asian NICs' economic growth has been input-driven, that is, not attributable to technical progress or "efficient growth"; therefore, it presents no economic miracle; Two, such growth "is inevitably subject to diminishing returns," similar to what the former Soviet economy experienced, which eventually collapsed; Three, therefore; there may not be an Asian-centered world economy and geopolitics.

This chapter examines Krugman's first argument, which is based on total factor productivity (TFP) studies of other economists. This chapter carefully compares their results with other similar calculations of TFP growth rates. Section 6.2 recaptures the essence of the so-called Asian miracle in terms of real GDP growth rates. Section 6.3 explains total factor productivity (TFP). We then compare TFP growth rates and the TFP contribution of the Asian NICs (hereafter, also called simply "NICs") and some OECD countries in Section 6.4. Comparison with similar estimates of other developing countries are given in Section 6.5. Section 6.6 presents some concluding remarks. The sources of data used in the figures are noted in the text.

6.2 The Nature of the "Miracle"

To understand the nature of the miracle, Figure 6.1 presents briefly the background of the Asian dynamism.[1] The columns show the average annual growth rates (in percent) of real GDP of four Asian NICs and individual Asian NICs, and of four ASEAN-4 and individual ASEAN-4, as well as that of China, Japan, the United States, the European Union (EU) and the World (average). The patterned columns show the long-run growth rates for 1981

---

1 The data in the diagram is taken from Table 5 of Sakura, 1995. The original data are based on World Bank, *World Tables 1994*; Asia Development Bank, *Key Indicators of Developing Asian and Pacific Countries* (1994); IMF, *IFS Yearbook* (1994); China Statistics Publisher, *Chinese Statistical Yearbook* (in Chinese), 1994; Bank of Japan, *Foreign Economic Statistical Yearbook* (in Japanese), 1993.

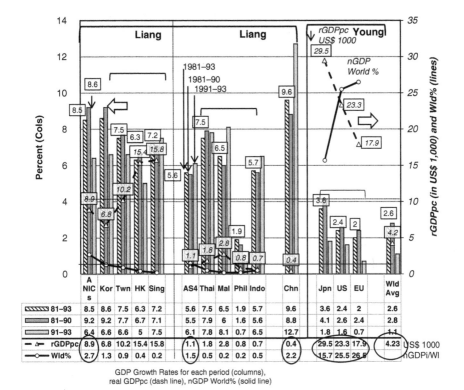

GDP Growth Rates for each period (columns),
real GDPpc (dash line), nGDP World% (solid line)

Figure 6.1 The Asian Miracle
GDP Growth Rates, rGDPpc and nGDP World Percentage. 1981–93, 1981–90 and 1991–93.
Annual. In Percent and US$ 1,000

to 1993; the adjacent darker columns show the short-run growth rates of the subperiod 1981–90; and the next lighter columns show those of the subperiod 1991–93. We also use a horizontal heavy dotted line as a benchmark to indicate the average world real GDP growth rate (2.6% per year) for 1981–93.

The figure shows clearly that the growth rates of the Asian NICs, the ASEAN-4 and China were much higher than the average growth rate of the world. During the 13-year period from 1981 to 1993, the average Asian NICs (at 8.5%) and China (9.6%) grew more than three times faster than the world average.

Among the NICs, Korea's growth is the highest (8.6%), followed by Taiwan (7.5%), Singapore (7.2%) and Hong Kong (6.3%). In another calculation (Young, 1995), which we refer to later in Figure 6.2, the 25-year-period (1966–90) growth rates of Korea, Taiwan, Hong Kong and Singapore are a whopping 10.3%, 9.4%, 7.3% and 8.7%, respectively (see the height of the column). The sustained high rates of economic growth for such a long period by so many countries are unprecedented in recent history. Thus, it is indeed[2] a "miracle."

Following the footsteps of the Asian NICs, the average growth rate of the ASEAN-4 countries during the whole period (1981–93) is 5.6%, slightly twice higher than the world average, although not as spectacular as the Asian NICs or China. These may be compared with Japan (3.6%), the United States (2.4%) and the EU (2.0%). The high growth rates of the Asian NICs, the ASEAN-4 and China, along with Japan, gave rise to Asian economic and social dynamism of the previous two decades, especially in contrast with other developing regions[3] during the 1980s: Latin America (1.3%), sub-Saharan Africa (1.9%), the Middle East (3.6%) and Eastern Europe (0.9%).

Naturally, the rate of growth of GDP depends on the size of GDP. Generally speaking, the smaller the relative size of GDP, the higher the rate of growth of GDP. This general trend is also revealed in Figure 6.1. The line with circle markers in Figure 6.1 indicates the relative size (in percent) of nominal GDP of each country or region in the world nominal GDP, which is estimated at US$23 trillion. The percentage rate of GDP growth for each country and region is shown as columns, and can be read from the left-hand-side Y-axis. As shown in the last row of the attached table below the chart (circled), the Asian NICs, the ASEAN-4 and China have only 2.7% ($0.6 trillion), 1.5% ($0.3 trillion) and 2.2% (0.5 trillion), respectively, of world GDP, while the OECD countries, that is, Japan, the United States and the EU have a huge 15.7% ($3.7 trillion), 25.5% ($6 trillion), 26.5% ($6.2 trillion), respectively, of world GDP. This explains, at least partially, the high GDP growth rates of the Asian countries and the low rates of the developed countries.

Due to the high growth rate of GDP and the low net growth rate of population, per capita GDP of Asian NICs also increased steadily during the last 25 years. The dotted line with triangular markers (also see the table below the figure) in Figure 6.1 shows real GDP per capita in 1992 US dollars, measured from the right (secondary) Y-axis: Korea had $6,700; Taiwan $10,200; Hong Kong $15,380; and Singapore $15,750. Those figures are 1.6 to 3.7 times higher than the world average of $4,230 (see the last circle on the right). The remarkable feat is that the per capita GDP of these countries converges[4] to that of developed countries. In fact, those of Hong Kong and Singapore are only about $2,000

---

2 Some economists give the reason for a miracle as "combining rapid, sustained growth with highly equal income distribution" among the Asian NICs and the ASEAN countries, excluding the Philippines. See Page, 1994, 222.

3 The figures are for 1980–90. Incidentally, the figures during the same period are 8.3% for the Asian NICs, 5.8% for the ASEAN-4 and 5.5% for South Asia (Bangladesh, Bhutan, India, Nepal, Pakistan and Sri Lanka). For details, see Stallings, 1995, 24–25.

4 The convergence of a subset of developing countries is discussed in Sachs and Warner, 1995.

lower than the average per capita GDP ($17,886) of the EU countries. They are, however, still far behind Japan ($29,460) and the United States ($23,344).

As newly industrializing countries, the average per capita GDP of the ASEAN-4 countries is only $1,061, well below any of the Asian NICs, and still only a quarter of the world average. Malaysia has the highest per capita GDP at $2,790, followed by Thailand ($1,840), the Philippines ($770) and Indonesia ($670). China has the lowest, at $426. Thus, if the achievement of the Asian NICs can serve as an indication, the ASEAN and other Asian countries have much more room to grow in the future.

6.3 On Total Factor Productivity

If real GDP, denoted as Q, is given as a function of labor (N), physical capital (K), human capital (H) and time (t) explicitly, then we may write an aggregate production function as

$$Q = F(N, K, H, t). \tag{6.1}$$

According to the growth accounting procedure (Barro and Sala-i-Martin, 1995, 346–52), the GDP growth rate may be written in terms of a growth equation:

$$\hat{Q} = s_N \hat{N} + s_K \hat{K} + s_H \hat{H} + \tau \tag{6.2}$$

where $\hat{X} \equiv X'/X$, and $X' = dX/dt$, the growth rate of variable X, and $s_x \equiv F_x X/Q$ is the (input) X elasticity of output. Here, τ is called the *total factor productivity (TFP) growth rate*, or the *(disembodied) rate of technological progress*. In a special case when H is a constant and the production function is measured in terms of efficient labor BN, with labor efficient factor B = B(t), and efficient capital CK, with capital efficient factor C = C(t), then the production function (6.1) becomes

$$Q = F(BN, CK). \tag{6.3}$$

In this case, τ in (6.2) can be expressed as[5]

$$\tau = s_N \hat{B} + s_K \hat{C}.$$

---

5 Note that it can be shown that $(\partial F/\partial(BN))(BN/Q) = sN$.

In particular, when B = C = A, under neoclassical assumptions,[6] the production function becomes

$$Q = AF(N, K), \tag{6.4}$$

and so

$$\tau \equiv A'/A.$$

A is called *total factor productivity* (TFP), or the *level of technology*. The other terms on the right-hand side of (6.2) are contributions of the factors of production toward the GDP growth rate. Under neoclassical assumptions (of constant returns to scale), s_x is the factor share of X, and all factor shares sum to one.

Since the data are given in discrete instead of continuous time, a translog production function is usually adopted. By assuming a translog production function with two factors of production, labor and capital, taking into account quality changes in labor and capital as weighted average of the growth rates of their subinputs, Kim and Lau (1994) estimate the TFP growth rate of the production function of form (6.3), and Young (1995) estimates that of form (6.4). Both estimates derive the TFP growth rate as a residual,

$$\tau = \hat{Q} - s_N \hat{N} - \left(1 - s_N\right)\hat{K} \tag{6.5}$$

Both estimations obtain similar results. For simplicity, we only discuss the latter.

Under the assumption of profit maximization, changes in the TFP represent shifts in the productivity curve (the production function) for given inputs. However, since the TFP growth rate is defined as a residual, shifts in the productivity curve may occur due to change in the quality of labor and capital, the scale of economy, imperfection of factor and product markets, restriction in factor movements and so on (Kawai, 1995, 47). Although recent studies of TFP try to incorporate quality changes in labor and capital, difficulties in statistical measurements still remain, and there is hardly a consensus on the best measurement.

Young first estimates the labor share and the weighted factor growth rates in (6.5), and then subtracts it from the GDP growth rate, which is calculated separately from national income account. He finds that "the rise in participation

---

6 That is, positive marginal productivity of factor X, $F_X > 0$, the law of diminishing return, $F_{XX} < 0$, the constant return to scale, and perfect competition in factor markets.

rates, investment to GDP ratios, and educational standards and the intersectoral transfer of labor from agriculture to other sectors" can explain most of the growth of the Asian NICs (ibid., 645 and 675), leaving little room for technological contribution. Young then concludes that

> while, with the exception of Singapore, productivity growth in the NICs is not particularly low, it is also, by postwar standards, not extraordinarily high. (ibid., 671)

This latter finding is rather surprising, as the Asian NICs' "virtually unprecedented" growth of output and manufacturing exports might suggest the contrary.

Based on the results of Young and similar results of Kim and Lau (1994), Krugman (1994) then presented his syllogism by focusing on the "small" rate of technical progress to the GDP growth rate. How small is it? Is it really small?

6.4 On Percentage Contribution of TFP

To focus on Krugman's argument, we slightly reorganize Young's results in terms of the TFP contribution. The percentage contribution of the TFP growth rate toward the GDP growth rate is simply the proportion of the TFP growth rate in the GDP growth rate when the latter is taken as 100 for each country. We will call them the *TFP contribution* (to the growth rate of a country). The remaining part of the GDP growth rate will then be *input (labor, capital, etc.) contribution*. For convenience we denote the TFP contribution as TFPC and the input contribution as IPC. Since the growth rates differ from country to country, as we have seen in Figure 6.1, and sometimes fluctuate widely, the TFPC seems to be a better measure of the role of technology in economic development within a country than the straight TFP growth rates. It should be noted, however, for predicting the growth of an economy and convergence, the TFP growth rate, not TFPC, is what counts.[7] Thus, we present both numbers in this chapter.

Figure 6.2 shows the decomposition of the growth rate of GDP of NICs (Young, 1995) and those of some OECD countries (Jorgenson, 1995, 243). The TFP growth rate is shown by a lower black bar, and the input growth rate in each period is shown by a lighter black column above the black column. The GDP growth rate is the sum of the TFP growth rate (the lower black portion of the

---

7 If Taiwan's GDP growth rate is 10% and the TFP growth rate is 3%, then Taiwan's TFPC will be 30%. However, if US growth rates are 1% and 0.6%, respectively, then US TFPC will be 60%. Thus, a comparison of TFPC alone is misleading.

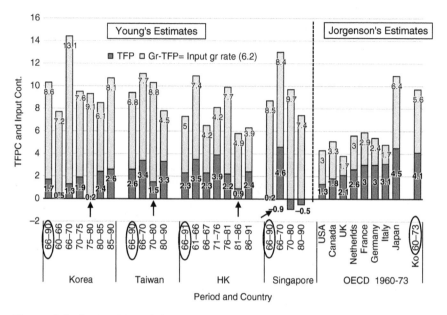

Figure 6.2 Composition of GDP Growth Rate
Various Periods and Countries. In Percent

column) plus the input growth rate (the lighter upper portion of the column), and is the height of the column. Young also estimates both growth rates of NICs for equally based subperiods. For example, there are six equally spaced five-year subperiods for Hong Kong, starting from 1966. They are presented on the right of the total period growth rate (see the circled years).

Clearly, the growth rates differ from country to country and period to period. Thus, exact comparison is impossible. However, generally speaking, Figure 6.2 shows that NICs' TFP growth rates (the lower black columns), with the exception of Singapore, are roughly comparable, if not higher, with those of the OECD countries..

However, if we compare the proportion of input growth rates, they seem much larger in four NICs than those of some of the OECD countries. The construction of Figure 6.3 is the same as that of Figure 6.2, except that it shows only the TFPCs. On the left-hand side of Figure 6.3, we calculate Young's TFPC of the Asian NICs, and present them as the filled columns for the period shown on the X-axis. They are the following:[8] Korea 16.5%, Taiwan 27.7%, Hong Kong 32.1%, Singapore 2.3% (the circled columns). The other filled columns

---

8 The percentages are calculated from Tables VII, VIII, V and VI in Young (1995).

on the right-hand side of each country column show the TFP contribution in subperiods.

The right-hand side of the heavy dotted columns in Figure 6.3 shows the estimates by Jorgenson and his associates[9] of the economy-wide TFPC for some OECD countries and Korea: the United States (30.2%), Japan (41.3%), the United Kingdom (55.3%), France (50.8%), Germany (55.6%), Canada (35.3%), Italy (64.6%), the Netherlands (46.4%), Korea (42.3%). Clearly, the TFPCs of the Asian NICs are generally lower than these OECD countries. In fact, the average TFPC of the four Asian NICs is 19.6%, as compared with 47.4% of these OECD countries (shown by the slanted line with circle markers in Figure 6.3). If the data is restricted only to manufacturing TFPC of the three NICs (not shown), the average manufacturing TFPC is even lower, at only 6.3% of the GDP growth rate, as shown by the black circle in the diagram. This probably has prompted Krugman's assertion[10] that East Asian economic growth has been input driven, is not attributable to technological progress and consequently presents no economic miracle. This is the same as saying that if a student spends all the time just studying (input driven), of course he/she will earn[11] straight A's.

Even using Young's, or similar, statistical data and results, Krugman's assertion is not convincing.

1. In Figure 6.2, the TFP growth rate of Korea (1.7%) is higher than that of the United States (1.3%) and very close to that of Canada (1.8%). The TFP growth rate of Taiwan (2.6%) is higher than that of the United States, Canada and the United Kingdom (2.1%), and is the same as the Netherlands (2.6%). Only the TFP growth rate of Japan (4.5%) is significantly different from that of Taiwan. Similarly, Hong Kong's TFP growth rate (2.3%) is also respectable. It is higher than the United States and Canada, and is the same as the United Kingdom. Thus, as observed by Young himself, it is difficult to say that the TFP growth rates of Asian NICs are especially low and that their growth is merely input driven.

2. In Figure 6.3, while it is true that NICs' TFPCs are evidently generally lower than those of the advanced countries, the long-run TFPCs of Hong

---

9 Young also makes some comparisons of the TFP growth rates of other developing and developed countries. However, since he does not list the GDP growth rates in these tables, we cannot calculate the TFP contributions.

10 Note that TFPCs, rather than TFP growth rates, seem more suited for Krugman's assertion.

11 However, every teacher probably knows that this may not always be true. The student's "TFP" will be manifested in learning skill, extracurricular activities, volunteer work or gained employment.

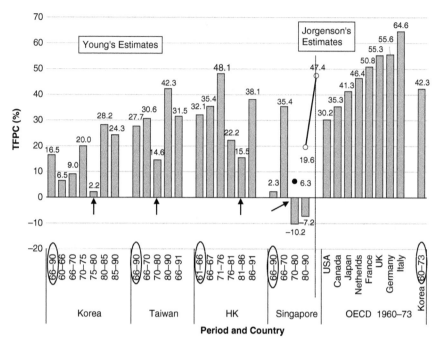

Figure 6.3 Total Factor Productivity Contribution (TFPC)
Various Periods and Countries. In Percent

Kong (31.5%) and Taiwan (27.7%) are very close to that of the United States (30.2%) as estimated by Jorgenson and his associates from 1960 to 1973. Furthermore, the average TFPC for Asian NICs is low because of the negative performance of Singapore. Without Singapore, the average TFAC increases from 19.6% to 25%. Thus, it is not clear how low the TFPCs should be to assert there is no future for the Asian NICs.

3. In Section 6.2, we have shown that the rate of growth of GDP depends on the size of GDP. On the one hand, the high level of GDP and per capita GDP of developed countries, as shown in Figure 6.1, may be an indication that the economic mobilization of inputs has reached a saturation point, and that the major source of (low) GDP growth will come from the TFPC. On the other hand, the low level of GDP and per capita GDP in developing countries may be an indication that there still is a margin for input mobilization to achieve rapid growth. If this is the case, it is nothing unusual that the growth of developing countries is input driven, and that the TFPC is small.

In fact, large TFPC is a luxury most of the developing countries cannot afford. Thus, the only fair way to compare the TFPC of Asian countries today is to calculate the TFPC of the developed countries when the latter were at the same stage of development as the Asian countries are today. If our conjecture is true, then if the East Asian economies are input driven, so were the former Soviet economy *and* the earlier economies of developed countries. Thus, it is too hasty to put down the future economy of Asian NICs by comparing their growth rates of TFP and the TFPCs only with those of the former Soviet Union. The growth of Asian NICs and their environments are much closer to those of the earlier economies of developed countries than to that of the former Soviet economy.[12]

4. It is more revealing if the long-run period is divided into several short-run subperiods, as done by Young. For all Asian NICs, the second part of the 1970s, that is, 1975–80 for Korea, 1970–80 for Taiwan, 1981–86 for Hong Kong (may be due to extended crisis) and 1970–80 for Singapore, as noted in Figures 6.2 and 6.3 by upward arrows, had the lowest economy-wide (as well as manufacturing[13]) TFPCs, probably due to world-wide oil crises during that period.[14] However, if we ignore these periods, with the exception of Singapore, Figures 6.2 and 6.3 show that there is a general tendency that the economy-wide (as well as manufacturing) growth rates of TFP and also the TFPCs increase with time. Even using Young's own statistics, we can discern a general increase in TFP growth rates, although erratic, over the long-run period in the case of Korea and Taiwan (Figure 6.2). If this trend continued, there would be continued growth in these two countries.

5. Jorgenson and his associates also estimated the TFP growth rate for Korea at 4.1% from 1960 to 1973, much higher than the estimate by Young (1.7%), and higher than any other developed countries in Figure 6.2 except Japan (4.5%). The TFPC is 42.3%, as shown by the last bar in Figure 6.3. It is slightly higher than that of Japan (41.3%) and much higher than that of the United States and Canada, but lower than the Netherlands (46.4%). In terms of Young's estimation, the time period of

---

12 One suggestion is to compare the TFP growth rates and the TFPC of the take-off period of the advanced economies with those of post–World War II NICs.

13 Manufacturing TFPCs are not shown in the figures.

14 In Taiwan, the impact of the first oil crisis appeared in 1974. The real GDP growth rate plunged to mere 1.2% per year in 1974 compared with 19% in the previous year, and the current balance of trade registered deficits of US$ 1.3 billion, the largest after the war. The recovery from the oil crisis was rather erratic during the rest of the 1970s. The second oil crisis started in 1979, the real GDP growth rate dipped to mere 1.0% in 1981 and to −1.8% in 1982. However, the Taiwanese economy, and probably other Asian NICs, recovered quickly, and attained a real GDP growth rate of 25.3% in 1986 and a whopping 39.7% in 1987. See Hsiao and Hsiao, 1995, 226–28.

Jorgenson et al. corresponds more or less to Young's first three periods, 1960–66, 1966–70 and 1970–75. The simple average of TFP for the first two periods is 7.8%, and that of the three periods is 11.8%, far below the estimation of Jorgenson et al. Since the result of estimation depends on the time period, and also the estimation methods and data used, it is difficult to compare the statistical results of different authors. However, if we can assume that Jorgenson and his associates use their method and data consistently with Korea and other developed countries—and we have no reason to believe they did not—their result on Korea is much more optimistic than Young's result.

6.5 Other Estimates of TFP Growth Rates and Contribution

We have seen above that, as in any statistical work, different authors have different estimates of TFP contribution, and we have discussed the problems of comparing TFP growth rates and the TFPCs between the Asian NICs and some advanced countries. This section introduces some more estimates that compare TFP growth rates and the TFPCs of other developing countries. We also compare the growth accounting composition of the GDP growth rate of Taiwan in detail.

Figure 6.4 shows three different recent estimations of TFP growth rates along with the GDP growth rates. The structure of the diagram is the same as that of Figure 6.2. The first column (K) for each country is recent growth-rate estimates by Kawai (1995) [15] of the Institute of Developing Economies, which, in addition to the Asian NICs, includes the ASEAN-4 and China. The second column (W) for each country is the estimates by the World Bank (1993; Page, 1995), which include the growth rate of the Asian NICs and the ASEAN-4, except the Philippines. The third column (Y) for each country repeats Young's estimates, which are the same as those in Figure 6.2 and are included here for comparison. In all cases, the TFP growth rates are, as in Figure 6.2, denoted by filled black columns, and the input growth rates are shown as the lighter black columns. The sum of both rates are GDP growth rates, and are shown by the height of the column and also shown along the horizontal axis.

Among the three estimates for the Asian NICs, Young's estimate of TFP growth rate (black column) is the lowest, and in the case of Singapore, his estimate is less than one-fifth of the other two estimates. However, his estimate of

---

15 Kawai's numbers in Figure 6.4 are also in EPA, 1995, 193, and Taniuchi, 1995, 11. Young's results here have been updated in accordance with his paper, Young (1995).

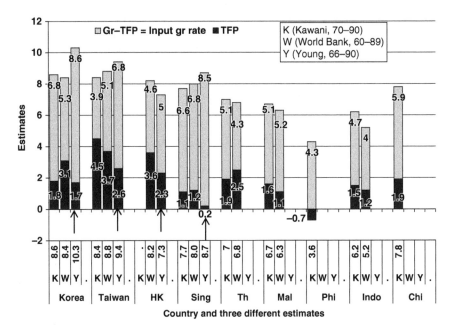

Figure 6.4 Estimates of GDP Growth Rate and Its Composition
TFP and Input Growth Rate, Three Different Estimates. In Percent

GDP growth rates, as shown by the height of the whole columns, is the highest for Korea, Taiwan and Singapore, and in the case of Korea, his estimate (10.3%) is 16% higher than the next highest estimate (8.6%) by Kawai. These lead to his low estimate of the TFPCs for the Asian NICs.

In fact, Figure 6.5 shows that Young's estimate of the TFPC is the lowest among the three, and in the case of Singapore, it is only about 16% of the other two estimates. Except for Korea, Kawai's and the World Bank's estimates are more or less close to each other. Despite large differences in terms of the levels of the TFPC, the rankings of the three estimates among the three Asian NICs are the same: Taiwan has the highest TFPC, followed by Korea and Singapore.

Among the ASEAN-4 countries, the negative TFPC of the Philippines may be expected, although its magnitude is rather surprising. Another surprise is that Malaysia's TFPC is consistently lower than that of Thailand for the two estimates, although the difference in Kawai's estimates may not be significant. China's TFPC is respectable; it is as high as many other Asian countries, although it is less than half of Taiwan's TFPC as estimated by Kawai.

Figure 6.5 also lists some other earlier estimations of the TFPCs. Korea has two additional estimates: one is 40.8%, denoted as C40.8 with a black

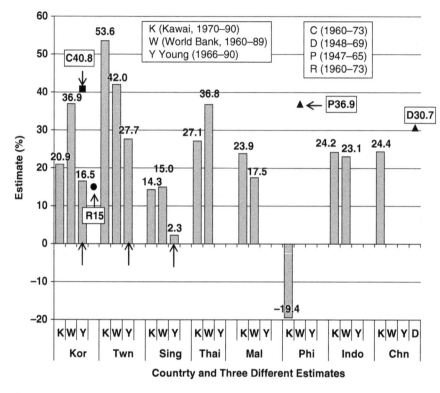

Figure 6.5 Total Factor Productivity Contribution (TFPC)
Various Periods and Countries. In Percent

square marker in Figure 6.5, and is estimated by Christensen and Cummings (1981) for the period 1960–73.[16] The estimate is surprisingly close to that of Jorgenson et al. shown in Figure 6.3. The other estimate is 15%, denoted as R15 with a black circle marker, which is estimated by Kim and Roemer (1979, 92) for 1960 to 1973. The estimate is much closer to Young's. Thus, with such a large difference, it is very difficult to make any conclusion about Korea's TFPC.

Williamson (1969) estimates the Philippines' TFPC for 1947–65 and obtains 36.9%, as denoted by P36.9 in Figure 6.5, which reverses Kawai's estimation of −19% during 1970–90. This may explain the Philippines' economic decline and dismal performance during the last two decades. Denison's estimate[17] of

---

16 Young (1995, 665) includes a discussion of Christensen and Cummings's method.
17 See Denison (1974, 127). Here, 30.7% is obtained by growth rate of "advances in knowledge and n.e.c." (1.19) divided by "total actual national income" growth rate (3.87). See also Denison (1967, 281–82) on residuals.

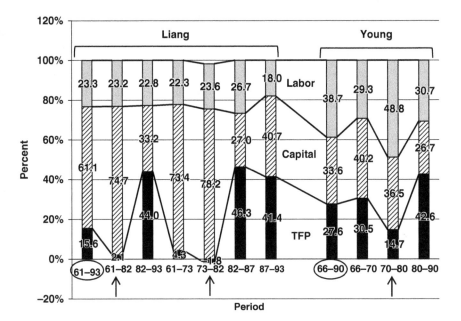

Figure 6.6 Growth Accounting, Taiwan
TFP, Capital and Labor Contributions

the US TFPC at 30.7% for 1948–69, denoted as D30.7 in Figure 6.5, is almost the same as the estimation (30.2%) by Jorgenson et al. in Figure 6.3. Thus, even using Young's low TFPC estimates of TFP growth rates and TFPCs, the TFP performance of Taiwan and Hong Kong has been as respectable as that of the United States and Canada, and Krugman's criticism of input-driven growth seems to be unfounded, unless we also consider that the growth of the United States and Canada is also input driven.

In response to Krugman's argument, Liang (1995), using Young's method, estimates Taiwan's labor, capital and TFP contributions to the GDP growth rate for a 33-year period. To see the "different characteristic of the subperiods," he estimates the various contributions for two and four subperiods. The result is shown as the stacked columns on the left-hand side of Figure 6.6. The bottom layer gives the TFPC, the middle layer displays the capital contribution and the top layer presents the labor contribution. The three layers should add up to 100%. To compare these layers with Liang's estimates, we also calculate the various contributions to GDP growth rate from Young's Table VIII, which only gives aggregate estimates for 25 years and three subperiods. Thus an exact comparison is not intended.

Like the previous two figures, no regular pattern seems to emerge immediately from these two estimates. The impact of the first oil crisis has different effects on these two estimates. The crisis of 1973 occurred during Liang's subperiods of 1961–82 and 1973–82, and during Young's subperiod of 1970–80 (see the arrows). The effects seem much more severe in Liang's estimates than Young's, probably because the former estimate considers energy input explicitly in the formula. This may also contribute to the much lower estimate of the aggregate TFPC for Liang (15.6%) as compared with that of Young (27.6%). In general, if the oil crisis is ignored, we may conclude that the TFPC (and also TFP growth rates, not shown in the diagram) did increase over each subperiod for all cases, although, in Liang's four-period estimate, the TFPC (and also TFP growth rate) decreased somewhat during 1987–93. This general increasing trend of the TFPC (and TFP growth rates) gives hope for continuous growth of the Asian NICs.

In both estimates, since the labor contribution has been more or less constant, the increase in the TFPC comes at the expense of the capital contribution. Thus, capital and technology are substitutes in both estimates. There is, however, a great discrepancy in the two estimates during the oil crisis. In Liang's estimates, capital is a complete substitute of technology, while in Young's estimates, labor is a mild substitute. Liang's detailed calculation of sectoral TFP growth rates does not seem to help in explaining this discrepancy.

In general, we have shown that, with all these numbers, it is an irony that we still cannot conclude whether the growth of Asian NICs has really been input driven, since some of them have high TFP growth rates and TFPCs, and there are no criteria to ascertain whether they are really low or high. Unlike Krugman, we do not think the TFP growth rates and TFPCs of the emerging East Asian economies are very low, and, like Young, we think they are not extraordinary either. The jury is still out on this subject. In the current state of art, it is not convincing to make any prediction based on a few statistical results.

6.6 Concluding Remarks

In this chapter, we have reviewed the nature of the Asian miracle and examined Krugman's first proposition of his syllogism. The assertion that the growth of Asian NICs has been input-driven, and not attributable to technological progress, is based on two recent statistical estimations that are still not conclusive, as other estimations have different (higher) results. Several estimates show that some Asian NICs' TFP contributions are as high as the United States and Canada, and it is not clear what is the appropriate size of the TFP growth rate and the TFPC for a developing country. The subperiod analysis also shows a general trend of increase in the TFP contribution.

Krugman's second proposition is that in input-driven growth, the law of diminishing returns will eventually set in, as the former Soviet economy once did and its economy declined. Elsewhere (Hsiao and Hsiao, 1996), we have shown that there are three major strategies to delay diminishing returns: improvement in education, expansion of domestic research and development, and promotion of openness. Until the mid-1990s, the Asian NICs relied mainly on the first and the last strategies to counter diminishing returns and achieved rapid economic growth, the "miracle." It has been shown in detail that technology could, and, in fact, did, transfer through import and export activities, and also through (inward) direct foreign investment in the Asian NICs (M. Hsiao 1992). The Pacific trade triangle formed among East Asian NICs, Japan and the United States (M. Hsiao 1996); East Asian NICs' industrial upgrading to higher value-added manufactured good exports; and increased flows of foreign direct investment in the Asian countries, especially from East Asian NICs to Southeast Asian countries and so forth, have enhanced intra- and interregional economic integration in recent years and contributed to today's dynamic economic activities in the Asia-Pacific area, as compared with Latin America and the sub-Saharan African countries. Thus, barring unforeseen political disturbances and economic disaster, like missile tests conducted by China in the early 1990s, it is rather difficult to imagine that, like the Soviet economy, the economic vitality of the Asian NICs, and of the Asia-Pacific region, will cease in the foreseeable future.

Acknowledgments

We would like to thank Professor Chi-Yuan Liang and Messrs. Takabumi Suzuoki and Kenichi Yanagi for help in references. Part of this chapter was written when the first author was a visiting scholar at the Fairbank Center for East Asian Research, Harvard University. His thanks go to the Center staff and faculty, especially Professors Ezra Vogel and William C. Kirby, for providing him an excellent research environment. This chapter consists of the first part of the original paper, which was presented at the Seventh Biennial Conference on US–Asia Economic Relations, Kuala Lumpur, Malaysia, May 1996. We are grateful for the helpful comments from the participants at the Conference, especially Professors M. Jan Dutta and Arnold C. Harberger, for their comments and suggestions. This research project is partly supported by the Center for Research on Economic and Social Policy, University of Colorado Denver, and the McGuire Center of International Studies and the Center of Economic Analysis, University of Colorado Boulder. All errors of omission and commission are the authors'.

References

Barro, R. J., and X. Sala-i-Martin. (1995). *Economic Growth*. New York: McGraw-Hill.

Christensen, L. R., and D. Cummings. (1981). "Real Product, Real Factor Input, and Productivity in the Republic of Korea, 1960–1973," *Journal of Development Economics* 8(3): 285–302.

Denison, E. F. (1967). *Why Growth Rates Differ: Postwar Experience in Nine Western Countries*. Washington, DC: Brookings Institution.

——— (1974). *Accounting for United States Economic Growth, 1929 to 1969*. Washington, DC: Brookings Institution.

Economic Planning Agency (EPA) (1995). *Asian Economies 1995* [in Japanese]. Tokyo: Ministry of Finance Publishing Bureau.

Hsiao, F. S. T., and M. C. W. Hsiao (1995). "Taiwanese Economic Development and Foreign Trade." In Taiwan Studies Workshop, ed., *Harvard Studies on Taiwan: Papers of the Taiwan Studies Workshop*, vol. 1: 199–270. John K. Fairbank Center for East Asian Research, Harvard University. Also in John Y. T. Kuark, ed. (1995). *Comparative Asian Economies, Contemporary Studies in Economic and Financial Analysis*, vol. 77 (part B). *An International Series of Monographs*. Greenwich, CT: JAI Press, 217–308.

——— (1996). "Diminishing Returns and Asian NICs' Growth." Paper presented at the Seventh Biennial Conference on US–Asia Economic Relations, Kuala Lumpur, Malaysia, May 1996.

Hsiao, M. C. W. (1992). "Direct Foreign Investment, Technology Transfer, and Industrial Development—The Case of Electronics Industry in Taiwan." In M. Dutta, ed., *Asian Economic Regime: An Adaptive Innovation Paradigm*. Research in Asian Economic Studies. 4A, Greenwich, CT: JAI Press, 145–64.

——— (1996). "Pacific Trade Triangle and the Growth of Korea and Taiwan—Cointegration and Causality Analyses." Paper presented at the 1996 Meetings of the Eastern Economic Association, Boston, MA.

Jorgenson, D. (1995). *Productivity*, vol. 2. Cambridge, MA: MIT Press.

Kawai, Hiroki. (1995). "International Comparison of Economic Growth—Trade Liberalization and Productivity" [in Japanese]. In Shinjiro Urata, ed., *Trade Liberalization and Productivity Growth in Asia and Latin America*. Institute of Developing Economies Monograph, #448. Tokyo: Institute of Developing Economies.

Kim, J. I., and L. J. Lau (1994). "Economic Growth of the East Asian Newly Industrializing Countries," *Journal of the Japanese and International Economies* 8(3): 235–71.

Kim, K. S., and M. Roemer (1979). *Growth and Structural Transformation: Studies in the Modernization of the Republic of Korea, 1945–1975*. Cambridge, MA: Council on East Asian Studies, Harvard University.

Kim, W. C., and P. K. Y. Young, eds. (1987). *The Pacific Challenge in International Business*. Ann Arbor, MI: UMI Research Press.

Krugman, P. (1994). "The Myth of Asia's Miracle," *Foreign Affairs* 73(6): 62–78.

Liang, C. Y. (1995). "Productivity Growth in Asian NIEs: A Case Study of the Republic of China, 1961–1993," *APO Productivity Journal*. Publication of Asian Productivity Organization. Winter: 17–40.

OECD (1979). *The Impact of the Newly Industrializing Countries on Production and Trade in Manufactures*. Report by the Secretary-General. Paris: OECD.

Page, J. (1994). "The East Asian Miracle: Four Lessons for Development Policy." In S. Fischer and J. J. Rotenberg, eds. *NBER Macroeconomics, Annual 1994*, 9:   219–82. Cambridge, MA: MIT Press.

Park, Y. C., and W. A. Park. (1989). "Changing Japanese Trade Patterns and the East Asian NICs." In P. Krugman, ed., *Trade with Japan: Has the Door Opened Wider?* Chicago: University of Chicago Press, 1991, chapter 3.

Sachs, J. D., and A. Warner. (1995). "Economic Reform and the Process of Global Integration," *Brookings Papers on Economic Analysis, 25th Anniversary Issue*, 1–118.

Sakura Institute of Research (Sakura Sogo Kenkyujo), Center for Pacific Business Research. (1995). *Reading New Century's Asian Economies* (Sinseiki Ajia Keizai o Yomu). Tokyo: Daiamondo Sha.

Stallings, B., ed. (1995). *Global Change, Regional Response: The New International Context of Development*. Cambridge: Cambridge University Press.

Taniuchi, M. (1995). "East Asian Growth and Efficiency Gains: A Critique of Krugman's 'The Myth of Asia's Miracle'," *APO Productivity Journal* Winter: 3–16.

Williamson, J. G. (1969). "Dimensions of Postwar Philippines Economic Progress," *Quarterly Journal of Economics* 83(1): 93–109.

World Bank. (1993). *The East Asian Miracle, Economic Growth and Public Policy*. A World Bank Policy Research Report. New York: Oxford University Press.

———— (1989). *World Development Report 1989*. New York: Oxford University Press

Young, A. (1995). "The Tyranny of Numbers: Confronting the Statistical Realities of the East Asian Growth Experience," *Quarterly Journal of Economics* 110(3): 641–80. Also in NBER Working Paper Series, No. 4680, 1994.

Chapter 7

"MIRACLE GROWTH" IN THE TWENTIETH CENTURY: INTERNATIONAL COMPARISONS OF EAST ASIAN DEVELOPMENT

Abstract

Using Maddison's extensive long-run data, we compare levels and growth rates of real GDP per capita between Korea and Taiwan, along with Japan, and 53 other countries in the world, covering the prewar and postwar periods (1901–92). Both countries, along with Japan, experienced very rapid growth in both periods, especially Korea, whose growth rates ranked third or fourth in the world in the prewar period.

After World War II, however, Korea fell steadily below Taiwan, and both fell continuously behind Japan until 1970 when they simultaneously began to catch up. Finally, using Perron's test, we analyze structural changes or continuity between the two periods. Both domestic and international economic conditions are examined to explain the findings. The gist of this chapter is that colonialism has unexpected results, and that the often-touted "rags to riches" or "Economic Miracle" of Taiwan and Korea is not a postwar phenomenon. It all started during the colonial period long before World War II, and both Taiwan and Korea took almost a century of development to become advanced countries of today.

7.1 Introduction

It is now well known that South Korea (hereafter referred to as Korea) and Taiwan are the only two noncity-state countries that have both achieved and maintained rapid modern economic growth since the end of World War II. The question "How did they do it, and can other developing countries learn from their experiences?" has been one of the most discussed and studied issues in recent economic literature. While recognizing the differences in their growth performance and industrial structures, most studies combine them as if they were twins, in consideration of both countries possessing similar cultural backgrounds, and having the status of Japanese colonies prior to World War II.

During the early 1990s, however, several "revisionists sought to trace various political and economic continuities between the Japanese colonial period and the rapid growth that began—or began again—in the 1960s" (Haggard, Kang and Moon, 1997, 867). The problem of continuity is important, as can be seen from Perkins's preface to Suh (1978): "a great deal happened to Korea's economy during that colonial period, and it is doubtful that one can really understand the current economic achievements without some knowledge of what went before." This also has been pointed out by Kohli (1994), although it has been criticized by Haggard et al. (1997).

In a similar vein, the same can be said of Taiwan. In Taiwan, revisionist work is being carried out by scholars at National Taiwan University through the construction of long-run economic time series dating from 1912. Elsewhere, we have also considered the agricultural development of Taiwan (Hsiao, 1997) and briefly reviewed the industrial and institutional development during the Japanese period (Hsiao and Hsiao, 2002a) as well as the postwar period (Hsiao and Hsiao, 2001b). In Korea, this work is done by the Naksongdae Research Institute in an attempt to demonstrate the structural similarities between these two periods (Haggard et al., 1997). While the "revisionists" have added depth to the research and broadened the scope of these studies, the majority of them examine the prewar and postwar economic development of each country separately, without attempting to relate the interwar periods (Ka, 1995; Suh, 1978; Twu, 1975), and still remain restricted to the study of one individual country. There are no comparisons and links made between prewar and postwar periods, nor are comparisons made between the long-run development of Korea, Taiwan and other countries.[1]

This chapter attempts to fill this gap by comparing statistically the similarities and differences in the levels and the growth rates of real GDP per capita between Korea and Taiwan during the long-run economic development, along with Japan, the United States and other countries in the world, within the spans of the prewar and postwar periods. Since one of the major concerns in the literature has been the continuity of economic growth between the prewar and postwar periods, we have tested the statistical continuity of the time series of real GDP per capita growth rates of Korea, Taiwan, Japan and the United

---

1 For a comparative study of postwar development, see Hattori and Sato (1996).

States. Based on our statistical findings, we give plausible explanations, which are mostly drawn from other sources, especially from our previous works.

Due to the limitations of data and space, our analysis, unlike that of Kohli (1994), is necessarily confined to the most important, although controversial, macroeconomic indicator, namely, GDP per capita.[2] By using the term "long-run," we mean to include the prewar and postwar periods, covering the years 1910–92, almost a century long, while we clearly distinguish the difference between prewar and postwar economic development. Since Singapore and Hong Kong are city-states and are not in possession of long-run data, the term "East Asian countries" includes only Korea, Taiwan and Japan, with emphasis placed on the first two. To allow for tractability of our analysis, and also because we are limited by the available comparable data from the pre-war period, this chapter deals only with a long-run time series of real GDP per capita. This means that we investigate the major characteristics of modern economic growth: high rates of growth of per capita product (Kuznets, 1973) of these countries. Japan and the United States are chosen because these countries have been the most important trading partners of Korea and Taiwan following World War II, and Korea and Taiwan were Japanese colonies prior to the war.

The chapter is developed as follows. Section 7.2, based on a recent OECD publication, compares the real GDP per capita growth of Korea and Taiwan with that of 10 Asian as well as 12 OECD countries. In that the data are readily available from the OECD, we have presented the level of long-run real GDP per capita diagrammatically, in order to dramatize the world's general patterns of growth. Section 7.3 then focuses on Korea and Taiwan and compares the levels of real GDP per capita of Taiwan and Korea, along with those of Japan, the United States, the Netherlands and China. Section 7.4 shows that there are differences among these "miraculous" countries. We confirm that the availability of the OECD data provides a challenging question regarding falling behind when Taiwanese and Korean real GDP per capita is compared with that of Japan over a long-run period. Section 7.5 briefly examines the differences in changes in the real GDP per capita ratios of Taiwan, Korea, Hong Kong and Singapore (the four "Asian NIEs") with that of Japan, from domestic and international economic perspectives during the 1970s. Section 7.6 tests econometrically the long-run structural changes of real GDP per capita series of the logarithmic levels and its growth rates series at the breakpoint between the

---

2 Elsewhere we have discussed in detail the problems of using GDP per capita as a measure of production and welfare under colonialism in Korea and Taiwan (Hsiao and Hsiao, 2000).

prewar and postwar periods. For the purpose of international comparisons, these tests included the real GDP per capita series of Taiwan, Korea, Japan and the United States. The final section of the chapter presents concluding remarks.

7.2 International Comparisons of Real GDP per Capita

In recent years, Maddison (1995, Appendix D) has compiled internationally comparable real GDP per capita of 56 countries from 1900–92 based on 1990 Geary–Khamis dollars,[3] which are based on international purchasing power parity. His data on real GDP per capita for Korea is based on the series compiled by Suh (1978), Kim and Roemer (1979), Mizoguchi and Umemura (1988) and others. "The figures are adjusted to exclude the impact of territorial change" (Maddison, 1995, 126). This is especially important in the case of Korea, which, following the Korean War, was divided into North and South Korea.

For Taiwan, Maddison's data are based on Mizoguchi and Umemura (1988), Ho (1978) and others. In addition to Maddison, Wu (1995) also estimated real GDP per capita of Taiwan in New Taiwan dollars (NT$) from 1910 to 1990, based on 1937 constant prices.[4] Mizoguchi (1997) also compiled real GDP per capita in New Taiwan dollars from 1912 to 1990 in 1960 constant prices. Elsewhere (Hsiao and Hsiao, 2000) we have shown that despite the fact that the data compiled by Maddison measure GDP per capita in international prices, it has essentially the same time series properties as the other two series measured in New Taiwan dollars (Hsiao and Hsiao, 2000). In that the focus of this chapter is on international comparison, Maddison's time series data for Taiwan has been adopted.

For Korea, Maddison's data is also based on Mizoguchi and Umemura (1988), Kim and Roemer (1979), Suh (1978), World Bank and others. In addition, Mizoguchi and Nojima (1996) also estimated per capita domestic gross expenditure and per capita domestic net product (DNPpc) in the Korean won for a limited time period, 1911–38 and 1953–83. For the comparable parts, we find that, despite the difference in currency units, the shape and trend of their DNPpc corresponds very well to Maddison's data, except that their DNPpc becomes steeper than Maddison's GDPpc after 1970.

---

3 For the discussion of the Geary–Khamis system and references, see Kravis, Heston and Summers (1982, 89–93). See also Appendix 9A.1 of this book.

4 Another estimation of real GDP from 1937 to 1950 is given by a group of statisticians in the Bureau of Statistics of Taiwan.

7.2.1 Comparisons of real GDP per capita level

How do real GDP per capita data of Korea and Taiwan compare with the corresponding data from other Asian and OECD countries? Figure 7.1 dramatizes the long-run growth of real GDP per capita among 10 Asian countries as follows: Korea (K), Taiwan (T), Thailand (Th), Indonesia (Indo), the Philippines (Ph), Burma (Bm), China (C), India (Indi), Bangladesh (Ban) and Pakistan (Paki). Both Figures 7.1 and 7.2, which will be explained shortly, are congested and it is difficult to distinguish among the respective countries. The major purpose here is, however, to focus more on the general trend of the Asian and the world economies and less on individual countries (see Table 7.1 for summary).

In examining Figure 7.1, it becomes clear that the long-run growth of real GDP per capita of Taiwan (the heavy solid line) and Korea (the heavy dashed line) has been extraordinary between these countries, most especially during the postwar period. Both Thailand (Th) and China (C) have also experienced steady growth, but only in recent years, and they still lag far behind Korea and Taiwan in real GDP per capita.

The growth of Korea and Taiwan accelerated during the 1970s and the 1980s, while the Philippines and Burma stumbled, and Pakistan, India and Bangladesh experienced either slower growth or no growth throughout the prewar and

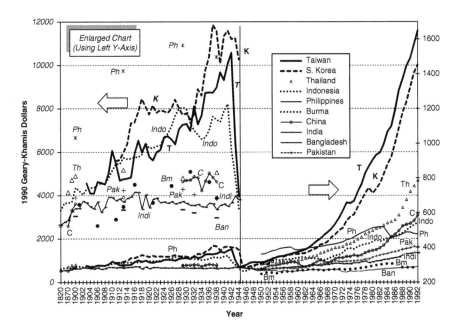

Figure 7.1 Levels of GDP per Capita in 10 Asian Countries
1820–1992

Table 7.1 Real GDP per Capita Growth Rates, World Regions
Prewar and Postwar Periods, 1901–92

Period Years No. of Yrs		Early 1901-10 10			Prewar 1911-40 30			Transition 1941-50 10			Postwar 1951-92 42		Long 1911-92 82			Postwar and prewar difference
Rk/no. rked			Rk/42			Rk/49			Rk/46			Rk/56		Rk/49			Rk/46
Row No. Country		Avg grrt	a	Notes	Avg grrt		Notes	Avg grrt		Notes	Avg grrt		Avg grrt		Notes	=(12)-(6) Diff
(1)	(2)	(3)	(4)	(5)	(6)	(7)	(8)	(9)	(10)	(11)	(12)	(13)	(14)	(15)	(16)	(17) (18)
East Asia																
1a	Korea	0.50	31	01-11	2.03	4	12-40	-6.14	46		5.80	2	2.98	3	12-92	3.8 3
1b	Mizo(NDPpc)				2.25	3	12-38	-0.57	36	39-53	4.94	54-83	2.78		12-83	2.7 10
2a	Taiwan	2.33	8		1.18	19		-3.92	44		6.03	1	3.04	2		4.8 1
		(1.37)	(17)	01-11	(1.51)	(12)	12-40									(4.5) (1)
2b	Mizo				1.26	17	13-40	-2.06	41		6.41	51-90	3.47	1	13-90	5.2 1
2c	Wu				1.65	8		-6.89	46		6.12	51-90	2.82	5	11-90	4.5 2
3	Japan	1.00	25		2.64	2		-3.89	43		5.57	3	3.34	1		2.9 9
	Average	*1.27*			*1.95*			*-4.65*			*5.80*		*3.12*			*3.8*
		(0.96) b			*(2.05) b*											
	Asia															
4	Indonsa	1.25	21		1.14	21		-3.76	42		2.73	19	1.44	33		1.6 24
5	Burma	-1.41	42	02-11	0.73	31	12-38	-4.63	45	39-50	1.53	40	0.35	48	12-92	0.8 35
6	China	0.41	35	01-13	0.49	35	14-38	-1.97	40	39-50	3.85	8	1.90	20	14-92	3.4 5
7	Philipps	2.44	6	01-13	0.22	41	14-38	-1.22	39	39-50	1.28	43	0.56	47	14-92	1.1 30
8	Thailand	0.32	36	01-13	-0.06	45	14-38	0.16	30	39-50	4.07	4	2.17	12	14-92	4.1 2
9	India	0.96	26		-0.11	46		-0.72	38		1.94	33	0.82	46		2.0 15
10	Pakistan	0.46	33	01-13	-0.28	48	14-38	-0.38	34	39-50	2.21	24	1.03	42	14-92	2.5 10
11	Bangldh	0.46	32	01-13	-0.30	49	14-38	-0.31	33	39-50	0.64	51	0.20	49	14-92	0.9 33
	Average	*0.61*			*0.23*			*-1.60*			*2.28*		*1.06*			*2.1*
	Advanced Capitalist Countries															
12	Norway	1.52	15		1.98	5		2.90	9		3.00	14	2.62	6		1.0 31
13	Finland	1.34	19		1.75	7		2.78	11		3.01	13	2.52	7		1.3 27
14	Sweden	1.52	16		1.63	10		3.27	3		2.19	26	2.12	14		0.6 42
15	Germany	1.18	23		1.51	12		-2.59	41		3.59	11	2.08	15		2.1 14
16	Switzerld	1.42	17		1.46	13		3.48	2		2.04	30	2.00	17		0.6 41
17	Italy	2.67	3		1.36	14		-0.01	31		3.70	9	2.39	8		2.3 12
18	USA	1.93	12		1.15	20		3.10	5		1.93	34	1.79	24		0.8 37
19	UK	0.26	39		1.09	23		0.45	29		1.98	31	1.47	30		0.9 34
20	Denmark	2.05	11		1.08	24		3.06	6		2.40	22	1.99	18		1.3 26
21	France	0.30	37		1.03	25		2.65	12		2.94	15	2.21	10		1.9 20
22	Canada	3.34	1		0.93	27		3.26	4		2.25	23	1.89	21		1.3 25
23	Nthlds	0.42	34		0.82	30		2.16	16		2.53	20	1.86	22		1.7 23
24	Austria	1.32	20		0.62	32		-0.66	37		3.63	10	2.01	16		3.0 7
25	NewZeal	2.13	10		0.57	33		2.94	7		1.18	45	1.17	40		0.6 39
26	Belgium	0.86	28		0.38	36		1.80	20		2.78	18	1.78	25		2.4 11
27	Australia	2.61	4		0.21	42		1.95	17		1.93	35	1.30	35		1.7 22
	Average	*1.55*			*1.10*			*1.91*			*2.57*		*1.95*			*1.47*

Table 7.1 *(Cont.)*

Period Years	Early 1901-10			Prewar 1911-40			Transition 1941-50			Postwar 1951-92		Long 1911-92			Postwar and prewar
No.of Yrs	10			30			10			42		82			difference
Rk/no. rked		Rk/42			Rk/49			Rk/46			Rk/56		Rk/49		Rk/49
Row	Avg			Avg			Avg			Avg		Avg			=(12)-(6)
No. Country	gr rt		Notes	gr rt		Notes	gr rt		Notes	gr rt		gr rt		Notes	Diff
(1) (2)	(3)	(4)	(5)	(6)	(7)	(8)	(9)	(10)	(11)	(12)	(13)	(14)	(15)	(16)	(17) (18)
South Europe															
28 Greece				1.94	6	14-39	2.42	14	43-50	3.96	5	2.34	9	14-92	2.0 16
29 Turkey				1.11	22	14-40	-0.17	32		2.92	16	1.91	19		1.8 21
30 Portugal	-0.30	41	00-13	0.93	26	14-38	1.85	18		3.93	6	2.67	5	14-92	3.0 8
31 Ireland	0.70	30	00-13	0.52	34	14-38	1.01	23	38-50	2.86	17	1.84	23	14-92	2.3 13
32 Spain	0.27	38		0.29	38		0.47	28		3.93	7	2.18	11		3.6 4
Average	*0.22*			*0.96*			*1.12*			*3.52*		*2.19*			*2.6*
Latin America															
33 Venezuel	0.76	29		5.06	1		6.07	1		0.50	53	2.85	4		-4.6 49
34 Peru	1.83	14	01-13	2.09	3	14-40	2.16	15		0.55	52	1.28	36	14-94	-1.5 47
35 Brazil	1.22	22		1.64	9		2.51	13		2.43	21	2.15	13		0.8 36
36 Colombia	1.84	13	01-13	1.58	11	14-40	0.97	24		2.09	29	1.78	25	14-92	0.5 43
37 Chile	2.38	7		0.92	28		1.61	21		1.52	41	1.31	34		0.6 40
38 Argentin	3.27	2		0.28	39		1.81	19		1.01	47	0.84	45		0.7 38
39 Mexico	2.15	9		0.22	40	14-40	2.93	8		2.14	28	1.58	28	14-93	1.9 19
Average	*1.92*			*1.69*			*2.58*			*1.46*		*1.68*			*-0.2*
East Europe															
40 USSR	0.87	27		1.35	15	14-40	2.79	10		1.19	44	1.45	32	14-92	-0.2 45
41 Czech	1.37	18		1.33	16	14-37	1.50	22	38-50	1.60	38	1.50	29	14-92	0.3 44
42 Yugo				1.22	17	14-39	0.82	26	40-50	2.20	25	1.68	27	14-92	1.0 32
43 Hungary	1.17	24		0.83	29	14-40	-0.64	36		1.96	32	1.25	39	14-92	1.1 29
44 Poland				0.34	37	30-38	0.96	25	39-50	1.57	39	1.27	37	30-92	1.2 28
45 Bulgaria				0.12	43	14-40	0.58	27		2.14	27	1.26	38	14-92	2.0 17
46 Romania				-0.11	47	27-38	-0.41	35	39-50	1.84	36	1.08	41	27-92	2.0 18
Average	*1.14*			*0.73*			*0.80*			*1.78*		*1.36*			*1.1*
Africa															
47 Ghana	2.60	5	01-13	1.65	8	14-50				-0.40	55	0.86	44		-2.1 48
48 SAfrica				1.19	18	14-50				1.02	46	0.95	43	14-92	-0.2 46
49 Egypt	-0.02	40	01-13	0.05	44	14-50				3.13	12	1.46	31		3.1 6
50 Nigeria										1.77	37				
51 Kenya										1.31	42				
52 Morocco										0.88	48				
53 Tanzania										0.81	49				
54 Cote										0.66	50				
55 Ethiopia										0.19	54				
56 Zaire										-1.40	56				
Average	*1.29*			*0.96*						*1.22*		*1.09*			*0.3*
Grand Avg	*1.15*			*1.09*			*0.02*			*2.66*		*1.78*			*1.6*

Notes: (a) average continuous growth rate per year during the period and (b) average growth rates of the three countries with the Taiwan's figures in the parentheses.

Source: Maddison (1995) and the authors' calculation.

postwar periods. Thus, in comparing these Asian countries, it is indeed unusual that Korea and Taiwan have been able to sustain their levels of economic growth at such a rapid pace over such a long duration since the onset of the twentieth century.

The curves in the upper part of the left-hand side of Figure 7.1 are more revealing, albeit less dramatic. These curves are measured from the right-hand side Y-axis, and are the enlarged part of the clustered curves of the lower part of the figure. For the first time in the literature, with unequivocal data rather than conjecture, we can point out that, by the end of the 1930s, Korea and Taiwan had already achieved higher real GDP per capita than all of the other major developing Asian countries.

Korea is very special: its real GDP per capita exceeded all Asian countries, except Japan, after the second part of the 1930s, exceeding the Philippines, which seemed to have the highest standard of living in Asia (even exceeding Japan) during the early part of the twentieth century until the mid-1930s, and even in the 1950s. The level of real GDP per capita of both countries accelerated during the second part of the 1930s, corresponding to Japan's expansionist foreign policy. Thus, despite the talk of colonial exploitation, Korea and Taiwan had already greatly improved and exceeded all the developing countries[5] in Asia prior to World War II.

If the long-run growth in Korea and Taiwan appears extraordinary in comparison with other developing Asian countries, what comparison can be made with some OECD countries? Figure 7.2 depicts the long-run growth of 12 OECD countries: Australia, Austria, Belgium, Canada, Denmark, Finland, France, Germany, Italy, Japan, the Netherlands and the United States, along with Korea and Taiwan. This figure illustrates that three Far Eastern countries—Taiwan, Korea and Japan (the line with white circle markers)—originated from more or less the same threshold during the early years of the twentieth century. In fact, according to Maddison, in 1910, real GDP per capita of Japan was $1,254, while that of Taiwan was $958, or about 76% of that of Japan. In 1911, real GDP per capita for Japan, Korea and Taiwan

---

5 For Taiwan, this was also observed in a report to the United States Congress by Conlon Associates (1959, 139), which stated, "Taiwan did not enter the post war era without advantages. Progress under Japan had been extensive. Prior to World War II, the Taiwanese had a standard of living second only to that of Japan itself in Asia. The people had acquired many industrial and agrarian skills. The years immediately after 1945, however, were years of chaos."For Korea, however, which was written in the aftermath of the Korean War, the report merely stated that "Japan contributed much to economic progress in Korea but it also shaped the overall economy in a typically colonial fashion, bequeathing to independent Korea a sharp economic imbalance," on which the Report did not elaborate (110–11).

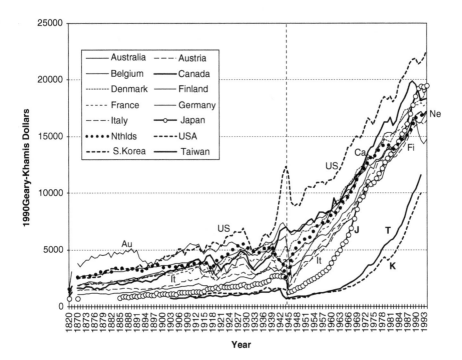

Figure 7.2 Real GDP per Capita of OECD Countries
Taiwan and Korea, 1820–1992

was $1,304, $898 (69% of Japan) and $882 (68% of Japan), respectively. In 1915, real GDP per capita of Korea even reached 81% of that of Japan.[6] Afterward, Japan, however, grew at a faster rate than both Korea and Taiwan, accelerated during the prewar period, and continued its acceleration throughout both the 1950s and the 1960s, while Korea and Taiwan grew at slightly slower rates in the prewar period, and stagnated from the early postwar period up until the mid-1960s. As shown in Figure 7.2, the accelerated growth rates of Korea and Taiwan established themselves only after the 1970s, and most notably during the 1980s.

The fact that the real distinction in growth among the three countries came about only after the war is rather surprising, as Japan was generally regarded as much more advanced than either Korea or Taiwan, both of which were

---

6 Even until the early 1960s, Japan was classified as an "underdeveloped" country, only slightly (one step) more advanced than Taiwan and Korea. This is consistent with our observation that Taiwan, Korea and Japan were close in terms of per capita income and living standard in the early twentieth century and immediately after World War II (see Higgins, 1968, 852; Adelman and Morris, 1967, 88).

"exploited" under Japanese colonialism prior to the end of World War II. As in most of the Western world,[7] the implication here is that the Japanese seemed unable to benefit greatly from colonialism, and that all three countries experienced accelerated growth only after becoming independent from one another.

7.2.2 Real GDP per capita growth rates

More specifically, Table 7.1 calculates the real GDP per capita growth rates of 56 countries.[8] It covers all six categories or continents listed in Maddison. Since our main concerns are the three East Asian countries, they are listed in the first three rows, with emphasis on Korea and Taiwan.

The first isolated data on Taiwan and Korea are available only in 1900, and their continuous data are available only after 1903 for Taiwan and only after 1911 for Korea; therefore, we have divided the time into four periods. One is from 1901 to 1910, which we call the Early Period, and another is from 1911 to 1940, which we call the Prewar Period (that is, pre–World War II period). Since World War II inflicted severe damage to the economies of the three countries, we have designated 1941–50 as the Transition Period, and 1951–92 as the Postwar Period, with the data ending in 1992. We have also calculated the average growth rates for 1911–92 and call that period the Long Period in Table 7.1. (Note that, in this chapter, when we specifically refer the prewar and postwar periods of Table 7.1, we capitalize the words, as Prewar Period and Postwar Period).

Since there are many isolated entries in the earlier period of Maddison's data, we use the continuous growth rates in each year for each country so that average growth rates (GrRt) per year can be calculated for the missing years.[9] In Table 7.1, the simple average of the growth rates for each region for each

---

7 Maddison (1991, 81). Hayami and Ruttan (1970) show that Korean and Taiwan rice induced Japanese agricultural stagnation. Japan is not alone. See Copland (1990, 174). After releasing the colonies, the colonial "empires began to seem more like burdens that had been cast off" (Osterhammel, 1995, 118).

8 According to Maddison (1995, 17), these 56 countries "accounted for 93% of world output, 87% of world population and world exports in 1992."

9 The growth rate (r100) in this chapter is defined in terms of the logarithmic difference of variables in the consecutive years ($r_t = \ln X(t) - \ln X(t-1)$). In this case we have $X(t) = e^r$ $X(t-1)$, which means that $X(t)$ is compounded continuously from $(t-1)$ to t at rate r. Thus, GDP is produced at every moment of time, not suddenly at the end of the year, as in the case of discrete growth rate, which is, $g_t = (X(t) - X(t-1))/X(t-1)$. Naturally, g_t is only an approximation of r_t. Note that if X takes 100, 80, 50 and 100, then average $r_t = 0$ from 100 to 100, but average $g_t = 0.14$ from 100 to 100, namely, the average growth rate g_t from 100 to 100 is 14%, which is counterintuitive. The long-run growth literature generally uses continuous growth rates, see e.g., Kremer (1993). r_t (= Δgdppc) is used in Equation (7.1) in this chapter.

period are given at the end of each region in italics. The beginning and ending years of the irregular time period are noted in the separate "Notes" column. The overall ranking (Rk) of the average growth rate of each country among the 56 countries in each period is also given in the column in italics next to the column of average growth rates. The numbers below row 2a in parentheses are the comparable average growth rates of Taiwan if the Early Period of Taiwan is taken as the same time range (1901–11) as that of Korea.[10]

For comparison, the corresponding average growth rates of Korean Net Domestic Product (NDP) per capita for each period based on Mizoguchi and Nojima (1996) are calculated in row 1b. Similarly, we also calculate corresponding average growth rates of Taiwanese GDP per capita from Mizoguchi (1997) and Wu (1995) in rows 2b and 2c. Rankings in these rows are based on the ranking of Maddison's world data. Since our emphasis here is on prewar development, the entries in the table are sorted by the average growth rates of the Prewar Period.

Maddison's data of the 56 countries indicate that, among all countries in the world, the performances of Korea, Taiwan and Japan in the Prewar, Postwar and Long periods are indeed unique and extraordinary.

In the Early Period, during 1901–10 (columns 3 to 5, Tables 7.1), the economic performances of Korea and Japan are lackluster. During this 10-year period, real GDP per capita growth rate of Korea was only 0.50% per year, ranked 31st among the 42 countries for which we have data. It was a time of political and economic turmoil in Korea, which eventually led to Japanese annexation of Korea in 1910. The performance of Japan was only slightly better, with the average real GDP per capita growth rate of 1.00% per year, ranked 25th among the nations, which was lower than most of the Latin American countries.

Taiwan's performance was much better: 2.33%, ranked eighth in the world. There is a concern that this high rate of growth might have been due to the development under the Ch'ing dynasty just before the Japanese takeover.

---

10 Note that the growth rates of real GDP per capita of Taiwan increased to 8.04% in 1909 from the negative growth rates of the previous two years, reaching its local high of 14.6% in 1910, the final year of the Early Period. The growth rates plunged during the following two years in 1911 (−8.27%) and 1912 (−11.4%). (A severe typhoon in August 1911 damaged the southern region of Taiwan, and also in August 1912, the northern region was damaged. The economy was devastated in these two years.) Since the ending year of the Early Period is 1910 and the beginning year of the Prewar Period is also 1910, this results in a large average growth rate during the Early Period (2.33%) and a smaller average growth rate for the Prewar Period (1.18%), as shown in Table 7.1 (row 2a). This points to the arbitrariness of the definition of the Period and also shows a limitation of the period analysis. Since we do not have information on other countries, we can only take the average growth rates of Taiwan at face value.

While it is true that Taiwan experienced a kind of commercial revolution by the end of the nineteenth century (Hsiao and Hsiao, 1999, 484–87), and the government built some railroads, harbors and coal industries, it "was still economically backward, and its modernization would require basic institutional and structural modifications" (Ho, 1978, 16–24). Thus, during the initial period of Japanese occupation (1895–1905) of Taiwan,[11] land surveys, land registration and land reform were completed. The Bank of Taiwan was established in 1899, financing the improvement of transport and communications.[12] "Once a part of the larger and more dynamic Japanese economy, Taiwan found its market considerably expanded" (Ho, 1978, 25). Substantial inflow of material, human capital and new technology into Taiwan greatly increased productivity (Ho, 1978, 25), especially in sugarcane production (Mizoguchi and Umemura, 1988, 49), resulting in rapid growth of real GDP per capita in the Early Period

During the Prewar Period (1911–40, columns 6 to 8, Table 7.1), the growth rate of average real GDP per capita of Korea ranked 4th in the world at 2.03%, behind only Venezuela,[13] Japan and Peru in the world. But Mizoguchi-Nojima's Korean data shows 2.25%, even higher than Peru, and Korea ranked 3rd in the world. Japan was 2nd at 2.64%.

Taiwan's ranking is rather problematic. It ranked 19th (1.18% in row 2a) or 12th (at 1.51% if we skip 1911) among the 49 countries for which we have data. At 1.51%, Taiwan's average growth rate was lower than Norway's (5th at 1.98%), Finland's (7th at 1.75%) and Sweden's (10th at 1.63%), but the same as Germany's (12th at 1.51%).

If we take Taiwan's unadjusted lower rate (1.18%), it ranked 19th in the Prewar Period, which was still higher than many countries in Asia, almost the same as South Africa (18th at 1.19%), lower than Switzerland (13th at 1.46%), Italy (14th at 1.36%), but higher than the United States (20th at 1.15%), the United Kingdom (23rd at 1.09%) and France (25th at 1.03%). Mizuguchi's data give a slightly higher growth rate, 1.26%, ranked 17th, and Wu's data give an even higher growth rate, 1.65%, ranked 8th. Thus, while Taiwan's

---

11 The era of Taiwan's modern capitalism had to wait until the Japanese colonial government to drive away the foreign capital; to modernize transportation, communication and the land and banking systems; and to attract Japanese capital from Japan. Yanaihara (1929, 43–50), Hsiao and Hsiao (1999, 489).

12 Hsiao and Hsiao (1996, 216). According to Maddison (1995, 33), technical progress, especially transport and communications as well as the spread of electricity and the use of power, is the most important factor influencing growth performance.

13 Venezuela started producing petroleum and natural gas commercially in 1917 by foreign firms. It also has large deposits of iron ore, mined by US firms in the 1940s, in addition to nickel ore, diamonds and gold.

performance in this period was not as stellar as Korea's and Japan's, it was still better than that of most of the countries in the world.

In general, while Japan's economic performance may not be surprising, the findings of prewar average growth rates for Korea and Taiwan are quite astounding. Few scholars have recognized Korea's strong performance relative to other countries in the world. Like most nationalists, the basic tenet of Haggard et al. (1997, 867, 870 and 878) is based on the notion[14] that "the growth record under Japanese occupation was more modest than is often thought." While Kohli (1997) was able to repudiate most of the counterarguments by Haggard et al. (1997), he was unable to rebut their basic notion and show the superb performance of Korea. Das (1992, 20) remarked mildly that "during the colonial period the Korean economy grew slowly but steadily." We have shown that the prewar growth of Korea was indeed not slow; rather, it was in fact exceptionally fast, ranked third or fourth in the world.

In the Postwar Period (columns 12 and 13), Taiwan ranked clearly number one at 6.03%, above Korea, which was second at 5.8%, and even Japan, which was third at 5.57%, and almost 2% higher than the fourth-ranked Thailand (4.07%). While Korea and Taiwan have been considered fast-growing countries in the Postwar Period, these findings about their rankings are still quite unexpected: their postwar real growth rates have even surpassed that of Japan!

For the postwar performance, the rankings by other scholars are also very similar. The Mizoguchi and Nojima (1996) data show 4.94% for Korea, ranked just below Japan but above the fifth-ranked Greece. Both Mizoguchi (1997) and Wu (1995) give Taiwan even higher growth rates, 6.41% and 6.12%, respectively. Taiwan is unquestionably number one in the postwar world. Its real growth rate in general has been higher than that of Japan.

The rapid growth of real GDP per capita of Korea, Taiwan and Japan is also reflected in the long-run growth covering both the Prewar and the

---

14 Another example of their way of thinking is revealed in the statement that "agricultural performance in the postwar period was distinctly superior to the prewar period in every regard" Haggard et al. (1997, 870). This is also true for Taiwan. So far as Taiwan is concerned, however, the rapid postwar growth was based on economic development during the prewar period and the postwar Pacific trade triangle, in addition to technological innovation, mechanization and rapid expansion of livestock production in the new era of the postwar period, not necessarily due to freedom from Japanese colonialism (Hsiao and Hsiao, 1996, 243; Lee and Chen, 1978). In terms of GDE in Mizoguchi and Umemura (1988, 8), the grand averages of the five-year average annual GDE per capita growth rates among the three countries were 2.9% for Korea for 1914–38 and 2.0% and 2.1% for Taiwan and Japan for 1904–38. If the same period (1914–38) is taken, the grand averages for Taiwan and Japan become about 2.5%. In any case, according to them, Korea grew much faster than Japan, and Taiwan grew at the same rate as Japan.

Postwar Period (columns 4 to 16, Table 7.1), including the Transition Period. Overall, Japan ranked first at 3.34%; followed by Taiwan, second at 3.04%; and Korea, ranked third at 2.98%. Note that the long-run average growth rates of Taiwan and Korea are very close to each other. Thus, for almost a century, their real GDP per capita, either at the levels or at the growth rates, grew together like twins.

Overall, the long-run average growth rates calculated from Mizoguchi's data give 2.78% for Korea and 3.47% for Taiwan, ranking Korea fifth and Taiwan first, even higher than that of Japan. Wu's data rank Taiwan fifth at 2.82%, slightly lower than Venezuela. Here again, the long-run performances of the three countries during these 82 years are indeed a miracle of the century.

We may further point out that the results in Table 7.1 show unequivocally that the so-called postwar East Asian miracle, in which we include Korea, Taiwan and Japan, already existed in prewar times; thus, it is not a postwar phenomenon alone (we exclude Hong Kong and Singapore due to lack of prewar data for comparison). The postwar miracle, in terms of real GDP per capita growth rates, is simply a continuation of the prewar miracle when the economies of these three countries recovered from the war and from the early postwar noise.

Table 7.1 also reveals that the large negative growth rates of Korea (−6.14%), Taiwan (−3.92%) and Japan (−3.89%) during the 10-year Transition Period (1941–50, columns 9 to 11) are exceptionally severe from the world economic point of view. During this period, the growth rates of real GDP per capita of Korea plunged to the bottom of the world, 46th out of the 46 countries that had statistics, followed by Taiwan (44th at −3.92%) and Japan (43rd at −3.89%). The results from Mizoguchi–Nojima data for Korea are quite different, only −0.57%, but still rank Korea at 36th in the world, close to the bottom. There are also differences in Mizoguchi's and Wu's data, but their Taiwan growth rates during this period are still either at the bottom or near the bottom in the world.

This abysmal performance during the Transition Period also shows the uniqueness of these three countries. As we discuss later, this is due to the depressed economies of these countries during the war, the effect of the Korean War in Korea and severe misalignment and confusion in the transition from wartime to peacetime in Korea and Taiwan. The rapid recovery of the economies of these three countries from the bottom of the world in the Transition Period to the top of the world in the Postwar Period may also be regarded as an "economic miracle" in its own right.

However, other Asian countries, except Thailand, were also hit hard by the war. Considering their low or negative rates of growth in the Early and Prewar

Periods and mostly negative growth rates during the Transition Period, as compared with positive and respectable rates of growth in the Postwar Period, the praise for "postwar Miracle Growth" after a long period of stagnation should also go to these Southeast Asian countries, especially Thailand.

Most other countries, especially Venezuela, Switzerland and Sweden, benefited from the war or recovered quickly from the wartime interruption and increased their real GDP per capita growth rates during the Transition Period.

Table 7.1 also shows the average growth rate by region. In the Early Period, average growth rates of real GDP per capita of the three East Asian countries (1.27%, column 3) lagged behind Latin America and advanced capitalist countries. But they became the highest (1.95%, column 6) during the Prewar Period, became lowest (−4.65%, column 9) in the Transitional Period, and then recovered to become the highest again (5.80%, column 12) in the Postwar Period. In both the Prewar and the Postwar Period, their average regional growth rates were almost twice the corresponding world average growth rates (1.09% for the Prewar Period and 2.66% for the Postwar Period). Here again we see the regional dynamism of the East Asian countries in the Prewar and Postwar Periods, and it is clear again that the "East Asian Miracle" started in the Prewar Period.

7.2.3 Coefficients of variation

Since the smaller the variability of the growth rate of real GDP per capita, the better, we have selected 32 major countries of Asia, advanced capitalist countries and South Europe, and ranked the absolute value of the coefficients of variation (CV) in ascending order (to avoid cluttering, the CV and ranking are not shown in Table 7.1). In the Prewar Period Korea (fourth) and Japan (second) fared much better than Taiwan. This result proves Das's statement that during the colonial period the Korean economy grew steadily (Das, 1992, 20). Taiwan ranked 13th (when the average growth rate is 1.18%, at 548% CV) or 9th (when the average growth rate is 1.51%, at 420% CV). The higher variability of Taiwan is explained by the fact that, while the emphasis of pre-war development of Korea and Japan was on industry rather than agriculture, Taiwan's emphasis of agricultural production until the later Prewar Period was exposed to monsoons, typhoons, earthquakes and droughts, resulting in rather unstable national production (Hsiao, 1997). In the Transition Period, the CV of growth rates in Korea and Japan were almost the same as that of Taiwan (16th for Korea, 20th for Japan and 18th at 484% CV for Taiwan), indicating a similar degree of war effect during the end of the Prewar Period and immediate Postwar Period. In the Postwar Period, Taiwan had the smallest CV (47%) among the 32 countries, showing almost a steady state growth.

Japan followed closely (3rd at 57% CV) and Korea followed at a distance (13th at 87% CV), showing uneven growth of the Korean economy.

Overall, throughout the Prewar and Postwar Periods, Korea's CV for the Long Period ranked 17th at 351% CV, worse than that of Taiwan, which is 12th at 277% CV, and of Japan, 11th at 274.2% CV.

7.2.4 Comparisons of the prewar and postwar growth of countries

In general, both Figures 7.1 and 7.2 show that, in both developed and developing countries, economic growth in the prewar years was very slow and it accelerated only after the war. This is also shown in column 17 of Table 7.1 by the difference in average real GDP per capita growth rate between the Postwar Period and the Prewar Period (column 12–column 6), Table 7.1). Almost all countries for which the data are available, except Venezuela, Peru, Ghana and South Africa, increased their growth rates from the Prewar to the Postwar Period. Compared with the Prewar Period, Taiwan's average growth rates increased somewhere between 4.5% and 4.8%, which led to it being ranked number one in the world. The growth rates of Korea and Japan increased by 3.8% (third) and 2.9% (ninth), respectively. Despite the high growth rates in the Prewar Period, the average difference in the average growth rates of the three countries is 3.8%, well above any other regions in the world. The growth of the three countries indeed accelerated considerably from the Prewar Period to the Postwar Period.

Such a performance cannot be taken for granted. Note the depressed post-war performance of countries in Latin America, East Europe and Africa, as compared with countries in Asia and advanced capitalist countries between the two periods.

Broadly speaking, while there could be many factors contributing to the differences between the prewar and postwar performance, the most important factor is the different pace of world technological progress and innovation, and the type of technology between the Prewar and the Postwar Periods. This is one of the most important topics for economic historians. Suffice it here to point out that slow growth in the prewar time and rapid growth in the post-war era are a general trend of the world economy, as shown on the left-hand side of Figures 7.1 and 7.2, and not the direct result of a particular system or government, or specifically related to colonialism. More on the world trend is discussed in Section 7.5 below.

In recent years, the close relationship between economic openness and growth has been emphasized (Dollar, 1992; Sachs and Warner, 1995). In particular, it has been found that opening trade with industrial countries is effective in increasing the total factor productivity of a developing country, and that with whom the trade is conducted is also important (Coe, Helpman and Hoffmaister, 1995). This is one of the reasons for the rapid growth of Korea and Taiwan in both the prewar and the postwar period. The Korean and Taiwanese cases are exemplary. In the prewar era, Japan invested heavily in Korea and Taiwan (Mizoguchi and Yamamoto, 1984) and they traded almost exclusively with Japan, although one may say they were exploited by Japan. After the war, Japan continued to be the major trading partner of Korea and Taiwan until the mid-1960s, and then the United States became another major trading partner of the two countries after the mid-1960s. The foundation of human capital and social infrastructure built before the war,[15] and which continued after the war; the continuation of trading with Japan, the world's second-largest and rapidly growing economy, as the major source of capital equipment and intermediate raw materials; and the opening of the vast and growing market of the United States, the largest economy in the world, undoubtedly catapulted these two countries into extremely rapid growth (Hsiao and Hsiao, 1996). As discussed below, Korea and Taiwan have indeed been fortunate to associate with the United States and Japan, their two distinguished neighbors, in trade and economy. We have called their relationship the Pacific trade triangle, which is the major driving force of the growth of Korea and Taiwan (Hsiao and Hsiao, 1996; Hsiao, 1998; Twu, 1995).

7.3 Long-Run Comparisons of Taiwanese and Korean Development

Figures 7.1 and 7.2 are rather cluttered and it is hard to make a detailed individual comparison of them. We now select real GDP per capita of six countries: Korea (K), Taiwan (T), Japan (J), the United States (U), the Netherlands (N) and China (C). They are presented in logarithmic scale in Figure 7.3. The Netherlands is included since, in addition to its colonial relation with Taiwan in the early seventeenth century, its area and population are very similar to those of Taiwan.[16] Several interesting features come out of Figure 7.3.

---

15 These include an extensive irrigation system, effective farm organizations, pervasive educational system, massive electric generating facilities and extensive transportation and communication networks (Hsiao and Hsiao, 1996, 219–21. Also, see Chapter 5 of this book). Naturally, institutional reforms were not affected by physical damage inflicted by the wars in Korea and Taiwan.

16 The Dutch ruled Taiwan from 1624–62 and introduced Taiwan to global trade in the seventeenth century (Hsiao and Hsiao, 2002a). The area and population of the Netherlands in mid-1978 were 41,000 km² and 14 million, respectively, while that of Taiwan were 36,000 km² and 17 million, respectively (see WDR (1980, 111)).

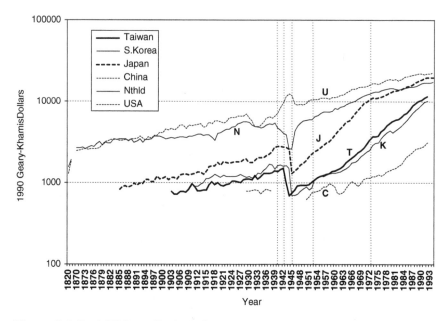

Figure 7.3 Real GDP per Capita in Log Scale (gdppc Series)

7.3.1 Slow postwar recovery

In an earlier paper (Hsiao and Hsiao, 1998), we observed that the Taiwanese standard of living did not recover to the prewar peak until the mid-1960s.[17] In Figure 7.3, Maddison's data also confirm that Taiwanese real GDP per capita in Geary–Khamis dollars reached the prewar peak in 1942 ($1,522) and did not fully recover until 1963 ($1,612). Korea's recovery was late for three more years. Its real GDP per capita did not recover until 1966 ($1,738) to the prewar peak of 1941 ($1,649), due to its being interrupted by the Korean War. According to Maddison (1995, 19), the world's "best performance was in the postwar golden age 1950–73 when per capita income improved dramatically in all regions, the second best was 1870–1913, and the third best 1973–92." Unlike Japan, which recovered quickly to the prewar peak of 1940 ($2,765) in

---

17 Wu's data (1995, 635) show that real GDP per capita in NT$ reached the prewar peak in 1939 and recovered only in 1965. Also see Figure 7.2 in Hsiao and Hsiao (1998). The prolonged recovery of real GDP per capita was partly due to the sudden influx of Chinese refugees in and after 1949 and the natural increase in the Taiwanese population. This is indicated by the fact that the aggregate level of real GDP recovered to the prewar peak much earlier, in 1954, in Wu's estimation (1995, 636) (also see Hsiao and Hsiao, 1998, Figure 1) and Maddison's estimation (1995, 191).

1956 ($2,868), as indicated in Figure 7.3, the best performance of Korea and Taiwan occurred only after the mid-1960s. Thus, international comparisons reveal that, in the early stage of the postwar era, Taiwanese and Korean economic growth stumbled and did not take the full advantage of the postwar "golden age."

7.3.2 The take-off point

Figure 7.3 reveals that the postwar accelerated growth, or the take-off of the economy, apparently occurred shortly after Japan, Korea and Taiwan recovered from the prewar peak performance: The acceleration of growth started at the mid-1950s for Japan, the mid-1960s for Taiwan, and the late-1960s for Korea. The later takeoff of Korea can be explained by the effect of the Korean War and the country's unstable political system. The sequence shows the East Asian "flying-geese pattern" of economic development. In contrast, the United States reached its prewar peak in 1944 ($12,348), a year before the war ended, and reattained its peak only in 1964 ($12,687) and after. In contrast, the Netherlands achieved its prewar peak around 1939 and then plunged to only about one-half of the prewar peak level in 1945, but recovered very quickly within four years in 1949 and after. While there is a different story for every country, the postwar recovery of the Korean and Taiwanese economies to their prewar peak did not occur soon. The column of the Transition Period in Table 7.1 shows that, while damage to the Taiwanese economy was almost the same as that to the Japanese economy, Taiwan's recovery was delayed considerably compared with Japan, the industrial base of which suffered as much, if not more, damage during the war.

7.3.3 The Korea–Taiwan reversal

Figure 7.3 also shows that real GDP per capita of Korea and Taiwan has been consistently lower than that of Japan throughout the prewar and postwar eras. Real GDP per capita of Japan, in turn, has been consistently lower than that of the United States, although Japan's nominal GDP per capita was already about 10% (in 1990) or 5% (in 1999) higher than that of the United States (WDR, 1992, 2000/2001). Korea's growth is very much similar to that of Taiwan: they have grown together. However, a distinct pattern appears between the prewar and postwar times: Korea's real GDP per capita was uniformly higher than that of Taiwan in the prewar period (except 1932), but consistently lower than that of Taiwan after 1945 in the postwar period (except 1953–55). The figures show that their differences seem to be increasing, although they tended to be constant after the mid-1980s.

The reason for the reversal of real GDP per capita of the two countries in the prewar and postwar periods is not clear.[18] One plausible explanation, however, is that when Japan annexed Korea, Korea was an independent state that was not far behind Japan in economic, political and social levels (Cumings, 1984, 486–88 and 491). After annexation, the colonial government in Korea invested largely in manufacturing and mining, relying on large capital inflow and subsidies from Japan (Mizoguchi and Yamamoto, 1984, 407 and 411). Rapid industrialization[19] in Korea during the 1930s as compared with slower and later industrialization in Taiwan kept Korea's real GDP per capita higher than that of Taiwan. But Korea's electricity industry was built in the northern region, and Korea had a much smaller agricultural sector and ineffective agricultural policy (Mizoguchi and Yamamoto, 1984, 406–7).

In contrast, the colonial government in Taiwan invested heavily in the agricultural sector and produced a large trade surplus (Mizoguchi and Yamamoto, 1984). By the end of the 1930s, Taiwan already was one of the most advanced agricultural countries, if not the most advanced one, in the world.[20] Taiwan's success in modernizing its agricultural sector in the prewar era and continued development of that sector after the war until the mid-1960s built a sound foundation for the industrialization of Taiwan after 1970. Thus, the division of Korea into North and South Korea after the war, the deprivation of industrial bases and the inheritance of a weak agricultural sector made Korea disadvantaged compared with Taiwan in the postwar era.

Recently, Hsiao and Park (2002) compared the productivity performance of the Korean and Taiwanese manufacturing industries at matched manufacturing sectors. They found that, using the data for 1979–96, the output productivity growth of the Korean manufacturing industry came more from efficiency improvement than from technical change, and the productivity improvement of the Taiwanese manufacturing industry occurred more from technical change. Since modern economic growth is closely related to technical progress in the

---

18 The case of Korea and Taiwan is not unique. The same reversal occurred between the United States and the United Kingdom, and the United States and Australia in the early twentieth century (see Maddison, 1995, 28).

19 For Korean society and industrialization, see Cumings (1984, 487) and Eckert (1991). "Japan was the only imperial power that systematically built up an industrial colonial economy in its colonial empire" (Osterhammel, 1995, 79).

20 According to Hsiao (1997, 507), by the end of the 1930s, the world ranking of Taiwan's production was as follows: bananas and canned pineapple ranked third; sugar and sweet potatoes fourth; tea sixth; rice and peanuts tenth; and salt thirteenth. Indeed, few countries in the world were endowed with so many kinds of products in such large quantities. The highly developed Taiwanese agricultural sector sustained the Taiwanese economy in the face of a massive influx of Chinese refugees in the 1950s, and catapulted it to rapid growth in the 1960s and 1970s.

manufacturing industry, this provides another explanation of the slower real GDP per capita growth of Korea as compared with that of Taiwan.

7.3.4 On the war damage

Another feature revealed by international comparisons in Figure 7.3 is that, as expected, the Korean economy fared better than the Taiwanese economy during World War II, as it escaped the Allied bombing.[21] Due to Allied air raids, wartime misallocation and encirclement by Allied forces, Taiwan's industrial output had almost came to a halt by 1945 when Japan surrendered, although it quickly recovered to 20% and 38% of the 1937 industrial output level in the following two years (Hsiao and Hsiao, 1996, 219). The Taiwanese real GDP per capita reached its prewar highest level in 1942 at $1,522, started declining precipitously in the following year to $1,011 and then reached its lowest level in 1944 at $693.

We have estimated that Taiwan's war damage (replacement cost) due to Allied air raids up to December 1945, was 40%–50% of its 1945 GNP, and that civilian causalities were 16,000–30,000 persons. The damage (replacement cost) to major industrial facilities was estimated as $506 million in Taiwan dollars, which was 42% of the value of the total fix assets in manufacturing at that time.[22] The decline of the Taiwanese standard of living started in 1942, two years before the end of the war, and unlike Japan, but like Korea, as we have observed before, the recovery was painfully slow until the mid-1960s.[23]

---

21 The major reason that Allied bombing took place in the agrarian Taiwan rather than the more industrialized Korea is that the original plan called for the Allied invasion of Japan to be staged in Taiwan, not Okinawa (Kerr, 1965, 28–33). Furthermore, Taiwan was the operating base of Japan's Southward Movement during World War II (Kerr, 1965, 29; Hsiao and Hsiao, 2002a, 183). The Korean economy was not damaged by the Allied air raids during World War II.

22 No official total estimation is available for Taiwan. According to Chang (1999, 172–73), by the end of December 1945, the total damage to factories, utilities and other tangible assets was about $729 million Taiwan dollars, and to private houses about $952 million. The level of nominal GDP in 1945 is estimated as $3,906 million (real GDP = $314 million) x (GDP deflator = 1241.7) / 100) (see Wu, 1995, 635). Thus the total damage is estimated, conservatively, as 43% of 1945 GDP. There is no indication on the unit of money (New Taiwan $ or Old Taiwan $) in Chang. We took it as New Taiwan Dollar (1NT$ = 40,000 OT$). According to the government-general, the casualties of the air raids were about 16,000 persons, and among them, 6,100 died and 435 were missing. Chang (1999, 161–62) states that these figures were greatly underestimated.

23 In addition to the misallocation of wartime resources and the distortion of a wartime economy, the expatriation of Japanese skilled labor, the discontinuity of imports and exports from Japan and postwar confusion, the inefficiency of huge public enterprises and government corruption and instability played an important role in economic decline in postcolonial Korea and Taiwan (Brown, 1973, 30; Hsiao and Hsiao, 1996, 222–24). Szczepanik (1958, 5), comparing the slow economic growth of Taiwan in the 1950s with that of Hong Kong, ably observed that the Chinese who were "the newcomers to Taiwan [...] had difficulty in merging with the predominantly Fukienese

In contrast, the Korean real GDP per capita inexplicably plunged below the Taiwanese economy in 1945 to $687, from a high of $1,484 in 1944, but started a slight and slow recovery after 1946. The Korean War (1950– 53), which devastated almost the entire Korean economy, did not damage the level of Korean real GDP per capita as much as we might have expected. It was estimated that during 1950–53, the civilian causalities were close to one million and the civilian war damages were from 86% to 200% of the 1953 GNP,[24] and 42%–44% of prewar manufacturing facilities were destroyed (Kim and Roemer, 1979, 30–33). Nevertheless, Korean real GDP per capita even slightly exceeded that of Taiwan during 1953–55 (as can be barely seen from Figures 7.2 or 7.3), the only three years of such better performance of Korea after World War II.

While many scholars have some reservations about, or simply dismiss, the comparability of the Korean and the Taiwanese economies due to Korea's experience of devastating war in the early 1950s, it appears that both Korea and Taiwan were on the same footing by the mid-1950s, and thus we may justify a one-to-one comparison of the process of economic development of these two countries.

7.3.5 Japanese legacy

We have shown statistically in the previous section that Korea and Taiwan had already achieved an "economic miracle" in the Prewar Period. Why this was the case, and what is the extent to which a Japanese legacy actually remained when both countries experienced another dramatic growth in the Postwar Period, are very important questions to ask. This is a controversial topic, as evidenced by Kohli (1994) and Haggard et al. (1997), and was in fact one of our major concerns in the case of Taiwan elsewhere (Hsiao and Hsiao, 1996, 1998, 2002a, b). For our purpose in this chapter, we present an overview of the literature with an emphasis on prewar and postwar linkages.

We note first that Japan's humiliating treaty of extraterritoriality with the world powers ended only in 1899, and that its treaty tariffs were terminated in 1910. As the latest newcomer among the colonial powers, Japan had a vested interest in showing off the difference between its "Asiatic" colonialism and the

---

indigenous population, speaking a different language and thinking in different political terms […] the refugees who went to Taiwan were […] a group ready to rule or fight but not to work."

24 Korean population in 1953 was 20.8 million (vs. 8.8 million for Taiwan), and its real GDP in 1990 Geary–Khamis dollars was $24 billion (vs. 10.4 billion for Taiwan) (see Maddison, 1995, 115 and 191).

"exploitative" Western colonialism (Itaya, 1997, 90–91 and 94; Peattie, 1984, 14). Thus, the Japanese felt the need to derive prestige from developing their colonial societies and economies. In later years, Japan's military expansionism forced it to build industries in the colonies. While imposing humiliation, discrimination, exploitation and authoritarianism on the colonial people, the colonial governments at the same time improved health and technical education and created modern industries, facilities and institutions (Peattie, 1984, 42–43 and 47), which Japan itself had experienced in the early Meiji era.

Kohli (1994, 1279) asserts that "Japanese colonialism in Korea helped establish […] [a] highly bureaucratized, penetrating and architectonic state, and a state-dominated alliance of state and property owners for production and profits, and repressive social control of the working classes," which survived more than a 15-year interlude. Then, "South Korea under Park Chung-Hee fell back into the grooves of colonial origins, and traveled along them, well into the 1980's" (ibid., 1269). Under the development state of Park,[25] the government nurtured and colluded with chaebols. With help from Japanese capital and technology,[26] chaebols have become the vanguard of capitalistic development under strict control of labor.

In Taiwan, political continuity ensued immediately. The Japanese colonial regime was replaced by the Chinese émigré regime[27] after the war. The

25 Haggard et al. (1997) questioned the influence of Japan after such a long elapse of time. But according to Eckert, Lee, Lew, Robinson and Wagner (1990, 392), "the ROK-Japan Normalization Treaty […] in 1965, was […] a resumption of a historic relationship under new condition […] South Korean official and private contacts with Japanese counterparts mushroomed, with Japanese speaking Korean bureaucrats and businessmen of colonial vintage leading the way and working through a network of ex-colonial officials in Japan […]. Park, […] who was himself an elite product of the colonial military system, […] deeply influenced both intellectually and emotionally by his training during Japan's period of Asian military-industrial supremacy, […] to continue this process after seizing power in 1961." This was also the case for businessmen (but not for the Chinese bureaucrats) in Taiwan (Hsiao and Hsiao, 1996, 268, 274 and 284–85). This point is generally neglected in the literature. Note that Mason, Kim, Perkins, Kim and Cole (1980, 86) observed that the long chaotic interlude "was also partly the heritage of Japanese colonialism. At a crucial point in Korean history, Koreans had been deprived of the opportunity to develop effective political institutions of their own."

26 See Eckert et al. (1990, 392–94 and 411–12), Eckert (1991, 254–59) and Cho and Kim (1991, 9).

27 Cheng and Haggard (1992, 3) wrote that "the new political order in Taiwan in the immediate postwar period resembled in many ways a colonial one. An outside power, the KMT, established political control over the domestic politics of subject people largely excluded from political representation." With the rise of Taiwanese identity and nationalism, although few want to acknowledge it, the new regime is merely another colonial regime (like South Africa), and it started to crumble only slowly after Teng-hui Lee, who is, like Chung-Hee Park, of Japanese "colonial vintage," was elected democratically as the President of Taiwan in 1996.

Chinese government confiscated the Japanese-owned public and private firms and banks, and combined and converted them into 50 or so public (government or Kuomintang, that is, KMT) enterprises, managed and controlled by non-Taiwanese-speaking, mostly incompetent, retired Chinese generals and refugees (Hsiao and Hsiao, 1996, 238).

In view of imminent Chinese communist invasions, martial law was declared in 1949, and the government maintained a strictly controlled wartime colonial economy inherited from the Japanese regime (Chen, 1996; Hsiao and Hsiao, 1996, 234–38 and 242–43; Huang, 1996; Twu, 1975, 499). At the same time, the new regime rebuilt and expanded industry on the foundation of the world-class agricultural sector that was established during the Japanese period (Hsiao, 1997; Hsiao and Hsiao, 2002a).

Like Korea, after a 15-year interlude, in the early 1960s the government moved from an import-substitution policy, which was an extension and expansion of the Japanese policy before the end of World War II (Hsiao and Hsiao, 1996, 230), to an export-promotion policy under US influence (Hsiao and Hsiao, 1996, 239). As in the Japanese period, and like the postwar Korea, the success of the export-expansion policy in the 1960s and the 1970s depended on strict control of farmers and workers (Deyo, 1989), and both countries benefited from the postwar formation of the Japan–Taiwan/Korea–US Pacific trade triangle (Hsiao and Hsiao, 1996, 258–69).

Unlike in Korea, the very nature of the émigré regime kept the local Taiwanese enterprises small and fragmented (Hsiao and Hsiao, 1996, 276–84; Hsiao and Hsiao, 1999, 498). Many of the Taiwanese business elite, the *laobans*, read Japanese and were mostly alienated from the non-Taiwanese-speaking government bureaucrats (Numazaki, 1997). Thus, once contact with Japan was re-established, as with South Korea's elite, Japan "continued to be a source of the latest information on everything from fashion to economic trends and industrial technology" (Eckert et al., 1990, 392). Japan has been the major provider of joint venture and technology transfer, and the model for emulation (Hsiao and Hsiao, 1996, 274 and 285). Eventually, the *laobans* became the leaders of Taiwan's export drive (Hsiao and Hsiao, 1996, 280; 1999, 475–77) and catapulted the Taiwanese economy into rapid growth.

More importantly, the Japanese legacy of institutional reforms, in addition to the construction of tangible assets and infrastructures, has remained crucial to prewar and postwar economic and social development in both countries. These reforms include eradication of infectious diseases, attention to public health and private hygiene, the upholding of law and order, respect for manual labor and technical education, habits of keeping time and being on time and so on.[28] These reforms were enforced through schools, factories and police actions. By the end of World War II, 81% of the boys and 61% of the girls (or 71% on average) among Taiwanese school-aged children were enrolled in primary schools (Hsiao and Hsiao, 1996, 220). The corresponding average primary school enrollment for South Korea was a respectable 48%.[29] By 1942, about 57% of the Taiwanese population spoke Japanese, while in Korea, the literacy rate was 22%.[30]

In 1941, there were about 130,000 Taiwanese manufacturing factory workers working in about 8,000 factories.[31] In contrast, in 1940, there were nearly 300,000 Korean factory workers in Korea working in 7,142 factories.[32] They consisted of about 2.4% and 1.3% of the population in Taiwan and Korea, respectively. The percentage may not be large, but the point is that Taiwan and Korea were left with a "substantial cadre of experienced workers," "residing

---

28 Hsiao and Hsiao (2002a) and Cho and Kim (1991, 2–13). Huer (1989, 7) lists reform programs that included virtually every aspect of traditional Korea: abolition of social class, slavery, early marriage and class privilege; permission for the *yangban* to participate in business and for widows to remarry; and use of merit and qualification as the basis of official appointment. In Taiwan, hygiene includes no spitting, having clean toilets and so forth to ensure a healthy labor supply. The statement of these institutional reforms during the Japanese period is now included in middle school textbooks in Taiwan.

29 Kimura (1997, 49). The enrollment ratio surged considerably immediately after the war, to 87%, and the literacy rate to 88%, in 1955, showing the resistance of Koreans against the forced Japanese education (ibid. 49). For comparison with India on institutional reform under colonialism, see Hsiao and Hsiao (2002b).

30 See Wu (1992), which is his PhD thesis submitted to the National Taiwan Normal University in 1986. Wu estimated the ratio indirectly by using the number of graduates of the primary schools plus the graduates of Japanese language classes minus current primary school enrollment. This is close to the figure of 53% obtained directly from the 1940 Population Census; see Ho (1978, 322). The Korean figure is from Kimura (1997, 49).

31 This number is derived as follows. In 1938, there were 7,291 Taiwanese-owned factories employing 47,800 workers, and 719 Japanese-owned factories employing 45,900 workers (Mizoguchi and Umemura, 1988, 52). Assuming 10% of Japanese-owned factory workers were Japanese, we estimate that there were 90,000 Taiwanese factory workers in that year. By the end of 1941, total manufacturing workers increased to 138,000 (Ho, 1978, 329). If, as in 1938, about half of them were working for the Japanese-owned factories, then there were about 130,000 Taiwanese factory workers.

32 Factories for Taiwan and Korea are here defined as a factory that employs five or more employees, or a factory that uses power or has enough facility to employ five or more workers (Mizoguchi and Umemura, 1988, 51). The number of Korean factories comes from Mizoguchi and Umemura (1988), and the number of Korean factory workers from Mason et al. (1980, 77). The population of Taiwan in 1941 was 5.5 million (Ho, 1978, 312), and of Korea in 1941 was 23.5 million (Mason et al., 1980).

in cities and often employed in modern sectors," facts that were not seen in many other African and Southeast Asian countries after the war (Mason et al., 1980, 77–79). These students and workers were indeed the stock of human capital available for postwar development.

7.4 Falling behind the Japanese Growth

This and the following section discuss that there are great differences among the miraculous Far Eastern Countries. We have pointed out that real income per capita of Taiwan lagged behind that of Japan during the postwar era, despite the "miraculous" development (Hsiao and Hsiao, 1996, 220 and 231). The income referred to in the previous papers was in nominal US dollars. Wu (1995, 616) compared long-run real GDP per capita between Taiwan and Japan by converting Japanese yen into New Taiwan dollars. He found that the real GDP per capita ratio of Taiwan over that of Japan showed a decreasing trend until 1970 and that it turned upward afterward.[33]

This section shows that this finding still holds when the real GDP per capita of Taiwan is measured in international dollars. Furthermore, we demonstrate that our international comparisons have revealed that Taiwan is not unique, as Korea also had the same experience. In the next section, we extend the comparisons to Hong Kong and Singapore.

It may be argued that, by the end of the 1930s and beyond, Japan was so well developed that it does not make sense to compare Korea and Taiwan with Japan. However, that argument is spurious and historically naive. In fact, Japan, along with Korea and Taiwan, was one of the 74 underdeveloped countries in the survey sample of Adelman and Morris (1967, 10). According to Maddison's data (1995), real GDP per capita of Canada surpassed that of the United Kingdom in 1945, and so did that of the United States as early as 1905, that of Australia in 1965 and that of New Zealand in 1981–84.

The catching-up process of Japan was much more dramatic. After ending the treaty of extraterritoriality in 1899 and treaty tariffs in 1910, Japan surpassed Russia in 1961, Ireland in 1963, Finland in 1969, Italy in 1971, the United Kingdom in 1980, the Netherlands in 1983, France and Norway in 1988, Denmark and Sweden in 1989, Canada in 1991 and, finally, Germany in 1992. In turn, Hong Kong exceeded Japan in 1987–92, and Singapore surpassed Japan after 1995.

---

33 Wu's calculation (1995, 636) shows that T/J reached as low as 25% in 1970, and that it was merely 44% in 1990.

Even with its enormous economic, political and military dominance, real GDP per capita in 1992 US dollars was outperformed by Norway, Denmark, Sweden, Japan and Switzerland (WDR, 1994, 163). Indeed, international economic competitiveness does not depend on military prowess, the size of territory or population, or even possession of natural resources.

Thus, while we are fully aware of the difference in the initial conditions of past exploited/exploiter relations, there is no reason to believe that Korea and Taiwan will never be able to surpass their former colonial power, Japan, and it will be interesting to see how the economies of these two countries evolve compared with that of Japan. In the early 2000s, the possibility of their catching up has seemed more likely, in view of the fact that the Japanese bubble economy collapsed in 1992 and still was unable to recover fully in 2002, while the performance of the Taiwanese and Korean economies continued to remain strong before and after the recent financial crisis in 1997–98 (Hsiao and Hsiao, 2001a).

7.4.1 Real GDP per capita ratios

Figure 7.4 presents comparisons of real GDP per capita ratios, and indirectly real GDP ratios, in international dollars. The two curves with triangle and

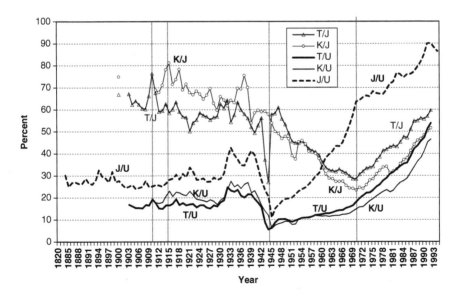

Figure 7.4 GDP per Capita Ratios in East Asia

circle markers in the upper part of Figure 7.4 present the ratios of Taiwanese and Korean real GDP per capita (denoted as T and K) by taking that of Japan (J) as 100 (T/J, or K/J). They show that Taiwan's real GDP per capita reached about 75% of Japan's in 1910, and that of Korea reached 81% of Japan's in 1915, both in the early period of Japanese occupation. Figure 7.2 illustrates that, compared with other countries at the beginning of modern economic growth, all three countries had low levels of GDP per capita and the differences among them were small.

In the prewar period, both ratios of real GDP per capita, T/J and K/J, fluctuated with a tendency toward decreasing gradually, especially for Korea. But Taiwan maintained an average of 58%, ranging from 49% in 1940 to 75% in 1910. Korea's ratios are generally higher: it had an average of 68%, ranging from 54% in 1939 to 81% in 1915.

While nationalists attribute the declining trend to colonial exploitation, it is also due to the difference in population growth and social and economic conditions. In view of our finding of the dynamic and rapid development of Korean and Taiwanese economies during the Prewar Period in Table 7.1 as compared with other countries in the world, and the fact that the ratios slipped further even after liberation from Japanese colonialism, we submit that the explanation of colonial exploitation alone is not sufficient, or even relevant.

7.4.2 The transition period

The uniqueness of the Taiwanese economy among these three countries is shown unequivocally during the Transition Period. Admittedly, Taiwan, Korea and Japan all experienced a change in regime in 1945, and all three economies were distorted and devastated by the war as shown in Figure 7.3. But in terms of the ratios of real GDP per capita, as compared to average growth rates of GDP per capita, Korea was able to maintain a relatively stable transition as compared with Japan, while Taiwan suffered much more than Japan or Korea.

Taiwan's welfare relative to that of Japan, as measured by the real GDP per capita ratio, plummeted deeply in 1944 (only 27% of that of Japan), recovered rapidly in 1945 (58%), and even increased in the following two years. After 1947, the ratios deteriorated again rapidly. In addition to the possible exhaustion of resources alluded to at the end of the last section, mismanagement of the economy (Wu, 1997), a misguided ideology of state capitalism (Kirby, 1990; Liu, 1975) and exploitation of the economy for China's civil war efforts before and long after 1949 by Taiwan's government (Glass, 1963) are some major causes of the Taiwanese suffering.

7.4.3 A common turning point

As shown in Figure 7.4, the real GDP per capita ratios for both Korea and Taiwan relative to Japan dipped continuously and considerably after the war until both reached their lowest points, 29% for Taiwan and 23% for Korea, in the same year of 1970. After 1970, both ratios then turned upward simultaneously and increased steadily. By 1992, Taiwan just barely surpassed its prewar average (60%),[34] but Korea (52%) still lagged far behind the prewar average.

Up to now, scholars have tended to compare the postwar developments and argue that Korea and Taiwan are "small" economies, not comparable to a large economy like Japan, thus taking it for granted that they could never catch up with Japan. Here, our long-run comparisons show that they not only did not catch up, after 50 years of independence from Japanese colonialism, but also even fell behind the record of average relative income ratios that they had attained previously during the prewar time. Furthermore, considering many smaller European countries that have higher real GDP per capita than that of Japan, and considering the Korean and Taiwanese ability to turn upward and grow faster than Japan after 1970, Korea and Taiwan could have caught up or even surpassed Japan shortly after World War II.

Comparing real GDP per capita of Korea, Taiwan and Japan with that of the United States reinforces our observations on their ability. While the real GDP per capita ratios of Korea and Taiwan relative to Japan declined immediately after the war, the real GDP per capita ratios relative to the United States (heavy and light solid lines in the lower part of Figure 7.4) increased gradually over 1945–70 and accelerated after 1970. This implies that Korea and Taiwan have demonstrated the ability to catch up with the United States, not only in the prewar period but also in the postwar period (see Table 7.1).

Note that the real GDP per capita ratios of Japan relative to the United States (the heavy dotted line) accelerated immediately after the war. Thus, considering the high degree of development achieved since the prewar period, as indicated in Figure 7.1 and Table 7.1, the real GDP per capita levels of Korea and Taiwan could have surpassed that of Japan. In fact, the postwar average growth rates of the real GDP per capita of both countries exceeded that of Japan (Table 7.1), and we may expect this trend to continue.

---

34 Wu (1995, 616–617, 636) shows that, measured in New Taiwan dollars, Taiwan did much better in the Japanese period. During 1911–42, Taiwan's real GDP per capita was, on average, 70% of that of Japan.

7.5. International and Domestic Environments

The synchronous turning point of Korea and Taiwan relative to Japan in 1970 seems to suggest that the economic growth of the two countries was most likely due to external factors rather than to the significant consequence of any particular domestic economic policy. This observation can be corroborated from other international data and the development of Hong Kong and Singapore around the 1970s, the other two rapidly growing economies in Asia in the postwar period, but with quite opposite economic policy orientations.

7.5.1 Performance of Asian NIEs vis-à-vis Japan

Based on the data from the Penn World Table (PWT5.6, 1994) that uses international dollars with the base year at 1985, Figure 7.5 shows the postwar real GDP per capita ratios of Hong Kong, Singapore, Taiwan and Korea relative to Japan.[35] It indicates that all four of these newly industrializing economies (NIEs) had their lowest GDP per capita ratios during 1968–70: Taiwan, 30% in 1970; Hong Kong, 62% in 1970; Korea, 22% in 1969; and Singapore, 40% in 1968. After these benchmark years, the ratios turned unequivocally upward and continued increasing, although not as dramatically as the ratios shown in Maddison's data[36] in Figure 7.4.

It is very difficult to consider such a coincidence either as random or as a deliberate coordinated act among the governments of the NIEs. There may be many explanatory factors. The timing of the turnaround in the early 1970s also coincided with the loosening of political control and the beginning of democracy in Taiwan (Moody, 1992, 6). At the same time, the basic ideology of free market and private investment, which was strongly advocated by the US Agency of International Development in Taiwan, gained momentum in the 1970s.[37]

---

35   PWT5.6 (1994). There are several definitions of GDP per capita in PWT5.7. The difference is minimal for the three countries. Here we take RGDPCH, that is, "real GDP per capita in constant dollars (chain index) expressed in international prices, base 1985."

36   The PWT data show that Hong Kong surpassed Japan in 1987, and that by 1992, it was 9% over Japan, but that Singapore was still 84% of Japan. Korea and Taiwan are very similar to the results from Maddison's data: their 1990 real GDP per capita was about 56% and 47% of Japan, respectively.

37   Hsiao and Hsiao (1996, 239). In Taiwan, "Emphasis on State-led, import-substituting, defense-related heavy industrial growth dominated until the late 1950s [...] A cautious, if not hostile, attitude toward private foreign investment lasted until the late 1960s [...] Strong protection of key import substitutes has continued until the 1980s" (see Kirby, 1990, 136).

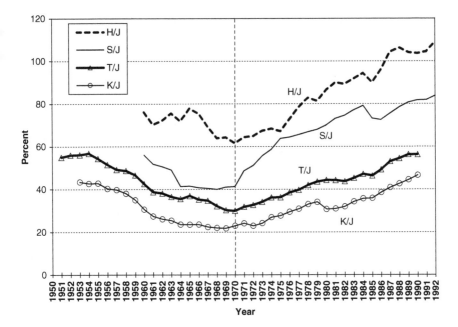

Figure 7.5 Relative Performance to Japan
Hong Kong, Singapore, Taiwan and Korea (Japan = 100)

In Korea, the government initiated the New Community Movement in the rural sector in 1971 and emphasized heavy and chemical industries instead of light industries in the urban sector (Pae, 1992, 90–91). A series of financial and investment laws were enacted in the early 1970s in Korea to encourage domestic saving and foreign direct investment (Pae, 1992, 93–96).

The international economic environment also led to the upgrading of exports of these four economies from labor-intensive products to technology and capital-intensive products in trade with Japan and the United States (what we called the Pacific trade triangle) from the late 1960s to the early 1970s (Chow and Kellman, 1993, 17). This transition made the year 1970 a landmark.

7.5.2 The world development

The most plausible explanation of simultaneous turnaround in 1970 could be changes in the international economic environment. The early 1970s were the threshold of a new world economy. In the 1960s, the major technological development was in the area of resource-intensive heavy and chemical industries. In the early 1970s, however, the world experienced the first oil price crisis (1973), and industrial development plans based on cheap oil were no longer feasible.

The 1970s were the beginning of the era of energy saving as well as resource-saving high-tech industries. It was the era of electronics and computers. Japan was the most successful country to transform from the development of steel and iron, shipbuilding and household electric equipment in the 1960s to that of small automobiles and electronics in the 1970s (Aoki, 1987).

The Japanese success set an example for the Taiwanese as well as the Koreans (Hsiao and Hsiao, 1996, 284; Eckert et al., 1990, 408) and spilled over to Korea and Taiwan through the rapid increase in foreign direct investment[38] from Japan and the United States and their ever-increasing imports. The subsequent formation of the Pacific trade triangle, the Japan–Asian NIEs–United States trade nexus,[39] helped the economic success of Asian NIEs. This is the major factor in the simultaneous upward trend of the economic tide of the Asian NIEs vis-à-vis the Japanese economy in 1970 and after.

On the other hand, the Japanese economy experienced a slowdown in the early 1970s and later. This can be seen clearly from the heavy dotted line (J) in Figure 7.3. The slowdown, however, was a world phenomenon among the advanced capitalist countries, as the real GDP per capita levels of all other OECD countries also declined.[40] The collapse of the Bretton Woods fixed exchange rate system, the emergence of strong inflationary expectations, the two oil price shocks and so on were given as reasons for the worldwide slowdown (Maddison, 1991, 177).

In Japan, 1957–69 was the period of an upswing, the "era of rapid economic growth" (Kosai, 1986, 4; Minami, 1986, 48), and it reached its postwar peak in 1970 (Shinohara, 1991, 132). Labor shortage and the narrowing of income differentials became pronounced after 1968 (Kosai, 1986, 140).

---

38 To avoid the evaluation of yen after the "Nixon Shock" of opening relations with China (1972), Japanese exporting companies went offshore. Japanese private outward foreign direct investment (FDI) was more than doubled in one year, from US$ 0.9 billion in 1971 to US$ 2.3 billion in 1972, and the FDI cases were also doubled from 904 cases to 1,774 cases in the same period, and were nearly doubled again to 3,097 cases in 1973. The bulk of FDI went to Asian NIEs, followed by ASEAN countries. The amount of FDI increased steadily afterward (see SEC, 1989, 10–11).

39 Hsiao and Hsiao (1996) and Twu (1995). Economic historians also note this trade nexus, e.g., see Coates (2000, 237 and 239) on the role of the US home market and Japanese capital in the East Asian miracle.

40 Maddison (1991, 128). It may also be related to the underperformance of the US economy as the United States has been Japan's largest export market. For debating US underperformance, see the survey in Coates (2000, 32–36).

Furthermore, as a resource-poor country, Japan was probably the hardest hit by the two oil price shocks during the 1970s and the early 1980s. Thus, in summary, in the 1960s, the slow economic recovery of the Asian NIEs and the rapid growth of the Japanese and world economies contributed to the relative decline of the Taiwanese and the Korean economies. After 1970, however, the rapid growth of Korea and Taiwan and the slowdown of the Japanese and world economies contributed to the upward trend of the income ratios for both Korea and Taiwan vis-à-vis Japan.

7.5.3 Why did Korea and Taiwan fall behind Japan?

Finally, a comparison of the GDP per capita ratios between Figure 7.4 and those in Figure 7.5 is revealing. Figure 7.5 alone cannot reveal the peaks of the relative income ratios achieved in the prewar period. For all the talk of miraculous growth in Korea and Taiwan, the continuous losses of the income ratios relative to Japan of these two countries in the postwar period before 1970 is puzzling. Cumings (1984, 492) seems to blame it on the conservative but powerful Korean landlords, who survived during the colonial period and prevented rapid changes in the rural social structure after the war until the 1960s.

Korean economists, like most scholars in Taiwan, also tend to marginalize (Kim and Roemer, 1979, 20), if not negate (Song, 1990, 38–42) or even ignore (Sakong, 1993, 1), the economic achievements of the Japanese colonial period (Haggard et al., 1997; Kohli, 1994). They attribute the postwar declining income ratios to Japanese colonial exploitation during the prewar period. But the steep relative deterioration in the postwar period is still hard to explain. One might argue that detrimental colonial institutions and heritage had plagued Korea and Taiwan long after the end of colonialism, and/or the sudden departure of Japanese administrators and skilled personnel.[41] This argument does not seem plausible, however. In view of the ever-changing international competitiveness among countries alluded to above, it is not clear why, after almost 50 years of emancipation from Japanese colonialism, Korea, and for that matter, Taiwan, are still unable to reach the real GDP per capita ratios that they achieved during the colonial period.

For Taiwan, an explanation by Wu (1995, 623) is more specific. He suggests that the Japanese wrongly developed the sugar industry in Taiwan through strenuous government protection.[42] Sugar and its by-products became the

---

41 This argument contradicts the assertion that, in the case of Korea, skilled labor fled from the North to the South during the Korean War, or that, in the case of Taiwan, the Chinese who fled from China filled in the gap left by the Japanese.

42 Twu (1975, 14) called this the "dependent" and "malformed" development of the Taiwanese economy under colonialism. No explanation was given. In fact, the

predominant industry in Taiwan in the early prewar period. He argues that the KMT government not only wrongly continued the same policy in the postwar period but also reorganized the industry as a public enterprise and monopolized sugar production completely, resulting in enormous inefficiency. As the sugar industry declined after the war, so did manufactured outputs based on the sugar industry, delaying the recovery of the manufacturing industry until the mid-1960s (Wu, 1995). The argument is interesting, but it does not seem to be convincing.

Elsewhere (Hsiao, 1997) we have argued that the Japanese developed agriculture, especially the sugar industry, in Taiwan not because Taiwan was its colony but because Taiwan had comparative advantages in agriculture. Taiwan's early industrialization also started with the developing of supporting industries for the sugar industry. After all, with the prewar world technology and poor natural resources, what else could Taiwanese industry specialize in at the initial stage of industrialization? It might be argued that Taiwan should not have relied so much and so long on the sugar industry.

In any case, more studies are called for as the findings of Figure 7.4 inevitably lead to a challenging and provocative question. Could the Japanese economic management system have been better? The answer might also provide a clue to the recent studies on the differences between Japanese colonialism and European colonialism.[43]

7.6 Regime Change and Structural Change

Figures 7.2 and 7.3 reveal that the real GDP per capita level of Taiwan plunged from the prewar peak level of $1,522 in 1942 to $693 in 1944, and to $748 in 1945. The 1944 and 1945 values were even lower than the $759 achieved in the more primitive year of 1900.[44] Similarly for Korea, its real GDP per capita also dipped from $1,681 in 1937 to a mere $694 in 1946, which was much lower than $850 in 1900. In terms of real GDP per capita

---

Taiwanese economy also gained from Japan. Taiwan's alternative would have been either independence or under the Chinese regime, which was, as Figure 7.1 shows, stagnant, unstable and marked by endless civil wars. Even in the early postwar period (1946), industrialization of Taiwan was not part of China's national economic plan (Hsiao, 1997).

43 Myers and Peattie (1984). Also see Ka (1995, 181) for a review. Elsewhere we tried to compare the British colonialism in India and the Japanese colonialism in Taiwan (Hsiao and Hsiao, 2002b).

44 Elsewhere we have suggested that the postwar proponents of Taiwan's "rags to riches" miracle growth have often ignored the country's prewar achievements (Hsiao and Hsiao, 1998).

growth rates, the decrease in the Transition Period is more dramatic. The plunge in both countries was indeed precipitous, and gives rise to the misleading contention of a postwar "economic miracle" for those who only know the Taiwanese and Korean economic development after World War II, as we observed in Section 7.1.

The plunge, however, when viewed over 1903–92, as shown in Figure 7.3, seems to be a minor variation in the long history of economic growth. Yet the plunge, combined with the postwar accelerated growth, does seem, at first glance, to suggest structural changes in the economy between the prewar and the postwar period (in this section, we define the two periods by the years before and after the plunge defined in Section 7.6.1 below).

In this section, we would like to test econometrically whether there were statistical structural changes in the Korean and Taiwanese economies using real GDP per capita time series. For the purpose of international comparisons, we would also like to test the real GDP per capita series of Japan and the United States.[45]

7.6.1 The Perron test

Perron (1989) has shown that when there are a one-time break and structural changes in the time series, as we have seen in Figure 7.3, the Augmented Dickey–Fuller test (Dickey and Fuller, 1979) for stationarity tends to show that the series has a unit root, while in fact, the series may be trend stationary, that is, the series may be stationary along a trend line. He then derives a method of combining the tests of a unit root with structural change in one model.

Perron's test equation is the following:

$$y_t = a_0 + a_1 y_{t-1} + a_2 t + \sum_{i=1}^{k} \beta_i \Delta y_{t-i}$$
$$+ \mu_1 DP_t + \mu_2 DL_t + \mu_3 DL_t * t + \varepsilon_t, \qquad (7.1)$$

where y_t in this chapter is either the logarithmic value of real GDP per capita series (gdppc) or the first difference of gdppc series (Δgdppc), which is also the

---

45 For Taiwan, aside from the statistical curiosity, the political implications of the regime change in 1945 may be noted. Wade (1990, 74, fn, points out, "Those who are pronationalist party [...] may be inclined to highlight the contributions of the Nationalist government and the liberalization reforms to the subsequent prosperity. Those who are opposed may do the opposite." Note that structural changes are defined here in terms of time series analysis, not in terms of broader socioeconomic sense, as noted by Kuznets (1973).

growth rate series of a country's real GDP per capita (see Footnote 10). DP_t is a pulse dummy variable, taking 1 at the year $(t_B + 1)$ for the one-time break at the year t_B and 0 otherwise.[46]

Based on the data, for Korea's real GDP per capita series, t_B is taken at the year 1944 at $1,484, as it slipped to $697 in 1945. For Taiwan, t_B is taken at the year 1943, although its real GDP per capita reached the prewar peak of $1,522 in 1942, decreased to $1,011 in 1943 and then stumbled to its minimum at $693 in 1944. For Japan's real GDP per capita series, t_B is taken at the year 1944 at $2,558, as it fell to its minimum at $1,295 in 1945. For the United States' real GDP per capita series, t_B is taken at the year 1945 at $11,722, as it decreased to $9,207 in 1946. From these real GDP per capita series, we can see that the effect of the war on the US economy was not at all severe compared with its effect on Japan, Korea and Taiwan.

DL_t is a level dummy variable (which measures the structural change in intercept after the breakpoint), taking 1 at the year $(t_B + 1)$ and after, and 0 otherwise. Variable t is the time trend, and the product DL_t*t is an interaction variable (which measures the structural change in time trend). y_{t-1} is the one-period lag of the dependent variable, and its coefficient a_1 will be used in the unit root test. Δy_{t-i} is the ith lag of the first difference of the dependent variable. The value of optimal lag length k for the augmented terms was selected by Perron's method.

In Equation (7.1), for the unit root test, the null hypothesis is H_0: $a_1 = 1$, against the alternative hypothesis, H_1: $a_1 < 1$. For other coefficients, the standard t-test is applied. For all four countries, we first perform the tests using samples for 1911–92. For Taiwan only, we did an additional test using a longer series from 1903 to 1992, which avoided the irregularity we have mentioned in the construction of Table 7.1 in Section 7.2.2.

Table 7.2 presents the estimated coefficients and their t-statistics, along with the adjusted R^2 for the gdppc (real GDP per capita) and the Δgdppc (growth rates of GDP per capita) series. The value of λ is the ratio of the observations up to the breakpoint to the total observations in the sample. It determines the critical value in Perron's test of the unit root.

7.6.2 The real GDP per capita series

In the upper part of Table 7.2, the unit root test results show that we cannot reject the null hypothesis in all gdppc series. Therefore, they are all nonstationary. Thus, the test results of structural changes based on these gdppc series may be spurious, and should be interpreted cautiously (they are listed here just

---

46 For the choice of t_B, see Perron (1989).

Table 7.2 Perron's Test of the Unit Root with Structural Change 1911–92

			Stationarity	Structural Change					
Var	Obser		y_{t-1}	const	t	DP	DL	DL*t	adj
Coeff	No.	λ k	a_1	a_0	a_2	μ_1	μ_2	μ_3	R^2
Eq. gdppc									
1 **Kor**	73	0.41 8	0.849	1.042	0.003	-0.598	-0.416	0.008	0.996
			(-2.54) (1)	*(2.55) b*	*(1.67) c*	*(-7.81) a*	*(-2.71) a*	*(2.71) a*	
3A **Twn 1911-92**									
	77	0.40 4	0.707	2.020	0.003	-0.272	-0.764	0.017	0.995
			(-3.36)	*(3.47) a*	*(1.23)*	*(-2.84) a*	*(-3.66) a*	*(4.20) a*	
3B **Twn 1903-92**									
	85	0.46 4	0.701	2.005	0.004	-0.225	-0.875	0.016	0.995
			(-3.54)	*(3.62) a*	*(2.19) b*	*(-2.36) b*	*(-3.75) a*	*(4.10) a*	
5 **Jpn**	80	0.41 1	0.961	0.303	0.0005	-0.745	0.035	0.0005	0.998
			(-1.03)	*(1.12)*	*(0.41)*	*(-15.6) a*	*(0.44)*	*(0.30)*	
7 **USA**	80	0.42 1	0.858	1.187	0.003	-0.199	0.028	-0.001	0.990
			(-2.63)	*(2.60) b*	*(2.93) a*	*(-3.69) a*	*(0.75)*	*(-0.78)*	
Eq. Δgdppc									
2 **Kor**	73	0.41 7	-0.293	0.008	0.0003	-0.743	-0.047	0.002	0.801
			(-7.28) a	*(0.28)*	*(0.19)*	*(-14.0) a*	*(-0.92)*	*(1.00)*	
4A **Twn 1911-92**									
	77	0.40 3	-0.426	0.070	-0.003	-0.446	-0.082	0.004	0.436
			(-7.34) a	*(2.31) b*	*(-1.93) c*	*(-5.16) a*	*(-1.54)*	*(2.65) a*	
4B **Twn 1903-92**									
	85	0.46 3	-0.376	0.045	-0.001	-0.408	-0.070	0.003	0.395
			(-7.12) a	*(1.71) c*	*(-1.27)*	*(-4.72) a*	*(-1.21)*	*(2.17) b*	
6 **Jpn**	79	0.41 1	0.046	0.030	-0.0005	-0.767	0.105	-0.001	0.809
			(-14.2) a	*(1.80) c*	*(-0.66)*	*(-18.0) a*	*(3.40) a*	*(-0.89)*	
8 **USA**	77	0.42 3	0.074	-0.011	0.002	-0.209	0.039	-0.002	0.372
			(-5.64) a	*(-0.48)*	*(1.59)*	*(-3.82) a*	*(1.01)*	*(-1.62)*	

Notes: (1) t-ratios are in parentheses. $t(a_1) = (a_1 - 1)/se(a_1)$. a, b and c denote that we can reject H_0: $a_1 = 1$ (a unit root) at 1%, 5% and 10% level of significance, respectively. At $\lambda = 0.4$, the critical values are -4.81, -4.22 and -3.95 for 1%, 5% and 10% level of significance, respectively. At $\lambda = 0.5$, the critical values are -4.90, -4.53 and -3.96 for 1%, 5% and 10% level of significance, respectively, see Perron (1989). (2) For all coefficients, except a_1, the null hypothesis is that the coefficient equals to zero in the standard t-test. a, b and c denote that the test is significant at 1%, 5% and 10% level, respectively.

for reference). With this caution in mind, we may notice that, for the gdppc series, broadly speaking, Korea and Taiwan as one group have similar patterns, and Japan and the United States as another group have different results. However, all four countries have significant one-time pulses (DP) in the level of the real GDP per capita series near the end of World War II.

Furthermore, the test results show that there are significant structural changes in real GDP per capita growth rates during the prewar period and continuing up to the postwar period (i.e., coefficient a_2 and μ_3 are significant) in Korea and Taiwan. In view of this, the upward changes of real GDP per capita in the postwar period could be viewed as being induced by the long-run trend from the prewar period. In other words, the prewar development came to bear fruit and induced structural changes in real GDP per capita in the postwar period. This interpretation is consistent with Kohli (1994) in the case of Korea and with Hsiao and Hsiao (1996, 1998) in the case of Taiwan.

7.6.3 The real GDP per capita growth rate series

From the lower part of Table 7.2 in the Δgdppc series, the unit root tests show a strong rejection of H_0: $a_1 = 1$ for all four countries. Hence, all the Δgdppc series are stationary. The coefficient a_2 of the variable t is not significant in the growth rate series[47] of Korea, Japan and the United States in the prewar period. In addition, the coefficient μ_3 of DL*t is also not significant for these three countries, implying that there is no significant structural change in the time trend of the growth rates of these three countries during the postwar period. We explain the other findings in the lower part of Table 7.2.

Only the case of Taiwan (Equation 4A) has a small negative coefficient ($a_2 = -0.003$), which is (weakly) significant at the 10% level. This means that the growth rate of real GDP per capita before 1944 decreased slightly for Taiwan. But when the data for a longer period are used (Equation 4B), then the trend coefficient a_2 becomes -0.001 and is not significant at the 10% level. Thus, for Taiwan, if we consider that the longer data series is more reliable, then Taiwan's growth rate series also has no significant time trend in the prewar period. This is consistent with the other three countries.

The coefficient (μ_1) of DP is negative and is significant at the 1% level in all four countries. This implies that there is a significant downward pulse at year ($t_B + 1$) in the growth rate series for all four countries, as shown in Figure 7.3. Thus, the negative effect of the war on the four economies cannot be ignored.

The coefficient (μ_2) of DL shows that only the intercept of Japan's growth rate has a significant upward shift of 0.105 at 1945 and after, as may be seen from Figure 7.3. This means that there is a structural change in the sense that the average growth rate has increased in 1945 and after, as compared with the

---

47 In Equation (7.1), if y_t is taken as Δgdppc, which is the growth rate, then the coefficient a_2 or $a_2 + \mu_3$ is the derivative of y_t with respect to time, and is the change (slope) of the growth rate Δgdppc along the regression line. It is, so to speak, the average growth rate of the growth rate series.

average growth rate before 1944. This agrees with the fact that the Japanese economy recovered fast and grew almost immediately after the war, despite the heavy war damage. For Korea, Taiwan and the United States, there is no significant change in the intercept after the breakpoint, showing a continuous and gradual recovery from the war.

The coefficient (μ_3) of the cross product DL*t gives a mixed result. We find that only Taiwan has a positive and significant coefficient (Equation 4A (0.004) and Equation 4B (0.003) in Table 7.2). Thus, there is an upward change in time trend in 1944 and after. Since the postwar trend of the growth rates is the sum of a_2 and μ_3, we may say that, for Taiwan, the postwar growth rates have a slight tendency to accelerate at about 0.001 (= $a_2 + \mu_3$ = −0.003 + 0.004) or 0.002 (= −0.001 + 0.003) in 1944 and after.

This result is different from the other three countries in the tests. In the postwar period, the growth rates of Korea, like Taiwan, also tend to increase slightly, and those of Japan and the United States tend to decrease, but all these changes in the time trend are not significant.

In general, so far as the structural changes of the growth rate series of real GDP per capita are concerned, our test results demonstrate that the pre-war trend of the growth rate series is not significant, and that there is a very significant one-time drop in the series due to the war in all four countries.

There is a partial structural change in the postwar trend in the growth rate series of Taiwan, but no such structural change is detected in Korea, Japan and the United States. If no structural changes in the intercept and the time trend of the growth rate can be interpreted as the continuity[48] of the economy from the prewar period to the postwar period, we have shown that the economies of Korea and the United States had continuity before and after the war.

This is rather surprising for Korea, since the general perception is that there is a discontinuity before and after Korea's independence (Haggard et al., 1997). Table 7.1, however, provides a clue to the result. Korea had rapid growth in the prewar period and relatively slower growth in the postwar period, and the growth accelerated only after almost two decades of faltering. Thus, the econometric results show no significant change in its growth trend and intercept.

The economy of Japan had partial continuity in the trend but discontinuity in the intercept, which implies that the GDP per capita growth rates of Japan shifted upward almost immediately after the war and continued afterward

---

48 We have some reservation in this interpretation. "Continuity" usually implies continuity in the real GDP per capita level (gdppc) instead of its growth rate (Δgdppc). But our results show that the level series are not stationary, and so may be spurious. The econometric interpretation can only be based on the growth rate series.

in the same trend as in the prewar period until the 1970s. The Taiwanese economy had continuity in the intercept but discontinuity in the trend, which implies that there is no significant change in growth rates immediately after the war, as, like Korea, its economy lapsed for almost two decades. But the trend of the growth rates between prewar and postwar periods changed rather significantly in the 1970s as compared with the prewar growth trend.

7.7 Concluding Remarks

This chapter takes long-run (prewar and postwar) economic growth seriously. By the long run we mean the prewar and postwar periods. It traces the growth experience of the Koreans and the Taiwanese under a strict and harsh colonial regime and their emancipation during almost a century of continuous capitalistic development. While their successful capitalistic development may be comparable to many OECD countries in the past, their rapid growth under colonialism and its continuation after World War II is unique and illuminating in the history of world economic development. The international comparison of the long-run real GDP per capita reveals that some popular views about the capitalistic development of the Taiwanese and Korean economies are untenable, and, at the same time, unveils some interesting and important features of the growth process of both countries.

Most economists in Korea and Taiwan hold the view that economic growth in both countries was slower in the prewar period, was repressed and declined during World War II, continued to decline after the war, and then accelerated after the recovery. The former is presented as evidence of the evil of colonialism, and the latter, as the fruit of liberalization or policies of the new government after the war.[49] This is untenable. As demonstrated in Figures 7.1 and 7.2 and Table 7.1, other countries, whether developed or developing, have shared the same pattern of growth before and after the war. It has been a worldwide economic trend, not due to any particular case of colonialism, liberalization or a "wise" government.

What is relatively unknown, as revealed again by international comparison from a very long-run perspective, is that it took a significantly long time for Korea and Taiwan to recover up to the prewar peaks of real GDP per capita. Another interesting finding is that, while it is true that both Korea

---

49 This is not uncommon in world history. A new regime tends to claim its legitimacy by emphasizing that it brings in a new and progressive era and smears the replaced regime as old and regressive. This also happened after the 1868 Meiji Restoration in Japan and after the 1949 communist revolution in China.

and Taiwan have more or less the same level of real GDP per capita and the same growth pattern, the fact that Koreans were consistently better-off than the Taiwanese before the war and have been continuously worse-off after the war has eluded scholarly attention in the literature. In view of the different responses of these two countries to the 1997 Asian financial crisis (Hsiao and Hsiao, 2001a), their differences in growth pattern and economic policies call for more attention.

When the real GDP per capita growth of Korea and Taiwan in international dollars is compared with that of Japan, another intriguing feature appears. If we take Japan's real GDP per capita as the base and compare it with that of Korea and Taiwan, then the real GDP per capita ratios for Korea and Taiwan were much higher during the colonial period than those after independence, and the ratios continued to deteriorate up until 1970. In that year, the ratios of both countries fell below 30%, then turned around simultaneously in that year and increased steadily afterward. But, until 1992, real GDP per capita of Korea and Taiwan still remained only between 50% and 60% of that of Japan. While for Taiwan, this has been pointed out by Wu (1995) using constant New Taiwan dollars, this chapter corroborates his finding in terms of constant international dollars. We also find that Hong Kong and Singapore had the same turning point vis-à-vis Japan around 1970, and we explained this from changes in the world economy.

We have suggested that it is the change in the world economic conditions and the steady growth of neighboring partner countries, such as Japan and the United States,[50] with whom Taiwan and Korea were fortunate to form the Pacific trade triangle, rather than the role of any specific economic policy, that triggered the rapid growth of Taiwan and other Asian NIEs.

Several scholars of Korean and Taiwanese economic development have contended that the modern economic growth of Korea and Taiwan begins in the postwar era, thus marginalizing, ignoring or even negating the prewar colonial development. Our study shows otherwise. The international comparison shows us that Korea, Taiwan and Japan were already rapidly growing countries in the Prewar Period. By the end of the 1930s, Korea, along with Taiwan, had achieved the highest real GDP per capita of any Asian country except Japan. In fact, we have shown further that the prewar growth of Korea was one of the fastest in the world, and that of Taiwan was also faster than that of most of the countries in the world. In sum, we submit that the "East Asian miracle" started in the prewar era, and that, thanks to the prewar

---

50 On the role of Japan in economic development of Taiwan, see Hsiao and Hsiao (1996); for Korea, see Kohli (1994).

linkages to the postwar era, the "miracle" continued in the Postwar Period only after the prewar peaks were recovered.[51]

Furthermore, we have conducted an econometric test to examine structural changes of real GDP per capita series and its growth rate series before and after the war. Perron's tests show that the growth rate series reflect continuity in the prewar and postwar periods for Korea, but we have detected only partial continuity in the postwar era for Taiwan. Considering the higher growth rates of Korea in the Prewar Period and the relatively slower rate in the Postwar Period, Korea's continuity in growth rates is not surprising. In contrast, considering Taiwan's slower growth rate in the prewar period and the accelerated growth only after the 1970s, discontinuity in the growth rate trend is also expected. Thus, in this chapter, we have found another difference in the long-run economic growth between Korea and Taiwan.

In summary, this chapter has used statistical methods to show that the modern economic growth of Korea and Taiwan started as early as the beginning of the twentieth century, only to be interrupted by World War II. There is no shortcut to growth. In reviewing the economic development of the Prewar Period of Taiwan and Korea, we also find that "institutional reform" for modern society is more important than the development of tangible assets and infrastructures, as most of these were destroyed by the war but were rebuilt after the war. Japan and Germany are other examples. A corollary to our finding is that rapid growth can also be achieved under a harsh colonial or authoritarian regime as an unintended consequence (Hsiao and Hsiao, 2001c). It is to be hoped, however, that other developing countries can achieve economic development without emulating the historical experiences of Korea and Taiwan.

Sources of Data

Data for Figures 7.1–7.5 and Table 7.1 are taken from Maddison (1995). Table 7.2 is authors' calculation.

Acknowledgments

A previous version of this chapter has been presented in seminars at Kansai, Kobe, Nagoya, Otaru and Tokai Universities, the International Center for the Study of East Asian Development (ICSEAD) and the Institute of Developing

---

51 A caveat is necessary for our strong conclusions. As in the case of any other empirical studies, our conclusions are mainly based on Maddison's data. While his data are consistent with other independently compiled similar time series (Mizoguchi, 1997; Mizoguchi and Nojima, 1996; Wu, 1995) and supported by other studies on economic and social conditions under Japanese colonialism, our strong conclusions must be qualified and be interpreted with caution. We owe this important caveat to one of the referees.

Economies (IDE) in Japan. We are grateful to Professors Tsong-min Wu and Toshiyuki Mizoguchi for making data available to the authors. Comments and suggestions from Professors Shigeyuki Abe, Ann Carlos, JoAnn Feeney, Natsuki Fujita, Takao Fukuchi, Shinichi Ichimura, Song-ken Hsu, Eckhart Janeba, Seiichi Katayama, Robert McNown, Naci Mocan, Motoaki Moriya, Masao Oda, Eric Ramstetter, Yukihito Sato, Ron Smith, Osamu Takenaka, Henry Wan, Jr., Tatsufumi Yamagata, Kenji Yamamoto and other seminar participants are greatly appreciated. The comments and suggestions by two referees were most helpful. All errors of omission and commission are the authors'.

References

Adelman, I., and C. T. Morris (1967). *Society, Politics, and Economic Development: A Quantitative Approach*. Baltimore: Johns Hopkins University Press.

Aoki, T. (1987). *Pacific Trade Triangle—Structural Adjustments among Japan, the United States, and Asian NICs* (in Japanese). Tokyo: Nihon Hyoronsha.

Brown, G. T. (1973). *Korean Pricing Policies and Economic Development in the 1960s*. Baltimore: Johns Hopkins University Press.

Chang, C. C. (1999). "War Damage of Taiwan during World War II," *Taiwan Historical Research* [in Chinese] 4(1): 149–94.

——— (1996). "The Legacy of Japanese Sociopolitical Control System in Post-war Taiwan." Paper presented at Conference on the Japanese Legacy in Post-Colonial Taiwan, St. Louis, MO, the Joint Center for East Asian Studies, Washington University, and University of Missouri.

Cheng, T. J., and S. Haggard (1992). "Regime Transformation in Taiwan: Theoretical and Comparative Perspectives." In T. J. Cheng and S. Haggard, eds., *Political Changes in Taiwan*. Boulder, CO: Lynne Rienner Publishers.

Cho, L. J., and Y. H. Kim (1991). "Political and Economic Antecedents to the 1960s." In L. J. Cho and Y. H. Kim, eds. *Economic Development in the Republic of Korea*. Honolulu: University of Hawaii Press, 2–13.

Chow, P. C. Y., and M. H. Kellman (1993). *Trade, the Engine of Growth in East Asia*. New York: Oxford University Press.

Coates, D. (2000). *Models of Capitalism: Growth and Stagnation in the Modern Era*. Cambridge, MA: Blackwell Publishers.

Coe, D. T., E. Helpman and A. W. Hoffmaister (1995). "*North-South R&D Spillover*." NBER Working Paper Series, No. 5048, March. Cambridge, MA: NBER.

Conlon Associates. (1959). "*United States Foreign Policy: Asia*." Studies No. 5, prepared at the request of the Committee on Foreign Relation, United States Senate. Washington, DC: US Government Printing Office.

Copland, I. (1990). *The Burden of Empire: Perspectives on Imperialism and Colonialism*. Sydney, Australia: Oxford University Press.

Cumings, B. (1984). "The Legacy of Japanese Colonialism in Korea." In R. H. Myers and M. R. Peattie, eds. *The Japanese Colonial Empire, 1895–1945*. Princeton, NJ: Princeton University Press, 478–96.

Das, D. K. (1992). *Korean Economic Dynamism*. New York: St. Martin's Press.

Deyo, F. C. (1989). *Beneath the Miracle: Labor Subordination in the New Asian Industrialism*. Berkeley: University of California Press.

Dickey, D. A., and W. A. Fuller (1979). "Distribution of the Estimators Autoregressive Time Series with a Unit Root," *Journal of American Statistical Association* 74(366): 427–31.

Dollar, D. (1992). "Outward-Oriented Developing Economies Really Do Grow More Rapidly: Evidence from 95 LDCs, 1976–1985," *Economic Development and Cultural Change* 40(3): 523–44.

Eckert, C. J. (1991). *Offspring of Empire: The Koch'ang Kims and the Colonial Origins of Korean Capitalism*. Seattle: University of Washington Press.

Eckert, C. J., K. B. Lee, Y. I. Lew, M. Robinson and E. W. Wagner (1990). *Korea, Old and New: A History*. Cambridge, MA: Harvard University Press.

Glass, S. (1963). "Some Aspects of Formosa's Economic Growth," *China Quarterly* 15: 12–34.

Haggard, S., D. Kang and C. I. Moon (1997). "Japanese Colonialism and Korean Development, A Critique," *World Development* 25(6): 867–81.

Hattori, T., and Y. Sato, eds. (1996). *Development Mechanism of Korea and Taiwan* [in Japanese]. Tokyo: Institute of Developing Economy. Also see the summary of the book in "Special Issue: Development Mechanisms in Korea and Taiwan," *The Developing Economies* 35(4): 1997.

Hayami, Y., and V. W. Ruttan (1970). "Korean Rice, Taiwanese Rice, and Japanese Agricultural Stagnation: An Economic Consequence of Colonialism," *Quarterly Journal of Economics* 84: 562–89.

Higgins, B. (1968). *Economic Development, Principles, Problems, and Policies*. New York: W. W. Norton Co.

Ho, S. P. S. (1978). *Economic Development of Taiwan, 1960–1970*. New Haven, CT: Yale University Press.

Hsiao, F. S. T. (1997). "Colonialism or Comparative Advantage?—On Agricultural Development In Colonial Taiwan." In *Proceedings of the National Science Council, Part C: Humanities and Social Sciences* 7(4): 497–513, Taipei: National Science Council.

Hsiao, F. S. T., and M. C. W. Hsiao (1996). "Taiwanese Economic Development and Foreign Trade." In J. Y. T. Kuark, ed. *Comparative Asian Economies*. Greenwich, CT: JAI Press, 211–302.

——— (1998). "Colonial Linkages in Early Postwar Taiwanese Economic Development." In W. C. Kirby and M. S. Weiss, eds. *Harvard Studies on Taiwan: Papers of the Taiwan Studies Workshop II*. Cambridge, MA: The Fairbank Center for East Asian Research, Harvard University, 91–117.

——— (1999). "The Historical Traditions of Taiwanese Small-and-Medium Enterprises." In F. S. Huang, and K. I. Ang, eds. *Taiwanese Commercial Traditions: Collected Papers*. Taipei: The Preparatory Office of the Institute of Taiwanese History, Academia Sinica, 464–524.

——— (2000). *Some Properties of Taiwan's Real GDP Per Capita Time Series Data, 1912–1990*. Working Paper. University of Colorado Boulder.

——— (2001a). "Capital Flows and Exchange Rates-Recent Korean and Taiwanese Experiences and Challenges," *Journal of Asian Economics* 12(3): 353–81.

——— (2001b). "Diminishing Returns and Asian NIEs—How They Overcome the Iron Law." In Institute of Economics, eds. *Conference Proceedings on Economic Development in Memory of Professor Mo-Huan Hsiang*. Taipei: Academia Sinica, 239–88.

——— (2001c). "Economic Liberalization and Development: The Case of Lifting Martial Law in Taiwan." In Taiwan Studies Promotion committee, ed. *The Transformation of an Authoritarian Regime: Taiwan in the Post-Martial Law Era*. Taipei: Academia Sinica, 353–79.

—— (2002a). "Taiwan in the Global Economy—Past, Present, and Future." In P. C. Y. Chow, ed. *Taiwan in the Global Economy: From an Agrarian Economy to an Exporter of High-Tech Products.* Westport, CT: Praeger Publishers, 161–222.

—— (2002b). "Colonialism, Learning, and Convergence: The Case of India and Taiwan." Paper presented at the 2002 Allied Social Science Association meeting, Atlanta, Georgia.

Hsiao, F. S. T., and C. Park (2002). "Korean and Taiwanese Productivity Performance— Comparisons at Matched Manufacturing Levels." Paper presented at the 2003 Allied Social Science Association meeting, Washington, DC.

Hsiao, M. C. W. (1998). "Pacific Trade Triangle and the Growth of Korea and Taiwan— Cointegration and Causality Analysis." Working Paper, University of Colorado Denver.

Huang, F. S. (1996). "The Japanese Legacy and the Nationalist Chinese Rule in Postwar Taiwan." Paper presented at Conference on the Japanese Legacy in Post-Colonial Taiwan, Joint Center for East Asian Studies, Washington University and University of Missouri.

Huer, J. (1989). *Marching Orders: The Role of the Military in South Korea's Economic Miracle, 1961–1971.* Westport, CT: Greenwood Press.

Itaya, S. (1997). "A Locus of Asian Development." In S. Itaya, K. Hirano, M. Kimura, I. Park, I. Yanagimachi and K. Nakajima, eds. *Chaos of Asian Development* [in Japanese]. Tokyo: Keiso Shobo, 65–114.

Ka, C. M. (1995). *Japanese Colonialism in Taiwan, Land Tenure, Development, And Dependency, 1895–1945.* Boulder, CO: Westview Press.

Kerr, G. (1965). *Formosa Betrayed.* Boston: Houghton Mifflin.

Kim, K. S., and M. Roemer (1979). *Studies in the Modernization of the Republic of Korea: 1945–1975: Growth and Structural Transformation.* Cambridge, MA: Council on East Asian Studies, Harvard University.

Kimura, M. (1997). "Primary Education in Modern Korea." In S. Itaya, M. Hirano, I. Kimura, I. Park, I. Yanagimachi, and K. Nakajima, eds. *Chaos of Asian Development* [in Japanese]. Tokyo: Keiso Shobo, 29–63.

Kirby, W. C. (1990). "Continuity and Change in Modern China: Economic Planning on the Mainland and on Taiwan, 1943–1958," *Australian Journal of Chinese Affairs* 24: 121–41.

Kohli, A. (1994). "Where Do High Growth Political Economies Come From? The Japanese Lineage of Korea's Developmental State," *World Development* 22(9): 1269–1293.

—— (1997). "Japanese Colonialism and Korean Development: A Reply," *World Development* 25(6): 883–88.

Kosai, Y. (1986). *The Era of High-Speed Growth: Notes on the Postwar Japanese Economy*, trans. Jacqueline Kaminski. Tokyo: Tokyo University Press.

Kravis, I. B., A. Heston and R. Summers (1982). *World Product and Income, International Comparisons of Real Gross Product.* Baltimore: Johns Hopkins University Press.

Kremer, M. (1993). "Population Growth and Technological Change: One Million B.C. to 1990," *Quarterly Journal of Economics* 108(3): 681–717.

Kuznets, S. (1973). "Modern Economic Growth: Findings and Reflections," *American Economic Review* 63(3): 247–58.

Lee, T. H., and Y. E. Chen (1978). "Agricultural Growth in Taiwan, 1911–1972." In Y. Hayami, V. W. Ruttan and H. M. Southworth, eds. *Agricultural Growth in Japan, Taiwan, Korea, and the Philippines: An East–West Center Book.* Tokyo: The Asian Productivity Organization, 59–89.

Liu, S. K. (1975). *An Analysis of the Postwar Taiwanese Economy* [in Japanese].Tokyo: Tokyo University Press.

Maddison, A. (1991). *Dynamic Forces in Capitalist Development: A Long-Run Comparative View.* Oxford: Oxford University Press.

———(1995). *Monitoring the World Economy, 1820–1992.* Paris: Development Centre, OECD.

Mason, E. S., M. J. Kim, D. H. Perkins, K. S. Kim and D. C. Cole (1980). *The Economic and Social Modernization of the Republic of Korea.* Cambridge, MA: Harvard University Press.

Minami, R. (1986). *The Economic Development of Japan: A Quantitative Study.* London: Macmillan Press.

Mizoguchi, T. (1997). "Revising Long-Term National Accounts Statistics of Taiwan, 1912–1990: A Comparison of Estimates of Production Accounts to Expenditure Accounts." Discussion Paper No. D97-8. Institute of Economic Research. Tokyo: Hitotsubashi University.

Mizoguchi, T., and N. Nojima (1996). "Estimation of Long-Term System of Accounts Of Taiwan and Korea (in Japanese)." Reprinted Paper No. R 96-6. Institute of Economic Research. Tokyo: Hitotsubashi University.

Mizoguchi, T., and M. Umemura (1988). *Basic Economic Statistics of Former Japanese Colonies 1895–1938.* Tokyo: Tokyo Keizai Shimposha.

Mizoguchi, T., and Y. Yamamoto (1984). "Capital Formation in Taiwan and Korea." In R. H. Myers and M. R. Peattie, eds. *The Japanese Colonial Empire, 1895–1945.* Princeton, NJ: Princeton University Press, 399–419.

Moody, P. R. Jr. (1992). *Political Change on Taiwan, A Study of Ruling Party Adaptability.* Westport, CT: Praeger Publishers.

Myers, R. H., and M. R. Peattie, eds. (1984). *The Japanese Colonial Empire, 1895–1945.* Princeton, NJ: Princeton University Press.

Numazaki, I. (1997). "The Laoban-Led Development of Business Enterprises in Taiwan: An Analysis of the Chinese Entrepreneurship," *The Developing Economies* 35(4): 440–57.

Osterhammel, J. (1995). *Colonialism: A Theoretical Overview.* Princeton, NJ: Markus Wiener Publishers.

Pae, S. M. (1992). *Korea Leading Developing Nations: Economy, Democracy and Welfare.* Lanham, MD: University Press of America.

Peattie, M. R. (1984). "Introduction." In R. H. Myers and M. R. Peattie, eds. *The Japanese Colonial Empire, 1895–1945.* Princeton, NJ: Princeton University Press, 3–57.

Penn World Table, Mark 5.6 (PWT5.6) 1994. Downloaded from www.nber.org/pwt57.doc. html. National Bureau of Economic Research.

Perron, P. (1989). "The Great Crash, the Oil Price Shock, and the Unit Root Hypothesis," *Econometrica* 57(6): 1361–1401.

Sachs, J. D., and A. M. Warner (1995). "Economic Reform and the Process of Global Integration," *Brookings Papers on Economic Activity, 25th Anniversary Issue,* 1–95.

Sakong, I. (1993). *Korea in the World Economy.* Washington, DC: Institute of International Economics.

Shinohara, M. (1991). "Growth and Cycle—The Pattern of Dynamism" [in Japanese]. In M. Shinohara, ed. *Dynamism of the Japanese Economy—Long-Run Economic Statistics and I.* Tokyo: Toyo Keizai Shimpo Sha, 123–57.

Softening Economics Center (SEC) (1989). *Softening of Japanese Economy and Asian NICs* [in Japanese]. A 1989 Report of Study Group of the Coexistence of the Softening of Japanese Economy and Asian NICs. Tokyo: Softening Economics Center.

Song, B. N. (1990). *The Rise of the Korean Economy*. Updated ed. New York: Oxford University Press.

Suh, S. C. (1978). *Growth and Structural Changes in the Korean Economy, 1910–1940*. Cambridge, MA: Harvard University Press.

Szczepanik, E. (1958). *The Economic Growth of Hong Kong*. London: Oxford University Press.

Twu, J. Y. (1975). *Taiwan under Japanese Imperialism* [in Japanese]. Tokyo: Tokyo University Press.

——— (1995). "The Asian Growth Triangle: Structure, Change And Perspective." International Economic Conflict Discussion Paper, No. 81. Nagoya, Japan: Economic Research Center, School of Economics, Nagoya University.

Wade, R. (1990). *Governing the Market, Economic Theory and the Role of Government in East Asian Industrialization*. Princeton, NJ: Princeton University Press.

World Bank (1980, 1992, 1994, 2000/2001). *World Development Report*. New York: Oxford University Press for World Bank.

Wu, T. M. (1995). "Long-Run fluctuations in Aggregate Outputs of Taiwan and Changes in Economic Structure" [in Chinese]. In K. J. Li, ed., *Modern Taiwanese History* [in Chinese]. Taipei: Taiwan Sheng Wenshian Weiyuanhui, 609–36.

——— (1997). "The Nationalist Government's Economic Policies Regarding Taiwan: 1945–1949" [in Chinese], *Taiwan Economic Review* 25(4): 521–54.

Wu, W. S. (1992). *A Study of Leadership Class of Taiwanese Society during the Japanese Occupation Period* [in Chinese]. Taipei: Cheng Chung Book Co.

Yanaihara, T. (1929). *Taiwan under Imperialism* [in Japanese]. Tokyo: Iwanami Shoten.

Chapter 8

CATCHING UP AND CONVERGENCE: ON THE LONG-RUN GROWTH IN EAST ASIA

Abstract

Continuing from Chapters 5 and 6, this chapter attempts to combine the traditional learning model with the recent theory of economic growth using Maddison's long-run real GDP per capita data of the three fastest-growing countries in East Asia: Korea, Taiwan and Japan.

We first explain the game of catching up among nations in the World. We find that catching up and falling behind among countries are the rule rather than the exception. We then explain the learning coefficients of Taiwan and Korea with Japan and the United States through periods before and after World War II. The model of learning leads to a logistic model of economic growth of convergence between two countries. Using time-series data, the coefficients of a logistic model are estimated to confirm that the real GDP per capita of Taiwan and Korea is converging to that of Japan and that of the United States, respectively. Similarly, Japan's GDP per capita converges to that of the United States. The time required for finite convergence, other things being equal, for these countries is also estimated.

8.1 Introduction

One of the most important challenges for developing countries is to catch up with developed countries. It is a question of economic convergence, and is generally framed in terms of the convergence of the level of real GDP per capita. Historically, poorer countries develop faster than (and so catch up and converge with) richer countries, if the former are closely associated with the latter.[1] Korea and Taiwan are good examples.

---

[1] Coe et al. (1995) have shown that opening trade with industrial countries is effective in increasing the total factor productivity (TFP) of a developing country. They also found that with which country is associated, is also important. "A developing country whose trade is more biased towards industrial countries that have large cumulative experiences in R&D has higher productivity." (ibid., 3) And among the developed

Before World War II, both nations were colonies of Japan, which was the fastest-growing economy in the world during the period 1911–40. Despite Japanese exploitation, both achieved high growth rates of real GDP per capita, and, by the end of the 1930s, their levels of real GDP per capita were higher than those of any other developing countries in Asia (Hsiao and Hsiao, 2003).

During the prewar period, Japan invested heavily in Korea and Taiwan (Mizoguchi and Yamamoto, 1984), and they traded almost exclusively with Japan (although one may say that they were exploited by Japan). After the war, Japan continued to be the major trading partner of Korea and Taiwan, and the United States had already been a major trading partner since the mid-1960s. The foundation of human capital and social infrastructure built before the war (Hsiao and Hsiao, 2002, 2003), and continued after the war; the continuation of trading with Japan, which is the world's second-largest economy and a major source of capital equipment and intermediate raw materials; and the opening of the vast and growing market of the United States, which is the largest economy in the world, all undoubtedly catapulted Korea and Taiwan into rapid growth (Hsiao and Hsiao, 1996).

In this highly competitive world, no nation can stand still. Elsewhere (Hsiao and Hsiao, 2001b) we have shown that, despite Krugman's assertion of factor-driven growth (Krugman, 1994), Korea and Taiwan, along with Hong Kong and Singapore, the so-called newly industrializing economies (NIEs), have been climbing the technology ladder during the last three decades of the twentieth century. They have learned and advanced their technological ability through education, foreign trade and inward and outward direct foreign investment, in order to stay competitive in the world and maintain their rapid growth.

In Section 8.2, we explain the source of the data and catching-up games among the nations. Section 8.3 attempts to measure how Korea and Taiwan learned from their powerful neighbors, Japan and the United States, using a popular but very simple model of learning. It can only be simple because the selection of the model is severely restricted by the availability of data (labor and capital) for the prewar period. Section 8.4 uses a similar model, the logistic model, to set up a nonlinear regression model to examine convergence of the Korean and Taiwanese economies with those of Japan and the United States. Section 8.5 derives the time required for convergence. Concluding remarks are in the last section.

---

countries, "The United States has by far the largest domestic capital stock [...], about five times as high as Japan, which is the country with the second largest effect" (ibid., 4).

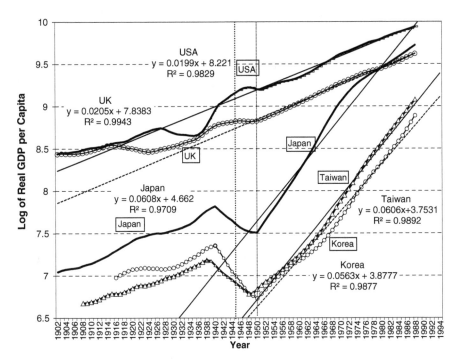

Figure 8.1 Real GDP per Capita of Korea, Taiwan, Japan, the United States and the United Kingdom. Ten-Year Moving Average

8.2 Games of Catching Up

The data we use are based on Maddison (1995, Appendix D), which gives internationally comparable levels of real GDP per capita of 56 countries between 1900 and 1992, based on 1990 Geary–Khamis dollars, which are compiled from international purchasing power parity. From Maddison's data, we see clearly that the ranking of countries can hardly stay fixed over time in this competitive world. Figure 8.1 shows the logarithm of the ten-year moving average[2] of the levels of real GDP per capita of Korea, Taiwan, Japan, the United Kingdom and the United States from 1902 to 1988. The slope of the curve at a given year shows the average growth rate of real GDP per capita over the 10-year period. It is interesting to observe that the patterns of the

---

2 For example, Korea's prewar period starts from 1916. Then, the level of real GDP per capita in 1916 is taken as the average of the levels from 1911 to 1920, and that of 1988 is calculated as the average of the levels from 1984 to 1992, and so on. The growth rate is calculated as the coefficient b in the regression line ln y $= a + bx$. The growth rate b of the postwar period is shown in Figure 8.1 as the slope of a line.

growth rates of the three Asian countries are very similar before, during and after the war.

The straight line along a curve in Figure 8.1 is an estimated regression line, using data from the postwar period. Here y is real GDP per capita, and the coefficient b is the average growth rate of real GDP per capita during the period. The three Asian countries grew steadily during the prewar and postwar periods, except during the transitional war period (we have fitted a regression line for each country for the postwar period).

The coefficient of x shows the growth rate of the postwar period up to 1988. There is a clear distinction between the East Asian countries, on the one hand, and the United States and the United Kingdom on the other. Throughout both the prewar and the postwar period, the real GDP per capita of the former group grew much faster than that of the latter group over a total period of almost one hundred years. Figure 8.1 also indicates that Japan's growth rate has tapered off in recent years, compared with those of Korea and Taiwan.

Since the levels of real GDP per capita of Korea and Taiwan have been lower than those of the other three countries, and that of Japan in turn has been lower than that of the United States, one may wonder whether Korea and Taiwan could one day catch up with Japan and the United States, and whether Japan could also catch up with the United States.

Historically, there are many examples of catching up and falling behind among nations. The levels of real GDP per capita of three former British colonies, the United States, Canada and Australia, surpassed that of the United Kingdom[3] in 1905, 1945 and 1965, respectively. The levels of real GDP per capita of other small countries, in terms of area and population, like Switzerland, Sweden and Norway, also surpassed the United Kingdom in 1945, 1957 and 1979, respectively.

The catching-up process of Japan has been more dramatic. Japan's 200-year seclusion policy ended in 1858, when Japan signed unequal treaties with the United States, the United Kingdom, the Netherlands, Russia and France. Japan's treaty of extraterritoriality ended only in 1899, and treaty tariffs terminated in 1910. By 1992, Japan had built up national wealth and strength, and had surpassed all these world powers.

While Japan has been busy catching up with other countries, few people are aware that Hong Kong and Singapore have been quietly catching up

---

3 At the height of the British empire in the early twentieth century, and even until 1945, the empire covered about 20% of the world area and 25% of the world population (Chamberlain, 1998, 3). No one would have dreamed that any of its colonies would one day surpass the United Kingdom.

with Japan. According to the Penn World Table (1994), the level of real GDP per capita[4] of Hong Kong exceeded that of Japan between 1987 and 1992. According to the World Bank (1999/2000), Singapore's real GNP per capita was higher than that of Japan by 1995. Even with the United States' enormous economic, political and military dominance, the real GDP per capita of the United States was outperformed by Switzerland from 1956 to 1976 and from 1980 to 1982.

In recent years, in terms of real GNP per capita in 1992 dollars, the World Bank (1994, 163) shows that even the United States has fallen behind Norway, Denmark, Sweden, Japan and Switzerland. Indeed, international economic competitiveness does not depend solely on gunboat policy, the size of territory or population, or even natural resource endowment.[5]

In short, while we are fully aware of the difference in the initial conditions of being the exploited versus being the exploiter, there is no reason to believe that Korea and Taiwan will never be able to surpass their former colonial power, Japan. Hence, it is of interest to consider how the economies of these two countries have evolved compared with those of Japan and the United States.

Is it true that, as some pessimists and fatalists may argue, "once behind, always behind"? In recent years, the possibility of Korea and Taiwan catching up has seemed more probable in view of the fact that the Japanese bubble economy collapsed in 1992 and Japan was still not fully recovered by 2002, while the performances of the Taiwanese and Korean economies have continued to be strong before and after the 1997 financial crisis (Hsiao and Hsiao, 2001a).

8.3 A Simple Model of Learning

One of the recent concerns in the literature on economic growth is whether the developing countries will catch up with the developed countries in the long run. Catching up can be achieved mainly through technology transfer and spillover between two trading partners through learning. In this section, we set up a simple model of learning between the developing and developed countries. It is "simple" since the data other than real GDP per capita, like capital and labor, are not available for the prewar period.

---

4 We use RGDPCH in PWT. It is "real GDP per capita in constant dollars (chain index) expressed in international prices, base 1985."

5 See Hsiao and Hsiao (2002). International competitiveness is defined as the capability of maintaining the high growth rate of a nation for the coming five to ten years. It may be evaluated in eight categories: labor, openness, technology, government, finance, infrastructure, institution, and management (WEF, 1999).

It is now well known that openness to trade can promote economic growth (Sachs and Warner, 1995). It is also important which country a developing country is trading with. Indeed, the formation of the Pacific trade triangle among Japan, Korea and Taiwan, and the United States has been an engine of growth for Korea and Taiwan (Hsiao, 2001). It is generally assumed that the wider the gap of real GDP per capita between the two trading partners, the faster the learning process and the stronger the effect of learning.

Let y and y* be real GDP per capita of developing and developed countries, respectively. Then

$$\ln\left(\frac{y*}{y}\right) = \ln y * - \ln y$$

is taken as an indicator of the "advantages of backwardness" (Gerschenkron, 1962), that is, of a technological gap that can be exploited by developing countries like Korea and Taiwan. Following Nelson and Phelps (1966) and, more recently, Verspagen (1994), the real GDP per capita growth rate of a developing country, denoted as d(ln y)/dt, is proportional to the discrepancy between developed and developing countries' real GDP per capita (in logarithm):

$$\frac{d\ln y}{dt} = r(\ln y * - \ln y), \tag{8.1}$$

where r is a constant coefficient that measures the degree of learning through technological transfer or imitation of industries, trading and foreign direct investment in the developing country (Gomulka, 1990). It is the usual speed of adjustment, ranging from zero to one, and r may be called more explicitly the coefficient of learning or catching up.[6] When r = 0, there is no learning, and so no growth takes place. When r = 1, the growth rate equals the income discrepancy (in logarithm).

The above equation may be written in discrete form for statistical calculation,

$$\ln y_t - \ln y_{t-1} = r(\ln y_{t-1} * - \ln y_{t-1}) \tag{8.2}$$

---

6 In this interpretation, the constancy of r is unrealistic as it implies that the "least developed country is most innovative" (Gomulka, 1990, 160). However, Hsiao and Hsiao (2003) show that Korea and Taiwan surpassed the threshold of development before World War II during the colonial period and possessed the ability to absorb foreign technology at the early stage of postwar development.

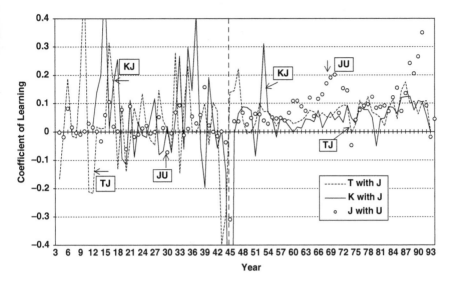

Figure 8.2 The Coefficients of Learning. Taiwan and Korea with Japan, and Japan with the United States

We use Maddison's data (1995) from the early 1900s to 1992 for Korea, Taiwan, Japan and the United States. Thus, we may also compare the coefficients of learning between the prewar and the postwar period. Figure 8.2 shows the values of r for the learning process of each pair of countries: Taiwan with Japan (TJ, the dotted line), Korea with Japan (KJ, the solid line) and Japan with the United States (JU, the circles) in each year. Similarly, we also calculate the coefficients of learning for Taiwan with the United States, and Korea with the United States (not shown in Figure 8.2. See Appendix 8A).

In general, the coefficients fluctuate more during the transition period (1941–50), especially those of Korea with Japan and Taiwan with Japan. For all cases, the coefficients fluctuate much more in the prewar period than in the postwar period. In particular, the coefficients of Korea and Taiwan with Japan fluctuate much more in the prewar period than during the postwar period, indicating a rather erratic transfer of technology from Japan to Korea and Taiwan during the prewar colonial period.

From Figure 8.2, during the prewar period, the positive learning coefficients seem to be cancelled out by the negative ones, but the net results seem to be positive. This explains the slow growth in the prewar period for all three East Asian countries. The postwar coefficients behave quite differently. The yearly coefficients are mostly positive. However, there is a clear difference among the three pairs of countries.

For the postwar and total periods, Japan's learning coefficients with the United States (the circles) are consistently the highest, especially during the late 1960s and the late 1980s. Taiwan's learning coefficients with both Japan (the dotted line) and the United States (not shown in Figure 8.2) are consistently higher than those of Korea with Japan (the solid line in Figure 8.2) and the United States (not shown) for the postwar and total periods. Apparently, the difference in the learning ability of Taiwan, Korea and Japan explains, at least partially, the difference in growth rates of the three countries during the postwar and total periods.[7]

Elsewhere we have estimated the long-run coefficients of learning between any two countries by using the Almon finite distributed lag model. The statistical estimates confirm that in the postwar period, Korea and Taiwan learned from Japan, and Japan, in turn, learned from the United States (Hsiao and Hsiao, 2003).

8.4 A Logistic Model of Convergence

Given the growth rates and the coefficients of learning in the past, we now look to the future and ask whether the levels of real GDP per capita of Korea and Taiwan could someday catch up with those of Japan and the United States. Many studies have been done involving a large number of countries, applying linear regression analysis after linearizing the growth equation under the assumption of a Cobb–Douglas production function (Temple, 1999). Instead of using the aforementioned method, we use time series analysis of two countries.

To compare the growth of two countries, we only need to modify equation (8.1) slightly, while reserving the basic form of the conventional growth analysis. Instead of real GDP per capita y on the left-hand side of equation (8.1), we replace it by the ratio p of real GDP per capita of developing and developed countries, $p = y/y^*$, where $0 < p < 1$. In this case, the right-hand-side variable of (8.1) can be written as

$$\ln\left(\frac{y^*}{y}\right) = \ln\left(\frac{1}{p}\right) = -\ln p.$$

---

7 Using Maddison's data (1995), Hsiao and Hsiao (2003) have shown that, during the postwar period from 1951 to 1992, the average annual growth rate of real GDP per capita measured in Geary–Khamis dollars of Taiwan was 6.03%, the highest among 56 countries in which long-run data are available. Taiwan's growth rate was above that of Korea, which ranked second at 5.8%, and even that of Japan, which ranked third at 5.57%, and almost 2% above the fourth-ranked country, Thailand (4.07%).

Write p = 1 – g, where g is a small positive fraction. Then by Taylor's approximation,

$$\ln p = \ln(1 - g) \approx -g = p - 1. \tag{8.3}$$

Substituting (8.3) on the right-hand side of (8.1), we have

$$\frac{d(\ln p)}{dt} = t(1 - p). \tag{8.4}$$

This is a simple S-shaped logistic model,[8] and has the solution,[9]

$$\ln\left[\frac{p}{1 - p}\right] = a + bt, \tag{8.5}$$

where we replace r by b in accord with the econometric convention. Equivalently, (8.5) may be solved for p as

$$p = \frac{1}{[1 + A \exp(-bt)]}, \tag{8.6}$$

where A = exp(–a), a constant of integration. According to (8.4), the slope of ratio p depends on the sign of b, and the point of inflection exists at t = –a/b.

If b is positive (b > 0), the slope of p is positive. From (8.6), the ratio p = y/y* converges to 1 as t goes to infinity. That is, y converges to y* as t increases.[10] In the early stage, when the difference in real GDP per capita between the developing and developed countries is large, the convergence is faster. In the later stage, when the difference is small, the convergence becomes slower and slower, but eventually the gap will be closed.

If b is negative (b < 0), the slope of p is negative, and the ratio p converges to 0, as t goes beyond any limit. That is, y diverges from y* more and more as

---

8 In Equation (8.4), d(ln p)/dt = d(ln y)/dt if y* is constant, and reduces to the learning Equation (8.1)

9 Equation (8.5) is the general solution of differential Equation (8.4), and a is a constant of integration. To solve (8.4), we simply separate the variables as dp/[p(1 – p)] = bdt, and note that the left-hand side is dp[(1/p) + (1/(1 – p))]. For some properties of the logistic model, see Johnston (1984, 72–73).

10 In this chapter, we define an absolute convergence. That is, real GDP per capita of a developing country converges to real GDP per capita of a developed country, not to the steady-state equilibrium real GDP per capita of the developing country, as formulated in Mankiw et al. (1992).

t increases. The divergence increases faster in the early stage, but it becomes slower in the later stage of development. Lastly, if b is zero (b = 0), no convergence or divergence is expected for any time period.

Note that Mankiw et al. (1992, 422) use a dynamic equation similar to Equation (8.1), which is the usual Gompertz curve, to investigate convergence or divergence of income per effective worker, y, of a country to its steady-state level, y*, which is a constant. In their model, k = (n + g + 8)(1 − α − β) is the product of the growth rates of labor (n), technology (g) and depreciation (δ) and the residual of factor shares (a + β). Both the logistic model and the Gompertz model belong to the family of three-parameter curves and can be derived as special cases of the Richards model (Ratkowsky, 1990, 140). Mankiw et al. (1992) use the Gompertz model since they expand their neoclassical dynamic model logarithmically around the constant steady-state value.

As we are interested in the long-run convergence when t goes to infinity, it does not matter whether we use the logistic model or the Gompertz model. Thus, our formulation of the dynamic model is basically the same as that of Mankiw et al., and instead of estimating the parameters using a linear regression method, we propose a nonlinear regression method.

Over the long period, real GDP per capita of Taiwan (or Korea) is, on average, about 50% of that of Japan, with the range between a high of about 80% in the prewar period and a low[11] of about 25% in 1970. The real GDP per capita of Korea and Taiwan is, on average, about 20% of that of the United States, with the range between a high of about 50% and a low of 6% (see Table 8B.1, Appendix 8B and Hsiao and Hsiao, 2003).

Figure 8.3 presents the logistic curves, ln [p/(1 − p)], for the five pairs of countries. Since visual inspection of Figure 8.3 shows that the time series are distinctly nonlinear, we have modified Equation (8.5) into a polynomial equation of degree 4 as follows:

$$\ln\left[\frac{p}{(1-p)}\right] = a + bt + ct^2 + dt^3 + et^4. \qquad (8.7)$$

Solving for p, we have

$$p = \frac{1}{[1 + A\exp(-bt - ct^2 - dt^3 - et^4)]}. \qquad (8.8)$$

---

11 Hsiao and Hsiao (2003) discuss the implication of this prewar and postwar difference.

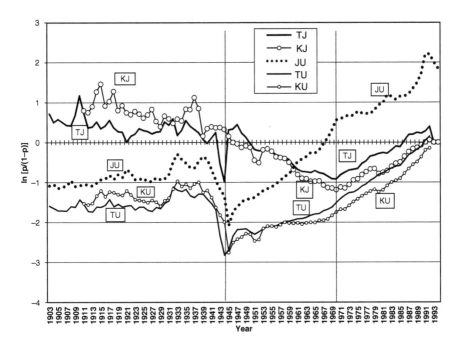

Figure 8.3 The Logistic Curves for Five Pairs of Countries

In Equation (8.8), t^4 is the dominant term, so the convergence of p depends ultimately on the sign of coefficient e, regardless of the signs of coefficients b, c and d. If e is positive, p approaches 1 as t goes to infinity, and y converges to y*. If e is negative, p tends toward zero as t goes beyond any limit, and y diverges from y*. If e = 0, Equation (8.7) becomes cubic, and the convergence of p depends on the sign of d, regardless of the signs of b and c and so on.

It is well known that many time series are nonstationary (i.e., they contain a unit root), so before estimating the logistic model, we first employ the augmented Dickey–Fuller (ADF) unit root test to examine the stationarity of ln $[p/(1-p)]$ series for the five pairs of countries. The general equation for the ADF test is

$$\Delta x_t = a_0 + a_1 x_{t-1} + a_2 t + \sum_{i=1}^{k} \beta_i \Delta x_{t-i} + \varepsilon_t, \qquad (8.9)$$

where x_t (level series) is $\ln[p/(1-p)]$, Δx_t is the first-difference series of x_t, x_{t-1} is the one-period lag of x_t for the unit root test, t is the time trend and Δx_{t-i} is the ith lag of Δx_t. We use k from 1 to 6, and the optimal lag length k is chosen by the minimum Akaike information criterion (AIC) (Stock and Watson, 2003).

Since major learning experiences among the countries occurred after World War II, we estimated the logistic curve using the data from 1947 to 1992. When we applied the ADF unit root test in Equation (8.9) on the five level series, we found them all nonstationary at the 10% significance level. Thus, we proceeded to do an ADF test on the first-difference series of $\ln[p/(1 - p)]$. We found that the five first-difference series were stationary at 1% or 5% significance levels. Hence, they are appropriate for use in the estimation of the logistic model of convergence.

Table 8.1 presents the estimated logistic curves for the five pairs of countries using the first-difference series of $\ln[p/(1 - p)]$. The logistic model of Equation (8.7) in the first difference series can be written as

$$\Delta \ln\left[\frac{p}{(1 - p)}\right] = a + \beta t + \gamma t^2 + \delta t^3. \tag{8.10}$$

In the first four cases in Table 8.1, the estimated coefficients of γ and δ are not significant at the 10% level, so a linear logistic model ($\gamma = \delta = 0$) of (8.10) is estimated. For this linear case, it can be shown from Equation (8.7) that $\beta = 2c$; hence, c and β have the same sign. For Korea and Taiwan with Japan, the β coefficients are about 0.004, and they are positive and significant at the 1% level. This indicates that the coefficient c in Equation (8.7) is also positive, which implies that the real GDP per capita of Taiwan (and Korea) is catching up with that of Japan.[12]

Similarly, for Korea and Taiwan with the United States, the β coefficients are about 0.002 (only one-half of the coefficients with Japan), and they are positive and significant at the 1% or 5% levels. This also indicates that the real GDP per capita of Korea (and Taiwan) is catching up with that of the United States, but their time for catching up is taking longer than with that of Japan.

For Japan with the United States, the estimated coefficients for β, γ and δ in Equation (8.10) are all significant. For this cubic equation, it can be shown from Equation (8.7) that $\delta = 4e$; hence, e and δ have the same sign. The coefficient δ is 0.00002. Although it is small, it is positive and significant at the 5% level. This also indicates that the real GDP per capita of Japan converges to that of the United States.

---

12 For some empirical evidence on the catching up, see Suzuoki (1996), Hobday (1995) and Hsiao and Hsiao (2001b;2003).

Table 8.1 Estimation of the Logistic Model and Convergence The First-Difference Series of $\ln[p/(1-p)]$, 1947–92

Pair of Countries	Method	const α	t β	t^2 γ	t^3 δ	R^2	DW-d
1 TwnJpn TJ	AR(1)	-0.0900 *** (0)	0.0040 *** (0)			0.525	1.923
2 KorJpn KJ	OLS	-0.0817 *** (0.01)	0.0037 *** (0)			0.216	1.618
3 TwnUSA TU	OLS	0.0024 (0.83)	0.0021 *** (0)			0.387	1.751
4 KorUSA KU	OLS	0.0087 (0.65)	0.0018 ** (0.02)			0.127	1.674
5 JpnUSA JU	OLS	0.0038 (0.95)	0.0198 * (0.08)	-0.0012 ** (0.04)	0.00002 ** (0.03)	0.153	1.842

Notes: AR(1) denotes the first-order autocorrelation method. p-values are in the parentheses. *** (** or *) denotes significant at the 1%% (5% or 10%) level.

8.5 Time Required for Convergence

In the above analysis, convergence is defined as the limit of p when t goes to infinity. It is unrealistic to say that convergence takes place at the infinite time horizon. A more realistic question would be how long it will take the current real GDP per capita of a developing country to converge, say, 5% or 10%, with the level of real GDP per capita of a developed country. To answer this question, we derive a formula to calculate the time length for convergence in a finite time horizon.

Since Table 8.1 shows that most logistic curves have positive and significant coefficients for the t^2 variable in Equation (8.7), we use the quadratic logistic model in (8.7) with d = e = 0. Differentiating both sides with respect to time t, we can derive $\hat{p} = (1-p)(b + 2ct)$, where $c = \beta/2$ and

$$\hat{p} = \frac{d(\ln p)}{p} = \left(\frac{dp}{dt}\right)\frac{1}{p}$$

is the percentage change of p from the previous year. Solving for t, we have

$$t = \frac{\left\{\left[\dfrac{\hat{p}}{(1-p)}\right] - b\right\}}{2c},$$

where[13] $\hat{p}t = \ln p_t - \ln p_{t-1} = \hat{y}_t - \hat{y}_t^*$, which is the difference of real GDP per capita growth rates of developing and developed countries. It may be called simply the deviation rate.
Let p_0 be the initial ratio at t_0, and p_n be the target ratio at t_n. Then

$$t_n - t_0 = \frac{\left\{\left[\dfrac{\widehat{p_n}}{(1-p_n)}\right] - \left[\dfrac{\widehat{p_0}}{(1-p_0)}\right]\right\}}{2c} = t(p_n) - t(p_0), \tag{8.11}$$

where, for convenience of calculation, we separate the right-hand side into two parts:

$$t(p_0) = \hat{p}_0 / [2c(1 - p_0)], \quad t(p_n) = \hat{p}_n / [2c(1 - p_n)].$$

Formula (8.11) shows that the time interval between the initial time t_0 and the terminal time t_n is inversely related to the coefficient c of t^2, but it does not depend on coefficients a and b in Equation (8.7). It also shows that coefficient c (or β) is indeed a measure of the speed of convergence: the larger the value of coefficient c, the shorter the time to reach the target of real GDP per capita ratio.

The "average" row of Table 8.2 lists the average of the ratios p, denoted as T/J, K/J and so on (that is, the ratios of real GDP per capita of the five countries), from 1988 to 1992 based on Maddison's data (1995) (for details, see Appendix 8C). We then calculate $\hat{p}$, denoted as g(T/J), g(K/J) and so on, in the table. Here, $\hat{p}_t = \ln p_t - \ln p_{t-1}$, the difference of ln pt in the consecutive years (see Appendix 8C).

We now take these p_t and $\hat{p}_t$ in the "average" row as the initial values p_0 (see A) and $\hat{p}_0$ (see B) and ask, other things being equal, how many years it will take if p_0 increases by, say, 5%, for Korea and Taiwan to catch up with Japan, and for all three countries to catch up with the United States, as indicated in the table (see E). We estimate c = $\beta/2$ from Table 8.1.

From average p_0 and $\hat{p}_0$, we calculate $t(p_0)$ in the "average" row as given in (8.11) (see C). We then assume that all the ratios increase by 5% (see D), and then calculate $\hat{p}_n = g(p_n)$ (see E) and $t(p_n)$ (see F). The difference, $t(p_n) - t(p_0)$, measures the time required to achieve the target and is shown in bold (see G). It shows that, for the estimated c given in row 2, it will take about 45 years for Taiwan from $p_0 = 0.57$, and 38 years for Korea from $p_0 = 0.49$, to narrow the

---

13 Since $p = y/y^*$, we have $\hat{p} = \hat{y} - \hat{y}^*$. Note that $\hat{p}_t = \ln p_t - \ln p_{t-1} = (\ln y_t - \ln y_t^*) - (\ln y_{t-1} - \ln y_{t-1}^*) = \hat{y}_t - \hat{y}_t^*$. We take $\hat{p}$ as a continuous growth rate, instead of a discrete growth rate, $(p_t - p_{t-1})/p_{t-1}$.

Table 8.2 Computation of Convergence Time Equation (8.11)

Pair of countries	Eq.(8.11) t(p)=g(p)/[2c(1-p)] Deviation rate	c= 0.002 / 0.002	0.001 / 0.001	0.01
		t(p0) ↓	↓	↓
A Varirable p0	**B** p̂0 ≡ g(p0)	**C** t(T/J) ↓ t(T/U) ↓ t(J/U)		
TJ KJ TU KU JU	g(T/J) g(K/J) g(T/U) g(K/U) g(J/U)	t(K/J)	t(K/U)	
avg 0.57 0.49 0.48 0.41 0.85	0.017 0.031 0.048 0.062 0.031	**D** 9.9 15.0 46.7 53.0 2.8		
(a) E pn = p0 + 5%	p̂n ≡ g(pn)=ln(pn)-ln(p0)	t(pn)		
+0.05 0.62 0.54 0.53 0.46 0.90	0.085 0.098 0.098 0.114 0.057	**F** 55 53 105 106 29		
No. of years required when p0 increases 5% = t(pn) - t(p0) =		**G** 45 38 59 53 26		
(b) A Policy Model	Control variable			
pn	**H g(pn)=** p̂0+0.01	t(pn)		
0.62 0.54 0.53 0.46 0.90	0.027 0.041 0.058 0.072 0.041	18 22 62 67 21		
No. of years required at 5% when p̂0 in B increses 1% =		**I** 8 7 16 14 18		

real GDP per capita gap with Japan by 5% (see F). Note that it takes a longer time for Taiwan to narrow the gap with Japan than for Korea, since Taiwan's initial ratio is higher than that of Korea at t_0.

The problem with this calculation is that the growth rate $\hat{p}$ is calculated as

$$\widehat{p_n} = \ln p_n - \ln p_0,$$

which is 45 years apart for Taiwan and 38 years apart for Korea, instead of the consecutive years at the terminal year, t = n.

Thus, we consider the deviation rate $\hat{p}_0$ as a policy variable by which the government can control the speed of convergence by promoting on-the-job training, innovation, licensing, technical cooperation with foreign countries and so forth. We assume that the deviation rate $\hat{p}_0$ increases by 0.01 to 0.027 (see H) to improve p_0 by 5%. In this case, it will take eight years for Taiwan to reach the target of closing the gap with Japan by 5%, and seven years for Korea to close the gap with Japan by 5% (see I). Note that the economies of Japan and the United States are also growing over time. Thus, the catching-up race is a moving target.

As may be expected, it will take more time for Korea and Taiwan to catch up with the real GDP per capita of the United States. Given the coefficient c = 0.001, it will take 16 years for Taiwan from p_0 = 0.48 and 14 years for Korea from p_0 = 0.41 to narrow the gap with the United States by 5% (see A and I).

The catching-up process of Japan with the United States is much more complicated. However, if we assume that it can also be represented by the quadratic form in (8.7), then from Table 8.2, Japan's coefficient c is 0.01. Since Japan's real GDP per capita on average is already as high as 85% of that of the United States in 1992 (see A), even with a much higher value of c, Japan still takes 18 years from $p_0 = 0.85$ to narrow the gap with the United States by 5% (see I).

8.6 Concluding Remarks

It is rather surprising that economists in Korea and Taiwan often take it for granted that prewar Japan was so strong and postwar Japan has grown so fast that Korea and Taiwan will never be able to catch up with Japan. This view is untenable. There are many examples from the history of world economic development of former colonies catching up with their former master countries. In fact, world competitiveness does not depend solely on size of population, military might or the amount of natural resource endowment.

Considering the recent experience of the long recession of the Japanese economy and relatively strong performances of Korea and Taiwan, we submit that it is time to examine when these countries can catch up with Japan and, for that matter, also with the United States.

For this purpose, we have attempted to combine the traditional learning model with the recent growth theory. We first set up a model of learning in accordance with the idea of the "advantages of backwardness" in terms of technology, which is interpreted as a function of the difference of real GDP per capita between developing and developed countries. From these models, we have calculated the coefficients of learning between the developing countries, Korea and Taiwan, with the developed countries, Japan and the United States. In addition, we also compute the coefficient of learning of Japan with the United States.

The innovative part of our model is that we have shown that the logistic model of convergence is an extension of the learning model and belongs to the same family of the dynamic equations used in the current literature, adopted to the case of time-series data. We then modified the solution to the logistic equation for the estimation of the coefficients in the logistic model.

The advantage of the logistic model is that the convergence process is formulated explicitly between the real GDP per capita of any two countries. It does not require the convergence of the real GDP per capita to the conjectured steady-state growth path of developing countries using cross-country data[14] or the unit root–based test of convergence (Bernard and Durlauf, 1996),

---

14 The problem of the cross-country data is that they are generally not comparable and the economic structure usually varies considerably across countries. Instead of putting 100 or so different countries on the regression lines, it appears more reasonable to compare directly the two closely related countries.

which, as in this chapter, uses the real GDP per capita exclusively, without being able to ascertain the time of convergence.

The logistic model is a nonlinear function, and its applications do not depend on the linearization of the Cobb–Douglas or CES production function, or on the initial condition of the country's GDP per capita but, more realistically, directly on the learning coefficient or similar coefficients (that is, the coefficients of time trend). Our model is simple and intuitive. It complements existing studies using cross-country growth regression and others.

The simple learning model and the logistic model are useful if the data for variables other than real GDP per capita are not available for the prewar and the transition period. However, data on labor and capital stock are available in the postwar period. These data may enable us to extend the logistic model to study the mechanisms behind the catching up in depth and will provide us with direction toward possible extensions of this chapter.

In general, using our simple models, we were able to show that the levels of real GDP per capita of both Korea and Taiwan catch up with those of Japan and the United States. Thus, while diminishing returns will eventually set in and the economic growth rate of the NIEs may be tapering off, the convergence of the Korean and Taiwanese economies with those of the advanced countries like Japan and the United States may, barring political turmoil and international disturbances, ultimately be realized.

Appendix 8A: On the Coefficient of Learning (r)

The average and the coefficient of variation (CV, in percent) of r are presented in Table 8A.1. For all cases except Taiwan with Japan, the transition period (1941–1950) has negative average coefficients, showing a rather unusual situation during the war period. Ignoring the transition period, for all other three periods—total, prewar and postwar—the coefficients of Japan with the United States generally have the highest average value (with the exception of the prewar coefficient of Korea with Japan), followed by Taiwan with Japan, Korea with Japan, Taiwan with the United States, and then Korea with the United States. These findings are consistent with our visual observations. They indicate that technology transfer from Japan to Korea and Taiwan is more effective than that from the United States to Korea and Taiwan.

Table 8A.1 Coefficients of Learning (r) and Variation

	TJ	KJ	TU	KU	JU
Total period (1911-1992) (a)					
Total Avera	0.044	0.044	0.025	0.023	0.063
CV (%)	243.8	416.3	186.4	215.8	134.0
Prewar period (1911-1940) (b)					
Average	0.024	0.075	0.008	0.015	0.026
CV (%)	536.1	225.8	493.0	273.9	192.5
Transition period (1941-1950)					
Average	0.002	-0.107	-0.012	-0.021	-0.015
CV (%)	12333.7	-371.3	-618.4	-416.4	-732.5
Postwar period (1951-1992)					
Average	0.069	0.058	0.045	0.039	0.108
CV (%)	52.5	100.9	64.8	85.4	66.5

Source: Maddison, 1995. (a) 1912–92 for Korea. (b) 1912–40 for Korea.

Table 8B.1 Ratios of GDP per Capita (p = y/y*)

Countries	T/J	K/J	J/U	T/U	K/U
Year	1903-1992	1911-1992	1903-1994	1903-1992	1911-1992
Sample	90	82	92	90	82
max	0.7640	0.8116	0.9011	0.5376	0.4643
min	0.2709	0.2337	0.1105	0.0561	0.0595
avg	0.4987	0.4927	0.4233	0.1977	0.1932
std	0.1159	0.1694	0.2164	0.0999	0.0841

Appendix 8B: Ratio of the GDP Per Capita

Descriptive Statistic of the data. See Table 8B.1.

Appendix 8C: Calculation of the Time Required for Convergence

Due to the limitations of space of the originally published article, many steps in Table 8.2 were curtailed. Table 8C.1 shows the step-by-step

Table 8C.1 Calculation Table of Convergence Time

							T/J	K/J	T/U	K/U	J/U
1 Original data											
2	Real GDP per capita					pt ≡ ratio at t					
3 year	Japan	USA	Taiwan	Korea			T/J	K/J	T/U	K/U	J/U
4 t	(1)	(2)	(3)	(4)			(5)	(6)	(7)	(8)	(9)
5 1988	17028	21463	9357	7829			0.55	0.46	0.44	0.36	0.79
6 1989	17757	21783	9955	8294			0.56	0.47	0.46	0.38	0.82
7 1990	18548	21866	10324	8977			0.56	0.48	0.47	0.41	0.85
8 1991	19240	21366	10957	9645			0.57	0.50	0.51	0.45	0.90
9 1992	19425	21558	11590	10010			0.60	0.52	0.54	0.46	0.90
10 avg	**18400**	**21607**	**10437**	**8951**	**A**		*0.57*	*0.49*	*0.48*	*0.41*	*0.85*
11						*p0 = avg ratio*					
12						$p^t = \ln p(t) - \ln p(t-1) \equiv g(pt)$					
13 Eq.(8.11)	$t(p^0)=p^0/[2c(1-(p0))]$						g(T/J)	g(K/J)	g(T/U)	g(K/U)	g(J/U)
14	$t(p^n)=p^n/[2c(1-(pn))]$						(10)	(11)	(12)	(13)	(14)
15							0.003	0.041	0.032	0.069	0.028
16	For p = T/J						0.020	0.016	0.047	0.043	0.027
17	$t(T/J)=g(T/J)/[2c(1-(T/J))]$						-0.007	0.036	0.033	0.075	0.040
18							0.023	0.035	0.083	0.095	0.060
19							0.047	0.028	0.047	0.028	0.001
20 Avg	**p^0 = avg deviation rate**				**B**		**0.017**	**0.031**	**0.048**	**0.062**	**0.031**
21	c (from Table 8.2)				**C**		0.002	0.002	0.001	0.001	0.01
22	Calculation of t(p^0)				**D**		**9.9**	**15.0**	**46.7**	**53.0**	**10.5**
23 *Case I* Target: pn = p0 + 0.05					**E**		0.62	0.54	0.53	0.46	0.90
24	**p^n = lnpn - lnp0**						0.085	0.098	0.098	0.114	0.057
25	t(p^n)				**F**		55	53	105	106	29
26	tn - t0 = t(p^n) - t(p^0)				**G**		**45**	**38**	**59**	**53**	**19**
27	= (row 25) - (row 22)										

Note: Lines A to G correspond to those in Table 8.2.

^ in $\hat{p}_0$ or $\hat{p}_n$ denotes "p hat 0" or "p hat n," showing the logarithmic difference.

derivation of the time required for convergence. Rows A to I in Table 8C.1 correspond to the rows A to I in Table 8.2. In Table 8C.1, the original data from Maddison (1995) are shown in rows 5 to 9, and the ratios of the real GDP per capita pt are calculated in columns 5 to 9 (see part A). The average of the ratios from 1988 to 1992 is taken as the initial ratio p_0 in part A. We then calculate $\hat{p}_t$, the logarithmic difference between the ratios over time, in rows 15 to 19, and denote them as $g(T/J)$, $g(K/J)$ and so on. (see B). Here, $\hat{p}_t = \ln p_t - \ln p_{t-1}$ is the difference of $\ln p_t$ in the consecutive years. The first row, row 15, is calculated from 1987 data in Maddison (not shown).

We now take these p and $\hat{p}$ in the "Avg" row (rows 10 and 20) as the initial values p_0 (in row 10, see A) and $\hat{p}_0$ (in row 20, see B). We then explore that, other things being equal, how many years it will take if p_0 increases by, say, 5%, for Korea and Taiwan to catch up with Japan. We do the same for all three countries to catch up with the United States, as indicated in row 23. We estimate $c = \beta/2$ in C in row 21 from Table 8.1.

From average p_0 (in A) and $\hat{p}_0$ (in B), we calculate $t(p_0)$ in row 22 (see D). We then assume that all the ratios increase by 5% to obtain p_n in row 23, and then calculate $\hat{p}_n$ and $t(\hat{p}_n)$ in rows 24 and 25. The difference, $t(\hat{p}_n) - t(\hat{p}_0)$ in row 26 (see G), measures the time required to achieve the target. Note that in the table, $\hat{p}_n$ is written as p^n and so on.

Sources of Data

The original datasets for all the figures and tables are taken from Maddison (1995). Tables are based on the authors' calculations.

Acknowledgments

We are indebted to Professors Song-ken Hsu, Robert McNown, Naci Mocan and Ron Smith for valuable comments and suggestions. All errors of omission and commission are the authors'. In this chapter, three Appendixes are added to the original paper. Table 8.2 has been expanded to Table 8C.1 to show the calculation procedure in detail.

References

Bernard, Andrew B., and Steven N. Durlauf (1996). "Interpreting Tests of the Convergence Hypothesis," *Journal of Econometrics* 71: 161–73.

Chamberlain, Muriel Evelyn (1998). *The Longman Companion to European Desalinization in the Twentieth Century*. New York: Addison Wesley Longman.

Coe, David T., Elhanan Helpman and Alexander W. Hoffmaister (1995). "North-South R&D Spillovers," NBER Working Paper, No. 5048. Also in *Economic Journal* (1997), 107(440): 134–49.

Gerschenkron, Alexander (1962). *Economic Backwardness in Historical Perspective.* Cambridge, MA: Harvard University Press.

Gomulka, Stanislaw (1990). *The Theory of Technical Change and Economic Growth.* London: Routledge.

Hobday, Michael (1995). *Innovation in East Asia: the Challenge to Japan.* Brookfield, VT: Edward Elgar.

Hsiao, Frank S. T., and Mei-Chu W. Hsiao (1996). "Taiwanese Economic Development and Foreign Trade." In John Y. T. Kuark, ed. *Comparative Asian Economies: Contemporary Studies in Economic and Financial Analysis.* 77 (Part B). Greenwich, CT: JAI Press, 211–302.

——— (2001a). "Capital Flows and Exchange Rates: Recent Korean and Taiwanese Experience and Challenges," *Journal of Asian Economics* 12: 353–81.

——— (2001b). "Diminishing Returns and Asian NIEs: How They Overcome the Iron Law." In Sheng-Cheng Hu, ed. *Conference Proceedings on Economic Development in Memory of Professor Ma-huang Hsing.* Taipei: Institute of Economics, Academia Sinica, 239–86.

——— (2002). "Taiwan in the Global Economy: Past, Present, and Future." In Peter C.Y. Chow, ed. *Taiwan in the Global Economy: From an Agrarian Economy to an Exporter of High-tech Products.* Westport, CT: Greenwood Press, 161–222.

——— (2003). " 'Miracle Growth' in the Twentieth Century: International Comparisons of East Asian Development," *World Development* 31: 227–57.

Hsiao, Mei-Chu W. (2001). "Pacific Trade Triangle and the Growth of Korea and Taiwan: Cointegration and Causality Analyses," Working Paper, University of Colorado Denver.

Johnston, J. (1984). *Econometric Methods.* 3rd ed. New York: McGraw-Hill.

Krugman, Paul (1994). "The Myth of Asia's Miracle," *Foreign Affairs* 73(6): 62–78.

Maddison, Angus (1995). *Monitoring the World Economy, 1820–1992.* Paris: Development Centre, OECD.

Mankiw, N. Gregory, David Romer and David N. Weil (1992). "A Contribution to the Empirics of Economic Growth," *Quarterly Journal of Economics* 107(2): 407–37.

Mizoguchi, Toshiyuki, and Yuzo Yamamoto (1984). "Capital Formation in Korea and Taiwan." In Ramon H. Myers and Mark R. Peattie, eds. *The Japanese Empire, 1895–1945.* Princeton, NJ: Princeton University Press.

Nelson, Richard R., and Edmund S. Phelps (1966). "Investment in Humans, Technological Diffusion and Economic Growth," *American Economic Review* 56: 66–75.

Penn World Table (PWT) (1994). Mark 5.6, National Bureau of Economic Research. Available at: www.nber.org/pwt56.doc.html.

Ratkowsky, David A. (1990). *Handbook of Nonlinear Regression Models.* New York: Marcel Dekker.

Sachs, Jeffrey D., and Andrew Warner (1995). "Economic Reform and the Process of Global Integration," *Brookings Papers on Economic Analysis*, 25th Anniversary Issue. 1–118.

Stock, James H., and Mark W. Watson (2003). *Introduction to Econometrics.* New York: Addison Wesley.

Suzuoki, Takabumi (1996). "From Flying Geese to Round Robin: the Emergence of Powerful Asian Companies and the Collapse of Japan's Keiretsu," Discussion Paper, Program on US–Japan Relations, Harvard University.

Temple, Jonathan (1999). "The New Growth Evidence," *Journal of Economic Literature*: 37(1): 112–56.

Verspagen, Bent (1994). "Technology and Growth: the Complex Dynamics of Convergence and Divergence." In G. Silverberg and L. Soete, eds. *The Economics of Growth and Technical Change: Technologies, Nations, Agents*. Brookfield, VT: Edward Elgar.

World Bank (1994, 1999/2000). *World Development Report*. New York: Oxford University Press.

World Economic Forum (WEF) (1999). *The Global Competitiveness Report*. Cambridge, MA: Harvard Institute of International Development.

Chapter 9

EPILOGUE: FROM EMERGING EAST ASIA TO AN ASIA-CENTERED WORLD ECONOMY

Abstract

From the previous chapters of this book, we may wonder what the recent development of catching up and convergence are in East Asia. We may also wonder whether the East Asian economies are still viable or whether they dropped out of the scene like many other newly industrializing countries (NICs) did several decades ago. As we predicted in Chapters 2 and 3, Korea's high-tech industry has continued to grow. In fact, Korea eventually caught up with Taiwan. Korea's GDP per capita in current US dollars exceeded Taiwan's in 2010. Thus, in particular, we want to know whether and when the GDP per capita in purchasing power parity (PPP) of Korea can catch up with that of Taiwan, or whether the GDP per capita of Korea and Taiwan will converge to Japan or the United States.

More interestingly, we ask what the comparison of their economic performance is with some other advanced OECD countries like the United Kingdom, Germany, France and the Netherlands. Applying cross-section and time-series data, this chapter discusses these questions using some recent international statistics published by the IMF, the World Bank and the US CIA. The data were taken from 1980 to 2020. From the study of these datasets, it appears that East Asia is still emerging, and there seems no reason to discount the possibility of an Asia-centered world economy.

9.1 Introduction

In Chapters 6, 7 and 8, we have pointed out that Japan, Korea and Taiwan had high average growth rates in the world before World War II (1911–40) in terms of real GDP per capita in Geary–Khamis dollars (see the explanation and derivation in Appendix 9A), but had the lowest average growth rates during the transition period (1941–50). However, these countries had the highest average growth rates in the world during the postwar period (1951–92) in the order of Taiwan (6.03%), Korea (5.8%) and Japan (5.57%).

In terms of long-run average growth rates including the prewar and postwar periods (1911–92), the three also ranked the highest in the world, in the order of Japan (3.34%), Taiwan (3.04%) and Korea (2.98%) (see Table 7.1). Looking at the level of real GDP per capita in Geary–Khamis dollars, Japan's GDP per capita was consistently higher than both Taiwan's and Korea's throughout the prewar and postwar periods, and Korea's GDP per capita was consistently higher than that of Taiwan during the prewar period. However, Taiwan caught up with Korea during the postwar period, at least until 1992, the year in which the Maddison data ended (Figure 7.1).

From our previous analysis of the manufacturing industry of both countries from 1978 to 1996, overall production and industrial structures were very similar between Korea and Taiwan, especially in the structure of valued-added output shares in the traditional and high-tech industries (Chapter 3). However, at disaggregated levels, we found that Korea's productivities in the basic and traditional sectors were consistently lower than those of Taiwan, but Korea had an extraordinary growth of productivity in the high-tech industry during this period (Chapter 4). The "innovators analysis" also revealed that Taiwan had more frontier sectors in the traditional category and that Korea had more in the high-tech category, especially in the electronics sector, showing the consistent productivity superiority of Korea's high-tech industries (Chapter 4). Our analysis was based on data from the 1980s to the 1990s (Table 4.2). We asked whether such differences at the disaggregate levels of the two countries had any effect on the long-run economic development of the two countries.

We also studied the catching up and convergence among Korea and Taiwan with Japan and the United States, respectively, and Japan with the United States, in terms of the real GDP per capita (the same below), and estimated the time required for convergence. Our learning models in Chapter 5, using the dataset from the mid-1940s to the mid-1990s, showed that the Taiwanese economy was converging with Japan's (Table 5.5, Chapters 5), and so was the Korean economy (Table 8.1, Chapter 8). Furthermore, both economies, along with the Japanese economy, were also converging with the US economy (Table 8.1).

We then calculated, using the Maddison data from 1988 to 1992, the time required to converge. Our calculation showed that, in terms of the real GDP per capita, it took Taiwan 45 years, and Korea 38 years, to converge on the Japanese GDP per capita by 5%. It appeared to take too long to converge. However, if the government could control the speed of convergence, the time could be reduced to eight and seven years, respectively. This would be a more reasonable prediction (Table 8.2).

In this chapter, we ask what happened to these analyses and studies from the vantage point of current (2016–17) economic development. More generally, we are interested in what the results of catching up and convergence games are among the four newly industrializing East Asian countries, among these Asian countries with the United States and some advanced countries in Europe, and also some more advanced countries in the ASEAN.

In what follows, Section 9.2 uses cross-sectional data of 2014 to compare GDP per capita in purchasing power parity (PPP) and in nominal US dollars among these countries. Section 9.3 uses time-series data from 1980 to 2020 to compare GDP per capita in PPP and in nominal US dollars among these countries. Section 9.4 summarizes the catching up and convergence among these countries, and points out some recent problems in the mid-2010s facing Taiwan, Korea and the world. While we recognize the current economic slowdown in Section 9.5, and the dichotomy of the world PPP GDP per capita distribution, we conclude in Section 9.5 with the possibility of an Asia-centered world economy. Lastly, we added a Question and Answer section, Section 9.6, as a postscript to this chapter to answer some of the questions posed by the three prepublication reviewers.

Since the use of purchasing power parity (PPP) only became popular in recent years, and its concept is hard to understand without knowing the method of its derivation, we explain in detail (for the first time in the literature) the method of deriving PPP in Appendix 9A. Then, we explain its relation with the so-called Big Mac Index in Appendix 9B. Appendixes 9C and 9B relate to the questions posed in Section 9.6 and highlight the seldom known fact that Taiwan is indeed the "Republic of Technology."

9.2 Cross-Section Comparison of GDP per Capita

In the previous analysis, the Maddison's data on catching up and convergence were based on the internationally comparable real GDP per capita measured in 1990 Geary–Khamis dollars. It is also called GDP per capita in international dollars, written as int$, or the purchasing power parity PPP value of GDP or GDP per capita (see Appendix 9A for explanation and derivation). We call it PPP GDPpc for simplicity. With advancements in computer capabilities, the PPP method gained popularity in recent years. It is used by several international organizations, such as the International Monetary Fund (IMF), the United Nations, OECD, the World Bank, the CIA and so forth to compare GDP and GDP per capita of the countries in the world.

In this chapter, we use an IMF dataset for our analysis since it is the only organization that includes data on Taiwan. We are interested in GDP per capita since it is an important, if not the most important, indicator of economic performance as well as the cost of living, or the standard of living, of individual countries (Schreyer and Koechlin, 2002).

For comparison, we also use the traditional method of comparison, namely, nominal GDP per capita, written briefly as nominal GDPpc, which is obtained by deflating GDP in national currency by the US dollar exchange rate[1] (for calculation, see Appendix 9A).

The left panel of Figure 9.1 compares PPP GDPpc among the four Asian NIEs, along with the United States, Japan, China, India and the four major European countries, Germany, France, the United Kingdom and the Netherlands. The data are measured in 1,000 international dollars (int$), and are taken from IMF (2014), as listed in *Wikipedia* (2016a, 2016b). Each group is arranged according to the size of GDPpc.

We list the country ranks across three rows on the horizontal axis as collected from three different sources/organizations: Row A is based on the IMF's data. Row B has two different sources. The left panel is PPP GDPpc based on the CIA's data, and the right panel is nominal GDPpc collected from the UN's data, as indicated. Row C is collected from the World Bank. Hong Kong's GDPpc was estimated but not ranked by all these four organizations.

Figure 9.1 shows that, in 2014, the average PPP GDPpc of the four NIEs was 54.9 ((measured in the unit of Int$ 1,000. Thus, 54.9 means Int$ 54,900. Same as below), as shown in the enclosed label above the horizontal line-patterned column), which was slightly higher than that of the United States (54.4). The average PPP GDPpc is well above the PPP GDPpc of Japan, the Netherlands, Germany, France and the United Kingdom (the upward line-patterned columns). The PPP GDPpc of China and India are still very much below the Asian NIEs. Among the Asian NIEs, Singapore ranked third in the world at 83.1, followed by Hong Kong (not ranked) at 55.1, Taiwan in the nineteenth rank at 46.0, and Korea in the thirtieth rank at 35.4.

Note that, as shown below the horizontal axis, the rankings of the countries among the four organizations (IMF, WB, UN, CIA) are more or less close to each other; thus, we only show the ranking of IMF, which is on the first line below the horizontal axis. We also note that Korea, at 35.4, ranked #30 in the world (here, # indicates the number of the ranking), is still falling far behind Taiwan at 45.9, ranked #19. In terms of PPP GDPpc, these are the same as our previous findings in Chapters 6, 7 and 8.

For comparison, the right panel of Figure 9.1 shows nominal GDPpc measured in current US dollars. The values are generally lower than those

---

1 As shown in the PPP calculation in Appendix 9A, unlike the PPP method, the US exchange rate only reflects the prices of traded goods, which only include a very small part of domestic goods in a country. Thus, nominal GDP is greatly distorted.

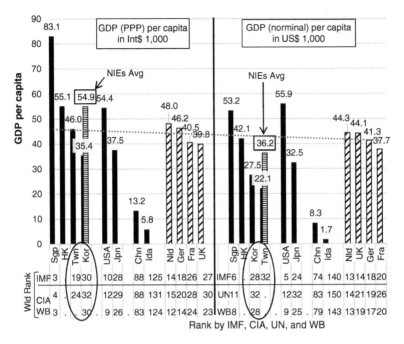

Figure 9.1 GDP per Capita in PPP and in Nominal US Dollar
NIEs and Selected Countries, 2014

measured in the PPP units, especially those for the NIEs. These values are almost the same for the United States, Japan and the EU countries in the chart. Note that the average GDPpc in terms of US dollars among the NIEs was only US$ 36,200, as shown in the enclosed number on the right panel of Figure 9.1. These values are much lower than that of the US (US$ 55,900, which should have been the same with US PPP GDPpc), and they are also below those of Japan and the four European countries. By comparing the two panels, for the NIEs, the PPP GDPpc on the left panel is generally higher than the nominal GDPpc on the right panel. This means that the general price levels, especially those of the nontraded goods of the NIEs, are generally lower than those in the United States or in Europe, and that the exchange rates of the NIEs may be undervalued (indicating that the nominal exchange rate of the NIEs per US dollar is too high).

Note also the reversal of ranking between Korea and Taiwan in 2014. The Korean nominal GDPpc in 2014 reached US$ 27,500 and a ranking at #28, in the world, surpassing the Taiwanese GDPpc at US$ 22,300 and a ranking at #32. This is different from those measured in PPP. We would like to know the relationship between the two countries over the decades and also when the reversal in nominal GDPpc occurred. To show this, the following section presents the time-series of the GDPpc.

9.3 Time-Series Comparison of GDP per Capita in PPP

In this section, we study the catching-up and convergence process of the NIEs, China, India, the four EU countries and the four ASEAN countries over time. The IMF dataset ranges from 1980 to 2014 and then forecasts the GDPpc up to 2020 (see the Sources of Data at the end of this chapter). In the following figures, the Japanese GDPpc, denoted as 1Jpn in the legend of the figures, is drawn in the columns to avoid clustering and to make comparison easy. In this chapter, the GDPpc of the 2USA is drawn in a light solid line, that of 3Korea in a dashed line, that of 4Taiwan in a heavy solid line, that of 5Singapore in a light dotted line and that of 6Hong Kong in a long dashed line. The lines for other countries vary. The column for 1997 is filled with a dark color to show the year of the 1997 Asian financial crisis (see Chapter 2), and the filled column of 2014 shows the end of the actual data from the IMF. The data after 2015 are projection by the IMF. Figures 9.1 and 9.2 present the PPP GDPpc and the nominal GDPpc separately for easier comparison.

9.3.1 Comparison among Asian NIEs, Japan, the United States, China and India

Figure 9.2 shows the trend of the PPP GDPpc of the eight countries. The figure indicates that Korea, Hong Kong and Singapore were affected by the 1997 Asian financial crisis, in contrast to Taiwan and large countries like the United States, China and India, which were not affected. However, all countries were affected by the 2008 world financial crisis, except for China and India, but the affected countries recovered very quickly.

Taiwan's PPP GDPpc surpassed that of Japan in 2006 (circled), and the difference between the two countries appeared to be increasing over time. Taiwan's catch up with Japan is faster than we have predicted in Chapter 8. However, Korea's PPP GDPpc is still consistently below that of Taiwan, but it appears to surpass that of Japan in 2017 (circled).

It appears that Singapore's PPP GDPpc supassed that of Hong Kong in 1980, and even overtook that of the United States in 1992 (circled). It increased much faster than any other country's PPP GDPpc, and by 2018 (no forecasting data for 2019 and 2020 are available), Singapore's PPP GDPpc will be more than double that of Japan, and will be more than 30% higher than that of the United States.

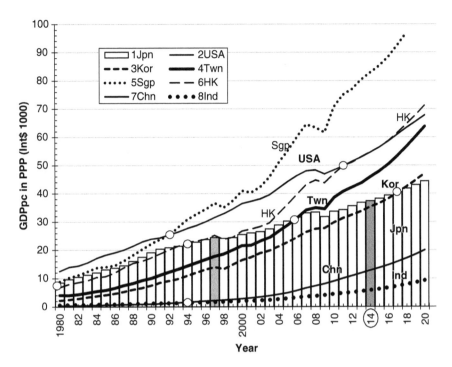

Figure 9.2 GDP per Capita in PPP
NIEs, Japan, the United States, China and India

Hong Kong is also growing fast. Its PPP GDPpc surpassed Japan's PPP GDPpc in 1994 (circled), it almost matches that of the United States between 2011 and 2017, and it is expected to overtake that of the United States after 2018.

Both China's and India's PPP GDPpc are far below these countries, and the difference seems to increase over time, despite the recent talk of high growth rate in China and India. China's PPP GDPpc was slightly below India's PPP GDPpc between 1980 and 1993, but surpassed India and gradually grew faster than India after 1994. Apparently, all the Asian NIEs are still very much "alive and kicking."

We see in Figure 9.1 that the GDPpc in PPP and in nominal US dollars are quite different. It appears that Korea, in terms of the nominal GDPpc, caught up with that of Taiwan some time before 2014. Figure 9.2 shows the time series of the GDPpc in nominal US dollars. Since the calculation of the PPP takes the US dollar as its reference, the shape of the PPP GDPpc and that of the nominal GDPpc for the United States are the same in both figures. Note that the PPP index measures the long-run trend (through the one

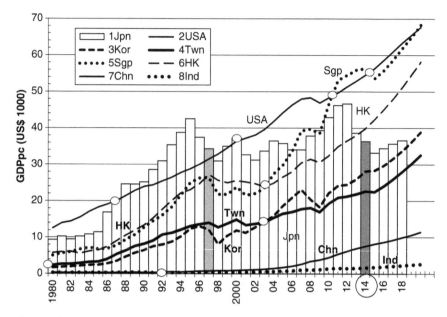

Figure 9.3 GDP per Capita in US Dollars
NIEs, Japan, the United States, China and India

price rule); thus, the shape of the PPP GDPpc for all countries mentioned in Figure 9.2 is much smoother than that of the nominal GDPpc of these countries in Figure 9.3.

In Figure 9.3, in terms of nominal GDPpc, the effects of the 1997 Asian fiancial crisis and the 2008 world financial crisis were much more pronounced, except for China, India and the United States in 1997.

The pattern of changes of the nominal GDPpc in Figure 9.3 is different from those of Figure 9.2. Korea's GDPpc came closer to Taiwan's after 1980, eventually caught up with Taiwan in 2003 (circled), and is expected to maintain the same distance over Taiwan after 2014. According to the IMF prediction, Korea is even expected to supass Japan in 2020 (circled). In addition, Japan's GDPpc surpassed the United States' between 1987 and 2000, and then fell behind the United States again after 2001 with a widening gap.

Furthermore, Hong Kong and Singapore's GDPpc were almost the same until 2003 (circled). After 2003, Singapore grew faster and eventually caught up with the United States around 2011 (circled), and it is expected to match the United States in the near future.

Lastly, as seen in Figure 9.2, both China and India remain far behind the other countries, and unlike in Figure 9.2, there is no indication that India is

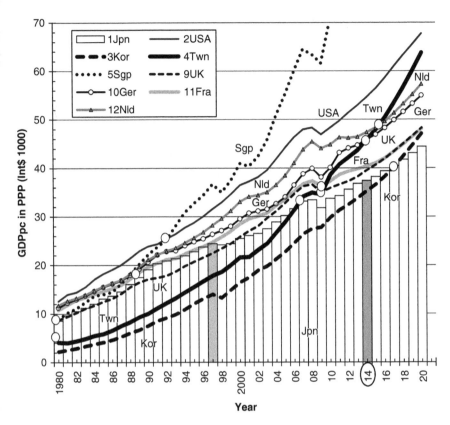

Figure 9.4 GDP per Capita in PPP
NIEs,* Japan, the United States and Four EU Countries
*To avoid cluttering, HK is not included in the figure.

catching up with China, nor that both countries are catching up with any of the other countries shown in the figure.

9.3.2 Comparison among Asian NIEs, Japan, the United States and the Four EU Countries

Figure 9.4 is the same as Figure 9.2 except that Hong Kong, China and India are substituted by the United Kingdom (9UK, the light dashed line), Germany (10Ger, the light line with circle markers), France (11Fra, the light black line) and the Netherlands (12Nld, the light line with triangle markers). It appears that these four countries have maintained more or less the same PPP GDPpc levels and growth rates since the 1980s, forming a steady upward-moving narrow interval (or band) each year between the trend lines of the United States and Korea. Contrary to some pessimistic views of the future of the world economy, the upward trend indicates the steady growth of the standard of living among the developed countries.

We also notice that Taiwanese economic performance in terms of its PPP GDPpc (the heavy black line) level and growth appears to be especially outstanding. Within the interval (or band) Taiwan's PPP GDPpc caught up with the PPP GDPpc of the United Kingdom in 2009, of France in 2010, of Germany in 2014, and is expected to catch up with that of the Netherlands in 2016 (all circled). Taiwan's PPP GDPpc level is even poised to converge with that of the United States after 2020.

In relation to this graph, Korean performance is also impressive. Its PPP GDPpc is expected to catch up with that of Japan in 2017 (circled) and the United Kingdom and France after 2020. Amid the world economic slump in recent years, the economic performances of Taiwan and Korea are indeed stellar.[2]

Note that Figure 9.4 should be read and compared with Figure 7.2 in Chapter 7. Both datasets were measured in Geary–Khamis dollars, but they are drawn on a different scale and range along the vertical axis.[3] From Figure 7.2, we can see that the PPP GDPpc of Taiwan, Korea and Japan accelerated during the postwar period. The same figure also shows that, by 1993, Japan (the solid line with circle markers) caught up with all the major Western countries, except the United States. However, the recent IMF data in Figure 9.4 show that Japan almost caught up with the four EU countries (except for the United Kingdom) from as early as 1989 (circled), but fell behind them after 1990, starting its "20-year long decession."

As we have seen above, both Taiwan and Korea continued to grow during the 1980s and the 1990s, and Taiwan's PPP GDPpc eventually caught up with that of Japan and the four EU countries. Thus, we have witnessed an example of catching up and falling behind in East Asia during the last two decades. All these four East Asian NICs are, as shown in Figure 9.4, still growing steadily.

---

2 Note that during this period, Taiwan's inflation rate (CPI) was very low. It increased from 66 in 1982 to only 107 in 2011 (2006 price = 100). This is indeed an achievement. See Hsiao and Hsiao (2015, 257).

3 We may also compare these two figures with Figure 8.1. Figure 8.1 shows that, when the data in Figure 7.2 are drawn as ten-year moving average, the postwar growth rate of PPP GDPpc for Japan was 6.08%, for Taiwan was 6.06% and for Korea was 5.63%, as compared with that of the United States at 1.99%, and the United Kingdom at 2.05%. It appears that these regressions predicted the future growth of these countries, except Japan, at least up to the end of the 2010s. Thus, what happened to the Japanese, Taiwanese and Korean economies since the early 1990s would be an interesting topic for research.

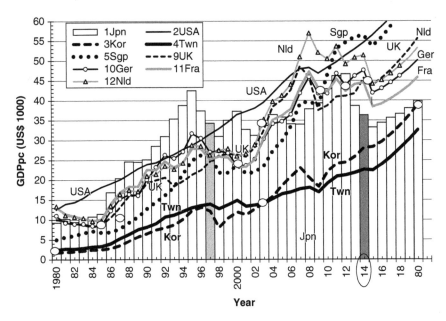

Figure 9.5 GDP per Capita in Nominal US Dollars
NIEs,* Japan, the United States and Four EU Countries
*To avoid cluttering, HK is not included in the figure.

The growth theorists often point out the importance of initial conditions for economic takeoff and driving to economic maturity. In Chapter 8, we showed that this was indeed the case for Taiwan and Korea, especially Taiwan (Hsiao and Hsiao, 2015). However, the economic slowdown of the Japanese economy defies such interpretation.[4]

Figure 9.5 shows the comparison of the nominal GDPpc of these countries. The lines are much more complicated and hard to read. However, we may discern three prominent patterns. First, the four European countries and Taiwan and Korea appear to be moving together in terms of their nominal GDPpc. Second, it appears that all of the countries on the chart (except for the United States in 1997) were greatly affected by the Asian crisis of 1997 and also by the world financial crisis of 2008–10, more so with the EU countries than with the four Asian countries. Note that, like the United States, the Taiwanese economy weathered the 2008 crisis very well. Third, the Taiwanese and Korean nominal GDPpcs lag far behind the European cluster. As we have noticed

---

4 Morishima (1999) has predicted the decline of the Japanese economy by pointing out several institutional and social factors, which appear to be shared by Taiwan and Korea.

in Section 9.1, this may be due to the undervaluation of the Taiwanese and Korea currencies.

We also find that, while the nominal GDPpc of the European countries has been lower than that of Japan after 1986 and during the 1990s, the nominal GDPpc of the Unied Kingdom and the Netherlands eventually surpassed that of Japan in 2003. The nominal GDPpc of Germany and France surpassed that of Japan after 2012 and thereafter. Like the PPP GDPpc, the figure shows that the trend line of the normal GDPpc of Japan deviates from that of the European countries more and more. Although Japan's nominal GDPpc, like its PPP GDPpc, is growing, there seems to be no indication that Japan will recover from its "20-year depression" and eventually catch up with the United States or the four major European countries again any time soon.

9.3.3 Comparison among Asian NIEs, Japan, the United States and the ASEAN-4 Countries

Up to this point, we have compared the PPP GDPpc of the Asian NIEs and Japan with the most advanced four European countries. How about the second-generation Asian developing countries, namely, the ASEAN-4 (Hsiao and Won, 2008)? Figures 9.6 and 9.7 compare the recent development of the GDPpc of the ASEAN-4 with that of Asian NIEs, Japan and the United States.

Figure 9.6 shows that, among the ASEAN-4 countries, the PPP GDPpc of Malaysia (13Mal, the light solid line) is the highest, and appears to be growing the fastest, followed by that of Thailand (14Thi, the line wih circle markers), Indonesia (15Idn, the heavy dotted line) and the Philippines (16Phi, the light solid line). All of these countries have been growing steadily but separately, with little or no catch-up or convergence among them. These countries' PPP GDPpc are far below those of Taiwan and Korea.

The effects of the 1997 and 2008 crises on the ASEAN-4 appear to be minor. While the ASEAN-4 have been developing since 1980 (namely, the lines are sloping upward), they still have a long way to go to catch up with Taiwan or Korea, since the latter are growing faster (the lines are steeper). Note that we cut the line for Singapore at 2010 to enlarge the other lines.

Figure 9.6 should be read and compared with Figure 7.1 of Chapter 7. Malaysia is not listed in Figure 7.1, but we see that by the 1990s, the order of economic performances among the other three ASEAN countries is the same, in the order of Thailand, Indonesia and the Philippines. We do not see catching up or convergence among the countries in Figure 9.6. It is interesting to notice that these four ASEAN countries maintained the same distance and grew together as a group for over two decades!

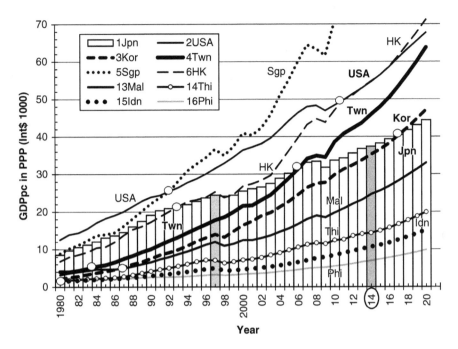

Figure 9.6 GDP per Capita in PPP
NIEs, Japan, the United States and Four ASEAN Countries

Figure 9.7 shows the time trend of the nominal GDPpc for the ASEAN-4. There does not seem to be much change across their growth relationship except that the nominal GDPpc of Indonesia and of the Philippines appears to coincide. Like the PPP GDPpc in Figure 9.6, the nominal GDPpc of all four of the ASEAN countries are much lower than those of Taiwan and Korea, implying the second-generation Asian NIEs still have a long way to go to catch up with the first-generation Asian NIEs in terms of the nominal GDPpc. Note that, like Figure 9.6, the effect of the Asian financial crisis in 1997 on these ASEAN countries seems very minor, and all aforementioned Asian countres discussed here recovered very quickly and continued to grow, demonstrating the strong resilience of the Asian economies during the last two decades.

9.4 Catching Up and Convergence in Emerging East Asia

In this chapter, we have seen that, whether the GDPpc is measured in PPP or in nominal US dollars, the economic performance of the four first-generation Asian NIEs has been outstanding since 1980, especially during the last decade, as compared with the European countries and the ASEAN

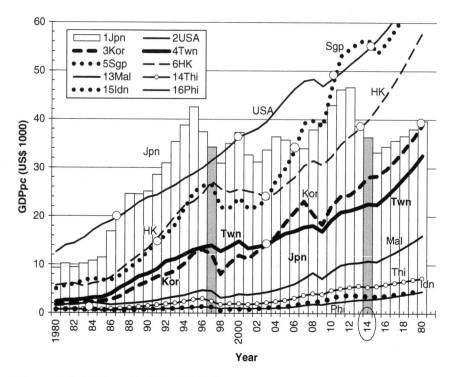

Figure 9.7 GDP per Capita in US Dollars
NIEs, Japan, the United States and Four ASEAN Countries

countries. From the steeper slope of the lines of both the PPP GDPpc and the nominal GDPpc from 2014 up to 2020, we also expect that they will continue to grow, catching up with and converging on the OECD countries, and thus gaining their place of importance in the world economy. In conjunction with our analysis in Chapter 6, we may state that the prospect of an Asia-centered world economy could continue into the foreseeable future, considering the slow but steady growth of the second and the third generations of NIEs, namely, the ASEAN countries and large countries like China and India.

Even if we put aside the two fast-growing city-states, Singapore and Hong Kong, the economic performance of Taiwan and Koria are stellar in terms of their PPP GDPpc, especially Taiwan. Taiwan's PPP GDPpc has already outperformed that of Japan and the four most advanced European countries, and is even poised to catch up with that of the United States, according to our prediction in this book (Chapter 8).

It should be noted that this finding is in stark contrast with the current domestic problems in both countries: low and stagnating wage rates, increasing inequality of income distribution, a hollowing out of domestic industries and languishing exports.[5] However, these seem to be problems facing all the developed and developing countries today and possibly will continue into the near future, and are not confined to Taiwan and Korea. While only time can provide more information, further investigation of the domestic and international conditions (e.g., Weiss, 2001) of these two countries is called for.

Aside from the domestic conditions, there is uncertainty with regard to the future of both countries under the world recession and the slowing down of exports. This is especially true for Taiwan, which, in addition, faces isolation from regional free trade agreements (FTAs) with its trading partners (Hsiao and Hsiao, 2007). World economic conditions are changing, and regional integration among countries in the Asia-Pacific is progressing rapidly. Countries are seeking FTAs to promote exports and policy coordination. Unless Taiwan can break the global isolation imposed on it by China, its future may be bleak and difficult.

Figures 9.2 and 9.3 show that China and India are also growing steadily, although not as fast as the first-generation Asian NIEs. Despite the talk of recent economic performance, there is no evidence that, at least in terms of PPP GDPpc, they will catch up with Taiwan or Korea anytime soon. Considering the century-long development of Taiwan and Korea (see Chapter 7), particularly for huge countries like China and India, they still have a long way to go. In addition, Figures 9.6 and 9.7 show that the second-generation NIEs, namely, Malaysia, Thailand, Indonesia and the Philippines, are also growing steadily, though also not as fast as the first-generation NIEs.

9.5 Conclusion—The Prospect of an Asia-Centered World Economy

From this perspective, it may be worthwhile to envision the position of the NIEs and the major Asian countries in the world economy today. Figure 9.8 shows the world frequency distribution of the PPP GDPpc of 188 countries (including Hong Kong but not including the World Average; see *Wikipedia*, 2016a) classified into 19 frequency intervals. All the data in the chart are normalized by taking the average PPP GDPpc of 34 OECD countries as 100%. Each interval has a closed upper boundary ("]") and an open lower boundary ("("). Thus, Interval 1, denoted as (0–10], means that there are 47 countries

---

5 For the case of Taiwan, see Hsiao and Hsiao (2015), Chapter 3, "Taiwan in the Global Economy—End of the 'Miracle'?"

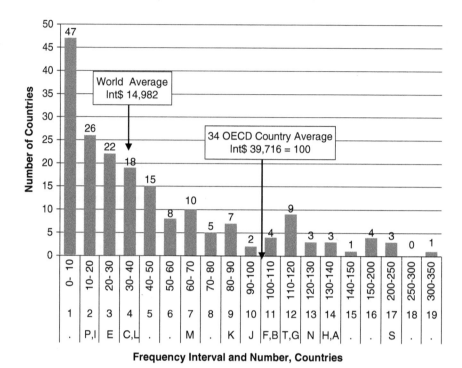

Figure 9.8 World PPP GDP per Capita Distribution
As Compared with OECD Average. 188 Countries/Regions
Notes: A = United States, B = United Kingdom, C = China, E = Indonesia, F = France,
G = Germany, H = HK, I = India, J = Japan, K = South Korea, L = Thailand, M = Malaysia,
N = Netherlands, P = Philippines. S = Singapore, T = Taiwan.

having 0% to 10% of the average OECD PPP GDPpc. The OECD average, Int$ 39,716, is taken as 100% and is located between Intervals 10 and 11 (the upper boundary of interval 10). The second row of the horizontal axis's labels depicts the interval numbers, and the third row shows the location of the 16 countries of interest we compared and discussed in the early part of this chapter.

Apparently there is a "GDPpc divide," or dichotomy, among these 16 countries, clustering around two poles. The first-generation NIEs along with the European countries consist of one group centered around the OECD average. The others, namely, the ASEAN countries, China and India, are centered around the average of World PPP GDPpc., Int$ 14,982, in Interval 4.

From Figure 9.8, we see that France (F) and the United Kingdom (B) are located about 10% higher than the OECD average; Japan (J) is about

10% lower than this average; Taiwan (T) and Germany (G) are about 20% higher than this average; and Korea (K) is about 20% lower than this average. Similarly, the Netherlands (N) is about 20 to 30% higher, Hong Kong (H) and the United States (A) are 30 to 40% higher, and Singapore (S) is 100 to 150% higher than the OECD average. From Figure 9.8, we can see that Singapore is an outlier and that all others are clustered around the OECD average.

We also show the world PPP GDPpc average[6], Int\$ 14, 982, which is only 37% of the OECD average, and is located in Interval 4. The ASEAN-4, China and India are clustered around or below the world average: China (C) and Thailand (L) are in Interval 4, the same as the world average, and Indonesia (E) is in Interval 3. Malaysia (M), an outlier, is located in Interval 7, the highest among the ASEAN countries. The Philippines (P) and India (I) are lowest among these countries, at only 10 to 20% (Interval 2) of the OECD average.

Table 9.1 shows the peer group in detail in each interval of Figure 9.8. For each country, we show its world rank and its PPP GDPpc in the unit of Int\$ 1,000 in the parentheses. To avoid clustering, from Interval 1 to 8, we only list some familiar countries (other countries are shown as three dots …).

As we have expected, all the first-generation Asian NIEs are on par with the OECD counties. The second- and third-generation Asian NIEs, except for Malaysia, and approximately 150 less-developing countries, are still very poor, even though they are not in the lowest interval (Interval 1). It may take a very long time for them to converge on the OECD average.

While these second- and third-generation Asian NIEs are located in the lower intervals, our figures point to a reason for optimism, namely, that all the ASEAN-4 countries as well as China and India are growing steadily, although slowly, especially after the Asian financial crisis of 1997 and the world financial crisis of 2008–10. Considering that they are some of the largest countries in terms of population and land area, and considering increasing manufacturing outputs and exports and foreign direct investment due to the recent "Information and Computer Technology (ICT)" Revolution (Hsiao and Hsiao, 2004, 2006, 2008; Hsiao and Won, 2008), we submit that their economies are already at the take-off stage for future development.

---

6 We took the world average Int\$ 14,982 from the one listed in the IMF dataset. However, our calculation shows that the world average including Hong Kong and the world average (divided by 189) is Int\$ 18,492. If the world average is not included (divided by 188), then the world average is Int\$ 18,510. Using our calculation, the world average will be 46.6% of the OECD average and will be located in Interval 5. However, our explanation of the "GDPpc divide" in this section does not change. It is not clear how the IMF calculated the world average. It may include some countries not listed in the dataset.

Table 9.1 World PPP GDP per Capita Distribution, 2014, NIEs, Japan, the United States, China, India, Four ASEAN and Four EU Countries, and Others

Int#	Interval	Freq.	cfrq	Rk range	Country
19	300-350	1	1	1	Qatar(1,137)
18	250-300	0	1		
17	200-250	3	4	2-4	Luxemboug(2,98), **Singapore(3,83)**, Brunei(4,80)
16	150-200	4	8	5-8	Kuwait(5,71), Norway(6,67), UAE(7,66), San Marino(8.61)
15	140-150	1	9	9	Switzerland(9,58)
14	130-140	3	12	10-12	**HK(10,55), USA(10,54)**, Saudi Arabia(11,52) (HK not ranked)
13	120-130	3	15	13-15	Ireland(12,51), Bahrain(13,49), **Netherlands(14,48)**
12	110-120	9	24	15-24	Austria(15,47), Australia(16,47), Sweden(17,46), **Germany(18,46)**,
					Taiwan(19,46), Canada(20,45), Denmark(21,45), Iceland(22,44), Oman(23,44)
11	100-110	4	28	25-29	Belgium(24,43), Finland(25,41), **France(26,41), UK(27,40)**
10	90-100	2	30	30-31	**Japan(28,38)**, Equatorial Guinia(29,37)
9	80- 90	7	37	31-38	**South Korea(30,35)**, New Zealand(31,35), Italy(32,35), Spain(33,34),
					Malta(34,33), Israel(35,33), Trinidad and Tobago(36,32)
8	70- 80	5	42	39-44	Cyprus(37,31), Czech Republic(38,30), ...
7	60-70	10	52	45-55	Portugal(43,27), Greece(44,26), **Malysia(47,25)**, Russia(50,24), ...
6	50-60	8	60	56-64	Chile(53,23), Argentina(55,22), Uruguay(57,21), ...
5	40-50	15	75	65-80	Turkey(61,20), Panama(62,20), Mexico(66,18), Iran (70,17), Brazil(74,16), ...
4	30-40	18	93	75-92	**Thailand(76,16), World Avg (15), China(88,13)**, South Africa(89,13), ...
3	20-30	22	115	93-114	Egypt(99,11), **Indonesia(102,11)**, ...
2	10- 20	26	141	115-140	**Philippines(119,7)**, **India(125,6)**, Myanmar(134,5), Pakistan(135,5), ...
1	0- 10	47	188	141-187	Bangladesh(142,3), Cambodia(145,3), ...

Notes: The first number in the parentheses is the rank of the country in the world distribution; the second number is PPP GDPpc in Int$ 1,000. We have added Hong Kong but excluded the World Average in 188 countries/regions.
Sources: IMF 2015. See Sources of Data. cfrq = Cumulative frequency.

In conclusion, as we have seen through the charts and the table of this chapter, the emerging Asia is still led by the Asian NIEs, followed by the ASEAN countries, and then by China and India, a clear pattern of the fly-ing geese model in East and Southeast Asia. Undoubtedly, there will still be catching up and convergence among these generations of Asian NIEs. The superlarge countries like China and India may eventually edge out, and when these two awakened tigers roar, they will certainly add to the role and stature of the Asian economy.[7] In any case, barring unforeseen political

---

7 Admittedly, our conclusion is rather optimistic. For discussions of economic, social and political problems facing Asia-Pacific area, see, for example, Weiss (2001). Recently, the Asian Development Bank (2016) calculated the potential growth of the Asia-Pacific area and simulated future potential growth to find "policies to invigorate potential growth."

disturbances and economic disasters, as we have concluded in Chapters 6 and 8, we may still expect that this century may indeed be the Asia-centered world economy.

9.6 Postscript—Q&A

As we have mentioned at the Introduction to this book, we have been very fortunate to have had three prepublication book reviewers. They have posed several interesting questions, comments and suggestions. Since several of the points they raised expand upon or supplement some integral points we have not explored in the book, they are explained briefly in this section in the form of the Questions and Answers.

Q1.   A reviewer wrote that "it seems that no one, or very few, would expect Taiwan or Korea to lead the Asian economy. Here the aggregate size of the economy is very important. When people are talking about G2, the authors are talking about Taiwan and Korea. I cannot see the point. In short, if we talk about an Asia-centered world economy, China, Japan and India are still expected to play a primary role."

A1.   Figures 7.1, and 9.2 to 9.5 show that Taiwan and Korea are still "leading" the pack of the Asia-Pacific region as reflected in their GDP per capita in terms of PPP and nominal values. We are simply explaining the facts and have nothing to do with G2. Undeniably, China, Japan and India will play a primary role in an Asia-centered world economy in the future if they continue to develop.

We have addressed the size of the economy in Sections 5.2 and 7.4 in this book. For catching up in terms of GDP per capita, economic size may not matter. The reviewer may be correct in talking about the most influential and powerful countries in the region or world. In that case, the "aggregate size of the economy" may matter, as people are now talking about the rising economies of BRICS or BRIICS (Brazil, Russia, India, (Indonesia), China and South Africa). Taiwan and Korea are not included in the discussions. Incidentally, note that three of the BRIICS countries are located in Asia. Thus, Taiwan and Korea aside, the rise of BRIICS, along with Japan, is consistent with our view on an Asia-centered world economy.

The "aggregate size of economy" may be taken as aggregate GDP, instead of the GDP per capita, of a country. Then, this is a good opportunity to extend our analysis to supplement our studies in this chapter, which is based on the GDP per capita.

According to 2016 estimates, the IMF data (*Wikipedia*, 2016c) show that the world rankings of Taiwan[8] and Korea are 22nd (Int$ 1,126b, b for billion, same below) and 13th (Int$ 1,916b), respectively, among 188 countries (including Hong Kong) in terms of real GDP measured in PPP. At #22 (hereafter, # indicates the number of ranking in the descending order)., Taiwan is comparable with Australia (#19, Int$ 1,189b) and Poland (#24, Int$ 1,052b). At #13, Korea is comparable with Italy (#12, Int$ 2,223b) and Spain (#15, Int$ 1,690b). Thus, both economies are indeed very large on the world scale. We submit that they are capable of "leading" the Asian economy.

Naturally, Taiwan and Korea cannot be compared with supereconomies like China (#1, Int$ 21,269 b), the United States (#2, Int$ 18,562b), India (#3, Int$ 8,721 b) and Japan (#4, Int$ 4,932b). Note the great gap in GDP between China and the United States (the talk of G2) on the one hand, and India and Japan on the other. These four countries are considered to be outliers, as seen in Figure 9.8, in the world GDP (PPP) distribution, which is extremely skewed to the right, namely, literally L-shaped, if it is ordered from high to low GDP.

In terms of the nominal GDP in 2016, the IMF data (*Wikipedia*, 2016d) demonstrate that the world ranking of Taiwan is 22nd (US$ 519 b) out of a total of 191 countries (including Hong Kong) in the world, which is the same rank it was given with regard to its GDP in PPP. Korea, however, is even better. It was ranked at 11th (US$ 1,404 b).

At #22, Taiwan is not only comparable with Saudi Arabia (#20, US$ 638b) and Switzerland (#19, US$ 662b) but also ranks higher than Sweden (#23, US$ 517b) and Belgium (#24, US$ 470b). Furthermore, at #11, Korea is comparable with Canada (#10, US$ 1,532b) and Italy (#8, US$ 1,853b), and is even ranked higher than Russia (#12, US$ 1,268b) and Australia (#13, US$ 1,257b). Thus, both the economies of Taiwan and Korea are indeed very large and important in the world. It will not be strange if Taiwan and Korea join G2, G7, G8 or G20! Some people still have an anachronistic Weltanschauung.

Naturally, Taiwan and Korea cannot be compared with supercountries such as the United States (#1, US$ 18,562b), China (#2, US$11,392b), Japan (#3, US$ 4,730b) and India (#7, US$ 2,251b). However, considering the much smaller size of the economies of Japan and India, the United States and China are outliers, as seen in Figure 9.8, in the world nominal GDP frequency distribution.

Q2.   "In terms of new technology, innovation, etc., I cannot see that Taiwan or Korea can deliver really spectacular performance. Taiwan

---

8 For the 2011 Taiwan GDP and GDP per capita in PPP in the world ranking, see Hsiao (2014) and Hsiao and Hsiao (2015, 239).

is doing worse than Korea in these aspects in recent years. The two economies' growth in the past was mainly a catch-up process, or copying the Western model."

A2.   The phrases "spectacular performance" and "recent years" are not clear. We have shown in Figures 7.1 and 9.2 to 9.5 that both countries indeed have delivered "really spectacular performances" in terms of their GDP per capita growth. Furthermore, in Chapters 3, 4, 5, 7 and 8 of this book we have derived the "learning coefficients" of Taiwan and Korea with Japan and the United States, and showed how "[t]he two economies' growth in the past was mainly a catch-up process, or copying the Western model."

In terms of manufacturing, Taiwan displayed "a spectacular performance" in terms of original equipment manufacturing (OEM), namely, designing and building products according to the specifications of other companies in advanced countries (like HP, Dell, Walmart and so on). With regard to original design manufacturing (ODM), Taiwan has also displayed "a spectacular performance" in designing and building products by Taiwanese manufacturers and supplying these products to other companies to sell under another company's brand name. Taiwan and Korea have "deliver[ed] really spectacular performance[s]" in terms of OEM and ODM, and advanced toward becoming developed countries.

Appendix 9C shows the evolution of Taiwan as the number one worldwide producer of dozens of high-tech products, and Appendix 9D presents Taiwan's inventive activities and the World Competitive Index (WCI). They are the telltale signs of a "really spectacular performance" regarding Taiwan's manufacturing industry, especially the ICT industry.

Recently, both Taiwan and Korea went one step further. Their industries have advanced beyond OEM and ODM to original brand manufacturing (OBM). Both countries now design and build products and sell under their own names, such as Taiwan's HTC (consumer electronics), Acer and Asus (both in computer), Trend Micro (software), Master Kong and Want Want (both in food and beverage), Giant (bicycle) and so on (Interbrand, 2012) as well as Korea's Samsung and LG (both electronics), Hyundai and KIA (both motors), SK Telecom (communication) and so forth (Interbrand, 2016). We submit that both Taiwan and Korea have "delivered really spectacular performance" in a short period.

It is usually thought that the general pattern of development of the manufacturing industry in a developing country is to advance from OEM to ODM and then to OBM. In terms of OBM, Korea appears to be ahead of Taiwan. However, each country has its own background, resources and comparative advantage, like Taiwan's small and medium-sized enterprises (SME) (Hsiao and Hsiao, 2015, Chapter 6) and Korea's chaebols. There are frequent debates about the pros and cons of SME versus chaebols. However, so far as the data are concerned, Taiwan's strategy of remaining mainly at the level of ODM apparently has not hampered its economic growth as compared with Korea or any other countries. *In any case, as shown in Figures 9.4 and 9.5, we submit that both countries have "delivered really spectacular performance."*

Q3. "Taiwan's government encouraged high technology industry development over the years, but it cannot be said to be successful at all. This situation is similar to that of China. At the same time, Taiwan's economic stagnation and social problems in the 2000s have not been seriously discussed. I cannot see where the optimism comes from. [...] the authors should not avoid addressing the lackluster performance of Taiwan in the 2000s."

A3. No, we repeat that the performance of the Taiwanese economy in the 2000s was excellent, as shown by Figures 9.2 and 9.4 and Appendix 9D. Although the recent performance of the Taiwanese economy is much less spectacular, as compared especially with Taiwan's own past and that of current China, as one of the authors also has observed recently (Hsiao, 2016).

In this respect, we first have to note that Taiwan is already an advanced country. As such, like any other advanced country, one should not expect Taiwan to maintain its 10% or so growth rates of the past. Furthermore, the world is currently in recession, and other countries, especially China, are also experiencing difficulties. This chapter shows that Taiwan is still ahead of other countries by comparison. We believe that the Taiwanese can overcome the latest (2016) setback.

Our optimism comes from the history of Taiwanese economic and political development (see Chapters 2, 7, 8 of this book; Hsiao and Hsiao, 2015, Chapters 1, 6, 13). The Taiwanese overcame the difficulties it encountered in almost every decade of the past 100 years: the World War II mobilization under the Japanese regime in the 1930s and the 1940s, the massive extraordinary influx of Chinese refugees (almost 30% of the then population) from China in the late 1950s and early 1960s, two world oil crises during the 1970s, being expelled from the United Nations in 1972, the US recognition of China in 1979, the unrest and transition to democracy in 1987, the Asian financial crisis in 1997–98, and the global world financial crisis in 2007–10, in addition to numerous violent earthquakes and typhoons. Each time the Chinese made a dire prediction of the collapse of the Taiwanese economy. However, Taiwan recovered quickly from all of these economic and political crises and disasters. While "the future's not ours to see, que sera sera," there are reasons for optimism.

Unlike the general perception in China and some quarter of Taiwan on the Taiwanese economy, we have pointed out in this chapter and also in Hsiao (2016) that Taiwan's performance is not "lackluster" at all. Rather, it is indeed stellar and astonishing, compared with any other country in the world (see Appendixes 9C and 9D).

Q4. "It is also better for the authors to emphasize the fact that Taiwanese economy relies quite much on the Chinese mainland."

A4. Short of colonial exploitation, benefits or gains from foreign trade and foreign direct investment are mutual and not one-sided: both sides "rely" on each other. In fact, the Chinese economy has "relied" on Taiwan heavily in the 1980s and the 1990s (Hsiao and Hsiao, 2004). In Marxist parlance and view,[9] American and Japanese capitalism and imperialism "exploited" Taiwanese and Korean workers and nurtured Taiwanese and Korean capitalism and imperialism, and Taiwanese and Koran capitalism and imperialism in turn exploited Chinese workers and "nurtured" Chinese capitalism and imperialism. In this sense, we submit that, as shown in Figure 9.2 and 9.4 as well as Appendix 9C, Taiwan is the country that benefited the most from practicing her "capitalism and imperialism."

In any case, the authors have discussed the economic relationship between Taiwan and China extensively in Hsiao and Hsiao (2015, Chapters 2 and 3; 2004; 2007). The readers can go directly to these sources.

Q5. "The only suggestion I would have would be to ensure that all the figures and tables have sources, which is presently not the case."

A5. Most of the figures and tables present the results of our statistical tests and estimations. All the data sources are explained in the text or at the end of the chapters.

---

9 See Pröbsting (1997). In Hsiao and Hsiao (2004), we call it the East Asian Circle.

Q6.   "I would also recommend that authors must add a concluding chapter in order to add value to this publication."

A6.   Thanks. The book is mainly a historical analysis. However, we have added Chapter 9 to update the data and show the past, current and future economic growth of Taiwan, Korea, the ASEAN-4, Japan, the United States, China, India and some major European countries as projected up to the year 2020.

Appendix 9A: Derivation of the Purchasing Power Parity (PPP) Exchange Rate

The dataset on economic growth used in this and other chapters of this book is GDPpc in PPP dollars (namely, Geary–Khamis dollars). The current literature on PPP GDP mainly focuses on a description of how the data are collected, instead of actual derivation of PPP. To help the readers understand the meaning and construction of PPP GDPpc, we explain its derivation in this Appendix based on the original paper by Geary (1958).

The PPP (purchasing power parity) is the exchange rate of a country in terms of the international dollar (denoted as Int$). To construct the PPP for country a, $a = 1, 2, \ldots, n$, we first derive the international price of a commodity i, $i = 1, 2, \ldots, k$, denoted as C_i, as the weighted average of all the international prices of commodity i in each country, namely, $E_a p_{ia}$'s (assuming the rule of one price prevails for each commodity), where E_a is the exchange rate of country a in terms of the international dollar, and p_{ia} is the domestic price of commodity i in country a. Here, the weight is taken as the proportion of the quantity bought in each country over the total quantities sold in the world.

$$C_i = \sum_{a=1}^{n} E_a p_{ia} \frac{q_{ia}}{\sum_a^n q_{ia}}, \tag{9A.1}$$

where $i = 1, 2, \ldots, k$.

The PPP for country a, E_a, is then derived by the ratio of the sum of all the weighted international prices C_i's over the sum of all the corresponding weighted domestic prices p_{ia}, in both cases, the weight being the proportion of the quantity of the commodity i bought in each country over the total quantities sold in that country.

$$E_a = \frac{\sum_i^k C_i q_{ia}}{\sum_i^k p_{ia} q_{ia}} = \frac{\sum_i^k C_i (q_{ia} / \sum_i^k q_{ia})}{\sum_i^k p_{ia} (q_{ia} / \sum_i^k q_{ia})},$$ (9A.2)

where $a = 1, 2, \ldots, n$. (9A.2) is similar to the Laspeyres price index. Note that all the prices and quantities are given constants collected by the statistics office of each country.

Mathematically, write (9A.1) in matrix form $C[kx1] = W[kxn]E[nx1]$, where W is a kxn matrix of weights. Write (9A.2) as $E[nx1] = V[nxk]C[kx1]$, where V is an nxk matrix of weights. After substitution, we have $E = AE$, where $A = VW$. Thus, the derivation of the PPP indexes is to solve the linear homogeneous system of equations $(I-A)E = 0$. For the numerical example given in Geary (1958), E_a or E can be derived easily by Microsoft Excel (Hsiao, 2011, 350–52 and 382–83).

The advantage of using the PPP is obvious from the above derivation of PPP. The basic macroeconomic condition is the following:

$$Y = C + I + G + (X - M),$$

where Y is GDP; C, consumption; I, investment; G, government expenditure; X, exports; and M, imports. Until recently, the domestic GDP is converted to US dollars by the US exchange rate, which is the price of the traded goods category, X and M. Instead of using the US exchange rate, or the GDP deflators, to deflate all the different categories, we can construct internationally comparable PPP indexes for separate categories of C, I, G, X and M separately to deflate the value of different categories of commodities. The advantage of using the PPP is clear.

Appendix 9B: On the Derivation of the Big Mac Index

It may be interesting to note that, in the case of only one commodity ($k = 1$) and two countries ($n = 2$), we can show directly from equation (9A.2) that, $E_2/E_1 = p_{11}/p_{12}$. Let $E_1 = 1$, then, we have $p_{12}E_2 = p_{11}$.

If the two countries are the United States ($a = 1$) and Taiwan ($a = 2$), and the commodity is Big Mac ($k = 1$). According to *The Economist* (2014), on July 24, 2014, $p_{12} = $ NT\$ 79, and $p_{11} = $ US\$ 4.795. The Big Mac PPP in Taiwan is $E_2 = 4.795/79 = 0.061$ (In\$). *The Economist* defines the "Dollar PPP" as $1/E_2$. Thus, $1/E_2 = 79/4.795 = 16.48$. According to *The Economist*, on the same day, the market NT\$ exchange rate was NT\$ 29.98 per 1 US\$, thus the NT\$ was undervalued by -45.05%.

GDPpc in Big Mac PPP

According to the IMF data, GDP in current Taiwanese currency (NGDP) in 2014 was NT$ 16,084 billion, thus GDP in Big Mac PPP is NGDP/Big Mac PPP = 16,084/16.48 = Int$ 975.97 billion. In terms of US dollars, using *The Economist* exchange rate above, 16,984/29.98 = US$ 536.49 billion. Both can be converted to the GDP per capita by dividing this number by Taiwan's population in 2014 (23.434 million). Thus, Taiwan's GDPpc in Big Mac PPP was Int$ 41,648, or US$ 22,894 in 2014.

In fact, according to the IMF data, in 2014, Taiwan's PPP exchange rate (PPPEX) was Int$ 14.909, very close to the Big Mac PPP of 16.48 calculated by *The Economist*. Thus, GDP in PPP (PPPGDP) by IMF was Int$ 1,078.79 billion. Dividing PPPGDP by population, we can derive the PPP GDPpc (= PPPPC of IMF) as Int$ 46,035.83, as listed in IMF table.

Appendix 9C: Taiwan as the "Republic of Technology" (ROT)

Taiwan has a long and distinguished history of economic development, from the first economic miracle during the pre–World War II Japanese period to the second economic miracle after the War (Chapter 7). Taiwan is an exemplary case of successful economic development in modern world history.

By the end of the 1990s Taiwan claimed the title of "number three producer of information technology worldwide, behind only the United States and Japan."[10] In a manner of speaking, one could say that, as the island entered the twenty-first century, Taiwan had become the "Republic of Technology" (ROT) in the areas of information and communications.

Table 9C.1 shows the products for which Taiwan was number one in the world market in the selected years during the 2000s. In 2009, Taiwan claimed 21 items as the number one producer in the world. The 21 items are arranged according to its world market share and the location of production in 2009 (the last category), and we trace the items backward to the years, 2005 and 2002. For example, in 2009, Taiwan produced 99% (in value) of world "mask ROM," which is an increase from 91% in 2005. The last column shows that the percentage is the same in 2008.

The "02 rk" in 2002 and "05 rk" in 2005 are the rankings of the world market share of the item in the year, respectively. For example, in 2002, the value of IC foundry production was ranked #2 in Taiwan's production, with 73% world market share. In 2005, its production ranking in Taiwan decreased to #4,

---

10 Cited in Hsiao and Hsiao (2002, 167). Original source: Institute for Information Industries, Market Intelligence Center, Taiwan.

Table 9C.1 Evolution of Taiwan as the Number 1 Worldwide Producer 2002–9

Yr	2002			2005			2009			08
	World Market Share (%)			World Market Share (%)			World Market Share (%)			
02 Rk	**14 items production**	%	05 Rk	**11 items, Excluding offshore production**	%	09 Rk	**7 items, Excluding offshore production**	%	%	
			1	Mask ROM (va)	91	1	Mask ROM (va)	99	99	
			5	*IC Testing (va)*	60	2	IC testing (va)	71	65	
2	IC Foundry (va)	73	4	Foundry Services (va)	67	3	(Wafer) Foundry (va)	67	64	
8	*Optical discs (va)*	40	2	*CD-RW Discs (vo)*	77	4	*Optical discs (vo)*	63	64	
1	*Recordable Optical*	83	3	*DVD-R (vo)*	71					
	Disk (va)		6	*DVD RW Discs (vo)*	59					
			9	*CD-R Discs (vo)*	44					
						5	Chlorella (vo)	51	51	
11	IC packaging (va)	32	8	IC packaging (va)	45	6	IC packaging (va)	46	47	
6	Routers (vo)	51	10	ED Cu (va)	36	7	ED Cu (va)	37	38	
			11	ABS Resins (vo)			TN/STN LCD Panels (va)	NA	34	
							14 items, Including offshore production			
3	*Motherboards (va)*	72		-----moved to China --->		8	*Motherboards (va)*	96		
5	*Notebook PCs (va)*	56		-------------------->		9	*Notebook PCs (vo)*	95		
14	Network Interface Cards (va)	25				10	Netbook PCs (vo)	91		
13	*Wireless LANs (va)*	30		-------------------->		11	*WLANs (va)*	81		
10	Cable Modems	34				12	Cable CPE (va)	79		
16	ABS Copolymer (va)*	11				13	PNDs (GPS, etc.) (va)	77	55	
15	Bicycles (va)	24				14	Golf heads (vo)	75		
4	*LCD monitors (va)*	59		-------------------->		15	*LCD monitors (va)*	72		
7	*xDSL CPE (va)*	45		-------------------->		16	*xDSL CPE (va)*	63		
						17	CRT monitors (vo)	59		
12	*Glass fiber (va)*	31	7	*Glass Fiber (va)* ---->48		18	*Glass fiber (va)*	41	31	
9	Huds (va)	39				19	Desktop PCs (vo)	39		
						20	Power wheelchairs and			
	23% in vo.						power scooters (vo)	37		
						21	Instant noodles (vo)	29		

Sources: TSDB, 2004, 10; 2007, 12; 2010, 12–14. va = production value, vo = production volume.

as its world share decreased to 67%. In 2009, however, its production ranking in Taiwan increased to 3, but its world market share remained at 67%.

In 2002, Taiwan's offshore production was not prevalent and the production classification did not distinguish whether production took place offshore or not. Thus, we assume all products were produced in Taiwan. In 2005, the data clearly indicate that the items listed excluded the offshore production, mostly in China.

However, by 2009, the offshore production becomes so prevalent that government statistics had to distinguish whether the item was produced in

Taiwan (upper part of the table in 2009) or produced offshore (lower part of the table in 2009). The table shows the very rapid change of the location of the Taiwanese manufacturing industry within a decade. It also indicates Taiwan's rapid outward foreign direct investment, mainly to China, during the 2000s.

Combining some items for the sake of discussion here, we can see that the production of three items (in shaded rows)—#4 (in 2009, same below) optical discs, #3 IC Foundry and #6 IC Packaging—were consistently number one products in the world with production facilities in Taiwan.

Three items in heavy boxes—#1 Mask ROM, #2 IC testing and #7 Electro-deposited copper foil ("ED Cu")—became prominent in the mid-2000s, and by 2009 the first two items almost completely monopolized world markets (99% and 71%, respectively). Incidentally, these three items were still produced in Taiwan in 2014.

The lower part of the table reveals that six items pertaining to the 2009 number one world products were already produced in Taiwan in 2002 (see the dotted lines connecting the items in 2002 and 2009), namely, #8 Motherboards (72% of 2002 world market share, same below), #9 Notebook PCs (56%), #11 Wireless LANs (30%), #15 LCD Monitors (59%), #16 xDSL CPE (45%) and #18 Glass Fiber (31%).

They moved to offshore production by 2009, mostly to China, to take advantage of low wages and low land prices in China. Consequently, the world market shares of these six products increased greatly, and some even more than doubled, indicating the vastly expanded production in China.

Other items in 2009, 5 Chlorella and TN/STN LCD Panels, were new products manufactured in Taiwan. Other items, 10 Netbook PC, items 12 to 14, 15 CRT monitors, 19 Desktop PCs and items 20 to 21 were some new Taiwanese products that started their production in China,[11] showing China is a primary location of the new Taiwanese production.

The last two columns compare the change in the world market shares from 2008 to 2009 where data are available. They show the general trend of increase in market share over the years.

Various issues of the annual *Taiwan Statistical Data Book* (2004, 2007, 2010, 2011) since 2002 list the products for which Taiwan ranked first, second or third in world production. Table 9C.1 only lists the products for which Taiwan was the number one world producer. More products are produced in Taiwan

---

11 From this table, it appears that the Taiwanese industry has moved to offshore production rapidly since 2009. As a reviewer pointed out, there is a problem of hollowing out domestically and of Taiwan's relying too much on production and markets in China, especially since China has territorial ambition regarding Taiwan (Hsiao, 2014, Hsiao and Hsiao, 2002; 2007). Such concerns led to the election of the new government in 2016.

with number two and number three world market shares. Considering its relatively small country area, the extent of the products and its volume are simply awesome and "spectacular." Most of them are related to information and communication technology, indicating that Taiwan is indeed a "Republic of Technology" in this critical area of modern manufacturing. While Taiwan has demonstrated excellent performance in the world, as the table shows, its production is moving away offshore to China for further expansion (as are the Korean and Japanese manufacturing industries).

It should be pointed out that the major actors in the Taiwanese achievements are, in addition to the hardworking Taiwanese workers, companies like Acer, Arima, ASUSTek, BenQ, Cmpal, Formosa Plastic, Hon Hai/Foxconn, Quanta, Inventec, Media Tek, TSMC, UMC, Wistron and so on (Hsiao and Hsiao, 2015, 243).

Appendix 9D: Taiwan's Innovative Activities and the World Competitiveness Index

A seldom known fact is that the Republic of Technology, Taiwan, was supported by her vigorous innovation and patent-related activities.

As shown in Figure 9D.1 below, according to the World Economic Forum (2010, 317), Taiwan has a large pool of scientists and engineers (#8 in the world, same as below) and has committed large company spending to R&D (#9).

In 2009, the patents per million population for Taiwan were 287 (see the right-hand side of the table and the heavy dotted line in Figure 9D.1), ranking Taiwan #1 among 139 countries, higher than Japan (279; #2) and the United States (262; #3) (ibid. 494). See the right-hand side table inside Figure 9D.1. This was truly a "spectacular performance."

The median innovation score among the 139 countries is 0.3 (Turkey), which is only 0.1% of that of Taiwan. The curve in Figure 9D.1, like most of the international statistics, is also strongly skewed to the right, and the long right tail is almost close to zero. This is further evidence of Taiwan's "spectacular performance" and a distinctive Taiwanese achievement and her contribution to the world economy and development, a fact rather unknown to the world.

Since most of the world patents are issued in the United States, the total foreign patents granted by the US Patents and Trademark Office (USPTO) listed in the SAUS (2011) shows that Taiwan's patents totaled 7,781 cases in 2009, with Taiwan thus ranked #4 across all countries. It was listed below Japan (38,100; #1), Germany (10,400, #2) and South Korea (9,600, #3), but far above Canada (4,400; #5) and the United Kingdom (4,000; #6).

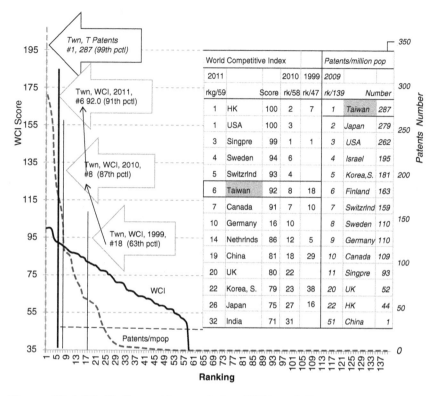

Figure 9D.1 World Competitiveness Index (WCI) and Number of Patents per Million Population (Patents/mpop)

The other index is the World Competitiveness Index (WCI), published annually by the Institute of Management Development (IMD) in Switzerland. It ranks a nation's business environment and analyzes its ability to provide an environment in which enterprises can compete (Hsiao and Hsiao, 2002, 203). Taiwan's WCI rating has fluctuated. However, as shown by the solid heavy line in Figure 9D.1, its rank improved from #18 (63 pctl, percentile, same below) out of 47 countries in 1999 to #8 (87 pctl) out of 58 countries in 2010, and then with a score of 92.0, #6 (91 pctl) out of 59 countries in 2011 (IMD, 2011, 19). Its world rank improved dramatically.

Note that, as shown by the left-hand side of the table inside Figure 9D.1, although Taiwan's WCI rating is high, it has been consistently behind the city-states, Hong Kong (100.0; #1) and Singapore (98.6; #3), but higher than that for South Korea (78.5; #22), China (81.1; #19) and Japan (75.2; #26). The 2011 median WCI score for the 59 countries is 29.5 (Czech Republic), less than one-third of Taiwan's score.

In short, Taiwan's outstanding economic performance and catching-up process as revealed in Figure 9.2 are by no means coincident. It was the achievement of hardworking Taiwanese people.

Sources of Data

The PPP GDPpc data in Figure 9.1 (left panel) were taken from the *Wikipedia* (2016a) website under "List of countries by GDP (PPP) per capita." It lists estimations by three organizations: the IMF (2014) for 187 countries, downloaded from the World Economic Outlook Database, October 2015; the World Bank (2011–2014) for 185 countries, downloaded from the GDP per capita, PPP (current international $), World Development Indicators database; and the CIA (1993–2014) for 198 countries, downloaded from the GDP-per capita (PPP), The World Factbook, https://www.cia.gov/library/publications/the-world-factbook/rankorder/2004rank.html.

The Nominal GDPpc data in Figure 9.1 (right panel) was taken from the *Wikipedia* (2016b) website under "List of countries by GDP (nominal) per capita." It also lists estimations by three organizations: the IMF (2015) for 184 countries, taken from the World Economic Outlook Database-October 2015; the World Bank (2014), for 183 countries, taken from http://data.worldbank.org/indicator/NY.GDP.PCAP.CD; and the UN (2014), for 194 countries, taken from the National Accounts Main Aggregates Database, December 2014 ("Select all countries," "GDP, Per Capita GDP—US Dollars", and "2014 to generate table"), United Nations Statistics Division.

The data for Figures 9.2 to 9.8 and Table 9.1 are taken from IMF "World Economic Outlook database, October 2015" downloaded on March 2016 from http://www.imf.org/external/pubs/ft/weo/2015/02/weodata/download.aspx.

The dataset on the PPP GDPpc was taken from the IMF category PPPPC, that on the nominal GDPpc was taken from category NGDPDPC, for Korea (KOR), Taiwan (TWN), Singapore (SGP), Hong Kong (HKG), China (CHN), India (IND), Germany (DEU), the United Kingdom (GBR), France (FRN), the Netherlands (NLD), Indonesia (IDN), Malaysia (MYS), Thailand (THA) and the Philippines (PHL). The "Big Mac" data in Appendix 9A are taken from website of *The Economist* (2014).

In Section 9.6, A1 (Answer to Q1), the latest estimation (2016) of PPP GDP of Taiwan and Korea is taken from *Wikipedia* "List of countries by GDP (PPP)," https://en.wikipedia.org/wiki/List_of_countries_by_GDP_(PPP) downloaded on October, 25, 2016. This website has the "List by the International Monetary Fund (Estimates for 2016)," along with the lists by the World Bank (2015) and the CIA World Factbook (1993–2015). The original source of the *Wikipedia* IMF data was taken from the *Report for Selected Country Groups and Subjects (PPP valuation of country GDP)*, which lists the ranking by alphabetical order.

In Section 9.6, A1 (answer to Q1), the latest estimation (2016) of nominal GDP of Taiwan and Korea is taken from *Wikipedia* "List of countries by GDP (nominal)" https://en.wikipedia.org/wiki/List_of_countries_by_GDP_ (nominal).

Downloaded on October, 25, 2016. This site has the "List by the International Monetary Fund (Estimates for 2016)," along with the lists by the World Bank, 2015, and the United Nations, 2014. The original source of the *Wikipedia* IMF data was taken from IMF "*World Economic Outlook Database.*" *International Monetary Fund*, which was available at the IMF site, lists the rankings by alphabetical order.

References

Asian Development Bank (2016). *Asian Development Outlook 2016: Asia's Potential Growth.* Manila: Asian Development Bank.

The Economist (2014). "The Big Mac Index: Historical Data from the Economist's Big Mac Index, July 24." Downloaded in April 2016, from http://bigmacindex.org/.

Geary, R. C. (1958). "A Note on the Comparison of Exchange Rates and Purchasing Power between Countries," *Journal of the Royal Statistical Society*, Series A. 121, Part I: 97–99.

Hsiao, Frank S. (2011). *Economic and Business Analysis: Quantitative Methods using Spreadsheets.* Singapore: World Scientific Publishing.

——— (2014). "Taiwan in the Global Economy: End of the 'Miracle'?". In Shyu-tu Lee and Jack F. Williams, eds. *Taiwan's Struggle: Voices of the Taiwanese*, NY: Rowman & Littlefield, 235–53. Revised and reprinted in Hsiao and Hsiao (2015), *Economic Development of Taiwan: Early Experiences and the Pacific Trade Triangle.* Singapore: World Scientific Publisher.

——— (2016). "How Bad is the Taiwan's Economy? Compared to other Economies around the World, Taiwan Is Doing Just Fine." *The Diplomat*, July 22.

Hsiao, Frank S., and Mei-Chu Wang Hsiao (2002). "Taiwan in the Global Economy: Past, Present, and Future." In Peter C. Y. Chow, ed. *Taiwan in the Global Economy: From an Agrarian Economy to an Exporter of High-Tech Products.* Westport CT: Praeger, 161–221. Also in Hsiao and Hsiao (2015), chapter 2.

——— (2004). "The Chaotic Attractor of Foreign Direct Investment—Why China? A Panel Data Analysis." *Journal of Asian Economics* 15(4): 641–70. Also in Hsiao and Hsiao (forthcoming).

——— (2006). "FDI, Exports, and GDP in East and Southeast Asia—Panel Data versus Time-Series Causality Analyses," *Journal of Asian Economics* 17(6): 1082–1106. Also in Hsiao and Hsiao (forthcoming).

——— (2007). "Prospects of a U.S.–Taiwan Free Trade Agreement—The China Factor and Critical Assessments." In Peter C.Y. Chow, ed., *Economic Integration, Democratization and National Security in East Asia: A Shifting Paradigms in U.S., China, and Taiwan Relations.* Northampton, MA: Edward Elgar. 2007, 191–239.

EPILOGUE   279

————— (2008). "The IT Revolution and Macroeconomic Volatility in Newly Developed
Countries: ARCH/GARCH–VAR Approaches." Paper presented at Joint International
Conference of American Committee for Asian Economic Studies (ACAES) and the
Rimini Centre for Economic Analysis (RCEA), Rimini, Italy. August 29–31, 2008. Also
in Hsiao and Hsiao (forthcoming).

————— (2015). *Economic Development of Taiwan: Early Experiences and the Pacific Trade Triangle.*
Singapore: World Scientific Publisher.

————— (forthcoming). *Trade, Investment, and Growth in East and Southeast Asia.* London:
Anthem Press.

Hsiao, Frank S., and Y. Won (2008). "Panel Causality Analysis on FDI: Exports-Economic
Growth Nexus in First and Second Generation ANIEs," *Journal of the Korean Economy*
9(2): 237–67. Also in Hsiao and Hsiao (forthcoming).

Institute of Management Development (IMD) (2011). *World Competitiveness Yearbook.*
Stephane Garelli and IMD, eds. Lausanne, Switzerland: IMD. "Scoreboard" retrieved
in August 2011 at http://www.vi.is/files/IMD%202011%20-%20listar_831280280.
pdf.

Interbrand (2012). *Taiwan Top 20 Global Brands. Ranked by Brand Value.* Singapore and
Taipei. Downloaded in October 2016 from the website http://www.rankingth-
ebrands.com/PDF/Interbrand%20Taiwan%20Top%2020%20Global%20
Brands%202012.pdf.

————— (2016). *Best Korea Brands 2016, Anatomy of Growth.* Omnicom Group. Downloaded
in October 2016 from the website http://interbrand.com/wp-content/uploads/2016/
04/BKB2016_REPORT_GLOBAL_FINAL.pdf.

International Monetary Fund (2014). *World Economic Outlook Database WEO Update: January
19, 2016.* Downloaded in March 2016 from website https://www.imf.org/external/
pubs/ft/weo/2015/02/weodata/index.aspx.

Morishima, Michio (1999). *Why Japan Will Decline* [Naze Nihon wa botsuraku suruka, in
Japanese]. Tokyo: Iwanami Shoten.

Pröbsting, Michael (1997). "Capitalist Development in South Korea and Taiwan."
Originally published in *Trotskyist International* No. 21, *Theoretical Journal of the League for
the Revolutionary Communist International.* Reproduced at the website of Revolutionary
Communist International Tendency. Downloaded in November 2016 at http://www.
thecommunists.net/theory/capitalism-in-south-korea-taiwan/.

Schreyer, Paul, and Francette Koechlin (2002). "Purchasing Power Parities-Measurement
and Uses," *Statistics Brief* No. 3, March. Paris: OECD.

Taiwan Statistical Data Book (TSDB) (2004, 2007, 2010, 2011). Council for Economic
Planning and Development, Executive Yuan, Taiwan. Also available at www.cepd.gov.
tw, retrieved in September 2011.

Weiss, Julian, ed. (2001). *Tigers' Roar: Asia's Recovery and Its Impact.* New York: M. E. Sharpe.

Wikipedia (2016a). "List of Countries by GDP(PPP) per Capita," *Wikipedia, the Free
Encyclopedia.* Downloaded in April 2016 from https://en.wikipedia.org/wiki/List_of_
countries_by_GDP_(PPP)_per_capita.

————— (2016b). "List of Countries by GDP (nominal) per Capita," *Wikipedia, the Free
Encyclopedia.* Downloaded in April 2016 from https://en.wikipedia.org/wiki/List_of_
countries_by GDP_(nominal)_per capita.

————— (2016c). "List of Countries by GDP (PPP)," Wikipedia, the Free Encyclopedia.
Downloaded in October 2016 from https://en.wikipedia.org/wiki/List_of_countries_
by_GDP_(PPP)_per_capita. See Sources of Data section for details.

———— (2016d). "List of Countries by GDP (nominal)," Wikipedia, the Free Encyclopedia. Downloaded in October, 2016 from https://en.wikipedia.org/wiki/List_of_countries_by_GDP_(nominal). See Sources of Data section for details.

World Economic Forum (WEF) (2010). *The Global Competitiveness Report, 2010–2011*. Klaus Schwab, ed. Geneva, Switzerland.

INDEX

GDP per capita (*cont.*)
Korea and Taiwan reversal 196
long-run, divide into 4 periods 186
nominal GDPpc 195, 250
OECD average 262–3
ratio p 141, 232
structural changes 177, 179, 211–12, 214–15, 218
World average 124, 159–61, 191, 263
world frequency distribution 261
GDP. *See* gross domestic product
GDPpc. *See* GDP per capita
Geary-Khamis dollars 137, 194, 247–8, 256, 270
Geary-Khamis dollars. *See* data, Maddison
geopolitics 158
GNP. *See* gross national product
golden age, postwar 194
Gompertz model of three parameters 234
government policy 40
government-led development 110
government-led unbalanced growth strategy 115
gross domestic product (GDP) 1–3, 5–6, 13, 23, 25, 28–30, 35, 54, 60–1, 63, 68, 70, 72, 86–8, 94, 106, 116, 119–22, 124, 126, 129, 131–2, 135, 137–41, 144–7, 158, 160–3, 165–6, 168–9, 171, 177–81, 184, 187–98, 202–6, 208–18, 225, 227–30, 232–4, 236–41, 244, 247–50, 265–7, 271–2, 277–8
gross national product (GNP) 12–15, 18, 20, 132, 197–8, 229
growth
average productivity 106, 115
between Korea and Taiwan 95
efficiency 59, 72–3, 77–9, 81, 83, 86–7
era of rapid growth (Japan) 208
GDP 2, 5, 30, 35, 54, 129, 160–3, 165–6, 168–9, 171
input-driven (Krugman) 171, 173
Korea and Taiwan
extraordinary 187
Korea, Taiwan, Japan
early period 188
postwar period 189, 191

prewar period 189
transitional period 190
long-run 5, 94, 158, 181, 184, 189
miracle 2, 60
output 78, 125
parallel
Taiwan and Korea 101
population 125, 129, 145, 204
productivity 3, 5, 59–61, 63, 71–3, 77–8, 81, 86, 95–7, 104–6, 110, 115, 163, 196
real GDP 5, 157–9
sustained, Korea and Taiwan 184
technology 59, 72–3, 77–9, 81, 83, 86–7, 93, 105–6, 110, 112, 115
unbalanced 146
growth accounting method 67, 96, 116
growth rate
continuous vs discrete 186
discrete 67, 98
efficiency (EG) 59, 67, 71, 73, 75, 77–82, 87, 98, 105–6
GDP 2, 5, 30, 129, 160–3, 165–6, 168–9, 171
Jorgenson estimation 163, 165–7, 170–1
Young estimation 158–9, 162–5, 167–72
GDP per capita 178, 186, 190–1, 211, 214
World ranking. Table 7.1, 187
long-run 190, 248
Malmquist productivity (MPG) 67, 71–3, 75, 77–82, 87, 98, 105–6
pure efficiency (PG) 98, 106
scale efficiency (SG) 98, 105–6
technology (TG) 67, 71–2, 75, 77–82, 86–7, 93, 98, 105–6
TFP 60, 67, 96, 98, 157–8, 161–5, 167–8, 171–2
as residual 162

health
condition in India 130
disease
epidemic 130
infectious 129–30, 200
hygiene 130, 200